THE AMATEUR

# Photographer's
# Handbook

The Grand Canyon, from a Kodachrome original.

*"The photographer can function as long as there is light; his work
—his adventure—is a rediscovery of the world in terms of light."*
— EDWARD WESTON

# THE AMATEUR

# Photographer's

# Handbook

By AARON SUSSMAN

SEVENTH REVISED EDITION

*Thomas Y. Crowell Company*

NEW YORK

# Foreword

All things change; but none more than photography.

Keeping pace with these changes, *The Amateur Photographer's Handbook* has gone through seven complete revisions since this present text was first published in 1941. The previous revisions appeared in 1948, in 1950 (with the help of the late *Bruce Downes,* Editor of *Popular Photography*), and again in 1952, 1955, 1958, and 1962.

This is the *seventh* revised edition.

It incorporates further changes and additions. Besides the corrections suggested by an alert and articulate readership, to whom we are grateful, there are all the revisions made necessary by the relentless improvements in this art-science-craft.

But photography today can be perfectly described by that sage French proverb which says: *the more things change, the more they are the same.* True, techniques have been improved; materials and equipment are better, faster, or easier to use. But the eye and heart of the photographer are still the same, and a box camera with ordinary film can still make great pictures if the artist sees clearly and presses the button at the decisive moment.

Photography is more than a means of recording the obvious.

It is a way of feeling, of touching, of loving. What you have caught on film is captured forever, whether it be a face or a flower, a place or a thing, a day or a moment. The camera is a perfect companion. It makes no demands, imposes no obligations. It becomes your notebook and your reference library, your microscope and your telescope. It sees what you are too lazy or too careless to notice, and it remembers little things, long after you have forgotten everything.

People have often asked me how I happened to take up photography. The fact is you don't "take up" photography.

It takes you up.

One day you're walking around grim and growling, like Herman Melville just before an escape to sea. Then, suddenly, you have a loaded camera in your hand and all is well.

v

I take to my darkroom out of affection for others.
There I make friends with the world again.
There I learn to look away, to focus on infinity.
There I play god with film, paper, chemicals, and lenses.
There, in the dark, I begin to see.

And finally, some acknowledgments: to Eastman Kodak, Ansco, and Morgan & Morgan, for making available charts, color plates, tables, and photographs; to Richard L. Simon, for inspiration and stimulation when it was needed; to Caryl Wallack, Leon Arden, Samuel Sugar, Lawrence Ferguson, Jack Deschin, Arthur J. Busch, Ralph Samuels, Robert W. Brown, John V. Adams, Henry M. Lester, Louis Bernstein, and John W. Doscher, for help in so many ways; to John Adam Knight, for changing his mind and being gracious enough to say so in print; to Ziff-Davis for permission to use the glossary. My special thanks to Dorothy Gelatt and Robert E. Mayer for gracious and timely aid in an emergency. The paragraph by Dr. Mortimer Adler is from *How to Read a Book,* and is used by courtesy of the publishers, Simon and Schuster. The paragraph by Lewis Mumford is from *Technics and Civilization* and is quoted with his permission.

AARON SUSSMAN

# *Contents*

# Photographic Illustrations

"Who would believe that so small a space could contain the image of all the universe? O mighty process! What talent can avail to penetrate a nature such as these? What tongue will it be that can unfold so great a wonder? Verily, none! This it is that guides the human discourse to the considering of divine things. Here the figures, here the colors, here all the images of every part of the universe are contracted to a point. O what a point is so marvelous!"

—LEONARDO DA VINCI

"Once you really commence to see things, then you really commence to feel things."

—EDWARD J. STEICHEN

"Every photograph, no matter how painstaking the observation of the photographer or how long the actual exposure, is essentially a snapshot; it is an attempt to penetrate and capture the unique esthetic moment that singles itself out of the thousands of chance compositions, uncrystallized and insignificant, that occur in the course of a day."

—LEWIS MUMFORD

"There is no particular virtue, it seems to me, in wasting time to find out for yourself what already has been discovered. One should save one's skill in research for what has not yet been discovered."

—MORTIMER J. ADLER

"The possibilities of natural light are so infinitely great they can never be exhausted. In a lifetime you could hardly exhaust all of the light-possibilities for a single subject. . . . The important thing is that you stay with whatever equipment you choose until it becomes an automatic extension of your own vision, a third eye. Then, through this photographic eye you will be able to look out on a new light-world, a world for the most part uncharted and unexplored, a world that lies waiting to be discovered and revealed."

—EDWARD WESTON

"We have been cocksure of many things that were not so."

—OLIVER WENDELL HOLMES

THE AMATEUR

# Photographer's

# Handbook

# 1

# *A Snapshot History of Photography*

Everybody likes to look at pictures. Even the ancients indulged. This led one among them, a kinsman of Confucius, to say that a thousand words could not tell as much or speak as eloquently as *one* picture. The multi-million sales of the picture magazines and newspapers seem to bear this out.

Those staggering circulations prove, if anything at all, that people haven't changed much. They're intensely curious about others, which is no more than neighborly; they continue to gape at the never-ending miracles of science, which is properly respectful; and they are always itching to go strange places and do new things even if only by armchair, which is *one* way of answering the call of adventure.

Until about a hundred years ago, and except for a few gifted men and women with artistic talent, there was no way for any of us to make a satisfactory permanent record of what we saw. This bothered many people for untold years, but nothing much was done about it until a young Frenchman by the name of Joseph Nicéphore Niepce discovered the secret of transferring and preserving the image seen with a mirror device used by artists. He died before his own picture could be taken, but not before giving *photography* its euphonious name and a magnificent start. What he did was to open up a new and wonderful world of self-expression for millions of perceptive, though sometimes inarticulate, people. But his story comes later. We are only concerned now with what he gave us.

*Photography is a means of recording forever the things one sees for a moment.*

It is better than memory, because it not only recalls things to *our* mind, but it enables us to show others, with *absolute realism,* what we have done, where we have been, what we have seen, even what we have thought. *And it is more accurate than memory.* With one glance, our eye can only take in the *big* things, and sometimes it even misses those, or fails to understand them. The camera lens, however, with what is often a fortunate disregard for *our* opinion of what's important, captures everything simultaneously. Then, with the aid of a little simple chemistry, it preserves that everything for us, to inspect as searchingly as we choose, wherever, whenever, or as often as we like. Which is not to say that such a facsimile cannot be altered to suit our fancy; it can, and in many ways, as we shall see later. But if we *wish* to picture it exactly as it was, we can do so with a photograph—and the least part of the scene registers on the film at the same moment as all the others, without any change whatever except that which we ourselves deliberately impose.

## HOW IT ALL STARTED

The history of photography is the history of a toy that was taken seriously. The toy is the *camera obscura,* a gadget consisting of a light-tight box with a mirror, a ground-glass or parchment screen, and a pinhole or lens. It is used by artists to help them convert large, three-dimensional scenes into small two-dimensional ones. We don't know who first invented it.

The principle involved seems to have been casually noted as much as ten thousand years ago, when the first civilized human beings, who were careful observers of nature, moved from the great plateau that is now Iran to such lands as Chaldea and Egypt. There, the sun burned more fiercely and people hid from its rays in darkened tents and still darker huts. Whenever there was a hole in the tent or a chink in the hut, and a sunlit camel or other object was in a line with it outside, the light was reflected back through the hole, making a colored, upside-down picture inside. Lying there, away from the hot sun, watching people and things move slowly by, must have been a pleasant relaxation for the tired Egyptian business man. Today, we have improved on this diversion somewhat. For one thing, the image is right-side-up, and brighter. For another, our scene is more varied, and we have added sound effects. But we have to sit up, instead of lying down; and, unless we are wealthy enough or important enough to demand privacy and get it, we have to watch these sights with thousands of others all crowded into one large room; and sometimes these others interfere with our pleasure in the sights and sounds. So, some ways considered, the Egyptians had the better of it at that.

Thousands of years after our Egyptian business man first noticed his inverted street show, Euclid, inventor of geometry, made use of the same idea to prove to his pupils that light travels in straight lines. Later, about 350 B.C., Aristotle, dozing under a tree one afternoon, noticed the sun's round image on the ground. He looked around and saw that the image was coming through a small rectangular hole made by an accidental arrangement of the leaves on a branch above him. He interposed a sheet of papyrus between the rays of light and the ground, and by alternating the distance between the papyrus and the hole in the leaves he found he could alter the size of the sun's image. But wise as was old Aristotle in other ways, he failed to appreciate what he had just discovered. He went no further with his experiments; in fact, he went back to sleep.

In the year 1267, the illustrious Roger Bacon described, in rather vague terms, an instrument that used a mirror for viewing pictures that *may* have been the first *precamera*. But it isn't until we come to that man of wonder, Leonardo da Vinci, in the early years of the sixteenth century, that we find an exact and full account of what we know today as the *camera obscura*. Leonardo, in his famous *Notebooks*,[1] showed a working diagram of the camera, explained how to operate it, but did not claim it as his own discovery.

For no other reason than that he was the first to popularize its use (he neither thought it up nor improved it), history seems to have thrust the honor of being the "inventor of the camera" on a precocious young Neapolitan, a writer of popular reference works, named John Baptista Porta. Porta was a sort of H. G. Wells or Lancelot Hogben of the sixteenth century. In 1553, when he was only fifteen, he published a work called *Natural Magic,* in which he described the *camera obscura* and suggested its use for a peep show! Actually, he did nothing more for the camera than mention it.

The man who first used a *lens,* instead of a pinhole, in a camera box was Daniel Barbaro, a Venetian nobleman, in the year 1568. He explained, in his book, *Practice of Perspective,* the value of using a smaller diaphragm opening to make the picture sharper, described how to move the paper screen until it came within the focus of the lens, and discussed the application of a method for drawing in true perspective. Here is what he says about the camera he invented:

1. Seeing, therefore, on the paper the outline of things, you can draw with a pencil all the perspective and the shading and coloring, according to nature . . .

2. You should choose the glass [lens] which does the best, and you should cover it so much that you leave a little in the middle clear and open and you will see a still brighter effect.

The lens he used was an old man's *convex* spectacle lens. He had tried a *concave* lens, but found that it wouldn't work. Barbaro's camera was

---

[1] A fine English translation by *Edward MacCurdy* was published by Reynal and Hitchcock in 1938.

nothing more than an artist's prop; he intended only to sketch the pictures projected on its screen.

Johann Kepler, the great astronomer, added much to the effectiveness of Barbaro's camera. In 1611, in a book called *Dioptrice,* he not only named Barbaro's instrument the *camera obscura,* but he also laid down certain laws by which both single and compound lenses projected images, explained why the image was reversed, and how one could go about projecting enlarged images on paper by the use of a concave lens set at the right distance behind the convex. From that time on better lenses, specifically designed for the purpose, began to be used in the camera.

## FIXING THE IMAGE

While all this was going on, another group of men, artists mostly ("terrible painters," M. F. Agha calls them), were hard at work trying to crack the seemingly insoluble problem of how to make the camera image *stay put.* Naturally, this would have been a great boon to all artists. Since their work was painstaking and slow, and since light conditions outdoors, and facial expressions indoors, changed rapidly and were hard to recapture, it would have been of tremendous help if someone could transfer the camera image permanently to another surface so that an artist might be able to study it later, at his leisure. I am sure that it was some such tempting picture as this which drove Louis Jacques Mandé Daguerre, a mediocre French painter, famous in Paris for the success of his *Diorama* (a show with huge paintings and marvelous light and sound effects, housed in a special building) to continue his experiments on the camera image for five, fruitless years. Finally, through the good offices of the optician in whose shop he traded, Daguerre met another customer who had been working on the very same problem but with little more success. The other customer was Joseph Nicéphore Niepce, of *Chalon* on the Seine.

Now, Niepce was a chemist, not a painter, but he had a son who was a painter; so the problem was still in the family. Besides, he used to putter around making lithographs—and one of his dreams was the multiplication of designs by means of light. The pictures produced by Niepce needed about a seven-hour exposure, so only still-life subjects were attempted. And that, incidentally, is why no photograph was ever made of Niepce.

The two men began to work together on the problem in 1829, and they kept at it for many years. Niepce's method was to coat a copper plate with a thin layer of asphaltum, place a drawing made on transparent paper in contact with it and expose it to the light of the sun. The sun hardened the asphaltum. Where the lines of the drawing obscured the light of the sun, however, the asphaltum remained soft, and this was the secret of his process. He washed away the soft asphaltum with a special solvent, which exposed the metal surface of the plate. Next, he etched the plate with nitric acid, removed all of the asphaltum, inked the plate, and then printed with it. This was the *heliogravure* process which Niepce had been trying to apply to the image of the *camera obscura*. It didn't work, because the asphaltum plate was not sensitive enough.

In 1831, the two men began to experiment with *silver plates* coated with *silver salts*, but their luck was no better. Niepce died in 1833, and Daguerre had to continue the experiments alone. It was not easy for him to do so. His wife had begun to nag him to go on with his painting and leave the camera alone. His income from portrait commmissions had ceased; and, most depressing, his savings began to run low. He seemed to be getting nowhere. Then, quite by accident, he stumbled upon it.

He had been experimenting with *iodized* silver plates. One sunny day he began to expose a plate as usual, but clouds blew up and obscured the sun. Discouraged, Daguerre packed up his equipment and went home. He started out the next morning to try again, but discovered to his confusion and delight that yesterday's underexposed plate, which he was about to throw away, had somehow, in the meantime, acquired an entrancing likeness of yesterday's scene. What a moment for Daguerre! But he still had to discover what had happened. Further experiments revealed that it was the fumes of *mercury*, in an open container in his cupboard, which had so magically developed the invisible image, and that Herschel's *sodium thiosulphate* (*hypo*, to you) could *fix* it. And so the thing was done.

## THE NEGATIVE

But no great discovery is ever left by nature to the efforts of just one man. Many people, working in different parts of the world, and independently of one another, suddenly attack a problem when the need for its solution arises. For example, when scattered populations make better and faster communication necessary, we have the telephone, invented in 1876 by Bell, but also in that same year by Elisha Grey, who worked it out quite independently of Bell. Again, we have the motorcar engine, invented in 1879 by Selden in America, but also in 1879 by Carl Benz of Germany; the electric lamp, invented in 1880 by Thomas A. Edison in America, and by J. W. Swan in England—both men having hit on the idea of using carbon filaments in a vacuum, though neither one was aware of what the other was doing.

And so it was with photography. While Daguerre was being honored in 1839, for his discovery, by the French Academy, an English scientist named William Henry Fox Talbot perfected, that same year, a way of printing pictures on white paper coated with silver chloride. Talbot was probably the first man to print through a paper *negative*. Daguerre's pictures, as you may recall, were *positives* and could not be duplicated. But Talbot's prints on silver paper were reversed, white to black, as our negatives are today, and could be used to make as many positives as he wanted to. He called his invention the *calotype process*, and his pictures *photogenic drawings*. We still nod to Talbot, you see, when we speak of a comely lady with shapely limbs as being *photogenic*.

Talbot was an ingenious experimenter. He was the first man to try *high-speed*, or *stroboscopic*, photography. In 1851 he attached a copy of the London *Times* to a whirring wheel upon which he had focused his camera. He loaded the camera, darkened the room, opened the shutter, and flashed a brilliant high-voltage electric spark. The photograph he got in this way stopped the motion of the wheel and made it possible to read, clearly, every word of the newspaper.

Talbot's discovery of the calotype process, like Daguerre's in this one respect, was an accident. His cat upset an extract of nutgalls (from which we get *pyro*) on some half-exposed papers coated with *silver chloride*. The rest was easy. Have you noticed, by the way, how nature has a habit of jogging a man's elbow if he doesn't get on with his work fast enough, or if he gets lost in the woods of experimentation? It's a comforting thought.

Other men, and one woman, who have contributed to the advance of the photographic process, are:

*The Alchemists,* who in the sixteenth century began a furtive search for ways of converting base metals to gold, and for an elixir of life to make men immortal. They found neither, but did discover *silver nitrate* (lunar caustic) which darkened in the sun (and gave us photographic film and paper), and they learned how to make clear glass for lenses (to sharpen the eyes of our cameras).

*Johann Heinrich Schulze,* an absent-minded German doctor, who forgot in 1727 to remove a flask filled with chalk, silver and nitric acid from his laboratory window; *the sun darkened it.* He tried this again in another way, by coating some paper with silver nitrate and exposing it to the sun; the same thing happened. By cutting out a stencil, he produced photographic lettering for the amusement of his friends. But the image disappeared after a time, and he never learned why it appeared or how it faded.

*Carl William Scheele,* a Swedish apothecary, who in 1777 was experimenting with the nitrate and chloride salts of silver and discovered that they turned brown under light because they had been converted to *metallic silver.* He also found, by throwing the rainbow of refracted light from a prism on these salts, that the violet end of the spectrum acted more quickly to darken them than the colors at the other end.

*Thomas Wedgwood,* a son of the famous potter of England, who experimented with silver nitrate, in 1802, and though he made pictures on paper with light, by using paintings on glass for negatives, he was unable to keep them from fading. His co-worker was *Humphry Davy.*

*Sir John Herschel,* the British astronomer, who discovered in 1819 that hypo was a solvent of silver salts. He also made the first silver chloride printing paper and introduced the words *photograph* and *photography.*

WHAT THE WELL-DRESSED PHOTOGRAPHER OF
1850 WORE

AND HOW THE LANDSCAPE CHANGED WHEN HE
UNPACKED

*Christian Friedrich Schoenbein,* a German chemist of the nineteenth century, who dissolved guncotton in alcohol and ether and produced *collodion,* the first base film for glass plates. It adhered well to glass, and could be sensitized.

*Joseph Petzval,* of Vienna, who designed the first, fast portrait lens in 1841. The lens covered a field of 25 degrees and had an aperture of $f\,3.4$. The previous landscape lenses used in the daguerreotype cameras had had a maximum aperture of $f\,11$. Petzval's lens was therefore ten times as fast!

*Frederick Scott Archer,* an Englishman, who made the first *collodion wet plate* in 1851 by adding potassium and iodine to the collodion and then dipping the coated plate in a solution of silver nitrate. The plates had to be exposed immediately after being coated, and developed within a few minutes after exposure. If you think the modern amateur carries a lot of equipment, look at what the well-dressed photographer wore, and carried, in those days.

*C. Piazza Smyth,* Astronomer Royal for Scotland, whose "little Egyptian camera," made in 1861 for a photographic trip to the Pyramids, was the first true *miniature camera.* The negative, a wet collodion plate, was one inch square; the lens, a perfectly corrected anastigmat of his own design, had a focal length of $1\frac{3}{4}$ inches and an aperture of $f\,4.5$; focusing was precise; and the shutter, a clever focal-plane arrangement, was adjusted to give longer exposures to foreground than to sky.

*Matthew B. Brady,* whose documentary photographs of the American Civil War, among the first such ever recorded, proved that a photographer's courage and daring have to exceed even his technical skill. Brady used the bulky, and therefore conspicuous, daguerreotype equipment; so he was constantly under fire.

*Dr. R. L. Maddox,* of London, who produced the first dry plate in 1871 by substituting gelatin for collodion.

*H. W. Vogel,* a German chemist, who found in 1873 that the addition of a dye to an emulsion made it sensitive to the light rays absorbed by that dye. *Orthochromatic* film (sensitive to all colors except *spectral red*) was the result of his discovery.

*Charles Bennet,* who further improved the dry plate by cooking the gelatin emulsion and thereby increasing its sensitivity. This ended the use of the wet plate, in 1878. By 1880, George Eastman was marketing dry plates in America.

*Hannibal Goodwin,* an American clergyman, who was the first to patent, in 1887, the invention of the modern transparent roll films. Eastman's roll film, marketed earlier, was really a paper film coated with a layer of soluble gelatin, which was in turn coated with the emulsion proper. The emulsion was later stripped from the paper base for use as a negative. It is interesting to reread what the *British Photographic Almanac* had to say about this in 1889:

The American films have been brought to that stage of perfection that very little improvement can be desired. Of course, we all hope to see the time when a transparent flexible film is discovered that will do away with stripping altogether, but while many efforts and experiments have been made in this direction, we believe nothing practicable has yet been found; and while there may be room for improvement in this respect, it cannot be denied that the present mode of stripping is both reliable and satisfactory in results, and is withal a very interesting operation.

*Hurter* and *Driffield*, two British amateur photographers, whose efforts, in 1890, to find out why equal increases of exposure did not produce equal increases in the density of the silver deposit on an emulsion, led to the discovery of the *characteristic curve*, known to most of us as the *H. and D. curve*. What this means is that, no matter what the exposure, there is an optimum developing time for best results with each emulsion, depending on the temperature of the developer. This easy *time and temperature* method of developing is the one we all use today.

*David Octavius Hill*, a Scotch artist, who was the first to use calotypes for portraiture on an extensive scale. Having been commissioned, in 1843, to paint a gigantic group portrait of 500 heads on a canvas twelve feet long, he decided to simplify the job a bit by using calotypes of the sitters to sketch from. He got a young chemist, Robert Adamson, to help him. The photographs were all taken out of doors in brilliant sunlight, and a mirror reflector was used to soften the harsh shadows. Hill posed and lighted the models while Adamson developed and printed the negatives. No one today remembers Hill's painting; but his camera portraits are still treasured as the finest ever made.

*George Eastman*, who is responsible for the fabulous spread of amateur photography. He manufactured the first compact roll-film camera, the *Kodak* (thus named because the word was odd, easy to remember, and sounded "like the click of a shutter"), as well as the first daylight-loading black-paper-backed roll film, and innumerable other devices and materials to make photography easy and pleasant.

*Dr. Paul Rudolph*, who in 1902 designed what has since become the most popular lens of all time, the Zeiss Tessar. According to some, however, the *finest* lens he ever produced is his Plasmat, offered by Meyer of Goerlitz in 1918.

*E. König*, a brilliant chemist in the dye works at Hoechst, Germany, who produced in 1904 the series of sensitizing cyanine-dyes that made *panchromatic* films (sensitive to *all* colors) possible.

*Alfred Stieglitz*, the grand old man of photography, whose magazine

*Camera Work* is one of the finest monuments ever erected to any art, as his own photographs are among the most perfect examples of that art. If Talbot is the father of photography, Stieglitz is spiritually its godfather. He did more to establish photography as an art than any other man living or dead. In 1924, the Royal Photographic Society of Great Britain conferred its highest honor, the Progress Medal, upon Mr. Stieglitz for "services rendered in founding and fostering Pictorial Photography in America, and particularly for the initiation and publication of *Camera Work,* the most artistic record of photography ever attempted."

*Oscar Barnack,* who wanted to become a landscape painter, but whose father persuaded him to start off as a mechanic's apprentice. The indirect result of this strange shift in careers was the invention of the Leica, which Barnack perfected in 1923, as an exposure pretester for movie film. It also replaced his bulky field camera on mountain hikes.

*Max Berek,* of Wetzlar, whose designs and calculations for sharp, fast lenses made *miniature camera* photography possible. He is responsible for the Elmar, the Summitar, and other superb lenses for small cameras.

*Harold E. Edgerton,* who perfected a high-powered stroboscope for ultra-high-speed photography, and made it possible for us to see what happens when a bullet passes through a light bulb, when a drop of milk hits a plate, and how a humming bird with stilled wings can rest on air. His usual *stroboscope* exposures, by the way, are *less* than 1/50,000 of a second . . . and recently, he made some at the incredible speed of a millionth of a second! When you consider that *quick as a wink* is no more than 1/40 of a second, you can see that the stroboscope exposures are really fast.

*Leopold Godowsky,* a violinist, and *Leopold Mannes,* a pianist, both enthusiastic camera amateurs, whose crude experiments in an improvised home laboratory, to find a film that could take pictures in color, attracted the attention of the Eastman Kodak Company in 1931 . . . and led finally to the discovery of *Kodachrome,* which was released to the public in 1935.

*Dr. Katharine B. Blodgett,* whose experiments on *glare* and reflected light, in the research laboratory of the General Electric company in 1939, led to the remarkable conclusion that glass could be made *invisible* and glareproof if properly coated. By applying a thin film of soap (one-quarter of a lightwave in thickness) to the surface of glass, Dr. Blodgett was able to remove all reflections. Most lenses lose about 25 to 30 per cent of the light they collect, by reflection. With Dr. Blodgett's glass treatment, they transmit *all* of this light.

*Dr. C. Hawley Cartwright,* young physics professor at Massachusetts Institute of Technology, who perfected, in 1940, Dr. Blodgett's method for glare control. He coated the lens, not with a delicate film of soap, but with a hard, durable coating of evaporated calcium, magnesium or other metallic fluoride about four-one-millionths of an inch thick.

*Douglas F. Winnek,* of New York, who in 1940 made *three*-dimensional photography (without the use of a stereopticon) possible. By *lenticulating* ordinary film (impressing on its momentarily softened surface many minute convex lenses in the form of cylindrical ridges) he is able to make transparencies so astonishingly lifelike that the petals of a flower seem to be falling right out of the picture. Under the wing of the U.S. Navy, Winnek perfected (and in 1947 demonstrated) his process for making three-dimensional prints in black-and-white and color.

*Edwin H. Land,* of the Polaroid Corporation, who in 1947 announced what he called a revolutionary photographic process by means of which a black-and-white paper print can be produced in a camera less than a minute after clicking the shutter. The trick is done by means of a sandwich consisting of a layer of light-sensitive material and a layer of positive paper between which is a pod of viscous chemical fluid. After exposure this sandwich is drawn through a roller in the camera, the pressure of which breaks the pod, spreading the fluid evenly over the two surfaces. The result is that the chemicals, consisting of hydroquinone and sodium thiosulphate, first convert the light-exposed silver bromide in the emulsion of the negative material into metallic silver grains, in the usual way, but instead of being dissolved and removed by the hypo, the metallic silver— and this *is* revolutionary—is transferred to the positive paper, which is not light sensitive, thus creating the black-and-white positive print. The print emerges slightly damp but dries almost immediately.

There are now many kinds of Polaroid cameras, including the new Electric Eye (Model 900) which operates automatically. Film speeds range from ASA 64 to 3000, and include a positive transparency at ASA 1000, and another (Type 55 P/N) that gives you a permanent negative along with the print in 15 seconds. All in all, a formidable attack on the mainland of photography, with all beachheads secured.

*Rowland S. Potter,* of the Dupont Corporation, who in May 1940 perfected a multilayer enlarging paper that is capable of yielding any grade of contrast from one negative, or prints of uniform quality from negatives of varying contrast or density. The gradations, between soft and hard, are produced by printing through blue, yellow, or other special filters. A high-speed *Varigam* appeared in 1951. Ilford introduced *Multigrade* in 1940; and Eastman, Ansco, and Haloid marketed their brands in 1957.

*Andrew Azan,* of the Aristo Corporation in Port Washington, N.Y., who pioneered in the development of cold-light grid lamps for enlargers and contact printers. In 1957 he perfected new light sources for both multi-contrast papers and type C color materials which eliminate all need for filters: the *Gradacon,* for monochrome photography, and the *Spectrocon* for color work.

*Alfred* and *Rudolph Simmon* (who prior to becoming two-thirds of the Simmon Brothers, manufacturers of precision photographic equipment, were respectively chief engineer at Westinghouse X-ray and master technician supervising the design of the Rolleiflex at the Franke and Heidecke plant in Germany). In 1957 they offered ingenious new solutions for two old photographic problems, contrast and scratches: 1. The Simmon Omega *Electronic Variable Contrast Timer* (for multi-contrast papers) which actuates a floating double filter attached beneath the lens of the enlarger. This is moved into position electronically by a "brain box," the dials of which can be set for simultaneous exposure time and contrast. 2. The *Refractamatic 35 Negative Holder,* which overcomes dust, fingerprints and film abrasions by washing *Refractasil* (see page 266) over the emulsion.

*The Western Union Telegraph Company,* which in 1947 announced a new light source for enlargers: the *Zirconium* concentrated arc lamp, which produces more brilliance and more detail than is possible with conventional enlarger lamps. The advantages of this powerful point-source light are that it gives almost ten times as much illumination as a tungsten lamp, maintains its original brilliance (at a color temperature of 3400-3600° Kelvin, which is perfect for Ektachrome, Kodachrome or Ansco Color) during its full life (800 hours), and is rated at only 25 watts. Its one serious disadvantage is its extremely harsh contrast, which will require special compensating techniques for developing the negative as well as the print. Sylvania subsequently arranged to market this lamp in 1952.

We have traveled far. We have made many wonderful advances. But sometimes, it seems, we go in circles. In 1838, Daguerre discovers that the fumes of mercury bring out the image on his iodized-silver plates; in 1938, two chemists in the Ansco Research Laboratories announce the discovery of a new method for the hypersensitizing of photographic emulsions, *by subjecting them to the fumes of mercury!* In 1851 Talbot succeeds in stopping ultrarapid motion with an electric flash; in 1940 Edgerton does the same with the flash of his stroboscope. In 1831 Niepce coats a metal plate and takes a picture for viewing by reflection; in 1940 another inventor announces the discovery of a way to coat *aluminum* film, for projection by *reflection.* So we're back where we started, having completed a circle.

But perhaps this isn't really a circle. Maybe, like one of the characters in Edwin Abbott's delightful little book, *Flatland,* we are trying to see it as a circle with our eyes closed. Perhaps it's that wonderful freak of nature, the *vortex.* Lord Kelvin said that atoms move in a vortex. Since life itself does, why shouldn't photography?

CHAPTER

2

# *The Magic of Light*

*"**Light** glorifies everything. It transforms and ennobles the most commonplace and ordinary subjects. The object is nothing; light is everything."*—LEONARD MISONNE.

Of all the wonders of the world, and there are many more than seven, none is more wonderful than the phenomenon of light. It not only creates life . . . the blade of grass, even man himself . . . but it puts on, daily, the most magnificent show which ever escaped a Hollywood producer, that colossal spectacle of forms and colors known as *the changing universe*.

Whether you are eager to discover what goes on in the vast spaces outside our world, or just curious about what goes on inside the atom, light says, "Here's the way it is. *Look!*" With the beams of an X-ray tube, you can see through impenetrable objects; with *infrared* light, you can cut through the haze of distance, take pictures in the dark, recover what has been blotted out or destroyed. Light can open doors, and close them; it can point things out, or hide them. And *this* is the amazing stuff which photographers use when they carelessly take a snapshot of a Sunday.

Since the function of photography is to reproduce the shape and tones of things, and since light is the substance which makes this miracle possible, it is important, right at the start, that we learn about light—what it is, how it acts, what it does, and how to control it.

A working knowledge of light and shade will clear up most of the troubles you have as an amateur. It cannot be said too often that light is the most important element in photography. Use it badly and all your technical skill is a waste of time; use it well and your technical shortcomings will never be noticed. And now for some interesting facts about light.

## WHAT IT IS

Scientists have concocted many odd and ingenious theories to explain the mystery of light, but the two generally accepted today, and the only ones about which we need concern ourselves, are the *corpuscular* theory suggested by an Englishman, *Sir Isaac Newton,* and the *wave* theory proposed by a Dutchman, *Christian Huygens.* It is the combination of these two theories, worked out more than two hundred fifty years ago, which best explains the various phenomena of light. Both theories make use of that strange, unknown and unseen substance which is supposed to permeate all space and all matter, the *ether.*

According to the *corpuscular* theory, luminous bodies throw off discrete particles of matter which set up an electromagnetic disturbance in the ether, just as a stone dropped in still water will start a series of concentric waves moving outward. Watch the water for a moment after the stone has hit it, and you will notice that the water bobs up and down but does not travel away, as the wave does; it is the *wave form* alone which spreads out in all directions. So it is with the ether.

According to the *wave* theory, light is just another form of electrical energy operating through the ether. Other electromagnetic impulses are *cosmic rays, gamma rays, X-rays, ultra-violet rays, infrared rays, radio waves.* Light waves differ from these others only in size; gamma rays being among the shortest, radio waves among the longest, and light rays, the ones visible to the eye, being about halfway between. See *Wave Length Scale, Fig. 1.*

Though light tears through space at the incredible speed of 186,000 miles a second, it takes time to travel. The light distance between the sun and the earth, to give you an illustration, is *480 seconds*—but then the geographical distance, according to the astronomers, is 93,000,000 miles! Even so, light moves fast. Just imagine a train going around the earth at the equator at a speed of 60 miles an hour; if you were riding on that train it would take you 17¼ days to get back where you started. Riding a light wave, you could travel the same distance in just one-seventh of a second! So you see that the *speed* of light is at least one factor you will not have to worry about in photography.

## WHERE IT COMES FROM

### NATURAL LIGHT

Practically all of the light that shines on the earth comes from the sun. The stars provide a little, and the moon reflects a bit of the light she herself gets from the sun;[1] but most of what we call natural light is direct or reflected sunlight; in other words, *daylight.*

---

[1] The exposure for scenes taken by full moon on a clear night have to be 150,000 times longer than the same scene taken by direct sunlight; that is, moonlight requires 25 minutes for each 1/100 second of sunlight.

We think of daylight as white light, but it's nothing of the sort. It's light composed of every color of the rainbow. When we see a rainbow, as a matter of fact, we are seeing the actual colors which, blended, produce white light.

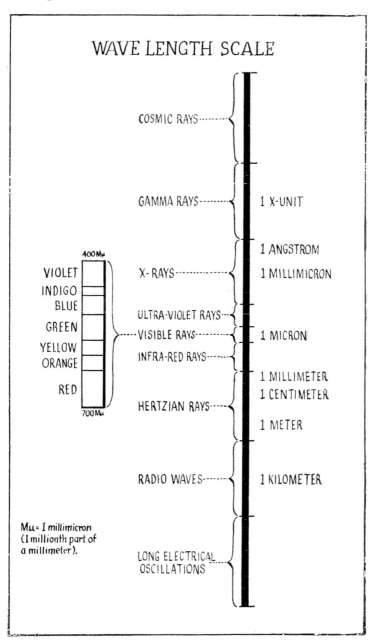

FIG. 1. VISIBLE RAYS PLAY ONLY A SMALL PART IN
THE UNIVERSE

Daylight changes in color from hour to hour and from place to place. At noon, with the sky clear, it is *blue-white;* in the mountains it is *violet;* while at sea level, at sundown, it turns *reddish.* We shall see, later, why all this happens.

## ARTIFICIAL LIGHT

That's the light which man has learned to make for himself: twig fires in ancient days, fluorescent tubes today. However, no matter how it is finally produced, it is still only secondhand sunlight. There are really only two ways to make artificial light: (1) by *chemical action,* and (2) by *electrical action.* All the other ways are combinations or variations of these two. But whatever the method, the sun can be credited with having supplied the material or the energy necessary for the action.

If it is light produced by burning one element in another, magnesium in oxygen for example, the sun is responsible since both elements came originally from the sun. If it is light made by burning oil, wood or coal, the sun is still responsible, since oil is a product of sun-nourished animal life, wood and coal are products of sun-nourished plant life, and oxygen we already know about. If it is light made by an electric current which is generated by steam or water power, the sun has created that too, since the fuel necessary to move the generators is produced from plant life; and if fuel is not used, then water power must be, in which case the sun has been at work again, making clouds which produce rain and swell the rivers that turn the dynamos which create the current that lights the lamps.

## THE KINDS OF LIGHT

There are ten kinds of light used in photography. They are:

| | |
|---|---|
| 1. Daylight | 6. Flash |
| 2. Carbon arc | 7. Fluorescent |
| 3. Mercury-vapor | 8. X-ray |
| 4. Incandescent | 9. Infrared |
| 5. Flood | 10. Stroboscopic |

Daylight includes: direct sunlight; the skylight created by the sun shining on the dust and vapor in the atmosphere; and reflected sunlight.

Carbon-arc lamps supply a light which, in color, is somewhere between sunlight and floodlight. To alter their light characteristics the carbons are sometimes drilled and then filled with a core of inorganic salts. They are inconvenient to use, however, being noisy and requiring attention.

Mercury-vapor lamps provide a *cold* light very rich in violet rays, and therefore very active photographically. They are available as *Cooper-*

*Hewitt* tubes or as *Sunlamp* bulbs, both forms requiring special transformers. They are excellent for portrait lighting and for enlarging.

Incandescent light is the glow produced by intense heat; sources for such light are *wax candles, kerosene lamps, gas burners, electric bulbs.* The incandescent electric lamps are, of course, the best and most popular of these. Easy to use, quite dependable, and very low in cost, they have a useful life of approximately 1000 hours if used at their normal rated voltage. The light supplied by the regular clear or frosted bulbs is constant though yellowish; but you can also buy bulbs that have been made with a blue-tinted glass.

Flood bulbs are also incandescent electric lamps. They differ from the others in that they have a slightly heavier filament and are used at about twice their rated voltage. This overburning shortens their working life to about two to six hours. However, their life can be extended to 1000 hours, provided they are operated at 65 volts instead of at the customary house voltage. For this reason many amateurs interpose a resistor transformer in their flood bulb lines, focusing under reduced voltage and exposing at the full voltage. This method of using flood bulbs is recommended to all amateurs who use them a great deal; it is not only easy on the pocketbook but easy on the eyes.

Flash bulbs are another form of incandescent lamp, but they have the shortest life of all—about 5/100 of a second. They are filled with oxygen and a metallic aluminum filament in the form of crumpled foil, ribbon or wire. They operate at any voltage from 3 to 120 volts, which means that they can be fired by dry cells as well as by the regular house current.[2] They produce an intense white flash, the peak of which is about 3/100 of a second. They can be synchronized with focal-plane or between-the-lens shutters.

Fluorescent tubes produce a soft, cold light of great photographic intensity. They are filled with *neon, argon, krypton* or *xenon* gas, or sometimes with a mixture of any of these. They require high voltage transformers, which are dangerous if you're clumsy or careless. They can be made to supply almost any color of light, consume very little current and produce almost no heat. Argon tubes have been used in enlargers, but the blue light, though strong actinically, is weak visually, which makes focusing very difficult. The new General Electric fluorescent tubes, used for the first time at the New York World's Fair, differ from the ones just described. In the G. E. tubes the gas is used only to *activate* a fluorescent substance with which the inner walls of the tubes have been lined. It is this substance, and not the gas, which furnishes the light. The color of the light depends on the kind of coating used.

X-rays are used by doctors and dentists and are of no real concern to

[2] See footnote page 362.

amateur photographers. However, if the subject arouses your interest, and you want to know all about it, see your doctor. He will undoubtedly be glad to show you how it works.

Infrared light is one of the by-products of incandescence. Good sources are sunlight, candlelight, gaslight, electric light—almost any kind of light that produces heat. Its use indoors is rather limited, unless you can afford expensive equipment. But outdoors all you need is a roll of *infrared* film and a special dark red filter (because the film is sensitive to other light rays). You can get some unusual pictures with this film: distant objects, invisible to the eye because of haze or fog, reproduce needle sharp; grass turns white, skies go black. In fact, using infrared rays you can take moonlight pictures in bright sun!

Extraordinary as are the feats of *stroboscopic light,* the explanation for them is quite simple. The stroboscope is a light that flickers! The secret, of course, is in the way it flickers. The flicker of an eye, you may remember, is about 1/40 of a second; a stroboscopic flicker is 1/1,000,000 of a second! At this speed even a bullet can be stopped in its tracks. An electric spark inside a gas-filled lamp produces the stroboscope light; the current which sets off this spark is fed first into an electrical reservoir, technically known as a condenser. While that gradually builds up, the inert gas with which the stroboscopic tube is filled begins to *ionize* (some of the molecules are converted into *ions*). When that has proceeded far enough to permit electricity to flow, the condenser is suddenly short-circuited, the stored-up current spills over and produces the lightning flash that takes the picture. Since 1/1250 of a second is the fastest speed you can get out of a modern camera shutter, and since that isn't fast enough to stop such action as a humming bird in flight or the drive of a golf club, no one was able to take any *ultrafast* pictures until Professor Edgerton, of the Massachusetts Institute of Technology, began to work on the problem. He neatly sidestepped the issue of a faster shutter by doing away with the shutter altogether. His lights blackout by themselves at a preset speed.

## HOW IT ACTS

### LIGHT TRAVELS IN STRAIGHT LINES

There are two ways you can test this for yourself. (1) Watch a beam of light as it passes through a hole in a darkened room. What you see is the atmospheric dust intercepting the light waves and reflecting them. If the room were dust free you could not see the beam, only the spot of light when the beam hit the floor or a wall. (2) Take a cardboard box, about the size and shape of a shoe box, remove the cover and use it to make a center wall that rests on the sides and can be moved up and down. Now, placing this center card flat against one end of the box, run a hatpin or a needle right through the box and the movable card. Do the same with

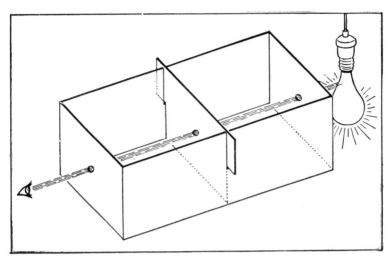

FIG. 2. AN EXPERIMENT TO PROVE THAT LIGHT
TRAVELS IN STRAIGHT LINES

the other end, using the hole made in the loose card to locate the position for the third hole. Finally, place a light at one end of the box and look through the other. If the holes are in a straight line, you will be able to see the light. But if you lift the loose card the least bit, the light will disappear.

## LIGHT LOSES INTENSITY

The further it has to travel the weaker it gets. Scientists have worked out a formula that accounts for this. It is called the law of inverse squares, and reads: *Light decreases as the square of the distance.* Let's see if we can make that any clearer. When the distance between a light source and a lighted surface is doubled, the light spreads out and covers four times the area, but each quarter gets only one-fourth as much light; at three times the distance, the light covers nine times the area but with one-ninth the intensity.[3] *Fig. 3* shows why this happens.

[3] This law applies, theoretically, only to *point* sources of light without reflectors. The rays from a point of light are cone-shaped (*divergent*), not cylindric (*parallel*). Whether light sources are one or the other makes a big difference, as you will see later when we consider such things as shade and shadow, why condenser enlargers give more contrast, and why the new reflectors for the small flash bulbs throw so much light. Though we rarely meet a point source of light as such in photography, we are constantly making use of the law of inverse squares. It applies in every case where the *area* of the light source is no more than a small fraction of the distance between the light and the subject.

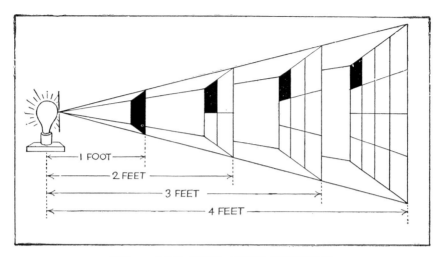

FIG. 3.  HOW LIGHT LOSES INTENSITY

### LIGHT AND CAMERA DISTANCE

There is one notable exception to the above rule which nevertheless confirms it, and that is *camera distance*. We do not alter the exposure for a subject each time we move the camera away from it. And the reason, believe it or not, is the law of inverse squares! Let's see how it works. Choosing a clear day without haze, let's take our camera outdoors and focus on an object 20 feet away; this produces a 2-inch image on the ground glass. Then, let's move back 20 feet and refocus; this creates a 1-inch image. (By *image* we mean, of course, the *object in the picture*. The picture naturally remains the same size, and the images within it become smaller as the camera moves away.)  If we examine the smaller image now, we notice that it seems brighter. Actually, it isn't. Each point on the 2-inch image corresponds exactly to each point on the 1-inch image.  There are just as many light rays; the beams are crowded together into a smaller space, that's all. The effect of increasing the distance is canceled out by what the lens does to the image. That's why the exposure remains the same in both cases. The emulsion, you see, gets just as much light, ray for ray, regardless of distance. Exactly the same thing happens indoors. That's why we never worry about the distance between the camera and the subject, but just the distance between the *light* and the subject.

### LENS DISTANCE

We have just said that the exposure remains the same, when the camera distance changes, but there's a catch to that.  It remains the same provided the distance between the lens and the film doesn't change either. But we know that it does. Normally, we don't have to worry about this at all because the distance between lens and film is increased so little in ordinary use that it's hardly enough to fuss about. (In the case of *close-ups,* however, it is sometimes enough to interfere. Later, when we consider the *factors affecting exposure* and *close-range work,* we shall find out what to do about this.)

### LIGHT IS REFLECTED

When you photograph a blazing bonfire or a burst of fireworks or the city at night, you are photographing *direct* light. What you do in each of these cases is to photograph the actual *source* of light. When you photograph the moon, or a curvy torso on the beach, or a face in a mirror, you are using *reflected light.* Practically all of the light used in photography is light reflected from objects.

There are three kinds of reflected light: (1) *specular* (or even), (2) *diffuse* (or ragged) and (3) *spread* (or mixed).

Specular light is the kind that is reflected from a smooth, highly polished surface like a sheet of glass or chromium plate. See *Fig. 4A.* When

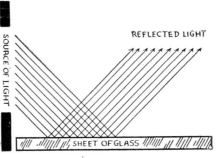

A. Specular reflection of light.

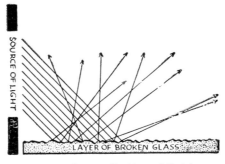

B. Diffuse reflection of light.

FIG. 4. THE KINDS OF REFLECTED LIGHT

specular light is reflected from an object, it is difficult to see the object. That's why coated paper is hard on the eyes and why glass-covered pictures are usually difficult to view.

Diffuse light is the kind you look at when you read a book printed on "wove" paper—each fiber of the paper presents a new surface to the light, sending the rays helter skelter all over the place. See *Fig. 4B* for an illustration of what happens when the glass used in *Fig 4A* is broken up and crushed.

The light reflected by this crushed glass will be diffused if all of it is ground to a fine white powder. If some shiny chunks remain, they will continue to reflect specular light. This combination of diffuse and specular light is called *spread,* or mixed, light. That's the kind of reflected light we use most of the time in photography.

Light rays reflect like bouncing balls. When they hit a hard smooth surface at an angle, they change direction. The angle at which they leave the surface is called the *angle of reflection;* the angle at which they hit it is called the *angle of incidence.* There is an exact relation between these two. The first law that governs this relation says: *the angle of incidence is equal to the angle of reflection.* This means that a ray of light, hitting a surface at thirty degrees to one side of an imaginary perpendicular set up at the point where the light touches the surface, will be reflected from that surface at an angle of thirty degrees on the other side of the perpendicular. The second law that governs it says: *the angle of incidence, the angle of reflection, and a perpendicular to the surface are all in one plane.*

Reflection increases with the polish of the surface or with the obliqueness of the angle of incidence. To prove the obliqueness part of this to yourself, take an ordinary sheet of white paper, one that does not have a shine to it, hold it near a reading lamp and tilt it at a sharp angle so that you will be glancing across the surface at the light source. You'll see a reflected image where only a moment ago there was just diffused light.

You can see an object better by diffused light than by specular light. That's why so many people have inadvertently walked through mirrors. What they saw was not the object itself (in this case the mirror) but the specular reflection of distant objects and light sources. This becomes what they call "an interesting problem" when you have to photograph bright metals, glassware, oil paintings, pictures under glass, or other shiny objects.

### LIGHT IS ABSORBED

Not all the light that shines on an object is reflected or transmitted. Some of it is absorbed and converted into heat. That's why the color and reflection characteristics of the object are fully as important in photography as the kind of light or materials being used. If the object is black and has an uneven surface, like black velvet, no more than 1 per cent of the light will be reflected; if it is white and smooth, like porcelain enamel, or if it has been coated with magnesium oxide, about 98 per cent of the light will be reflected. Colored objects present other problems in reflection and absorption; your red safe-light is red because it absorbs *all* other colors; your blood is red because it absorbs *green*. Why does this make it look red? Well, there are four principal colors—*blue, green, yellow,* and *red*. When spectral blue and yellow are mixed, the eye sees them as *white*. Since blood absorbs green light, that leaves only the red, which is the color we see. The *kind* of light absorbed and transmitted by any object, as well as the *intensity* of the light, determines how it photographs.

In general, a blue surface reflects nearly all of the actinic (i.e. chemically effective) light that strikes it, but absorbs a little; green reflects less and absorbs more; yellow reflects still less and absorbs still more; while red absorbs most and reflects least.

### LIGHT IS REFRACTED

When a ray of light travels through empty space outside the earth's atmosphere, or in a vacuum, it does so at a constant speed. But when it passes through a transparent substance like air, water, glass or quartz, it is slowed up. This slowing up depends on two things: (1) *the density of the new medium*, (2) *the wave length of the rays of light*. The denser the medium, the slower will the rays travel. And the longer the wave length of light, the less will it be affected.

As long as the ray of light stays in one medium, this slowing up causes no trouble. But when it starts moving from one medium to another, things begin to happen. One of these things is that the slowing up bends the rays out of shape. An easy experiment to prove this involves nothing more than a pencil and a glass of water. Put the pencil into the glass at an angle, and look at it from a sharper angle. The lower end will appear to be bent up. An old *disappearing coin trick* was based on this phenomenon: the coin was placed at the bottom of an empty opaque bowl and the bowl was moved away just far enough so that the rim hid the coin; when water was poured into the bowl the coin mysteriously reappeared.

One other stunt, and then we'll explain why all this happens. Take a piece of heavy plate glass, as thick a piece as you can get, hold it horizontally over a table, place a coin under it and then offer to give the coin to anyone who can, while looking through the glass, stab the exact center of the coin with something like a toothpick the moment you say, *"Ready!"* You'll get many volunteers, but the coin will still be yours when they've all had their try. Let them study the coin *through* the glass all they please; the more they do so, the more elusive will it seem when you give the signal.

And now for the explanation. When a ray of light travels horizontally, the waves which compose it move vertically at right angles. The wave fronts are all parallel, like a row of buttons strung on a thread. Looking at them sideways, they'd look like this:

As long as this wave travels through *one* homogeneous medium, the space between the lines, which represents the *wave length* of the ray, will remain the same. But let's see what happens when the light wave hits a medium of greater density. See *Fig. 5*. Here we see the wave passing from air,

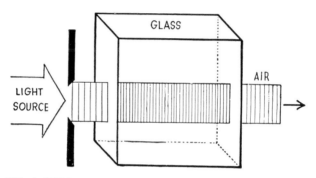

FIG. 5. HOW LIGHT PASSES THROUGH A TRANSPARENT OBJECT THE SURFACES OF WHICH ARE PLANE PARALLEL

through a cube of glass, and out into air again. The wave is slowed up, and so the lines are packed together more closely, which means that the wave is shorter. When the light leaves the glass, it picks up speed again; the distance between the lines increases, which means the wave is longer.

Now how does all this serve to explain the *bending* of light? See *Fig. 6*. We've taken our glass cube or prism and sliced one end of it away at an angle. The light now enters the prism obliquely. The first wave impulse to hit the glass makes contact at *A*. It's slowed up at that point. While that part of the wave starts to travel through glass, a denser medium, the rest of it is still in air. The result is that the wave begins to pivot at *A*, which changes its direction. When it leaves the glass again, *C* hits the air first and swings away, forcing the wave to pivot at *B*, thus changing its direction once more. Light is always bent toward the perpendicular of the surfaces when it passes from a rare to a dense medium. Obversely, it is bent away from the perpendicular when it passes from a dense to a rare medium. But something else happens to the light when it leaves the prism in *Fig. 6*. We shall see what that is in just a moment.

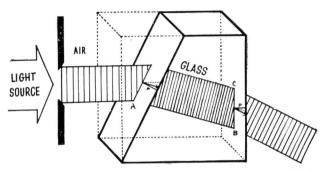

FIG. 6. HOW LIGHT IS REFRACTED AND PARTLY DIS-PERSED WHEN PASSING THROUGH A TRANSPARENT OBJECT THE SIDES OF WHICH ARE NOT PLANE PARALLEL

## THE CRITICAL ANGLE

When light passes from one medium to another *at right angles to the surface*, it is not refracted and only partially reflected. If one of the media is air and the other is a substance like glass, the unreflected rays of light stream through unchanged (except in *speed*, which we have already mentioned). But as we move the light source further from the perpendicular, we notice that the direction taken by the incident ray, *after* it hits the surface, seems to be erratic. To find out what happens, let's imagine a hollow glass sphere half filled with water and a source of light outside, as

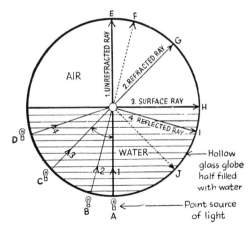

FIG. 7. ILLUSTRATING *THE CRITICAL ANGLE* OF RE-FLECTION AND REFRACTION (ANGLE *COA*)

A ray from *C* just skims the surface between both mediums.

in *Fig. 7*. (Since we can imagine the light source as a point, sending a ray at right angles to the surface of the glass, there will be no refraction as the ray passes from air through glass to water.) Now hold the light at *A* and an *unrefracted* ray will leave the globe at *E*. Move the light to *B*, and instead of seeing a ray at *F*, it will suddenly appear at *G;* it has been *refracted*. Move the light once more, this time to *D;* the *reflected* ray will appear, as you expect, at *I*. But if we move the light back to *C* and look for the ray at *J*, where a well-behaved, *reflected* ray should be (since the angle of incidence *COA* and the theoretical angle of reflection *AOJ* are equal), it will just not be there. You'll find it at *H, skimming along the surface of the water!* Angle *COA* is called the *critical angle;* it determines whether the ray is going to be reflected or refracted. This angle varies with the color of the light used; it is greater for the red rays than for the blue.

### LIGHT IS DISPERSED

White light is composed of seven spectral colors: *violet, indigo, blue, green, yellow, orange* and *red*. We see them as such because certain vibra- tions of light produce these sensations of color in our eyes. A wave length of 700 millimicrons, for instance, produces the sensation of red; a wave length of 400 millimicrons, the sensation of violet.

When they all travel together in parallel lines, as in *Fig. 5,* we get the sensation of white light. When they travel through a dense medium, the surfaces of which form an angle, the rays begin to be *dispersed,* or spread out; they no longer travel together in parallel lines. The result of this is shown in *Fig. 8*. To decompose white light, therefore, we use a *triangular* prism. Sir Isaac Newton was the first to try this experiment. It is simply a modification of the light-bending experiment we tried in *Fig. 6,* except that by cutting away both sides of the cube to make a triangular prism, we bend the light sharply and so disperse it fully.

Newton tried two other interesting experiments with prisms to test his theory that white light was *mixed* light. In the first, he duplicated the setup shown in *Fig. 8,* but instead of the white screen for the spectrum he used an opaque screen with a slit in it that would permit only the yellow rays to get through. On the other side of the screen he placed another triangular prism to refract the yellow light. *But he couldn't disperse it;* the yellow light remained yellow! He tried this also with the other six spectral colors, and discovered that none of them could be broken down. Only mixed light, he found, could be so dispersed. He concluded that the seven spectral hues were *basic* or primary colors.

In his second experiment, Newton took two prisms and arranged them so that the dispersed white light from the one would enter the inverted side of the other (the points of the triangles facing in opposite directions). In this way he showed that white light could not only be decomposed but *recomposed*. The second prism, as you guessed, gathered the dispersed

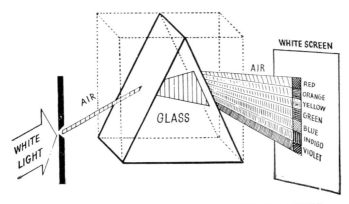

FIG. 8. HOW LIGHT IS DISPERSED WHEN PASSING THROUGH A PRISM

rays and refracted them to reproduce white light. Later, when we discuss color photography, we will see that we do not need all seven colors to produce white light.

## LIGHT IS POLARIZED

There is still another phenomenon of light that's of interest to photographers, and that is the mysterious one known as *polarization*. If we can imagine each pinpoint of light as an expanding cone and let that represent light waves spreading out in *all* directions, then polarized light (or light

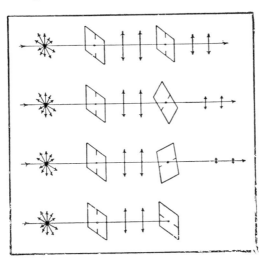

FIG. 9. THE POLARIZATION OF LIGHT

that travels in only *one direction*) can be represented by a plane which bisects this cone from its apex to the diameter of the base at infinity. This phenomenon was first studied by Huygens, who discovered that the crystals of certain translucent minerals had the property of stopping light when they were placed with their long axes at right angles to one another. The crystals act like optical slits which transmit only light vibrating in the plane of that slit. The degree of polarization can be controlled by the rotation of the crystals. *Fig. 9* illustrates the effect of rotating one Kodak Pola-Screen in relation to another. When the vibration plane of the second Pola-Screen is at right angles to the first, almost no light gets through.

### LIGHT BENDS AROUND CORNERS

Place two fingers close together, almost but not quite touching, and bring them up to your eye. Now look through the fingers at a light source and you'll see one of the strangest of all the phenomena of light. First you'll see what appears to be a shadowy aura around the edge of both fingers; as you move them closer together these shadows will become a series of parallel lines darker in intensity, and resembling somewhat the lines on a contour map. Just before the fingers touch, these contour lines will seem to jump toward one another, creating what appear to be little bumps on each finger. This phenomenon, known as *diffraction*, occurs whenever light hits an edge. It causes no end of trouble in photography, as you will find out when we take up the *diaphragm* and the *critical aperture* of a lens.

## WHAT IT DOES

Now that we know something about what light is and how it behaves, we can investigate some of the things it does. Chief among these, as far as photography is concerned, is its ability to (1) *cast shadows,* and (2) *create an image.* But before we take these up, let's dispose of a few questions that have troubled the curious for ages.

### WHAT MAKES A RAINBOW?

Unless we have forgotten all that we have just found out about refraction and dispersion, this one shouldn't be so tough to unravel. *The raindrops, of course, are responsible.* The few stragglers that are still up in the sky when the sun comes out act like so many tiny prisms to disperse the rays of sunlight. Those on the outside of the arc send red rays to the eye; those on the inside, violet ones. The other colors are transmitted from the intermediate drops. The bow or arc is really the circumference of the base of a crane, the apex of which is the observer's eye. If an imaginary line were drawn from this apex, through the center of the rainbow, and extended back far enough, it would hit the sun. The shell of the cone is composed of seven layers of color, one within the other, corresponding to the colors of the spectrum.

### WHY IS THE SKY BLUE?

Nature always seems to be splitting light into its many colors or wave lengths. The *blue* sky is one example familiar to most of us; another is the *red* sunset; still others are soap bubbles, mother of pearl, peacock feathers, the iridescent shells of certain insects, a film of oil on water, the sparkle of a diamond.

The blue sky is caused by the screening effect of the earth's envelope of atmosphere. This envelope extends upward about twelve miles, and the first four or five miles are packed with dust and water particles of all sizes hanging suspended in the air. Many of these particles are so incredibly small that they are almost the same size as the wave lengths of blue light, about 1/600,000 of an inch. In consequence, they *scatter the blue waves,* letting the others get through. See *Fig. 10.*

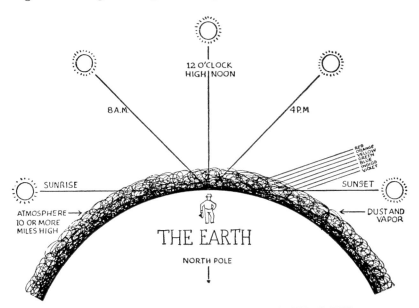

FIG. 10. WHY SKIES ARE BLUE AND SUNSETS RED

The illustration in *Fig. 10* also explains why morning and evening sunlight is redder than the light at high noon. When the sun is low on the horizon, the light has to push through a denser fog of atmosphere which scatters the violet, blue, green, and some of the yellow rays and lets the long red rays through. This change in the color of daylight, from morning to evening, will be much more important to us later when we take up the problems of *exposure, film sensitivity* and *filters*. In the meantime, all we need to remember is that the light between nine in the morning and four in the afternoon is best for normal use outdoors. Before nine or after four we have to make certain adjustments that will be discussed in subsequent chapters.

And while we're on the subject, the iridescence produced by soap bubbles, bird feathers, diamonds, and so forth (all of which are examples of dispersed light) can be distinguished from the ordinary absorption colors of substances because the iridescent colors change as the point of view changes.

### LIGHT CASTS SHADOWS

Almost as important to photography as light itself is the *absence* of light. Without shade or shadow, most pictures would be impossible. See the illustrations elsewhere in this chapter in which three geometric figures have been painted white, arranged against a black background, and photographed. They show that *shadow is part of the picture*.

### THE KINDS OF SHADOWS

There are two kinds, those made by a *point source* of light, and those made by a *large source* of light. The difference between them is that one makes a *hard* shadow with a sharp edge and the other a *translucent* shadow with a soft edge. If you will look at *Fig. 11* you will understand how this happens. Some photographers like to distinguish between the various dark areas, so they call the lighter part of a soft-edged shadow, the *shade*.

Short shadows are made by overhead lights; *long shadows,* by side lights (the lower the light, the longer the shadow). Changes in the shadows made by the sun illustrate this perfectly.

Contrast is increased between the light and dark areas of an object when the light is strong, close, raw, direct, or point source; *it is reduced* when the light is weak, distant, diffused, reflected (as from a wall or sheet or card), or large source.

Hard shadows can be softened by reflected light, by diffused or weak supplementary light, by moving the basic light further back, by changing the size and shape of the reflector (the larger the angle of the cone, the softer the light), and by changing the inside surface of the reflector (the more polished the surface, the harder the light).

And that's about all you have to know about shadows, except that there

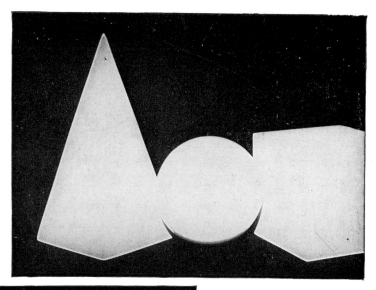

To illustrate the importance of the absence of light, these geometric shapes, have been painted white and arranged against a black background. Let's light them first to eliminate all shadows. This top figure shows what you would see. Nothing three-dimensional about that, is there? If the forms had been placed against a white background, there would have been even less to show you.

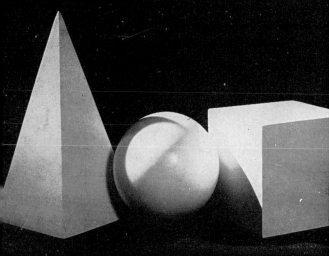

And yet there was plenty of light! Obviously, light alone cannot make a picture. Now let's take away, or intercept, some of the light. This one, in the middle, might be the result. But it's still not good enough.

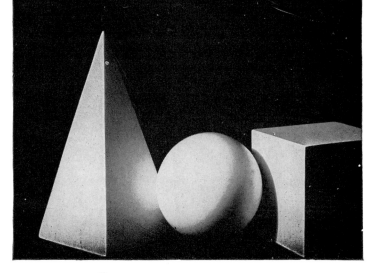

So we continue to play around with the lights until we get something we like better, such as this figure at the right.

are no absolute blacks in nature, that the whitest substances found outdoors (*chalk,* for instance) reflect only 85 per cent of the light that shines on them, and that the light intensities outdoors aren't as great as

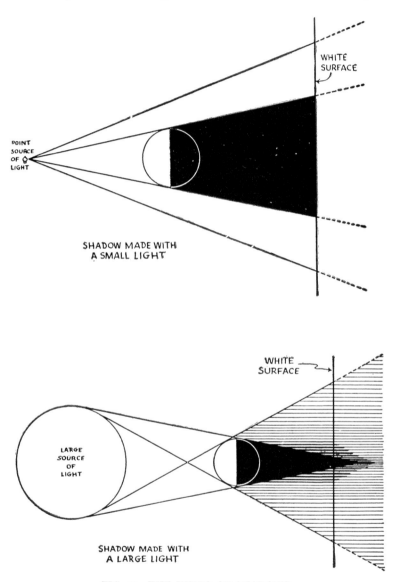

FIG. 11. THE KINDS OF SHADOWS

most amateurs think they are. The sky (I did *not* say the sun, now) is only thirty times as bright as the deepest shadow in strong sunlight, and the sunlit road you walk on is only six times as bright as your own shadow under an open sky. If you don't believe this, take your exposure meter outdoors and make some readings. We'll go into this more thoroughly later, when we take up *exposure*.

In the meantime, if you have nothing better to do, try to figure out why a bird flying over a man's head on a sunny day casts no shadow on the ground, or why no one can tell where the shadow of a church steeple stops. We've already given you a clue in *Fig. 11*.

### LIGHT CREATES AN IMAGE

The most interesting property of light, its ability to form an image, stems from the fact that it travels in straight lines. There are three ways in which an image can be formed: (1) by *reflection,* as in a mirror, (2) by *projection,* as through a pinhole, and (3) by *refraction,* as through a lens. The third way will be the subject of the next chapter, so we won't discuss that here, but we can take up the other two now.

First, let's consider *the mirror.* The kind we have in mind is one that has a *plane* glass surface. When light from any point on an object is reflected from such a mirror, it travels with those old friends of ours, *the laws of reflection.* That is, each ray hits the mirror and leaves it at precisely the same angle (the angles of *incidence* and *reflection*). How does this form an image? See *Fig. 12.* When a ray of light is reflected or

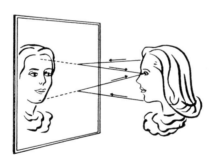

FIG. 12. HOW A MIRROR REFLECTS AN IMAGE

refracted, the direction it *seems to have* is the one taken by the ray just before it enters the eye. If we can, therefore, imagine the reflected cone of light which enamantes from a point, extending behind the mirror, all the rays composing it will meet at the same point. This will give us the impression that the point is on the other side of the mirror, and as far from the surface on *that* side as we are on *this.* Since this kind of image is nothing more than an optical illusion, it is called a *virtual* image, as distinguished from the *real* image made by a pinhole or a lens.

## HOW LIGHT AND A PINHOLE FORM AN IMAGE

If you have a ceiling light such as I have, with three bulbs in it, and your friends find you moving a card around between it and a white sheet of paper, you can show them this paragraph and the pinhole in the card to prove that there's nothing wrong with you. You are just trying to duplicate something first noticed by a tired Egyptian many years ago.

It is because light travels in straight lines that it is able to form an image on a screen when it passes through a small hole, and for the same reason the image will be upside down. This inversion of the image is made clear in the picture shown in *Fig. 13*. In the picture *A* and *B* represent

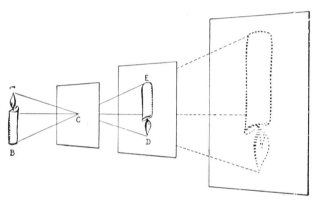

FIG. 13. HOW A PINHOLE CREATES AN IMAGE

two points of a lighted candle, *C* the pinhole and *D* and *E* the image on the screen. Now while light sends out rays in every direction, each ray moves in a straight line and it must, therefore, be clear that only the ray sent out from the point of the flame at *A* which is in a straight line with the pinhole *C* can pass through it and, hence, it must reach the screen at *D;* in the same way, the ray that starts from *B* which is in a straight line with *C* can only pass through it and this will reach the screen at *E*.

## THE SIZE OF THE IMAGE FORMED

The size of the image of an object depends upon the distance that both the object and the screen are from the pinhole. To prove this, you need only to move the screen forth and back. The farther away the screen is from the pinhole the larger will be the image and the fainter it will be. This increase in size is due to the fact that the rays of light from the object which pass through the pinhole diverge on leaving it, the *A D* ray (see *Fig. 13*) moving down and the *B E* ray moving up. The reason the image decreases in brightness as the size is increased, is that the very small amount of light that passes through the pinhole emerging as a cone must spread over a much larger surface.

The following formula will give you the size of the image at any given distance:

$$\frac{\text{Length of Object}}{\text{Length of Image}} = \frac{\text{Distance of Object from pinhole}}{\text{Distance of Image from pinhole}}$$

or in other words, you divide the length of the object by the length of the image, and this equals the distance of the object from the pinhole divided by the distance of the image from the pinhole.

### WHY A SQUARE HOLE FORMS A ROUND IMAGE

Aristotle, as you may recall, noticed that when the image of the sun came through a rectangular opening in the leaves of a tree under which he was resting, the image on the ground was round nevertheless. He couldn't explain it. But today we know that regardless of the shape of the hole, it is still only a pinhole in relation to the sun, and therefore the *real* image it produces must of necessity be a round one.

## HOW TO CONTROL LIGHT

Indoors, the control is pretty much in our own hands; there are many things we can do. Outdoors, however, the matter is not so simple. We cannot move the sun around the way we can a flood light, but there are other controls. The most important of these is *patience*. Yes, just that. There is a right and a wrong time to photograph everything. Study each subject and try to imagine how it would look if lighted differently. If it isn't lighted the way you'd like it to be the first time you see it, go back at another time when the light is more suitable, when the angle is better.

Alfred Stieglitz once spent months studying the effects of sunlight on an old stone well in a courtyard facing his home before he took even one picture. Another example of patience is the work of Joe Wiener, A.R.P.S. This wise and modest young businessman, whose hobby is the camera, has learned the full force of patience as a technique in photography. He does nothing hurriedly or slapdash. He has photographed one scene for four years under all conditions, and he's still not satisfied; he almost never snaps a scene as he first finds it. He tries to imagine how the scene would look earlier or later in the day, *and then he goes back*. The result is that his pictures have crashed every *salon* to which he has sent them, and now the *salons* are *inviting* him to contribute! Some interesting examples of his work are shown elsewhere in this book.

Later, we shall consider all of the specific techniques for the control of lighting, both indoor and out. But, in the meantime, here are some ideas to mull over: Turn your back on the *taboos* of photography. Everyone will tell you to avoid noon light outdoors or to get indoors when it rains. Pay no attention. Listen, instead, to one of America's great photographers, Edward Weston, explain why he could use *only* noon light for one of his famous photographs, "Bean Ranch": "The clarity and meaning of the picture would be lost if the neat black eclipses under the trees were sprawled out across the foreground and the furrows between the plant rows were so filled with shadows as to hide the important contrast provided by the texture of the plowed earth. Noon light is by no means the only popular taboo. I have been out with photographers who felt that the day's work necessarily ended when clouds obscured the sun or fog rolled in. . . . To know the phenomena of the photographer's world only as brilliant sunlight reveals them, is to know but a small part. Mist in the air, curtains of fog, clouds and overcast skies, the afterglow when the sun has set and the dawn light before sunrise provide him with different avenues of approach to his subject matter, or, more properly, provide him with different subject matter. For it cannot be too strongly emphasized that *reflected light is the photographer's subject matter.* Whether you photograph shoes, ships, or sealing wax, it is the light reflected from your subject that forms your image."

# All About the Lens

The eye was the first lens, and it's still the best. The most perfect lens ever made is just a clumsy affair compared to the sensitive, self-adjusting, *apochromatic* [1] mechanism that functions as the eye.

The curious thing about man's long search for the perfect lens is that he pursued this search with the only perfect lens there is, and never realized it. Each new basic discovery in lens design was just a rediscovery of optical and mechanical principles already at work in the eye. Some of these are: the *diaphragm* which is the *iris* of the eye; the *compound lens* which duplicates the *liquid* and *crystalline* lens formations of the eye; the *shutter,* which is a mechanical eyelid. The eye even has an *anti-halo* backing, a layer of some black substance behind the retina which absorbs all rays not needed or not wanted to create vision.

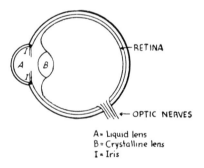

A = Liquid lens
B = Crystalline lens
I = Iris

FIG. 14. THE STRUCTURE OF THE EYE

When it's in perfect condition, the eye is a marvelous instrument: it does not suffer from *lens aberrations;* it sees no problem in *depth of focus;* it operates its *shutter* quietly; it overcomes *curvature of field* very simply by collecting the rays on a curved field (the retina); and it turns the continuously shifting upside down world right side up before register-

---

[1] Free from chromatic and spherical aberrations.

ing it, in full color, in the brain. The eye finally, if you're still not impressed, is "several hundred thousand times more light sensitive than the
fastest [2] photographic emulsion," according to laboratory scientists who
have tested both. *Fig. 14* shows the structure of the eye.

## HOW LENSES ACT

### HOW A CONVEX LENS REFRACTS LIGHT

In the preceding chapter we saw how a pinhole makes an image, and
how a prism bends light. By cementing the bases of two prisms together,
we have a very clear approximation to a convex lens. See *Fig. 15*. Let's
assume that the light rays leaving point *A* are all spectral yellow and that
they cannot therefore be dispersed. *Fig. 15* shows us how the rays would

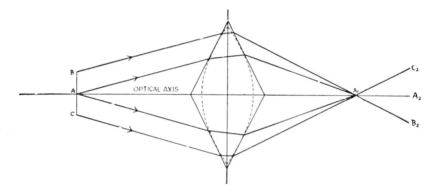

FIG. 15. THE ACTION OF LIGHT RAYS THROUGH TWO
CEMENTED PRISMS

travel. All the rays from point *A*, which is placed on a line with the axis
of the prisms, will meet again somewhere along that line after they leave
the prisms. Now, not only do all rays from a point on the axis meet again
on that axis, but rays from every point on a perpendicular through *A* will
meet again at $A_1$. Point $A_1$ is therefore the *point of principal focus*. The
distance from the center of the lens to $A_1$ is the *focal length*. The action
through that imaginary point duplicates exactly the action through a pinhole.

Though *focal length* is one of the most frequently used terms in photography, it is one of the most difficult to explain, if one is to judge by the
confusion that besets the innocent reader hunting for an accurate and

[2] In photography the expression "fast" concerns the ability to deal with light. Thus a
"fast" film reacts more quickly to light than a slow one—requiring less exposure. A "fast"
lens can be used with a wider diaphragm opening than a "slow" one of the same focal length,
thus admitting *more* light in a given time.

understandable definition. A check with all the dictionaries, most of the classic works on photography, and the service bureaus of Eastman Kodak and Ansco gives the most reasonable explanation as "the distance from the diaphragm (or roughly the center of the lens) to the film plane when the lens is focused at infinity." The *principal focus,* or the *point* of principal focus, is the closest the film plane can approach the lens and still be able to focus an *any* object. As the lens is moved away from the film plane there will be an infinite number of other possible points of focus, depending on the distance of the object from the lens. The closer the object to the lens, the greater the distance must be between lens and film plane. But at the shortest distance between lens and film (the principal focus) the object must be at *infinity.*

The convex lens can be considered as made up of an infinite number of prisms of varying angle. The composite surface of such an arrangement of prisms would resemble the surface of a convex lens. All camera lenses, no matter how complicated their structure, are in action no different from simple convex lenses; they bring spectral rays of light[3] to a point called the *focus.*

### HOW A CONVEX LENS FORMS AN IMAGE

All you have to do to form an image of an object on a screen of any sort is to let the light from an object pass through a convex lens that is placed between them. To get a sharp image of the object, you need only to move

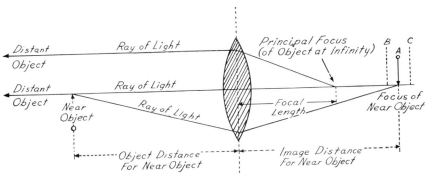

FIG. 16. HOW A CONVEX LENS FORMS AN IMAGE

the screen back and forth a bit, and you will soon find a point where it is clear and sharp. At that point the image is said to be *in focus,* and the process by which this point is found is called *focusing.*

The image formed by the lens, like the one made through a pinhole,

---

[3] All those, that is, which are in a plane at right angles to the path of light.

will be inverted, that is upside down on the screen, and for the same rea·· son (see *Fig. 16*).

But, unlike the pinhole, a lens lets a larger number of rays pass through it other than those that do so through its optical axis—as a glance at the diagram will show; thus rays coming from the top of the object which strike the upper part of the lens are refracted downward by it, while those that come from the bottom of the object and strike the lower part of the lens are refracted upward by it. These meet the rays coming through the center of the lens at a point between the *principal focus* (for objects at infinity) and any of the infinite number of *image foci* (for objects between infinity and the lens). The range of possible lens extensions (and therefore the size of the image) is determined by the construction of the camera and the lens; the greater the distance between the lens and the film plane, the larger the image of the object. The plane on which the image is focused is called the *focal plane,* and that is where the film is placed.

## HOW THE FOCUS AFFECTS THE IMAGE

From the diagram shown in *Fig. 16,* it will be clear that the image formed by a convex lens will be sharp only when the screen, or other surface on which the image is formed, is at a point where the rays of light that are refracted by the lens, and those that pass through its center in straight lines, meet. This is indicated by the arrow *A*. If the screen or other surface is placed ahead of this point, as shown by the broken line at *B*, or back of it, as shown by the broken line at *C*, the rays from the same point of the object will be separated since at *B* they will not as yet have met, while at *C* they will have met and spread apart. It must be clear, then, that at either of these points the image will not be sharp.

## HOW TO FIND THE FOCUS OF A LENS

A lens can make a sharp image of an object on only *one* plane. When the object is at *infinity* (a distance such that reflected rays from the object pass through the lens as parallel lines; for most cameras this would be beyond 100 feet) the rays come together at the principal focus. As the object moves closer to the lens (or vice versa) the distance between the lens and the focal plane must also be increased or the image will not be in sharp focus. That's why we rack or turn our lens out as we move up toward an object. The closer the object to the lens, the larger will be the image (until, at a lens extension of twice the normal focal length, the image would be the same size as the object). Since the focal length of a lens, therefore, controls both the *size* and *sharpness* of the image, it is important for us to know what this measure is, so that we can use the lens effectively. There are two ways of discovering this important fact.

(1) A simple way to find the point of principal focus of a lens, is to let the rays of the sun pass through it and fall on a sheet of cardboard so that they are brought to the smallest possible point of light just as you do when you are using it as a burning glass. This done, measure the distance from the spot of light to the center of the lens.

(2) To find the equivalent focus, image focus, or focal plane, of a convex lens, you need only to move the cardboard or other screen toward or away from the lens very gradually until you reach the point where the image is as sharp as you can get it, and then measure the distance from the screen to the center of the lens. (There are formulas for calculating these foci of a lens, but it is easier for the average person to find them experimentally.)

### OTHER SHAPES OF LENSES

Besides the double convex lens, there are five lenses of other shapes which are used in various combinations with each other to get better results than can be had by using single lenses; that is to say, lenses in certain combinations will let more light through them and at the same time reduce the numerous defects to a minimum.

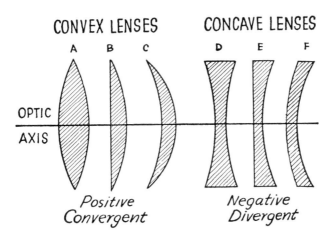

FIG. 17. THE DIFFERENT KINDS OF LENSES
(*A*) Double convex or biconvex. (*B*) Plano-convex. (*C*) Converging or positive meniscus. (*D*) Double concave or biconcave. (*E*) Plano-concave. (*F*) Diverging or negative meniscus.

These different lenses can be divided into two general classes, namely, (*A*) *convex lenses*, or *positive convergent lenses* to give them their scientific name, and (*B*) *concave lenses*, or *negative divergent lenses*. The first class, of which there are three, are those that curve out on one or both sides, and the second class, of which there are also three, curve in on one or both sides. These lenses are shown in *Fig. 17* and are (1) the *biconvex,* or *double convex,* (2) the *plano-convex,* and (3) the *converging,* or *positive meniscus.*[4] All belong to the first class.

Then there are (4) the *biconcave,* or *double concave,* (5) the *plano-concave,* and (6) the *diverging,* or *negative meniscus,* all belonging to the second class.

### THE OPTICAL DEFECTS OF LENSES

A double convex lens has seven defects that must be overcome if the image it produces is to be a true likeness of the object. These are: (1) *spherical aberration,* (2) *chromatic aberration,* (3) *astigmatism,* (4) *distortion,* (5) *curvature of field,* (6) *coma,* (7) *unequal illumination.*

*Spherical Aberration.* Now while all the rays of light that pass through a lens are refracted to practically the same extent, there is just enough difference in the refractive powers of different annular, (*i.e.,* ring-shaped) portions of a lens to prevent all the rays of light meeting at a single point on its optical axis. It is this difference in the refraction of a lens that produces what is called *spherical aberration.* See *Fig. 18.* Spherical

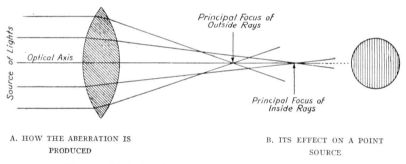

A. HOW THE ABERRATION IS
PRODUCED

B. ITS EFFECT ON A POINT
SOURCE

FIG. 18.  THE  CAUSE  AND  EFFECT  OF  SPHERICAL
ABERRATION

aberration is greater with a double convex lens than it is with a plano-convex one and, what is more, when the rays of light strike the flat side of the lens first, it is more pronounced than when it first strikes the curved side. Spherical aberration is, then, due to *the curvature of the lens* which makes it refract light unequally. The effect of this aberration, in small amounts, is to cast a haze of light over the image; in large amounts it spoils the overall sharpness of the image. This defect be-

---

[4] *Meniscus* means crescent-shaped.

comes more troublesome and more difficult to correct, the larger the aperture (speed) of the lens.

*Chromatic Aberration.* The light of the sun, as we have already seen, is made up of seven different wave lengths. When these strike the retina of the eye, they produce in the brain the sensation of color. We proved this by splitting up a beam of white light with a prism, forming the seven colors in a narrow band on a screen; further, we saw how the different colors of the spectrum can be recombined by another prism so that they will produce a beam of white light once more.

When light waves of different lengths, and therefore different colors, pass through a prism or a lens, they are refracted unequally, the shortest waves, which make violet light, being bent at a greater angle than the

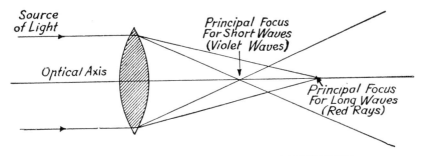

FIG. 19. THE CAUSE OF CHROMATIC ABERRATION

longest waves, which make red light, as shown in the diagram *Fig. 19.* The result is that each ray of white light which enters the lens is split up into its seven component wave lengths and each of these in turn comes to a focus at a different point on the optical axis of the lens. Since most subjects reflect light of all colors, the *final* result of all this is that *seven* images are formed, each of a different spectral color, and each on a different plane of focus (and therefore of a different size). This throws the *visual* image out of focus and blurs the edges with rings of color. A photograph made with such a lens could never be sharp, since *six* of the images would always be out of focus.

Which brings us to the problem of *visual* vs. *chemical* (or *actinic*) focus. Film is most sensitive to *violet* and *blue* light; the eye is most sensitive to *yellow* and *green*. If, then, we focus the lens visually, which is what we do when we use a ground glass as in a reflex camera, that part of the light which affects the film most is out of focus. The result: *an unsharp picture.* To avoid this, the lens has to be corrected, to bring all the seven images together on one plane of sharp focus (See below, *How Lenses are Corrected for Chromatic Aberration.*), or we must use a filter to screen out the other images. In the ordinary camera this is done quite simply by the use of a strong filter (dark green, orange or deep yellow) which cuts out most of the out-of-focus rays. The use of a filter has its limitations, however, because though we might in this way get a sharper picture, it would represent color values quite falsely. A *green* filter, for instance, would cut out most of the out-of-focus *orange* and *red* light, but the print would show these as *black* or *dark gray* patches, while the *greens* would show up as sharp white. The most effective use of this phenomenon is in enlarging, where a heat-resistant blue glass, placed between the light source and the lens, will noticeably increase the sharpness of a print by screening the red rays which fuzz it up. The newer projection anastigmats, notably the Kodak Ektar, are especially corrected to make *visual* and *chemical* focus coincide; with such a lens, the use of the blue glass would show no improvement. The projected image, in other words, would be sharp to begin with, and would not need such help.

*Astigmatism.* This, the most serious and yet the most difficult lens fault to correct, is also a by-product of spherical aberration. Astigmatism means that a lens will not bring horizontal and vertical lines to a sharp focus at the same time on a flat screen. The result is that if a lens is not corrected for this defect, the lines running in one direction or the other will not be sharp, thus blurring the image. While it cannot be so easily corrected by giving a lens of ordinary glass a particular shape, it can be rectified by using a special kind of optical glass. A lens which corrects this fault is called an *anastigmat,* or one without the error of astigmatism.

*Distortion.* This is a by-product of spherical aberration which takes place at the edges of the screen. Distortion means that if a rectangular

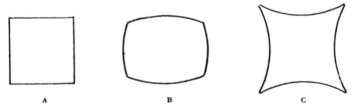

FIG. 20. THE EFFECTS OF DISTORTION

figure, as shown by *A* in *Fig. 20,* is projected on a screen by a lens, it may appear as a barrel-shaped figure as by *B,* or as a pincushion outline as by *C.*

*Curvature of Field.* Because lenses are spherical in shape, they create an image on a *curved field,* as in *Fig. 21.* Since the surface of a negative is *flat,* it is important that the image created by the lens also be flat; otherwise there will be a blur at all points not in focus on the plane of the negative.

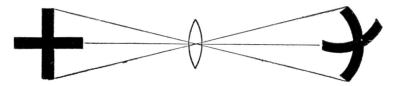

FIG. 21. THE EFFECT OF SPHERICAL ABERRATION

*Coma.* This is the variation in the size and location of the image produced by the various parts of the lens. The result of this lens fault is that *points* of light at the edges of the image, traveling obliquely through the lens, emerge as *tear drops* of light. See *Fig. 22.*

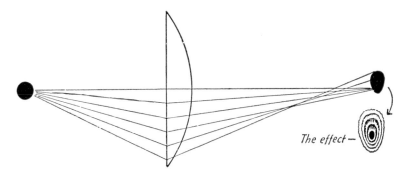

*The effect—*

FIG. 22. THE EFFECT OF COMA

*Unequal Illumination.* Hold an open tube before your eye and swing it to one side until the outer rim begins to cut off the view. The opening of the tube, which was a perfect circle, has now become an *oval.* This is one reason why a lens cannot deliver full illumination at the edges of an image; the rays passing through obliquely are cut off by the edges of the barrel which holds the lens elements in place. The cure for this is to make the barrel as compact as possible. Another reason for unequal illumination at the edges is *flatness of field.* Normally, a lens creates an image on a curved field (like the retina of the eye). When that happens, each point of light on that curved field having entered through a point in the center of the lens, travels the same distance to the field from the lens to the point of focus and thus delivers a proper share of the light. When the curved field is flattened, however, the light going to the outer edges has to travel farther, and is therefore weaker.

## HOW LENSES ARE CORRECTED FOR SPHERICAL ABERRATION

Different schemes have been tried out to overcome or reduce the defect of spherical aberration. The most successful of these is to grind the

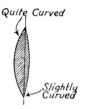

FIG. 23. HOW A LENS IS CORRECTED FOR SPHERICAL
ABERRATION

lens so that both of its surfaces have different curvatures (depending on the index of refraction of the glass), when, of course, one of them will be very much more convex than the other, as shown in *Fig. 23*. This is called an *aplanat* lens.[5]

## HOW LENSES ARE CORRECTED FOR CHROMATIC ABERRATION

The splitting up of white light by a lens, through refraction of the different wave lengths or colors, is caused to a lesser or greater extent by

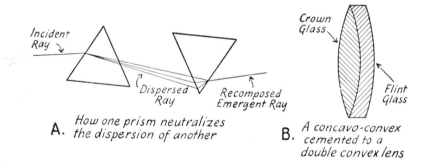

FIG. 24. HOW A LENS IS CORRECTED FOR CHROMATIC
ABERRATION

two things. These are: (1) the kind, or nature, of the glass from which the lens is made, and (2) the refracting angle of the lens. There are two ordinary kinds of glass used for making prisms and lenses: (a) flint glass and (b) crown glass. Flint glass is made by melting sand, lead and soda together, while crown glass is made by melting sand, lime and soda

[5] See page 51.

together. More recently barium has been added to these two to make additional kinds of glass with different refraction and dispersion indices. These kinds of glass are used because flint glass in general has high dispersive power with low refraction, while crown glass has high refractive power with low dispersion. The addition of barium alters these properties somewhat. The way that two prisms, one of which is made of flint glass and the other of crown glass, are arranged, so that the dispersion of the first is neutralized by the second, is shown by *A* in *Fig. 24.*

It follows, then, that since the same principles which apply to prisms also hold good for lenses, it is possible to make a lens that will do away with chromatic aberration in the manner described above. Such a lens, shown by *B*, is called an *achromatic lens.*[6]

## HOW LENSES ARE CORRECTED FOR DISTORTION

When a single convex lens is used, the distortion is the greatest. If you put a diaphragm (a device for controlling the size of the aperture

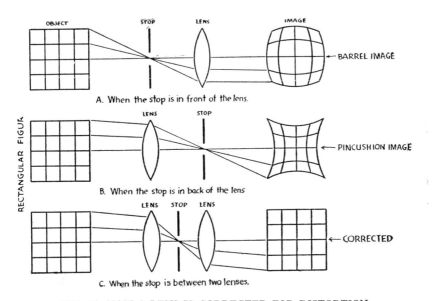

A. When the stop is in front of the lens.

B. When the stop is in back of the lens.

C. When the stop is between two lenses.

FIG. 25. HOW A LENS IS CORRECTED FOR DISTORTION

and hence the portion of the lens used) or *stop*[7] as it is commonly called, in front of it, the barrel-shaped distortion is increased as shown by *A* in *Fig. 25;* and if you put a stop back of it, the pincushion distortion is increased as at *B*. But when two lenses or components are used and you

[6] See page 51.
[7] See page 62.

put a stop between them, the distortion of each one reacts on the other and the effect is neutralized, as at *C*. Thus a photographic lens made with two achromatic components gets rid of the distortion. This forms what is called a *rectilinear*, or *symmetrical* lens.

## HOW LENSES ARE CORRECTED FOR ASTIGMATISM

The glass used for making lenses that correct astigmatism is of a special kind, and is the result of experiments made by Abbe and Schott in Jena, Germany, ending about 1884. The new optical glass which they originated includes barium, boron and phosphorous as the extra ingredients, and it is these which give the glass its special optical properties.

Lenses made of *Jena glass*, as it is called, can be corrected for astigmatism, chromatic aberration, and field curvature, and at the same time have high transmission. This, of course, makes for speed, while they give images that are uniformly sharp from the center of the plate to the very edges of it without being stopped down. Added to these good qualities the lenses are ground and combined in accordance with advanced optical formulas, as will be seen later.

## HOW LENSES ARE CORRECTED FOR CURVATURE OF FIELD

The best correction is by stopping down, making the diaphragm smaller thus cutting out the marginal rays. No lens made to date can claim a perfectly flat field; the anastigmats are better in this respect than the others, but none is *fully* corrected. Factors determining the extent of the curvative produced by a lens are the kind and thickness of glass used, the position of the diaphragm, the distance between the various elements, and the distance between the object and the lens.

## HOW LENSES ARE CORRECTED FOR COMA

There are two ways of correcting for this fault: (1) by the use of a *diaphragm*, as for curvature of field, which eliminates the oblique rays that produce coma, and (2) by *compensation*, which neutralizes the directional coma of one lens by the reverse coma of another. Thus, by placing two lenses together so that the coma of one corrects the coma of the other, this fault can be entirely eliminated.

## HOW LENSES ARE CORRECTED FOR UNEQUAL ILLUMINATION

Again the simplest correction is by the use of the diaphragm. Lens designers sometimes overcome this defect by increasing the diameter of the front lens, giving it a greater light-gathering power. This method was used in the design of the Summicron (see page 54). When a lens is corrected for curvature of field, the angular rays have to travel farther to reach the surface of the film. This weakens the oblique rays (law of inverse squares) which accounts for the loss of light, along the edges of the image. The corrections here are the use of the diaphragm, a larger front lens element, and a more compact unit with a shorter barrel.

## HOW LENSES ARE MADE

Less than fifty years ago a German mathematician proved that it was theoretically, and therefore practically, impossible to make a perfect lens. Such a lens would reproduce each point of light as a point, each line as a line, all objects in their original tones and colors, place the entire image on a flat field, and have an aperture large enough to make the photographer almost independent of light sources. This dream lens can only exist in the imagination. The modern lens maker, by devoting some time to intricate and intensive calculations preparatory to actually grinding his lens, can now eliminate most of the wasteful drudgery that went with the trial-and-error method of lens manufacture used in the past. With this new method, devised by Professor Abbe, Director of the University Observatory at Jena, the lens maker can have in his hand, before he begins to grind his first lens, all the data needed to make it. Unless you're familiar with the long, drawn-out, heartbreaking process used by opticians years ago (lenses were ground and tested, reground and tested, reground and tested again, until the repeated trials proved something, *or nothing*) the saving in time and human wear by this new method would be hard to appreciate.

Almost any lens can be made to simulate a perfect lens, if it is used *monochromatically* (with a filter that screens out all but one of the seven spectral colors), if it is used to view only a *narrow field,* and if it is used at a *small enough aperture* and at a great enough *distance*. But that, obviously, will never satisfy the requirements of photography today. Hence the search for new and better lenses goes on.

The first step in the making of a new lens is the selection of a design. This is usually based on some old design, the characteristics of which

are known, or on some modification suggested by the use of new materials. This design is then tested for aberrations *trigonometrically,* with
months or sometimes even years of computation. The design is then
changed, and the various aberrations checked again, mathematically.
More changes are made, until a formula is found which tests well *theoretically,* on paper. During all this testing, new kinds of optical glass, new
lens shapes, and all sorts of focal lengths and speeds are tried. Sometimes
a lens works better in one focal length than in another, in one speed better
than in another. The two-inch *f* 2.8 Tessar, for instance, is said by some
to be the best Tessar made; others claim this distinction for the *f* 4.5
Tessar in the six-inch size. At any rate, all these things are checked and
rechecked until a good formula is found.

A sample of such a lens is then carefully made, and just as carefully
tested. Too often, a lens which works out perfectly on paper is a dud in
the camera. To obviate this, the new lens is put through all its paces,
checked on a lens chart that exposes every one of its quirks and aberrations, it is tilted every which way to see how its definition stands up under
extremes of use, and then photographs are taken with it indoors and outdoors on the most difficult subjects that can be found. While all this is
going on, tests are also made for flare spots due to internal reflections, for
the accuracy of the focusing scale and diaphragm numbers, and for the
uniformity of the light it delivers. If the lens has any faults or weaknesses, these tests bring them out. Then, if all the tests show that the
lens is satisfactory for the use for which it is intended, manufacture in
quantity is begun. Even then, rigid tests all along the way check on the
maintenance of a quality equal to, or better than, the model.

### KINDS OF LENSES

Though a simple convex lens will form an image, it has so many optical
faults that it is not of much use to us in photography. The sort of lens
used in even the lowliest box cameras is made of special glass and ground
according to a special formula. Here are the basic types of lenses in use
today: meniscus, achromatic, rectilinear, anastigmat, apochromat (used
for color process and copying). Besides these, there are the lenses used
for *enlarging,* and the special-view lenses known as the *wide-angle* and the
*telephoto.*

*The Meniscus.* This is a simple lens made up of only one piece of glass,
and guilty of almost all the aberrations there are. As used in cheap box
cameras it can deliver an image of usable sharpness, provided the negative
is not enlarged. The *concave* side is usually turned toward the object,
with the diaphragm and shutter *before* the lens.

In order to understand why a lens can have a fixed focus, it is only necessary to remember that when it is focused on an object that is not too close, everything beyond that object and away from the lens will also be

  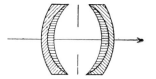

FIG. 26. THE MENISCUS LENS          FIG. 27. THE ACHRO-MATIC LENS          FIG. 28. THE RECTI-LINEAR LENS

fairly sharp. This holds good for *all* lenses. In small box cameras, the object distance is set at ten feet for the largest sizes, and about fifteen feet for the smallest sizes. See *Fig. 26*.

*The Achromatic.* This is a single lens made up of two or more pieces of cemented glass. It is partially corrected for *spherical* and *chromatic* aberrations, and produces a passably sharp image provided the aperture is not too large, so that the unreliable outer portion of the lens is not used (at about $f$ 12),[8] if only a *narrow angle of view* is used. However, depending on whether the diaphragm is used before or after the lens, it is still afflicted with distortion, which makes it unfit for use whenever a straight line has to be reproduced as such. The achromat is also known as the *aplanat* or the *symmetrical*. See *Fig. 27*.

*The Rectilinear.* By bringing two achromatic lens combinations together as a single unit and setting the diaphragm between them, it is possible to eliminate barrel and pincushion distortion. The resulting lens is known as the *rapid rectilinear*. Its corrections make it usable at openings larger than in the case of the achromatic (as large as $f$ 8). See *Fig. 28*.

*The Anastigmat.* When applied to a lens, the term *an*astigmat indicates that it is *not* astigmatic—or rather, that it is *free* from astigmatism. As the apertures of rapid rectilinear lenses were made larger, the aberration of astigmatism, caused by the rays which enter the lens at an oblique angle, became more and more of a problem. Though lenses made of crown and flint glass can be corrected for chromatic and spherical aberration and for coma, they cannot be cleared of astigmatism. On the other hand, barium glass lenses can be corrected for astigmatism, but still suffer

° These numbers preceded by $f$'s ($f$ 2.8, $f$ 12, etc.) are to designate the size of the diaphragm opening, the size of the hole controlling the amount of light that passes through the lens. When an "$f$ 4.5 lens" is referred to, as we have already referred to the "$f$ 4.5 Tessar," this relates to the largest diaphragm opening that the lens has—$f$ 4.5 in this case. (Such a lens would have other, smaller diaphragm openings, of course.) Notice that the larger the opening, the smaller the $f$ number. The larger the largest stop, the faster the lens is said to be. (This use of "fast" does not concern the speed of the *shutter*.)

from spherical aberration. This problem was solved in 1893 by Dr. E. von Hoegh, who worked out a formula for a lens to be made of the new barium glass, just then made available at Jena, in combination with crown and flint glass. When this lens was completed, it was found that astigmatism, the curse of all other lenses produced up to that time, had been reduced to a new and remarkable low. This lens was the Goerz Dagor, and it is still manufactured and sold here in America. It was the first lens that would form a sharp image on a screen at full aperture. See *Fig. 29.*

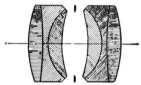

FIG. 29. ONE OF THE FIRST ANASTIGMATS—THE GOERZ
DAGOR

Following this lens came other anastigmats that were made of various kinds of the new glass according to the formulas of other celebrated mathematicians and constructed by the greatest lens makers. Of these, the Zeiss anastigmats have found great favor, one type of which, called the *Protar,* has convertible components as shown by *A* in *Fig. 30,* and the other, the *Tessar,* has non-convertible components as shown by *B.* The Tessar structure has become a basic design, being widely copied by other lens makers.

Most anastigmats, as *A* and *B* in *Fig. 30* show, are made with components formed of two or more lenses, some of which are cemented together, and others separated by air spaces; the purpose, however, of all of these variations in design is the same: to give an image of the best possible definition and the flattest field, and one that is free from spherical aberration, distortion, coma and color magnification. Diagram *C* in *Fig. 30* shows a lens that accomplished this with a rather simple design.

In the case of some anastigmats, notably the Dagor, the Protar, and the Plasmat, the front and rear components can be used independently of one another, as well as together, to get varying sizes of image from the same camera position.

The fastest anastigmats (*i.e.,* those which can be used with the widest apertures) for still cameras made today are the Zeiss Sonnar *f* 1.5 and the Leitz Summarit *f* 1.5 (*Fig. 31*). They are both made for use in miniature cameras, like the Contax and the Leica. Besides the *f* 3.5 Elmar and the *f* 3.5 Tessar, which are both good, one of the best corrected anastigmats for miniature camera use is the Summicron *f* 2. Its large front

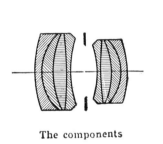

The components

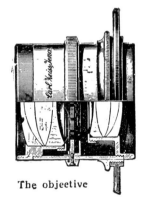

The objective

A. ZEISS DOUBLE PROTAR

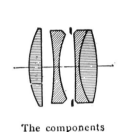

The components

The objective

B. ZEISS TESSAR

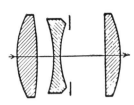

C. KODAK ANASTIGMAT

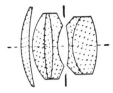

D. ZEISS SONNAR $f$ 2

FIG. 30. TYPES OF ANASTIGMATS

element is made of a new type optical glass which resists climatic changes, increases marginal illumination and improves definition. Another superb lens for miniature cameras is the Zeiss Sonnar $f$ 2 shown in *Fig. 30*. For wide-angle use with the Leica, there is the excellently corrected 35-mm. *Summaron f* 3.5; for the Contax, the brilliant and beautifully corrected

35-mm. Orthometar, $f$ 4.5, the design of which, by the way, duplicates that of the Plasmat. The Eastman Kodak Ektar, which is made in various speeds and focal lengths, is another splendid example of the anastigmat at

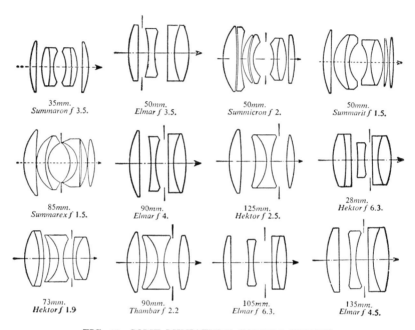

FIG. 31. SOME MINIATURE CAMERA LENSES

its best; based on the design of the Tessar, it has improved on the Tessar's already excellent corrections. In addition, all the inside air-glass surfaces have been treated to increase light transmission.

*The Apochromatic.* The exacting requirements of color process work, where the lens must produce a precise and perfect photographic copy of the object, has stimulated lens manufacturers further to improve the corrections of the anastigmat. The result is the *apochromat,* a lens so perfectly corrected that it not only produces images of equal sharpness on the same focal plane through all the various color filters, but the negative images are of exactly the same size so that color plates made from these negatives will register perfectly.

A good example of the apochromatic type of lens is the Goerz Artar, an air-space, uncemented combination consisting of four lens elements, two of which are symmetrically placed on each side of the diaphragm. It is said to be fully corrected for chromatic and spherical aberrations, coma and astigmatism; is free from zonal aberration and flare; and its symmetrical construction prevents linear distortion. (The maximum speed is $f$ 9 and it is made in various focal lengths from 4 to 70 inches.)

*Enlarging Lenses.* The normal *taking* lens for a still camera is corrected for infinity. That means that it gives its *best* performance for distant objects, when the lens lies closest to the focal plane. Though a well-corrected anastigmat can be used for close-ups, it does not give so flat a field, and because of the increase in oblique rays from short object distances there may be an increase of coma and other aberrations. For that reason most manufacturers recommend that a taking lens be stopped down when used for enlarging. A better way is to use another lens for this purpose— one that has been corrected especially for short distance focusing, and one that has a flatter field at those distances than the regular camera lens can possibly have. Good examples of such lenses are: The Bausch & Lomb Micro Tessar, the Kodak Projection Ektar, the Meyer Helioplan, the Schneider Componar, the Wollensak Enlarging Velostigmat, the Simmon Enlarging Lens. The Helioplan is especially well designed for this purpose, being constructed of four *uncemented*, heat-resistant lens components, which makes it a perfect lens for enlarging. See *Fig. 32.*

MEYER HELIOPLAN, *f* 4.5

FIG. 32. AN ENLARGING LENS

*Wide-Angle Lenses.* The normal lens of any camera has a focal length equal to the diagonal of the picture size. For a 4 x 5-inch negative, for instance, the correct lens would be one with a focal length of about 6½ inches. The angle of view of such a lens would be about 50 degrees. To get more of the scene in, without moving the camera back (which might be impossible in many cases) we must use a lens with a broader angle of view. Such a lens is called a *wide-angle* lens. As a rule, the curvature of such a lens is considerably greater, the components are mounted closer together, and its focal length, therefore, is less. Such lenses are especially useful for photographing interiors of buildings, and for exteriors where the space around them is restricted. Because it tempts you to get closer to objects, the wide-angle lens distorts perspective; that is not, however, a fault or property of the lens itself, but rather a fault in the way it is used. Perspective, as we shall see later, is not a property of the lens at all.

An example of an extreme *wide-angle* lens is the Zeiss Hypergon, shown in *Fig. 33*. This is a symmetrical lens consisting of two single com-

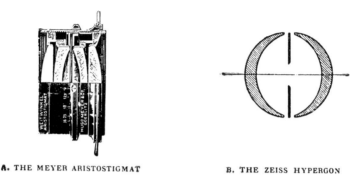

**A.** THE MEYER ARISTOSTIGMAT          **B.** THE ZEISS HYPERGON

FIG. 33. WIDE-ANGLE LENSES

ponents, hemispherical in shape. Its angle of view is 140 degrees, and its speed is *f* 22. The Meyer Aristostigmat is another excellent wide-angle lens. It has an angle of 105 degrees and a speed of *f* 6.3.

*Telephoto.* When you want a fairly large image of a distant object, a telephoto lens is called for. A good example of such a lens is the Eastman Kodak Telephoto shown in *Fig. 34*. It has a focal length of six

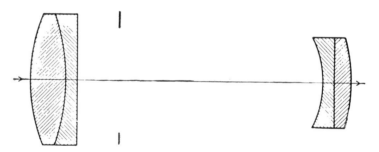

FIG 34. A TELEPHOTO LENS—THE EASTMAN KODAK

inches and a speed of *f* 4.5. In order to enable it to bring things closer, the lens is made on the principle of the telescope, with a convex, or converging, component in the rear. The difference between a telephoto lens and an ordinary lens of the same focal length is illustrated in *Fig. 35*. The telephoto, as you see, is much more compact. Since the weight of a camera fitted with a telephoto makes it difficult to hold steady by hand, it should be mounted on a tripod or other firm support; otherwise the image will be blurred.

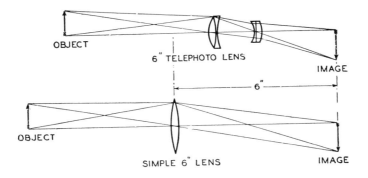

IMAGE DISTANCES FOR 6" SIMPLE AND TELEPHOTO LENS

FIG. 35. THE DIFFERENCE BETWEEN A LENS OF LONG
FOCUS AND A TELEPHOTO

*Auxiliary Lenses.* For certain types of lenses and cameras, especially those with double extension bellows, there are supplementary lenses available for shortening and increasing the focal length of the original lens. The Zeiss Distar, for instance, *increases* the focal length of a lens, making possible a larger image on the film from the same camera position; the Zeiss Proxar, on the other hand, reduces the focal length and the image size. The Proxar can also be used as a portrait attachment. Other such lenses are the Schneider Longar and Curtar, and the Eastman Kodak Portrait Lens.

Another supplementary lens available for amateur use is the *soft focus* or *diffusion disk.* This deliberately blurs the photographic definition and clarity that lens makers have tried so hard to give you. The use of them, quite a vogue years ago, makes no sense at all today. It's simple enough to diffuse your image when you enlarge it (by interposing some crumpled cellophane or a silk stocking stretched on a hoop, or by kicking the enlarger). Get the sharpest and clearest image you can on your negative; you can always lose that crisp definition later, *if you want to.* In fact, it's only too easy, as you will soon discover when you start to make enlargements.

### LENS COATING

Age, in combination with exposure to sun and air, frequently causes lenses to tarnish. When this occurs the surface acquires a perceptible discoloration, which has prompted some people to dispose of otherwise perfectly fine objectives. Not too many years ago it was discovered that this tarnish actually improves a lens, makes it sharper and somewhat faster. Optical scientists learned that the tarnish reduces light reflection, allowing more light to pass through the lens than was the case before it had become tarnished. Experiments finally led to one of the most important advances in the science of optics in the last twenty-five years—artificial aging, or lens coating.

Lens coating has been the subject of considerable discussion among amateur photographers, as a result of which many misconceptions about what it does have gained currency. Lenses that have been coated are definitely improved so far as practical picture-taking is concerned, but not so miraculously as some enthusiasts would have you believe. Here, roughly, are the facts about lens coating:

Photographic lenses consist of a number of elements. Some of these are single lenses, others consist of two or more single lenses cemented together. The points at which lenses lose efficiency in transmitting light are the free surfaces; those, in other words, which are in contact with air. Transmission loss at each such surface, according to Bausch & Lomb optical experts, is about 5 per cent due to reflections from the surface of the glass. If a lens structure has eight such surfaces the loss of light transmission through surface reflections may amount to as much as one-third. These surface reflections also give rise to internal lens reflections causing flare, which results from shooting toward the sun or other light source.

Coating the free surfaces of lenses greatly overcomes these reflection losses and the tendency to flare. The coating, which is about four-millionths of an inch thick, has a lower refractive index than the glass elements of the lens. Here, in the words of A. F. Turner, of the Scientific Bureau of Bausch & Lomb Optical Company, is how it works:

A ray of light striking the coated surface is partially reflected, the remainder passing through the coating. At the second surface of the coating it is again partially reflected. The latter reflection is one-half wave-length behind the first; the reflections interfere with one another, cancelling each other out, thereby reducing reflection and decreasing flare considerably. Not only that, more light is transmitted by the lens. Complex? . . . but it works.

From this it can be seen that the increase of efficiency to be expected from lens coating *depends entirely upon the construction of the lens.* A simple lens with only two free surfaces, or even one with several elements all cemented together but still having only two free surfaces, will not be greatly improved by coating. The greater the number of free surfaces in a lens the more apparent will be the increase in speed, sharpness and flare reduction.

The question frequently arises as to the advisability of having an old lens coated. Although there are reliable firms offering such a service, to do so is always to incur a certain amount of risk. The lens coating process requires that your lens be dismantled. In putting it together again there is always the possibility that the delicate adjustment of the lens may be disturbed in recementing the elements. While the work may be sincerely guaranteed, there is the danger that the elements may not be put together perfectly; and it would be difficult for you to prove that your lens had not been properly reassembled. Thousands of people have had their old lenses coated and have been satisfied with the results. But it is only fair to warn you of the slight risk involved.

While lens coating is a topic of discussion among photographers now, in all probability it will be taken for granted a few years hence. Practically all lens makers include a coating machine in their assembly line, so that all new lenses appearing on the market will be coated.

### BUBBLES

When you find bubbles in your lens you can be sure that it has been made with the best new optical glass. The chemicals used in making such glass form gasses which, inevitably, create bubbles. This cannot be avoided. But unless the bubbles are large and numerous, they do not affect the performance of your lens at all. They may obstruct a few rays of light, but the total amount of this loss would not exceed 1/5000 of the total light streaming through the lens, even if stopped way down, so there's nothing to worry about. To do as much harm as one of those old-fashioned diffusion disks or an inaccurately timed shutter, the lens would have to be so full of bubbles that you could hardly see through it.[9]

## CARE OF THE LENS

To get the best out of your lens, take good care of it: (1) Always keep it covered when not in use. If the design of your camera permits it, use lens caps for both the front and rear elements. (2) Never take it apart yourself for cleaning. The lens was put together in an air-conditioned, dust-free room. If *you* try it, you'll let dust and moisture get between the elements, with sad results. (3) Do not expose it to the sun for long periods. (4) Avoid keeping it in damp or warm places. (5) Do not subject it to extreme variations of temperature. (6) Don't put your fingers on its surface, *ever*. (7) Don't drop or jar it. (8) Never use alcohol or other solvents to clean it.

The best way to clean a lens is to brush its surface *gently* with a little camel's hair brush reserved only for that use, or to blow the dust away with a rubber ear syringe. If that doesn't do the trick, use some dry lens tissue, or an old linen handkerchief that has been freshly laundered, first

[9] In July 1956, Dr. Masao Nagaoka of Nippon Kogaku (Nikon) announced the invention of a new type of ceramic crucible that "virtually eliminates bubbles."

breathing on the lens (very, very lightly) and then *softly* wiping it with the tissue in a rotary motion. *Don't clean it too often or too hard.* You may scratch or dull the highly polished lens surface.

If you follow the directions above, you should never have to do more than dust it occasionally with the brush or syringe. If the lens needs much more than this to clean it properly, send it to one of the big camera shops for servicing. They have experts on their staffs who know how to do it, and the small charge they'll make for this service is well worth it.

## HOW TO BE SURE OF SHARP PICTURES

The lenses on most good cameras have greater resolving power (the ability to separate more lines per square inch of image) than any film now made. Why, then, is it so difficult for amateurs to get sharp pictures? Perhaps it's because they neglect such obvious precautions as these:

1. Be sure to focus exactly, whether by *distance scale* (this requires testing), by *range finder* (check this against a ground-glass image if your camera permits it, or have the manufacturer . . . Leitz, for instance, if you own a Leica . . . check it for you), or by ground glass (see *Some Focusing Hints* on page 190). A quick check for a range-finder camera is to set the lens at infinity and then snap some building beyond 500 feet. This test is not inclusive (for any other distance) or conclusive for infinity, but it's reassuring if you're out of reach of a repair shop.

2. Be sure not to jerk the camera. Tests by experts have shown that any shutter speed slower than 1/100 second is dangerous. *Use a tripod for slow speeds.*

3. Be sure to use the sharpest part of your lens, *the center.* You do this by stopping down to such median openings as *f* 5.6 to *f* 6.3 with a miniature, or *f* 8 to *f* 11 with a larger camera. Use the larger or smaller openings only for bad light conditions, special effects, or to get greater depth of focus.

4. Check your equipment frequently to be sure it's in good working order. See pages 332-340 (WHAT'S WRONG?).

5. Use sharp-resolution films (such as Panatomic X, Adox KB14 and KB17, Isopan F, and Plus X).

6. Use fine-grain developers that do not degrade the sharpness of the image (such as D76, Neofin blue, Willi Beutler's developer, D25, Windisch 665, Microphen, Clayton P60, Microdol, Promicrol, and X22).

# 4

## *The Mystery of "f"*

The sixth letter of the alphabet is the most frequently used symbol in photography, yet very few really know what it stands for. It does not, as some believe, indicate the focus or focal length. It is an abbreviation for the term *factor* and symbolizes an arithmetical proportion; the relation between the diameter of the lens opening, or *aperture,* and the *focal length* of the lens (given below in inches). For example, any of the following lens combinations would have a factor of 2, or be rated as *f* 2 lenses:

> a 1″ lens with an aperture of ½″
> a 2″ lens with an aperture of 1″
> a 3″ lens with an aperture of 1½″
> a 4″ lens with an aperture of 2″
> a 5″ lens with an aperture of 2½″
> a 6″ lens with an aperture of 3″

The "*f*," as you see, indicates the *speed* of the lens, or the amount of light it lets through in proportion to its focal length. Amateurs sometimes make the mistake of trying to determine the "*f*" value by measuring only the diameter of the front lens, without relation to aperture or focal length. The result is incorrect, of course, as you can realize from a study of the following list of lens factors; though they all vary, they apply to lenses that have exactly the same lens aperture—all *one inch in diameter:*

> Focal length 2″ = *f* 2
> Focal length 3″ = *f* 3
> Focal length 4″ = *f* 4
> Focal length 5″ = *f* 5
> Focal length 6″ = *f* 6

In addition to the lens factor which determines its speed at *full* aperture, each lens has marked on it somewhere a series of other lens factors which are controlled by a *diaphragm,* or *stop.* Let's investigate this stop and find out what it is, what it does, and how it works.

## WHAT A STOP IS

In its simplest form a *diaphragm,* or *stop,* is a metal plate with a hole in it which limits the amount of light that passes through the lens. In box cameras it may be nothing more than a strip of black metal with several holes of varying size punched in it; in the better cameras it is usually an iris diaphragm, patterned on the one in the eye, which provides a hole continuously variable in size.

## WHAT A STOP DOES

There are four good photographic reasons for using a stop:

1. To *make the picture sharper* than it would be with the lens wide open, especially if the lens is not an anastigmat.

2. To *equalize illumination,* from the edges of the image to its center.

3. To get *depth of field.*

4. To *control the exposure,* which is rather important with modern films.

### HOW TO MAKE THE PICTURE SHARPER

Since no lens, not even an anastigmat, can be considered perfect—that is, absolutely free from aberration, distortion and astigmatism—a stop helps to correct these faults by cutting off the rays of light that pass obliquely through the edge of the lens. As the only effective rays remaining are those that go through the middle, which is the area of least distortion or aberration, it is easy to see that this will form a sharper image. But since some of the rays of light are thus shut off from the film surface, the loss must be compensated for by increasing the exposure.

### HOW TO EQUALIZE ILLUMINATION

The oblique rays that travel from the outside rim of a lens have farther to go and are therefore weaker when they get there. The result is that the image seems brighter in the center and weaker around the edges. If the lens formula hasn't already compensated for this fault (a surprise byproduct of flatness of field), the only thing you can do is to close off the outer edge of the lens by stopping down the diaphragm and so restricting the light rays to the center of the lens. Extra exposure will be needed to compensate.

## HOW TO GET DEPTH OF FIELD

When you make a photograph of, say, a landscape with a lens wide open (at its largest aperture), only that part of the scene which you focus on, and other parts at the same distance (*i.e.,* in the same plane), will be perfectly sharp. It follows that objects in the foreground and background will not be equally sharp. For ordinary work this does not spoil the effect; in fact, it adds what some photographers, even today, call atmosphere or plasticity. The scene looks natural to the eye, for the simple reason that that is the way the eye would normally see it. The extent of apparent sharpness, from the nearest object to the farthest, is called the *depth of field.* To bring *foreground* and *background* into focus at the same time is quite a trick. To accomplish it, the lens must be stopped down. We shall explain in just a moment why this is so. The smaller the stop the greater the effect will be by increasing the depth of *focus* of the foreground and background objects. And again, this stopping down of the lens requires a longer exposure to compensate for the loss of light.

*What is Depth of Focus?* Technically, a perfect lens can give a sharp image of only one *object plane* at a time. This is known as the *plane of focus.* Every point on this plane is represented, theoretically, by another point on the *image plane.* When a lens is sharply focused, each point of light from the object plane has been brought together again as a point on the image plane. We know of course that each of these points of light is really a *cone* of light and that if the distance between the image plane (in this case the film) and the lens is increased or decreased, the points of light from the object plane will become cones again. Similarly, points of light from other object planes will also reach the image plane as sections of cones, the points of which will be on other image planes. As the object planes move forward so do the image planes, and in the same proportion. Since the film plane would slice transversely through these cones, the impression made on the film surface (except where it was in *focus*) would be that of little *circles* of light, instead of *points.* These circles are the famous *circles of confusion* you've heard so much about. The effort in photography (except by the stubborn gentlemen of the soft-focus school) is to keep these circles of confusion as small as it is humanly possible to do so.

The diameter of these circles is affected by the following:

1. The focal length of the lens; *the shorter the better* (since a lens of short focal length has a greater depth of focus).

2. The aperture of the lens; *the smaller the better.*

3. The distance between the plane of focus and other object planes to be represented; *the shallower the better*.

4. The distance between the object plane and the lens; *the greater the better*.

5. The resolving power of the lens (its ability to separate adjacent lines or points of an object); *the more highly corrected the better*.

6. The care with which focusing is done; *the finer the better*.

Now let's see how this works out in practice. If you will look at the diagram in *Fig. 36*, you will see that the solid black lines and the broken lines which represent rays of light start from the points marked *A* and *A₁* at different distances, or object planes, of the view you are taking.

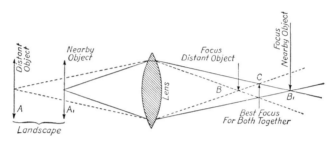

FIG. 36. WHAT DEPTH OF FIELD MEANS

at different distances, or object planes, of the view you are taking. After these rays pass through the lens, they come to a focus at two points marked $B$ and $B_1$, which, you will observe, are separated by a small distance, and, consequently, instead of focusing at either one as a sharp point of light, they produce those little patches of light called circles of confusion.

The point, then, where the rays from $A$ and $A_1$ come closest together is at $C$ which is between $B$ and $B_1$, and hence, the image formed there is the sharpest for the total landscape. Of course, this is only a compromise; a plane somewhere between $A$ and $A_1$, and closer to $A$, will be the only plane in absolutely sharp focus. The reason such a picture looks sharp to us, nevertheless, is that the eye cannot readily distinguish between a sharp point and a circle that does not exceed certain limits. These limits vary with the viewing distance, but as a general rule the eye will still see a circle as a point if, at whatever distance it is held from the eye, the angle made by its diameter does not exceed 2 minutes of arc.[1] For a Leica negative, for instance, this permits a circle of confusion of 1/30 mm., and so all the depth-of-field tables for Leica lenses are based on this figure.

Now let us see what happens when you put a stop in front or back of

---

[1] A minute of arc is 1/60 of a degree.

the lens at *D*, as shown in *Fig. 37*. It cuts off all the rays of light that pass through the edge of the lens and lets through only those that are in a line with the center of the lens. As the angles of these rays are more acute the

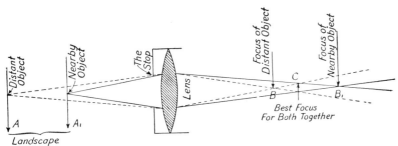

FIG. 37. HOW A STOP INCREASES DEPTH OF FIELD
Compare with Fig. 36.

circle of confusion is much smaller. If a screen is now placed between the points *B* and $B_1$, the image for both distances, or planes, will seem sharper, or in other words the depth of focus will be greater.

## HOW STOPS ARE MARKED

If you will look at the rim of your lens mount, you will see certain letters and numbers engraved there. One of these is the letter "f" (which may also be written as F or F/ or F: or *F*. or F= or f/ or f: or f= or *f*, or just the simple letter without diagonal, period, colon or crossbars). You already know the meaning of this letter,[2] it indicates that the number that follows is the lens *factor*, or *fraction*—a measure of the speed of the lens, found by dividing the focal length by the diameter of the aperture. In some old lenses you may find the letters "U.S." followed by a number. This stands for the "Uniform System" (not *United States*) of lens speed marking, now obsolete.

You may also find the letters "mm." or "cm." "Mm." stands for millimeter and "cm." for centimeter; both are metric indications of the

[2] When the *f* speed of a lens is given, it is usually indicated by a number preceded by one form of the letter "f" as given above. But lens makers themselves have been perpetuating a confusion by using f's indiscriminately to indicate both the lens *factor* and its *focal length*. For example, Zeiss in their circulars, etc. speak of an *f* 2.8 Tessar, but the lens itself is marked:

Tessar 1:2.8
f = 8 cm.

Leitz, similarly, speak of their *f* 3.5 Elmar, while the lens is marked:

Elmar 1:3,5
F = 50 mm.

To avoid further confusion, we shall distinguish between them by making the italic lowercase *f* the symbol for the *lens factor* (which it was, anyway) and the capital F the symbol for the *focal length*. This system of marking will be followed throughout this book.

focal length, an inch being the equivalent roughly of *25 mm.* or *2.5 cm.* Thus a 5-cm. or 50-mm. lens is a 2 inch lens; a 7.5-cm. or 75-mm. lens is a 3-inch lens.

### WHAT THE NUMBERS MEAN

There is, as we have said, a definite relation between the size of the stop (the diameter of the hole in it) and the focal length of the lens (the distance between the optical center of the lens and the image plane when the lens is focused on infinity). When the advantage of using stops to get sharper pictures was first discovered, the relation between the factors cited above was not worked out in detail, so the photographer used a stop of the size he thought would give the necessary definition, and then exposed the plate for the length of time he guessed would be about right. In other words, he had to depend entirely upon his judgment, or just plain luck, to guide him in making the right exposure. The vast preoccupation with methods for *reducing* and *intensifying* negatives in the past was due to this bungling.

Then someone found that if the stops were set so that the various aperture diameters were made proportionate in size to the focal length of the lens, the time of exposure could also be calculated proportionally. This simplified photography quite a bit; it had been pretty much of a guess-as-guess-can proposition up to that time. It now began to take on an aura of scientific exactitude which has stayed with it ever since. This has gone so far in fact that some otherwise good photographers have begun to lose sight of the main purpose of photography, the making of pictures, and have become bogged down or obsessed by laboratory technique.

The number after the letter, then, indicates the relation between the *aperture* of the stop and the *focal length* of the lens. Thus, if it is marked ƒ 11 it means that the hole in the stop has a diameter one-eleventh of the focal length of the lens; ƒ 16 means that the diameter of the stop is one-sixteenth of the focal length of the lens, and so on.

### THE ƒ SYSTEM OF LENS MARKING

This simple and accurate method for predetermining the changes in light intensity due to aperture changes was conceived by some members of the Royal Photographic Society of Great Britain in 1881. They adopted as the unit *one* an aperture of ƒ 4, and worked out a sequence of aperture ratios that gave each successive stop an area just half of the one which preceded it. Each numerical stop, therefore, lets through twice as much light as the next stop higher. The reason that these stops were halved, instead of quartered or divided by thirds, is that a light intensity must be *doubled* before the eye will recognize the change; this also has its application in the making of negatives, prints and enlargements, and it explains why amateurs are often told to alter their exposures, if at all, *only* by a factor of 2; that is, if you are taking some extra shots of a scene just to be sure, there's no use trying more than half, or less than double, any indicated exposure.

The higher the number marked on the stop, the smaller the hole, and, hence, the longer the exposure must be. It follows, conversely, that the lower the number, the larger the hole in the stop and the shorter the exposure can be. In the ƒ system, the numbers on a stop give only the proportion of the diameter of the hole to the focal length of the lens and, therefore, the numbers should really be marked 1/8, 1/11, 1/16 and so on; but the fractional form was dropped in practice and whole numbers were used instead.

From what has just been said, it will be seen that the ƒ number is not one of fixed size for all lenses, but that it varies with the focal length of the lens. Thus an ƒ 8 stop with a lens having an eight-inch focal length would have a diameter of one inch; while the same numbered stop with a lens having a sixteen-inch focal length would have a diameter of two inches, and so on.

The following table shows the chief sizes of stops used in the international ƒ system today.

| ƒ 1.4 | 2 | 2.8 | 4 | 5.6 | 8 | 11 | 16 | 22 | 32 | 45 | 64 |
|---|---|---|---|---|---|---|---|---|---|---|---|

These really represent fractions, as follows:

| $\frac{1}{1.4}$ | $\frac{1}{2}$ | $\frac{1}{2.8}$ | $\frac{1}{4}$ | $\frac{1}{5.6}$ | $\frac{1}{8}$ | $\frac{1}{11}$ | $\frac{1}{16}$ | $\frac{1}{22}$ | $\frac{1}{32}$ | $\frac{1}{45}$ | $\frac{1}{64}$ |
|---|---|---|---|---|---|---|---|---|---|---|---|

And the exposure ratios called for by these stops are:

| $\frac{1}{8}$ | $\frac{1}{4}$ | $\frac{1}{2}$ | 1 | 2 | 4 | 8 | 16 | 32 | 64 | 128 | 256 |
|---|---|---|---|---|---|---|---|---|---|---|---|

That is, it takes 128 times as long to make an exposure at ƒ 45 as it does at ƒ 4; 128 times as long to make an exposure at ƒ 16 as at ƒ 1.4. Some types of foreign lenses are marked with a different series of stops. These would take their places in a series this way:

| ƒ 1.5 | 2.2 | 3.2 | 3.5 | 4.5 | 6.3 | 9 | 12.5 | 18 | 25 | 36 |
|---|---|---|---|---|---|---|---|---|---|---|
| 1 | 2.2 | 4 | 5 | 9 | 18 | 36 | 70 | 144 | 280 | 576 |

### RELATIVE EXPOSURES

In this series you can determine the relation of one factor to another by comparing their relative exposures. Stop ƒ 4.5, for example, has a relative exposure factor of 9; ƒ 9, an exposure factor of 36. To find out how much *more* exposure to give *f* 9, divide its factor, *36*, by the factor for *f* 4.5, which is *9*. The answer would be *4*. Which means that you need four times as much light, or an exposure four times as long. Working it backwards, if you were using *f* 12.5 and wanted to find out how much less exposure you'd need at *f* 3.5, you would divide the factor for *f* 12.5, 70, by the factor for *f* 3.3, 5. Your answer would be 14. In other words, you'd need one-fourteenth as much exposure.

## THE U. S. SYSTEM OF NUMBERING STOPS

Though this system is no longer used, some of the older lenses still have such markings. You may run across one of these one day and will want to know something about it.

The difference between this and the *f* system is in the way the lens speed factor is arrived at. In the *f* system, the *diameter* of the stop is used; in the U. S. system, the *area*. The result is the same in both cases.

To simplify computation, the U. S. system is numbered in a geometric progression, beginning with the number 1 as the numerical stop for an aperture equal to *f* 4 (at that time they could conceive of none larger).

Whereas in the *f* system the factor is the ratio between aperture and focal length, in the U. S. system it is the ratio between the light intensity for the largest aperture (*f* 4) and that of any other succeeding one. Match up equivalent *f* and *U. S.* stops and they would run along this way:

TABLE OF EQUIVALENT STOPS AND RELATIVE
EXPOSURES *IN SECONDS*

| | *f* 4 | 5.6 | 8 | 11.3 | 16 | 22 | 32 | 45.2 | 64 |
|---|---|---|---|---|---|---|---|---|---|
| | U.S. 1 | 2 | 4 | 8 | 16 | 32 | 64 | 128 | 256 |
| RELATIVE EXPOSURE IN SECONDS | $\frac{1}{400}$ | $\frac{1}{200}$ | $\frac{1}{100}$ | $\frac{1}{50}$ | $\frac{1}{25}$ | $\frac{1}{12}$ | $\frac{1}{6}$ | $\frac{1}{3}$ | $\frac{2}{3}$ |

The first thing you will probably notice is that the *relative exposures* for the *f* series exactly duplicate the aperture numbers of the *U. S.* series. Another thing you may notice is that the factor *16* is the same in both systems. With these two clues as memory joggers in case of necessity, you can now proceed to forget all about the sane, but short-lived, uniform system.

## WHAT "LENS SPEED" MEANS

The term the *speed of a lens* refers to the *largest* opening or stop at which it can be used. For example the lens of a box camera has a *speed* of ƒ 16, which means that this is the largest stop that can be used with it. Consequently, the shortest exposure you can give a medium-speed film like Verichrome or Finopan with such a lens is about 1/25 of a second in sunlight.

The single achromatic lens which is used in small folding cameras has a speed of ƒ 11 and hence under the same conditions, with the lens fully open, it takes an exposure of only 1/50 of a second because an ƒ 11 stop is the largest that can be used with it, and this gives it twice the speed of the lens of a box camera. The reason for this, as we have seen, is that an ƒ 11 stop has twice as large a hole, or opening, in it as an ƒ 16 stop, and therefore, lets twice as much light through the lens. The speed of the 50-mm. Elmar is ƒ 3.5 and this makes it possible to use an exposure, if all other conditions are the same, of 1/500 of a second at ƒ 3.5 compared with the 1/50 of a second with the ƒ 11 achromatic.

## HOW A STOP IS MADE

Only three different types of stops are used in modern cameras. These are: (1) the fixed stop, (2) the sliding stop and (3) the iris diaphragm. (See *Fig. 38.*)

*The Fixed Stop* is found only in the cheapest box cameras. It consists

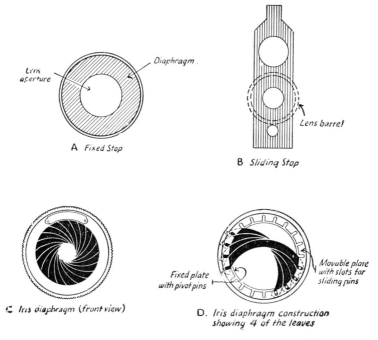

FIG. 38. THE KINDS OF DIAPHRAGMS OR STOPS

of a hole, slightly smaller than the lens aperture, punched out of a ring of black sheet metal which has been set permanently in front of the lens. Pocket magnifiers usually have such a fixed stop set between the lens elements.

*The Sliding Stop* is a thin strip of blackened metal which slides, in grooves, across the front of the lens. It usually has two or more holes of varying size to serve as apertures. This form of stop is used in the better grades of box cameras.

*The Iris Diaphragm* is a variable stop, rather ingeniously constructed, which is used in almost all other types of cameras. It consists of a number of curved leaves cut out of thin sheet metal overlapping each other and each pivoted to the inner circumference of the barrel of the lens. These leaves all work together, and by moving the knurled rim of the lens mount they can be made to slide back to the wall of the barrel, like the leaves of a fan. In this position they are wide open and give the lens its largest stop. By moving the rim the other way, the leaves close and you can reduce the opening to any size you want. The diagram, *Fig. 38 D,* illustrates the principle upon which it works.

## THE CRITICAL APERTURE

In all the discussion about diaphragms and stopping down we may have given the impression that all you have to do to get a good sharp image with almost any kind of lens is to stop it way down, and presto, the image is needle sharp. Well, and this may disappoint you, it's just not so. The sharpest definition, and the maximum resolving power, that it is possible to get out of any good lens is at the largest aperture which still removes the few aberrations not corrected when it was designed. This point, which is known as the *critical aperture,* varies with each type of lens, and depends on its original *f* speed and focal length. If the lens is stopped down beyond this point, *diffraction* sets in and begins to degrade the image.

Diffraction is not a lens aberration; it is a spreading of an image point caused by light rings which are formed by the rays bent at the edges of the stop; it cannot be corrected in the design of the lens, nor by closing the diaphragm. The critical aperture for most of the Leica lenses is about *f* 6.3; for the Zeiss Sonnar it is *f* 5.6; for most enlarger lenses it is about *f* 8 or *f* 11. With other lenses this point is about midway between the largest aperture and the smallest, favoring the largest.

By stopping down you will get increased depth of focus; but don't confuse that with sharpness. A pinhole camera has remarkable depth of focus, but absolutely no resolving power. By stopping your lens down until it resembles a pinhole, you are making it behave like one. To avoid this very thing, some lens makers take the necessary precautions in advance and prevent stopping down beyond a certain point.

## MORE ABOUT FOCAL LENGTH

There are three important lens characteristics which we haven't discussed as yet. These are: *image size, angle of view,* and *apparent perspective.* Since they are all dependent on the *focal length* of the lens, this is as good a time and place to take them up as any.

### IMAGE SIZE

With the camera remaining in the same position, the image size will vary in *direct* proportion to the focal length of the lens; or,

$$I \text{ (image size)} \propto \text{ (focal length)}$$

Mathematically translated, this becomes

$$I = KF$$

with the letter $K$ standing for the *proportionality constant*. If we want to find out what size image we should get if we increased or decreased the focal length at the same camera distance, this is how we should go about it. Suppose the image size produced by our 3-inch lens is just two inches high, and we want to know what a 6-inch lens will do. The formula becomes

$$2 = K\,3$$
$$\text{or, } K = \tfrac{2}{3}$$
$$\text{then } I = \tfrac{2}{3}\,F$$

Now, since the new $F$ is 6, we get

$$I = \tfrac{2}{3} \text{ of } 6$$
$$\text{or, } I = 4$$

The new image size, therefore, would be four inches. For a 12-inch lens the formula would be

$$I = \tfrac{2}{3} \text{ of } 12$$
$$\text{or, } I = 8$$

The image would then be eight inches high. The principle involved is illustrated by *Figs. 39* and *40*.

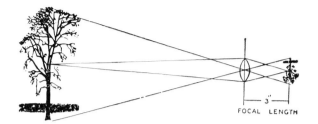

FIG. 39. HOW FOCAL LENGTH AFFECTS IMAGE SIZE—
SHORT FOCAL LENGTH, SMALL IMAGE

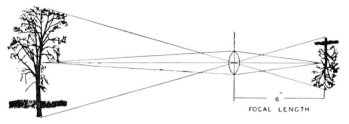

FIG. 40. HOW FOCAL LENGTH AFFECTS IMAGE SIZE—
LONG FOCAL LENGTH, LARGER IMAGE

The image size will also vary (focal length remaining constant) in *inverse* proportion to the distance between the object plane and the center of the lens. The formula for this is

$$I \text{ (image size)} \propto \frac{1}{D \text{ (object distance)}}$$

Mathematically translated, this becomes

$$I = K\frac{1}{D}$$

with $K$ again as the proportionality constant. We use this formula in exactly the same way that we did the one above. For example, a 2-inch image at 30 feet will become a 3-inch image at 20 feet and a 6-inch image at 10 feet, thus:

$$2 = K\frac{1}{30}$$

or, $K = 60$

substituting the value of the constant, $K$, in the above formula, we get

$$1 = \frac{D}{60}$$

at 30 feet, therefore, the formula is

$$I = \frac{60}{30} = 2$$

at 20 feet it becomes

$$I = \frac{60}{20} = 3$$

at 10 feet it becomes

$$I = \frac{60}{10} = 6$$

We can also combine both of these formulas into one single formula, thus:

$$I = K \frac{F}{D}$$

To photograph an object *same size*, or *natural size*, the lens has to be racked out to twice its focal length. The object distance then will also be twice the focal length. This rule applies to lenses of all focal lengths.

Here is a simple formula, and some variations, by which (the focal length remaining constant) you can figure out any *one* of four *object-image* dimensions if you know the other *three*:

$$\frac{A \text{ (object size)}}{B \text{ (image size)}} = \frac{C \text{ (object distance)}}{D \text{ (image distance)}}$$

The formula for *image size:*

$$B = \frac{A \times D}{C}$$

In other words, you multiply the object size by the image distance and divide that by the object distance, to get the size of the image.

The formula for *object size:*

$$A = \frac{B \times C}{D}$$

or, multiply the image size by the object distance and divide that by the image distance, to get the size of the object.

The formula for *object distance:*

$$C = \frac{A \times D}{B}$$

that is, multiply object size by image distance and divide that by the image size, to get the distance of the object.

The formula for *image distance:*

$$D = \frac{B \times C}{A}$$

which means, multiply image size by object distance and divide that by the object size, to get image distance.

Another formula for finding the *focal length* of a lens:

$$F = \frac{C \times D}{C + D}$$

or, multiply the object distance by the image distance and divide by the sum of the same integers, to get the focal length.

## ANGLE OF VIEW

The lens in the human eye has an angle of view of about 48 degrees (if you haven't a protractor handy, a rough approximation is the angle made by spreading out two adjacent fingers of one hand). Photographically, this is considered a normal angle and is about what we get when we use a lens with a focal length equal to the diameter of the negative area. The normal lens for a 4 x 5-inch negative, for example, would have a focal length of about 6½ inches. If we want to include more of the object in our picture we either have to move back, which is sometimes impossible, or increase our angle of view.

A lens that sees more of an object plane than the normal from any given distance is called a *wide-angle*. The eye of a fish has such a lens; it is flatter in shape and sees more in all directions. The normal lens for a Contax or Leica negative is one with a focal length of 2 inches, or 50 mm. The angle of view of such a lens is only 45 degrees to 48 degrees. To increase this angle we can use a lens with a shorter focal length, one of about 1⅜ inches or 35 mm. The wide-angle Elmar, Orthometar and Biogon, are all of this focal length, and have an angle view of about 65 degrees. For extreme wide-angle work in this size, there is the *f* 8 Tessar with a focal length of only 28 mm. and an angle of view of almost 76 degrees. In the larger sizes, the 4 x 5-inch for example, we can get wide-angle lenses even more extreme. The Aristostigmat, for instance, used to increase the angle of view in this size, has a focal length of 4 inches and a view of 105 degrees. The important things to remember about wide-angle lenses are that (1) while they increase the object angle, they reduce the image size in direct proportion (see *Figs. 39* and *40*); (2) they increase the apparent depth of focus by reducing the size of the circles of confusion; and (3) the angle of view can be increased slightly by racking the lens back and stopping down to compensate. The Dagor is used in this way.

To increase the size of an image, from a given point of view (especially if you can't get any closer), it is necessary to use, as we have already pointed out, a lens of longer focal length. Though strictly speaking not every lens of long focal length is a *telephoto,* it has become the custom to distinguish lenses of longer than normal focal length in that way. The lens in the eye of a bird is constructed like a telephoto; it is tubular in shape and sees less of any object than we do, but the image size is larger. There is quite a variety of telephoto lenses available for the Contax or Leica: the 85-mm. Sonnar or Triotar with an angle of view of 28 degrees; the 90-mm. Elmar with an angle of view of 27 degrees; the 105-mm. Elmar with an angle of view of 24 degrees; the 135-mm. Elmar with an angle of view of 18.5 degrees; the 200-mm. Telyt with an angle of view of 12 degrees (and a magnification of 4 x); the 135-mm. Sonnar with angle of view of 18.5 degrees; the 180-mm. Tele-Tessar or Sonnar with an angle of view of 13.6 degrees; the 300-mm. Tele-Tessar with an angle of view of 8 degrees; and the 500-mm. Zeiss Fern Long Distance, with an angle of view of only 5 degrees. In the larger picture sizes there are, in addition to the regular long-focus lenses, many combination sets, the separate elements of which have different focal lengths. The Plasmat and Protar sets, for example, each offer three different foci, depending on whether the front and rear components are used together or separately. The important things to keep in mind about telephoto lenses are (1) they increase size at the expense of depth of focus, (2) they not only magnify the image, but also *vibration;* for which reason (3) they should always be used with the camera set firmly on a tripod, and with an extra long cable release to avoid jarring the camera when making the exposure.

### APPARENT PERSPECTIVE

Despite a widespread belief to the contrary, all lenses give exactly the same perspective, no matter what their focal length, if they are used at the same distance. The *only* way it is possible to alter perspective is by changing the distance between the lens and the object. What our eye sees in any scene, therefore, is what any lens will see, whether wide angle, normal, or telephoto. The reason why wide-angle pictures often look badly distorted or unreal is that the photographer, in order to compensate for the inherently smaller size of a wide-angle image, comes too close to the object. You can duplicate this effect by stretching your hand out in front of you and looking at some distant object with one eye; gradually bring the hand back toward you and it will loom up larger and larger until it blots out everything else.

*Fig. 41* illustrates the meaning of photographic perspective. Two objects of the same size, *A* and *B,* are placed at different distances from the lens, *L*. The resultant images are shown by $A_1$ and $B_1$. The plane $F_1$ on which these images are formed is that for a lens of, say, normal focal length. The result of using a telephoto lens (or a normal lens if the other is a wide-angle) is shown at $F_2$ by images $A_2$ and $B_2$.

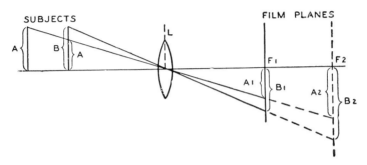

FIG. 41. ILLUSTRATING THE MEANING OF PHOTO-
GRAPHIC PERSPECTIVE

We can apply this to the solution of actual photographic problems in this way:

1. *To increase size of A without affecting size of B,* use a telephoto lens and move back until *B* is the size wanted.

2. *To increase size of B without affecting size of A,* use a wide-angle lens and move forward until *A* is size wanted.

3. *To reduce size of A without affecting size of B,* use a wide-angle lens and move forward until *B* is size wanted.

4. *To reduce size of B without affecting size of A,* use a telephoto lens and move back until *A* is size wanted.

5. *To increase apparent distance between A and B,* use a wide-angle lens and move forward until *B* is size wanted.

6. *To reduce apparent distance between A and B,* use a telephoto lens and move back until *B* is size wanted.

7. *To reduce violent perspective,* use a telephoto lens and move back until *B* is size wanted.

8. *To increase violent perspective,* use a wide-angle lens and move forward until *B* is size wanted.

The perspective effect produced by using a long focus lens can be duplicated simply by enlarging the picture taken with an ordinary lens.

# The Shutter

Basically, the photographic *shutter* is nothing more than a mechanical *light* chopper; something that lets light reach the emulsion for only a small and controlled fraction of time.

In the early days of photography, when sensitive plates were slow, they were exposed by simply removing the cap from the lens with the hand, keeping it off for the necessary length of time, and then putting it back on again. With the advent of faster films and better lenses, the need was felt for a device of some kind that would open and close the lens more quickly and with more precision than could be done with a cap. This led to the invention of the *shutter*.

## EARLY TYPES OF SHUTTERS

In its first form the shutter consisted of a thin strip of wood or panel, with a hole the size of the opening of the lens in its middle, and this slid in a grooved board that had a like hole in it and which fitted over the end of the barrel of the lens. When the operator wanted to make an exposure, he simply pushed the sliding strip or panel over until the hole in it was even with the opening in the lens, and after giving the time needed he pushed it back until the lens was closed.

There were other modifications of this type, notably the *drop shutter* which acted like a guillotine, the *rotary shutter* which is still used in some fixed-focus cameras, the *double-leaf shutter* which had two leaves pivoting at one end and was worked with compressed air by pressing on a rubber bulb. However, since most of these early before-the-lens shutters are now obsolete, we need not concern ourselves about them.

## MODERN TYPES OF SHUTTERS

This brings us to the three shutter types which are in use today, namely the *rotary shutter*, the *between-the-lens* (or *iris-diaphragm*) *shutter*, and the *focal-plane shutter*.

## THE ROTARY SHUTTER

This is the simplest of all. It consists of a hinged disk with a curved slot, pivoted in front of the camera, which by means of a spring-wired trigger release is made to cut across the supporting aperture plate. The trigger is moved *once* for each snapshot exposure. The speed of such a shutter is about 1/25 of a second (the aperture being *f* 16). It is self-setting, and has provisions for time exposure.

## THE IRIS SHUTTER

The iris shutter is built around the lens and contains both the diaphragm as well as the shutter. The latter consists of from three to five blades which are opened and closed at the center. These blades are controlled either by an air brake, as in the Compound shutter, or by an intricately meshed chain of gears, as in the Compur or the Eastman Kodamatic (see page 79).

As the iris shutter opens, it forms more or less of a star-shaped aperture depending on the number of leaves it has. This gives a better distribution of light all over than was possible with the old two-leaf shutters. The speed it is possible to get with such a shutter depends on the intricacy of its mechanism (which determines its price) and on its size. Those made for larger lenses are *dial-set* (that is, by means of two small dials that are pivoted on the front edge) and start at one second but only go up to 1/200 of a second and time; the others are *rim-set* (variations in exposure being controlled by rotating a knurled rim) and range from one second to 1/300 of a second and time. Among the faster shutters there are the Supermatic, which goes up to 1/400 and time, and the Compur-Rapid which goes up to 1/500 and time. All of these, unless built into the camera (as with the Automatic Rolleiflex which uses a Compur-Rapid shutter but encloses it within the camera body) are of the rim-set, pre-setting type. That is, adjustments for varying the exposure are made by rotating the rim of the shutter, and a lever has to be cocked each time to tense the spring before tripping it. The blades used in these shutters are made of exceptionally thin spring steel (those in the Supermatic being only .0015 of an inch thick); so they offer no resistance to air, have no inertia, and can therefore be opened and shut swiftly and accurately.

A special feature of the Supermatic is its two-color, speed-adjusting ring. Its eleven speeds are arranged in this way: from time, bulb and one second through 1/10 of a second, the six speed settings are marked in

red *as a warning that a tripod should be used;* from 1/25 to 1/400 second
the five markings are in black to indicate that hand-held exposures are
okay. (However, *play safe,* and for hand-held exposures *use nothing
slower than 1/100 of a second* if it is at all possible.)

Other types of iris shutters are the Kodamatic, which has seven speeds
from 1/10 to 1/200 second, including time and bulb; and the Diomatic,
which has six speeds, from 1/25 to 1/150 second, including time and bulb.

*Shutter releases.* There are four different kinds: (1) *the trigger* (or
*finger*) release, (2) the *cable* (or *antinous*) release consisting of a flexible
wire through a flexible tube. This tube is usually made of fiber, though
some have appeared with a flexible metal tube of a style similar to electric
cable. (3) the *bulb* (or *pneumatic*) release, which is a small air piston
connected by a rubber tube to a rubber bulb; pressure on the bulb com-
presses the air, which in turn moves the piston, which finally trips the
shutter. This type of release is now obsolete, having been replaced by the
*cable release.* (4) the *automatic* (or *self-timing*) release. This is a
delayed-action device which, after being tripped, postpones the actual
exposure for any preset interval of time. For those that are built into
cameras, as for instance in the Automatic Rolleiflex, the Contax II, the
Super Ikonta III, or in certain types of Compur shutters like the one
built into the Super Ikomat B, this interval is about 12 seconds. However, the Kodak self-timer, which is independent of the camera and is
attached to it by means of the cable release, offers variable delay intervals
from ½ second to 1 minute.

### THE FOCAL-PLANE SHUTTER

It is so called because it is fitted to the camera at or as near the focal
plane of the lens as it is possible to get it, without actually touching the
surface of the film. Since it is the fastest shutter made, giving exposures
as brief as 1/1000 of a second, it is largely used in reflex and press
cameras. Different from all other shutters in this respect, the *focal-plane
shutter,* or *curtain shutter,* or *roller-blind shutter,* as it has been variously
named, is used close to the film instead of *ahead* of or *between* the lens
components. This has its advantages, but it also presents many problems.

Essentially, the focal-plane shutter consists of a durable, light-tight
curtain with five rectangular openings or slits, only one of which moves
across the film in making the exposure. That part of the curtain which is
not covering or exposing the negative is wound on rollers at each end.
When the exposure is made, the curtain unrolls from the top and rerolls
at the bottom, where it is under tension. (See *Fig. 42.*) The exposure

FIG. 42. THE
FOCAL-PLANE
SHUTTER
CURTAIN

An iris shutter.

depends on the *width* of the *slit* and the *tension* of the variable spring
(with six possible tensions) which pulls the curtain when the shutter release is tripped. The exposures vary from 1/10 of a second to 1/1000
of a second, according to this table attached to the camera:

### FOCAL-PLANE SHUTTER SPEEDS

| TENSION NUMBER | CURTAIN APERTURE | | | |
|:---:|:---:|:---:|:---:|:---:|
| | **A** (⅛″) | **B** (⅜″) | **C** (¾″) | **D** (1½″) |
| 1 | 350 | 110 | 40 | 10 |
| 2 | 440 | 135 | 50 | 15 |
| 3 | 550 | 160 | 65 | 20 |
| 4 | 680 | 195 | 75 | 25 |
| 5 | 825 | 235 | 80 | 30 |
| 6 | 1000 | 295 | 90 | 35 |

In addition to these speeds, the curtain can also be adjusted to make a time exposure by winding the curtain or tripping the shutter release until the slit aperture window at the right shows T (*time*). The tension is set at 1, the camera mounted on a tripod, the shutter opened by tripping it once and closed by tripping it again. The latest *Speed Graphic* models are equipped with a new and simplified focal-plane shutter, which does away with the necessity for converting tension numbers into speeds. This one has a single winding key, where the old one had two, and the actual speeds are read directly from a small indicator.

*Something else to worry about.* The *effective aperture* of a lens is affected by the width of the slit in a focal-plane shutter; the wider the slit, the more accurate the exposure. When the slit is at its narrowest, it tends to cut off some of the pencils of light trying to reach the film. This would not be so if the shutter were actually moving in contact with the plate; in that case the efficiency would be 100 per cent. But since there is some distance, no matter how small, between these two planes, a narrow slit may cut partly through each cone of light that begins at the lens (varying with the diameter of the aperture) and ends as a point (when in focus] at the film surface. The effect this has, naturally, is to reduce the amount of light reaching the film, and hence change the *f* number. The cure for this is either a larger curtain slit or a larger lens aperture, or both.

*Miniature Focal-Plane Shutters.* Though basically the same in design and concept as the shutters used in the Graphic and Graflex cameras, the focal-plane shutters used in the Leica, Contax, Exakta, Nikon, and Canon cameras are smaller, and therefore more accurate and reliable.

For one thing, they are *self-capping,* which means that they are made of two blinds (instead of one) which separate as the exposure is made and lock together again when the shutter is rewound. This prevents the accidental fogging of film.

For another thing, these shutters offer a greater range of speeds; the Contax, for example, offering ten speeds from ½ second to 1/1250 second plus time, bulb, and delayed action; the Leica offering thirteen marked speeds from 1 full second to 1/1000 second as well as bulb and time, with the speeds from 1 full second to 1/20 second being continuously variable; the Exakta offering 27 speeds from 12 full seconds to 1/1000 second, as well as bulb, time and delayed action.

The Contax shutter is made of flexible, metal sections, and drops vertically across the surface of the film; both the Leica and Exakta shutters are made of a climate-resisting rubberized cloth, and move horizontally across the film surface. To avoid distortion with these, as with all focal-plane shutters, it is better to stop down. Another thing to remember, when following action with a miniature camera, is that the direction of the shutter curtain should match the direction in which the subject is moving. If it doesn't do that normally, simply turn the camera upside down and you'll find that it will.

## SHUTTER EFFICIENCY

The word *efficiency* when applied to a shutter means the amount of light it lets through during the time it takes to make an exposure. As an illustration: Suppose you have two shutters, and both of them open and close in exactly the same length of time, say 1/25 of a second, but the construction of the first is such that it lets more light through than the second. The first one clearly has a higher efficiency than the second one.

This difference in the efficiency of shutters results from the fact that some of them are so made that the entire opening of the lens is uncovered only for a very small fraction of the time that the shutter is making the total exposure, the rest of the time being taken up by the leaves' uncovering and covering up the aperture of the lens. To have one hundred per cent efficiency, a shutter would have to open and close absolutely instantaneously—that is, without any time element at all—and thus give the full aperture for the whole length of time. The focal-plane shutter comes the nearest to doing this of any that has been devised up to the present time. (See *Fig. 43.*) Each strip shows a series of flashes

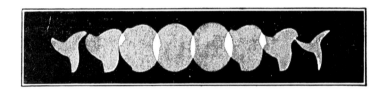

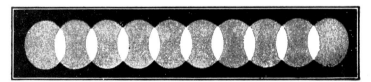

FIG. 43. RELATIVE EFFICIENCY OF FOCAL-PLANE AND
IRIS SHUTTERS

occurring at intervals of 1/1000 of a second and totaling an exposure of 1/100 of a second. The iris shutter is wide open during only the fifth and sixth flashes; the focal-plane transmits the full flash during the entire exposure. The efficiency of the iris shutter can be increased by stopping down. When that is done, the full aperture of the reduced stop opening remains completely uncovered for a proportionally longer time.

However, there are other considerations involved. One of the most important of these is *distortion of image*. In this regard the iris shutter is still supreme. When a fast-moving object (like a racing auto) is photographed at high speed with a focal-plane shutter, the wheels are apt to appear oval, and there may be other similar distortions. The reason for this is not hard to understand when you consider that the slit moves down across the surface of the film and only a narrow segment of the image registers on the film at any given moment. In the meantime, however, the image has also moved a little so that when the next portion registers it is not quite in line; hence the distortion. Though this sounds very bad in theory, the distortion involved (except for very fast-moving objects taken at too slow a shutter tension) is not too serious. Press photographers overcome this hazard to a great extent in three ways: (1) by using the highest tension, 6, at all times and varying only their curtain apertures, (2) by stopping down, which corrects the distortion of this type shutter as it improves the efficiency of the iris shutter, and (3) by following the action with the camera; swinging the lens, that is, to keep pace and direction with the object.

The earliest shutter was the lens cap, which was removed and replaced by hand. It wasn't until 1900 (six years after the appearance of roll film) that the single-blade shutter was found to be inadequate. The search for a means to stop fast motion started then (with the invention of the multiblade shutter) and has kept pace with emulsions ever since.

*Jet Speed Iris Shutter.* Kodak announced a revolutionary new type of shutter in 1951, the Synchro-Rapid 800—the fastest iris shutter ever made. It has ten speeds, from one full second and bulb to a breath-taking 1/800. It has flash-synchronization settings for all the currently available flash bulbs and strobe lights. The construction secret that makes the amazing top speed possible is the way in which each leaf of the shutter has been designed to swing in a complete circle of 360°, on its own axis—avoiding the mechanical jolt that a regular iris shutter gets when it opens, stops, and then closes. The design of the Synchro-Rapid shutter not only makes for smoother operation and a faster top speed, but it will undoubtedly prolong the life of the shutter. Kodak claims it will also give greater accuracy at all speeds. It synchronizes at any speed, including 1/800, with class M lamps; and up to 1/400 with class F lamps. For strobe lights it has an "X" setting. Another feature: there is no synchronized lever to cock. Once the lamp selector is set, the shutter is operated the same for flash as without it. Adjustments are possible to get peak synchronization for any bulb used.

*Light Value Scale (LVS) System.* Invented by the makers of the Compur shutter, and introduced in the 1955 Rolleiflex, this change in shutter synchronization represents what the British *Journal of Photography* considers "one of the most important developments of recent times in camera design." What it does is to link the iris diaphragm to the shutter mechanism in such a way that once the correct exposure is determined according to light conditions and film speed, this "light value" as set operates through the entire range of shutter speeds, by the simple shifting of only one ring or lever. Thus, if you've set your camera for an exposure of, let's say, $f$ 8 at 1/125 second (equivalent to light value 13) and you suddenly have to shift to 1/250 or even 1/500 because the object is moving rapidly, you merely turn the milled setting ring clockwise to 1/250 or 1/500, and you're still set for the correct exposure as previously determined.

If the light changes, however, you still have full freedom of choice to readjust to any other exposure by moving the iris diaphragm to another opening. This will automatically change your LVS setting to the new exposure, cross-linking the shutter and lens diaphragm to the new light-value reading.

## SOME SHUTTER HINTS AND CAUTIONS

1. Never *leave a shutter of any kind tensed;* you'll shorten its life if you do. If your camera is the type that prevents double exposure, which means that you have to ruin a shot when you release the shutter, find out how you can effect this release with your particular model, or leave the shutter unwound after each exposure. This is better practice in any case, since the new film brought up for use each time will not have had a chance to buckle.

2. When using the Compur shutter for bulb shots, don't make the mistake of setting it on time by mistake: *you'll ruin your negative.*

3. To remove tension from the shutter spring of the Automatic Rolleiflex, move the indicator to B *(bulb)* before closing the case.

4. Never use the delayed-action mechanism with the highest speeds.

5. Never try to rotate a shutter dial against an arrow; *you'll strip the gears.*

6. Don't change the exposure *after* cocking the shutter; it doesn't do the shutter any good. This does not apply, however, to the Contax, Leica, Nikon or Canon type cameras.

7. If your camera has two shutters (iris and focal-plane, as in the Speed Graphic) be sure to leave one *open* when the other is in use.

8. When rewinding a focal-plane shutter be sure, on the other hand,

that the iris shutter is *closed,* the lens capped, or the film holder covered by a slide. Otherwise you'll fog the film.

9. Never try to cock an iris shutter that is set for Time and is *open.*

10. Never move from any other setting to Time or Bulb, or vice versa, while the shutter is cocked.

11. When using the self-capping, focal-plane shutters (as in the Leica and Contax) be sure to continue winding until you feel a positive stop. If you don't do this your exposure will not be accurate, and your film will not be completely wound.

12. Never, under any circumstances, attempt to oil or clean a shutter of any kind yourself. The mechanism of a photographic shutter is just as delicate as that of a fine watch; if you wouldn't tamper with one, leave the other alone too. If your shutter needs adjusting or cleaning, let a skilled mechanic do it.

13. If you have a 35-mm. camera with a rubberized cloth focal-plane shutter (Leica, Nikon, Canon) don't walk around in the sun with the lens uncovered, especially if you have it set on infinity. *The sun may burn a hole in your shutter!* To avoid this, if you must leave your lens unprotected, shift your focus from infinity to close-up (about 4 or 5 feet).

A candid shot taken with a Contax and a 135-mm. Sonnar telephoto lens at a distance of well over 500 feet.

# What Camera Shall I Get?

Most amateurs devote more than half their hobby time and most of their spare cash to searching for, or trading toward, the "perfect" camera. That's why there are so many camera exchanges. The fact is, it doesn't matter what kind of a camera you get, provided that it's good of its kind and that you learn how to use it. Anyway, no one camera can serve for all purposes; so your effort to find the Universal Camera will become a never-ending search.

Cameras differ chiefly in *size* and *speed*. Otherwise, they all work alike. Get the best lens you can afford, because that *is* important, but don't worry too much about the style of the camera box. Styles change, and return. At one time it was a race between the 35-mm. cameras and the twin-lens reflexes; now it's a scramble between the single-lens reflex eye-level miniatures and the 127 Super-Slide cameras.

As you grow up in photography you'll notice that your demands on material and equipment become less and less exacting. That high fever of discovery that lures you from one miracle developer to another, from one print paper to another, from one new film to another, will finally burn itself out and leave you weaker but wiser. When it's all over you may find as I did, and as almost all amateurs inevitably do, that the manufacturers of photographic products really know what they're talking about. When they recommend a certain procedure with one of their products they do so because they secretly know that by following their suggestion you'll get such marvelous results that you'll continue to use the product. It's as simple as that. When the chemists at Eastman Kodak, for example, recommend that you develop Plus X in Microdol, they *know* that you cannot get better results or finer grain, or anything at all, by using one of the many magical supersoups now on the market. You can't, that is, without sacrificing something. You may get finer grain, but your pictures will not be as sharp. You may get more speed, but grain clumps will pepper your print. You may get more tones, but you will lose brilliance.

Exposure: 1/30 at *f* 14 (approximate).  Exposure: 1/30 at *f* 14 (approximate).

$3 CAMERA

Exposure: 1/25 at *f* 16.  Exposure: 1/25 at *f* 7.7.

$10 CAMERA

Exposure: 1/25 at *f* 16.  Exposure: 1/25 at *f* 5.5.

$50 CAMERA

*In the group at the left*, the background detail improves slightly as the price of the camera goes up, but, since each one of the three photographs was adequately exposed there is not a great deal of choice. These are contact prints; with enlargements there would be a big difference. *In the group at the right*, the meter called for 1/25 at *f* 5.6. The $3 camera had only a fixed speed for "instantaneous." Underexposure was the result and was responsible for the dead black portions.

Besides, you can duplicate any of these defects, if you really want to, by using D-76 and changing your exposure, your developing time, or the dilution of the developer.

And so it is with cameras. The law of compensation, as Emerson so beautifully pointed out, is the law of life itself. Every advantage has its disadvantage; every loss has its gain. Do you envy the man with the $f$ 1.5 lens? He can't stop down below $f$ 11; he almost never uses the lens wide open because he gets sharper pictures at $f$ 5.6. Do you envy the man with the focal-plane shutter and speeds up to 1/1000 second? When he takes a picture of a racing auto the image moves across the film so much faster than the shutter blind that distortion squashes the wheels and makes them look like eggs.

## GOOD PICTURES HAVE BEEN TAKEN WITH ALL SORTS OF CAMERAS

Dr. D. J. Ruzicka uses a folding Kodak; Maxwell Coplan uses a Graflex; Eliot Elisofon uses a Rolleiflex; Valentino Sarra uses a Speed Graphic on location, Ivan Dmitri uses a Leica; Edward Weston always uses a big view camera, and Philippe Halsman uses a 3¼ x 4¼-inch twin-lens reflex camera of his own design. Obviously, the secret of good pictures does not lie in the choice of camera. Is it the lens, then?

I was curious to see how much the lens had to do with success in photography, so I checked through seven hundred pictures shown at one of the Leica exhibits held at Radio City in New York. Here were pictures taken by all types of photographers, all over the world and under all sorts of conditions. There were pictures by professionals, press men and amateurs. What did they use? What speeds, what lenses? Well, the results were both disconcerting and heartening:

*78 per cent of the pictures were taken with the normal 50-mm. lens!*
10 per cent were taken with a wide-angle lens.
12 per cent were taken with a telephoto.
*89 per cent were taken at f 3.5 or slower.*
65 per cent were taken at $f$ 6.3 or slower.
11 per cent were taken at larger apertures than *f 3.5.*
*53 per cent were taken at 1/40 second or faster.*
27 per cent were taken at 1/100 second or faster.

Not many crumbs of comfort for the camera-swapping amateur in those figures. Almost 80 per cent of the pictures could have been taken with an $f$ 3.5 lens (which would have been stopped down to $f$ 6.3 in most cases) and with a shutter speed between 1/40 and 1/100 second. For that you certainly wouldn't need any fancy equipment. Just keep this in mind when you visit any photo exhibits in the future; notice how often the pictures are taken at speeds of $f$ 6.3 to $f$ 8 at 1/40 to 1/100 second.

## HOW TO CHOOSE A CAMERA

The first thing to keep in mind is something that was said by Edward Steichen after he had put together that monumental photographic exhibition, *The Family of Man:*

"No photographer is as good as
the simplest camera."

The modern amateur photographer is so concerned with gadgets and conveniences he often forgets that judgment—*his* judgment—is the only thing that really matters. There are many photographers who use the Leica; there is only one Cartier-Bresson. And it is his masterful, if sometimes mysterious, choice of the decisive moment that separates his great pictures from the mass of snapshots by the rest of us. We cover the same ground he does, but with such different results. No camera and no exposure meter has a brain of its own. It waits for us to give it the spark of life. What we decide makes the difference.

I have a hunch that there would be more Cartier-Bressons, Edward Westons, Ansel Adamses and Edward Steichens if we all had to start with a box camera and were made to prove that we could use that well, before we were allowed to touch another camera.

Unfortunately, the appeal of a camera is much like the appeal of a woman. It isn't enough for us that she knows how to cook; she has to have the right equipment. There is no doubt the modern cameras are made to look good and handle beautifully. But they don't take any better pictures. If you doubt this, look at some of the war photographs of Roger Fenton (who photographed the Crimean battlefields in 1855) and of Matthew Brady (who photographed the Civil War from 1861 to 1865) and then realize that these magnificent silver prints and daguerreotypes were exposed, developed and printed right on the battlefields, in clumsy covered wagons. Have we done any better lately, with all our fancy equipment?

This is not an argument to send us back a hundred years in time. I am simply trying to point out that the camera is less important than you are; than the two indispensable gadgets you are born with, your brain and your eye. Use these well and your box camera pictures will look like masterpieces; use them badly and your Hasselblad will function like a pinhole camera.

## BASIC CONSIDERATIONS

Your choice of a camera will depend, naturally, on what you can afford to pay, how much convenience you want for that price, and how many camera virtues you are willing to do without in exchange for that convenience. If you like the compactness and ease of handling of the miniatures, you will have to pay from 30 to 50 cents apiece for decent-sized enlargements, or get an enlarger of your own. Also, your lens will have to be better, and therefore somewhat more expensive. If you're not very good at judging distance, the blind cameras (that is, those having neither ground-glass nor coupled range finders) are not for you (unless you'd be satisfied with one of the fixed-focus box cameras). You'd do better to get a film-pack or view camera (that is, one with ground-glass focusing). If you want to "shoot the works," you can get a coupled-range-finder camera like the Leica or Contax, or you can pamper yourself with the new Swedish single-lens reflex, the Hasselblad.

If you like clarity and sharpness in your prints, get one of the larger sizes; if you're going in for photography on the run or in the dark, get a miniature of the 35-mm. size. A good compromise size for most purposes is, I feel, the Rolleiflex size. If you want speed in that size the new Rollei, the new Exakta 66, and the Astraflex II are all now fitted with $f\,2.8$ lenses. The Exakta in addition has shutter speeds from 12 seconds to $1/1000$ second. If you're more serious in your intentions, by all means get one of the film-pack or view cameras from $2\frac{1}{4}$ x $3\frac{3}{4}$ to 4 x 5 inches in size. Developing is less finicky; contact prints are often large enough for viewing; and focusing is exact and foolproof. Furthermore, many of these cameras can be equipped with accessory range finders that are coupled to the lens, if you prefer that type of focusing.

## A FEW CAUTIONS

It is easier to get good results with a larger camera than with a miniature. Excluding the cost of film, it is cheaper also. If you are not planning to do your own developing and enlarging (and even if you are) a large camera is a wiser choice because it requires less diligent processing methods. In any case, whatever the camera, get the best anastigmat lens you possibly can. If it's a miniature, $f\,3.5$ is fast enough; if it's a larger camera even $f\,4.5$ will do. Be sure, also, that the lens is set in a good, dependable shutter. The Compur and Compound shutters can always be relied upon to perform well, as can the new American-made Kodak Supermatics or Kodamatics, Ilex Acme Synchro, or the Wollensak Rapax, which also incorporates built-in synchronization. Though the lenses of minia-ture cameras have greater depth of focus, this advantage fades as we increase the size of the prints. Contact-print quality can only be obtained by a contact print (one made with the negative in *direct contact* with the print paper, as distinguished from an *enlargement* which is made by pro-jection); don't let anybody tell you otherwise. Obviously, then, it's best to enlarge as little as possible. A 4 x 5-inch Speed Graphic negative only needs a 2 x enlargement to make an 8 x 10-inch print; a 35-mm. negative has to be enlarged eight times to make a print of the same size. The larger cameras, especially the view types, have certain swing and tilt movements that are invaluable for still lifes, architectural pictures, etc., but they cannot as easily be used without a tripod. The smaller cameras, however, are much more rapid in operation, use cheaper film, are lighter in weight, are less conspicuous, can be hand held. If you can't make up your mind, flip a coin.

A VIEW OF NEW YORK. Taken by Rudolph Simmon with the Omega 120 camera and Plus-X film developed in Microdol.

HOW A TWIN-LENS
REFLEX CAMERA
WORKS
(The Rolleiflex)

A folding blind-focus camera.

A single-lens reflex camera.

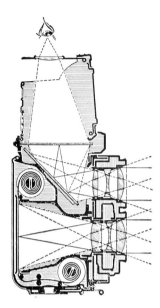

For ground-glass focusing and viewing.

A press-type camera.

A professional view camera.

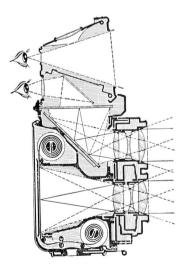

For eye-level focusing and viewing.

The Leitz version of what a perfect single-lens reflex should be: Leicaflex.

Film-pack adapter for view camera.

## OTHERS FACTORS IN CHOOSING A CAMERA

*Seeing the picture.* No matter how good the camera may be in other ways, if you find it difficult to *see* the picture in the viewfinder or on the ground glass, you'll get very little fun out of your photography. It would be like stumbling around in the dark; you might just bump into something good, but the odds are against it. A camera without a decent viewfinder is worthless. So check that first. Make certain that the picture you see in the viewfinder is the picture your camera sees (and that parallax errors are corrected, if it isn't a single-lens reflex or a camera with a ground-glass back). If you can't take the camera back off and check it with a ground glass, make certain that the dealer lets you test a roll of film before you have to make up your mind. Also, find out, by trying many types, which kind of viewer is best for your eye. Some cameras have a special eye compensator for near and far viewing; the Rolleiflex has an interchangeable focusing magnifier which can be ordered, without extra charge, in whatever diopter correction your eye needs (from minus 3 to plus 3 diopters). Both the Leica and Contax have provisions for attaching correction lenses to the viewfinder. If you wear glasses, this may be important. Your doctor's lens prescription can be filled by Leitz or Zeiss through your dealer.

*Judging distance.* Though it is perfectly true, as H. Postlethwaite once pointed out in *Camera World,* that you can get along with a piece of string knotted every foot, you'll enjoy your camera more if you can be sure of getting sharp pictures when you want them (though sometimes you may deliberately want to throw part of the scene out of focus). With a box camera, which is set to focus at about 15 feet, there is no problem and no choice. Everything from about 6 feet to infinity will be approximately though unchangeably sharp. With a lens of greater speed, however, and especially when you use it "wide open" for fast action, dim light, or to throw part of the scene out of focus, accurate focusing is a must. Here again you have to decide what is best for you as between blind-focusing (by distance scale), coupled rangefinder (split or superimposed image), ground glass (with or without accessory Fresnel lens), and the combination of both split-image and ground-glass focusing, as in the new single-lens eye-level reflexes, the Contaflex and Alpa 6. The Rolleiflex now has an accessory rangefinder, the Rolleimeter, which attaches to the front of the lens panel and rides along with it as you focus. This makes it possible to use the direct viewfinder while focusing (especially useful for sports shots and in poor light).

It is also important for you to check the manual mechanics of focusing.

In the Rolleiflex, for instance, the focusing knob is on the right; in the Rolleicord, it is on the left; in the Contax and Nikon it is done by a milled wheel at the top, which makes it easy to focus-and-shoot; in the Contaflex and the Graphic 35 there are push-button focusing knobs on both sides of the lens. Try all of these focusing methods before you decide. It may make a big difference to you, for instance, if you are left-handed.

Focusing in the Contaflex combines a split-image rangefinder (inner circle), conventional ground-glass focusing (outer circle) with the scene as seen by the viewfinder.

Finally, are the viewfinder and rangefinder images brought together in one large window as in the Leica M3 and the Contax, or are they separated, as in the Leica F and the Omega 120?

*Loading and winding the film.* Does the back of the camera swing away or come off, as in the Contax, Leica M3, Nikon, Rolleiflex, and others; or does the loading of film require an engineering degree and the skilled hands of a brain surgeon? If you're heavy-handed and awkward, stay away from the Hasselblad. Check on what kind of film cassettes are needed, especially in the 35-mm. cameras; you may want to bulk-load your own cartridges later. Felt-lined cassettes sometimes scratch, so it's better to avoid them. Does the camera have an automatic film transport as in the Rolleiflex and the Leica? Is it coupled to the shutter to avoid double exposure? Can it be uncoupled, if necessary, as in the Automatic Rolleiflex? Are all the moving parts smooth-working, without backlash? Is the film size available everywhere, or do you have to keep a large stock of it on hand yourself to avoid missing pictures? Does the film have to be rewound before removal, as in most 35-mm. cameras; or does it sensibly pass from one removable cassette to another removable cassette, as in the Contax?

*Picture size.* Later on we will discuss cameras that use six different popular film sizes. Those we have chosen are pleasing in their proportions, are available everywhere and in plentiful variety, and the enlargers needed for them are low in cost and are well constructed. The big unresolved question is: *square or rectangle?* The proponents of the rectangle say the square is a rectangle cut down; the others insist the rectangle is cut from the square. I remember something Alfred Stieglitz once told me when I commented on the fact that so many of his wonderful prints had the focus of interest in dead center: "That is the way the eye sees it."

Fritz Henle composes his pictures within the square Rollei shape, and prints them usually without alteration; Cartier-Bresson composes his Leica shots to the very margins and never permits any cropping.

*Flash synchronization.* Shutters take time to open, and bulbs take time to flash. The problem of synchronizing diaphragm (between-the-lens) shutters is to make certain the leaves are open at the very moment the bulb is at its brightest. With shutters marked M-X this can usually be accomplished at *any* speed using the M setting, and at 1/25 (or 1/50) using the X setting. Strobe can be synchronized *only* with the X setting; when used with the M setting, the shutter begins to open *after* the flash is over.

With focal plane shutters, this problem is further complicated by the way the curtain slit swings across the film plane, exposing the negative in successive strips instead of all at once. To avoid losing part of the picture, use the M setting for flash, 1/25 to 1/50 with small cameras, and not more than 1/25 with large cameras. For strobe, you can use your diaphragm shutter if you have one (remembering to leave your focal plane shutter open) at the X setting and at *any* of the shutter speeds, or your focal plane shutter at the X setting, but then only at the slower (1/25 to 1/50) speeds.

Where the light is mixed (daylight and flash or strobe) there is the additional problem of balancing or avoiding background exposure, especially at slow speeds. You do this by using the M setting (X for strobe) and adjusting diaphragm or shutter as explained on pages 214 and 215.

*What do the letters M-F-X and FP-S mean?* They describe the time-lag used to delay opening the shutter or to control the firing of the bulb: M for medium (20 milliseconds to reach full peak), F for fast (fires circuit when blades are half open, about 7-8 milliseconds), X for zero delay (fires flash at instant shutter blades are fully open), FP for focal plane (long-flash bulbs with a flat peak duration of about 40 milliseconds), S for slow (these bulbs do not reach peak until 30 milliseconds after contact; can be used with X setting at 1/10, with F setting at 1/15, with M setting at 1/25).

*Exposure meters.* The trend has been towards built-in or linked meters, as in the Leica M3 and the Yashica LM. But remember that there may be times when you'll be cussing out that built-in meter, especially after you have put your camera on a tripod and have to take a close-up reading.

*If you use a tripod,* and have occasion to shift your camera on and off quickly, get yourself a *detachable tripod mount.* There are quite a few good ones on the market: the Rolleifix, the Zip Grip, the Powerlock, etc.

*Shutter mechanism.* There are two kinds: *focal plane* and *between-the-lens.* Each has its advantages and its troubles, some of which have been mentioned previously. The important thing to check is the relation of the shutter to the lens aperture (1/25 at *f* 11, 1/50 at *f* 8, 1/100 at *f* 5.6, etc.). The exposure on the film in each case should be exactly the same.

*Shooting fast.* For taking sequence pictures you need some means of rapid film transport linked to the shutter-cocking mechanism. The Rollei-flex takes care of this with its LVS system of exposure control (since adopted by others) and its film-rewind and shutter-cocking crank handle; the Robot does this with its built-in spring motor; the Praktina FX with its detachable rapid sequence spring motor; the Leica with the Leikavit manual speed base and its Leica Spring Motor base or, as in the M3, with the rapid wind lever which moves the film and cocks the shutter with two fast flips of the thumb. The latest camera to join these "rapid fire" ranks is the Nikon, which offers an electric motor driven by pen-light batteries as an accessory power plant for rapid film-transport-and-shutter-rewind.

*Extra lenses.* For portraits that have the best "drawing" (no distortion), you need a telephoto lens; for narrow street scenes and cramped-quarter interiors you need a wide-angle lens. Unless your camera is built to take interchangeable lenses, you will have to use makeshifts, such as stepping back to where you would stand with a telephoto lens and then enlarging the smaller image to compensate, or taking cramped interiors and narrow exteriors always at an angle. A new trend in lenses is the use of *interchangeable front elements,* as in the Contaflex and Retina cameras. This cuts the cost of the extra lenses considerably and makes for more efficient camera design.

*Reflex or rangefinder; single or twin-lens?* When you start to shop for a camera you'll be overwhelmed by the variety of choice. One of the many types that is fast becoming popular is the single-lens reflex, like the Contaflex, the Retina, or the Exakta. One complaint against these is the *blackout* that hides the image as the mirror snaps up to let the exposure be taken. The Asahiflex has overcome this by a clever bit of engineering which returns the mirror to viewing position automatically the moment the exposure has been made. In other cameras, the mirror has to be wound back into position. Another improvement is the *automatic iris* which is preset, can be opened full for focusing, and then snaps back to the preset *f* opening you planned to use as you shoot.

As for methods of focusing, many cameras (notably the Contaflex, the Alpa 6, the Praktina, and the Exakta IIa) solve this problem of choice by combining mirror-prism ground glass and split-image rangefinders with their viewfinders.

This leaves the question of what kind of rangefinder: *split-image* or *superimposed image?* If you do not have perfect vision, you may find it a bit easier to use the split-image type, since with these the point of exact focus can be determined more readily. In any case, the best way is to try them both. The Leica uses a superimposed or merged image; the Kodak Chevron (for 2¼ x 2¼), a split-image.

*Parallax.* Since it is impossible for both the lens and the view finder to occupy exactly the same point in space, the use of a view finder always introduces the error of parallax, or image displacement. If your view finder is not corrected for this by some device built in by the manufacturer (as in the Leica M3 and the Rolleiflex), you can overcome it by placing the subject in the finder close to the sides nearest to the lens. This will tend to center the subject on the film. A few trials, preferably made on a tripod so that you can be sure of what you are doing, will tell you how extreme this correction must be in your case.

## HOW TO BUY A CAMERA

Don't forget that the cheapest Leica can make as good a picture as the latest model, if the lens in both is the same. And resist buying things you'll have no use for, such as slow speeds (if you know you're never going to try anything less than 1/25) or speeds above 1/500 (if you've never used anything faster than 1/200 before). I've had an expensive miniature for years and have yet to use the self-timer or the speeds above 1/500, yet I paid plenty to have both.

When the salesman first puts the camera in your hands, make sure you understand what each knob, wheel and lever does *before* you attempt to use it. *And don't force anything!* See that everything moves freely without sticking, and that the shutter mechanism works perfectly at each speed. If anything sounds wrong, insist on another camera or proof that the sound you heard is normal. Don't take the dealer's word for it that the stiffness or sticking will "work its way out in time." A camera is not an automobile motor; no breaking-in period should be required. And see that there is no backlash of lens-rotating or shutter elements.

If it's a secondhand camera, open the back and tap it gently over a piece of white paper. If a lot of dust and dirt falls out, don't buy it; it will probably give you trouble. Make sure the lens isn't marred or scratched, and look for any evidence that the camera has been dropped. If it was jarred badly, the lens elements as well as the rest of the delicate mechanism may be out of kilter. Such repairs are costly.

*Never buy a camera, new or old, without a written guarantee and a money-back trial period!* The way to avoid trouble in these matters is to deal with a recognized and reputable dealer. The extra discount you get from a sharp-shooting fly-by-night may turn out to be very expensive. Have the guarantee and the trial period arrangement written right on the bill. A reputable dealer will do this for you without question. If he argues that "it isn't necessary," or that you should "trust him," button up and get out fast.

As soon as you get the camera home, read the directions carefully. Then, go through a couple of dry runs before you load the camera with film.

When you do start the actual tests, make them complete and keep a record of everything you do. If your first test indicates that something is wrong, retest with another roll of film. It may have been your fault. Then, if you're sure that something isn't working right, take the film tests to the dealer with your camera, and have him explain, fix, or replace. But *don't* let him double-talk you out of getting a camera that's in perfect condition.

## HOW TO TAKE CARE OF YOUR CAMERA

The three chief enemies of a camera are: (1) careless handling, (2) dust, and (3) moisture. To give efficient service a camera must be treated as a scientific instrument should be, and that is with a good deal of care. A camera usually gets rougher usage than any other kind of optical instrument, and much of it is needless. A little thought on your part will insure its working and lasting qualities. One way to do this is to keep it in a carrying case except when it is actually in use. A waterproof canvas or plastic case will do, but a leather ever-ready case is much better.

After you have been out on a trip, it is a good scheme to wipe off all of the dust from the exposed parts with a soft piece of old linen, and you should occasionally remove the lens if you can, or open the back, and dust out the inside of the camera with a soft brush. It is the dust that finds its way into the camera which causes black spots to appear on the negative, and other mischief by reflecting the light that strikes it from the lens. Moisture spoils the real or imitation leather covering of a camera, and if the latter is built of wood, it makes the movements stick. Oil or grease should not be used to lubricate the sliding parts if these are made of wood and metal; a little *graphite* can be applied instead. The inside of the camera must always be a dead black, and if any light spots show up they can be painted over with a dead-black paint like #4 Brush Type Kodalak. If a pinhole appears in bellows, fix with Scotch tape #33.

*To preserve leather* (camera bodies, bellows, cases, straps, etc.) use one of these: *Collectors' Book Dressing,* an exceptional old formula, probably the best on the market, still made up by the Haas Pharmacy, 812 Madison Avenue, New York 21, N. Y.; *Leather Vita,* sold by Brentano's; *Lexol; Mel-O-Wax;* saddle wax; or almost any lanolin preparation. Follow directions, don't overdo it, and use *hand*-rubbing where called for.

## TYPES OF CAMERAS

### A SURVEY OF SOME PROS AND CONS

When George Eastman introduced his first Kodak in 1888 he could hardly have foreseen the tremendous consequences of his act . . . over 50,000,000 shutterbugs clicking away happily every year, in the United States alone. But that is what happened as a direct result of his putting *roll film* and the one-dollar Brownie *box camera* on the market.

This is a book for the amateur photographer, so it is proper to point out that some of the most unforgettable pictures of our time were all made by amateurs: the flaming end of the Zeppelin *Hindenburg,* the tilted confusion on the deck of the sinking *Vestris,* the crying child sitting among the ruins of atom-bombed Nagasaki, the stricken Frenchman tearfully watching the Nazis roll into his beloved Paris. Having once seen these, who can ever forget them?

Strange, but as we learn to see more vividly in order to photograph more effectively, we find ourselves becoming one with the thing we see, as did each photographer of those historic moments. Dr. Jacob Bronowski has explained it well in his *Science and Human Values:* "There are no appearances to be photographed, no experiences to be copied, in which we do not take part. We remake nature by the act of discovery."

Some photographers *take* the picture, others *make* it. No matter which kind you are, here is a rundown on the various types of cameras currently available, with some pertinent comments, and perhaps a few impertinent cautions, on their good and bad qualities.

### THE BOX CAMERA

This is the *only* foolproof camera made. It doesn't have to be focused; the lens is preset at about 15 feet, which makes everything sharp from 6 feet to infinity. The lens aperture is usually *f* 11, with two or three smaller stops possible; the shutter is set at 1/30 to 1/50 second, with additional *time* or *bulb* settings available in most models. The small aperture of the lens gives great depth of field, but since this is a feature that cannot be controlled, the amateur photographer using a box camera often runs into trouble with his backgrounds. This requires extra care in the choice of camera position and angle. Sensible use of a box camera is wonderful training in the seeing and creating of a picture. If you can learn to make good pictures with a box camera, any other kind will prove to be a cinch.

Most modern box cameras are either synchronized for flash, or have the flash unit built right into the camera; this makes photography easier, especially for indoor and night shots. Others are made like reflex cameras, to give you a large view of the scene.

Since most box cameras use 120 or 620 film, you get contact prints that are large enough for album use. A few models use 127 film in the Super-Slide size so that inexpensive color slides can be made with the new fast Ektachrome.

Because the new high-speed panchromatic films, like Tri-X, have ASA speed ratings of 200 or more, the usefulness of the box camera has been effectively increased, especially in dim light and at night. But, on the other hand, overexposure in bright sunlight becomes a serious problem when such films are used. For general use it is best to shoot with Veri-chrome Pan or All Weather Pan, reserving the faster film for poor light outdoors or "available light" indoors.

Besides the Kodak box cameras described and shown here, you'll find good, inexpensive cameras in this 120 size manufactured by Ansco, Argus, Bolsey, Zeiss, Ferrania, and Nomad.

TWO TYPICAL MODERN BOX CAMERAS

FIG. 44. BROWNIE STARFLASH, for 127 film. Direct view finder, automatic double-exposure prevention, built-in flasholder.

FIG. 45. BROWNIE STARFLEX, for 127 film. With a large hooded reflex viewfinder. Three metal prongs at right for the matched but detachable synchronized flasholder.

## SUPER-SLIDE CAMERAS

The success of Frank Rizzatti's *Super-Slide* (see chapter 17) has set off a series of surprising chain reactions. First Eastman announced the reiease of Ektachrome in the 127 size, which is the Super-Slide size without waste (Kodacolor was already available in that size). Ansco then announced that Anscochrome would also be available in that size. Almost simultaneously, Kodak put a new series of 127 box cameras on the market to make use of the new film.

Taking a tip from their own American distributor, Franke & Heidecke redesigned and modernized their 127-size baby Rolleiflex (4 x 4 cm.) which had been discontinued in 1938. Hasselblad followed with a new film magazine that uses the 120 size to produce 16 Super-Slide pictures, 1⅝ x 2¼ in size, with minimum wastage. And other manufacturers are now rushing to produce a series of 127 miniatures of the *rangefinder, pentaprism,* or *twin-lens reflex* type. Many of these should be available by the time this is printed.

The reason for all this excitement is the simple notion that when pictures made on a 120 size film are trimmed to the 127 size, they can be made into 2 x 2-inch slides which can then be shown in the 35-mm. projectors, *but with a picture that is 85% larger in total area!* Amateur and professional photographers have found this idea so attractive that the 127 size camera may become the best seller of the future.

The new baby Rollei has a few improvements worth mentioning: the body release is cleverly set at an angle on the side below the lens so that it can be pressed by the thumb as you hold the camera in the palm of your right hand; film loading has been improved so that the film can be attached to the take-up spool outside the camera and then both spools inserted simultaneously; except for the lens hood, all accessories that fit the bayonets of the 6 x 6 cm. *f* 3.5 Rolleis are interchangeable with this new model; all ten shutter speeds from 1 second to 1/500 are evenly spaced, to conform with the LVS system (see chapter 5); the Synchro Compur shutter is fully synchronized and has click diaphragm stops; the new type collapsible hood acts as a shutter safety catch when closed; film loading and operation is entirely automatic.

## THE 35-MM. CANDID CAMERA

It all started with the Leica, invented by Oscar Barnack in 1914 as a way of pretesting movie exposures to avoid costly mistakes. The model A appeared in 1924. It had no rangefinder, but it did use standard 35-mm. sprocket-perforated movie film (for a 1 x 1½-inch picture) and a focal-plane shutter that operated at a fixed speed of 1/40 second (like his movie camera). Later models added a rangefinder, a variable-speed shutter to 1/1000, and interchangeable lenses, but otherwise the first Leica did about everything the M3 does today; as far as taking pictures, that is. And it was such a comfort to take along on hikes, instead of that heavy view camera!

The popularity of the *miniature* or *candid* camera, as it has been variously called, stems from the fact that it is easy to carry, can be used swiftly and often invisibly, gives more leeway in focusing (unlike the larger, long-focus-lens cameras) since its normal or wide-angle lenses have tremendous depth of field, and it costs less to operate (because it uses inexpensive movie film and takes 36 pictures at one loading). Besides, it offers a tempting variety of accessory gadgets that are fun to play with.

THE LEICA M3 WITH COUPLED
EXPOSURE METER

THE CONTAX IIIA WITH
BUILT-IN EXPOSURE METER

A SINGLE-LENS PENTA-
PRISM REFLEX CANDID
CAMERA. The Contaflex IV,
with built-in exposure meter.

A RAPID-SEQUENCE MINIATURE
CAMERA. The Robot Royal 36, with
power-drive film transport, coupled
rangefinder, fully synchronized for flash;
takes 36 exposures of the full miniature
size (1 x 1½ inches).

Two problems that plagued the first users of the camera, *grain* and *excessive contrast,* have since been solved by the appearance of such thin-emulsion films as Adox KB14 and 17, Isopan F and FF, the new Pana-tomic X, Ilford's Pan F, and such matching developers as Neofin, Micro-phen, Microdol, Clayton P 60, and those dependable old-timers D 76, MCM 100, D 23, and D 25. Discovery of new, rare-earth-element glass has made it possible to design sharper and faster lenses, such as the $f$ 2.8 Elmar in the 5-cm. focal length, as supplied with the Leica G. The shutter mechanism and its flash-strobe synchronization have been improved. A fast-action film-transport lever has been added in some cases. The latest trend is toward built-in or linked exposure meters, and pentaprism mirror-reflex viewing (where the focal plane shutter has given way to a between-the-lens shutter).

The modern miniature is a superb photographic instrument. It's a delight to hold and a pleasure to operate. Skillfully used, it makes mag-nificent pictures. However, it requires faultless technique in exposure, developing and enlarging, and it demands absolute cleanliness at every stage. If you're inclined to be sloppy or careless, avoid miniature camera work. It is exciting and rewarding, but exacting. Any transgressions of procedure become magnified horrors.

The miniature is an ideal instrument for making color slides for view-ing or projection. Some magazine publishers still insist on larger trans-parencies, but few print any better color plates than does the *National Geographic,* whose photographers use 35-mm. Kodachrome exclusively.

The one serious defect of the miniature is its lack of camera movements (swings, tilts, rising and sliding front, and double or triple extension of the lens). This has been partially overcome by the use of extension tubes, close-up attachments, and mirror-reflex housings. Architectural distortion can often be corrected by a tilting lens board on the enlarger used in con-junction with a countertilt easel.

When you start to shop for a miniature you'll have to make a choice between these types: blind focus (Contina); rangefinder (Leica, Contax, Minolta, Nikon) and the single-lens reflex (Contaflex, Praktina). With a camera like the Contina you have to guess-focus by scale. Since the normal lens is a 45-mm., even slight stopping down corrects for any focus-ing errors. However, when you use the Contina 75-mm. interchangeable front element, focusing becomes more critical, so Zeiss supplies a *telephoto focusing finder* which is a combination rangefinder and telephoto view-finder. Since this is not linked to the lens, you have to transfer the dis-tance measured to the lens before you are in exact focus. If you forget: *no picture.*

A new trend in miniature camera construction is the single-lens mirror reflex with either an eye-level pentaprism viewfinder or the familiar waist-level ground-glass viewer with snap-up hood. Good examples of such cameras are the Leicaflex, Yashica, Kodak Retina Reflex, Zeiss Contaflex, Honeywell Pentax, Bell & Howell Canon, Minolta Reflex, Miranda, Nikon F. Almost all models take interchangeable lenses. The image is focused visually, not by scale. Some of the cameras offer two kinds of simultaneous focusing: ground-glass and split-image (as in the Contaflex). Such cameras are especially good for subjects in motion, where quick focusing is essential. The waist-level mirror-and-ground-glass type shows the image upright, but reversed left to right. The *pentaprism* not only turns the image upright but corrects it left to right. Since the prism is made in one piece, and of good optical glass, it operates accurately.[1]

Though there is no parallax problem in the single-lens reflex (you see exactly what you are taking) there are two other problems, equally serious: 1. If you stop down to the iris setting you plan to use, the viewing image may become too dim. Some cameras overcome this by a *pre-set iris diaphragm* which enables you to view the image at full aperture, the iris closing down to the correct *f* opening as you start to press the shutter release. 2. The second problem is the *blackout,* which hides the image a moment before exposure, when the reflex mirror swings up out of the way. Most single-lens reflexes have to be rewound before the mirror returns tc viewing position, which is a great nuisance and makes it difficult to tell whether you really got the picture. However, the *instant-return mirror* is becoming standard in many of the new models.

Other improvements in miniature construction and accessories which may be worth considering: interchangeable lenses (35-mm. wide-angle for architecture, landscape, and crowded interiors; the 85-, 90-, or 135-mm. telephotos for portraits, and for landscapes where you want to increase the size of background objects without altering the size of the foreground); fast-action lever film-transport which moves film and resets shutter quickly and automatically (as in the Konica III, where it is placed on the front of the camera and is operated by the left forefinger while the right forefinger snaps the release button); fast action film rewind lever (as in the Aires 35); power-drive film transport, as in the Robot, in the Leica (through a detachable motor base), and the Praktina (which offers not only a detachable spring motor but an electric motor with magnetic remote control as well). The power drive enables you to shoot a burst of up to ten exposures in rapid sequence, as fast as you can press the release button, without stopping to rewind or recock the shutter. An all-metal rotor shutter makes this possible in the Praktina.

Besides the Leica and the Contax, which were first in the field and are still the best, here are some other miniatures worth looking at when you start to shop: the Argus, Minolta, Canon, Nikon, Aires 35, Contaflex,

---

[1] *Pentaprisms* are also being made for two-lens reflexes with detachable hoods.

A candid shot taken with a Leica held at waist level, the focus having been preset.

Graphic 35, Kodak Signet, the Kodak Retina (with interchangeable front-lens components for *wide-angle* and *telephoto*) and the Asahiflex (with quick-return mirror and preset diaphragm which, with direct-view *penta-prism,* is now almost standard in cameras of various sizes).

## THE REFLEX CAMERA

The *camera obscura,* first noted by Leonardo da Vinci (see page 3), was the precursor of the modern reflex camera. The first such camera, the twin-lens Rolleiflex using 120 size film, appeared in 1928. It combined the speed and portability of the candid camera with the film-size advantages of the larger camera. As a result, it became the camera best seller of its time, with prices jumping to $500 for a secondhand camera in 1937 when no new ones could be imported. Half a million cameras were sold by 1947, and sales are steadily rising.

The twin-lens reflex deserves this immense popularity. Though professionals sometimes grumble about its bulk, its lack of interchangeable lenses and the square shape of its negative, almost all of them carry one or more Rolleis with them on their big assignments. And the tougher the assignment, the more certain is the Rollei to be one of the cameras chosen. It's a camera they rely on, as newsmen rely on the Speed Graphic.

*What are the advantages of a reflex camera?* In the twin-lens models, there is no time lag between the focusing of the picture and the exposure. You see what you are taking right up to and beyond the moment of exposure—and you see it large and clear, just as the negative will show it.

**A TWIN-LENS REFLEX**

The Rolleiflex 2.8E, with built-in exposure meter and LVS fully synchronized flash - strobe Compur Rapid shutter.

FIVE PICTURE SIZES IN ONE CAMERA. The Rolleicord Va now offers a choice of 5 picture sizes and 12, 16, or 24 exposures per roll of 120 film by supplying a set of interchangeable focal-plane and ground-glass masks and exposure counters, all easily interchanged.

You can therefore compose carefully, right up to the very edges, secure in the knowledge that parallax errors have been automatically corrected. The focusing and viewing lens is always wide open, and in most cameras it is a bit faster (has a larger *f* opening) than the taking lens at full aperture. This insures sharp pictures. Because of the square shape of the negative there is no need to turn the camera around to adjust to the shape of the picture. Most of the twin-lens reflexes can be used at eye level as well as at waist level. For candid shots, the camera can be turned sideways at waist level so that the subject is not aware of your interest. The camera can also be held upside down overhead, to get better composition or to see over an obstruction (as during a parade, if people are in the way).

*Among the drawbacks* (besides those already mentioned): When the taking lens of the twin-lens reflex is stopped down, the viewing lens cannot

THE HASSELBLAD

The "Rolls Royce" of single-lens reflexes, made in Sweden. Interchangeable lenses, film holders and focusing hoods make this one of the most versatile of the cameras using 120 roll film.

In 1958, Hasselblad released its sensational new 500 C model which dropped the focal-plane shutter entirely and substituted a series of synchro-compur shutters with automatic diaphragm (for wide-open focusing). Each lens is now fitted with its own shutter, thus making flash and strobe synchronization possible at all speeds. A baffle protects film between exposures.

show the scene truthfully; the scene is shown reversed, left to right (except in those cameras that incorporate *optical reversing systems*); parallax errors for close-ups cannot be completely corrected; like the 35-mm. camera, it lacks camera movements, but again these can usually be corrected in enlarging.

*What of the single-lens reflex?* Everything that was said about it in the candid camera section applies here. The most spectacular camera of this kind is the Swedish Hasselblad. It is equipped with interchangeable lenses *and* film magazines (wonderful for switching to color and back; a new magazine, the #16, makes 16 Super-Slide pictures on a 120 roll). The single-lens reflex is also available in the 3¼ x 4¼ and 4 x 5 sizes (the

A WINTER SCENE as recorded by a twin-lens reflex camera. Taken by a Rolleiflex on Super XX developed in Microdol.

Graflex, equipped with a focal-plane shutter, and with a revolving back which overcomes the problem of having to turn the camera when shooting vertical pictures). Undoubtedly, single-lens cameras in the 127 Super-Slide size will also appear soon.

Of the many good reflex cameras besides the Rolleiflex now on the market, these are especially worth investigating: the Rolleicord (which now offers 5 picture sizes and 12, 16, or 24 pictures per roll of 120 film, including 16 Super-Slides perfectly framed on each roll), the Minolta Autocord, the Ikoflex Favorit, the Bronica, the Kalloflex, the Ricohflex, the Exakta 66, the Rocca Automatic, the Yashica (in both the exposure-meter and automatic models), and the Mamiyaflex Professional (the only twin-lens reflex with true lens interchangeability, and no film fogging between changes. Four sets of viewing and taking lenses are offered; each pair comes complete with lens board and with the taking lens mounted in a flash-strobe-synchronized shutter to 1/500. Operation is semi-automatic. Viewing hood detaches to be replaced by direct-view *pentaprism* as in Rolleiflex and other similar reflexes. (See footnote p. 104.)

### THE FOLDING CAMERA

The special advantages of a folding camera are compactness (for its film size and focal length), lens interchangeability, and camera movements such as tilts, swings, rising and falling front, revolving back, and extra bellows extension for close-ups.

Some folding cameras, such as the Ansco Speedex and the Kodak Tourist, do have a bellows, but when the camera is opened, the front snaps out and falls rigidly into place and, except for the fact that the lens can be focused by scale, they are little more than box cameras that fold up. Most of these use 120 or 620 film, and produce 8 exposures, 2¼ x 3¼ in size. Some have built-in flash synchronization, and a few, like the Ansco Super Speedex and the Super Ikonta, even offer coupled range finders (which *do* take them out of the box camera class). But in general, though such cameras offer little in comparison with the *candid* and *reflex* cameras described previously, they cost as much, if not more. The Japanese imports, for instance, in both the candid and reflex types, cost less than most of these folding box cameras, and they are better cameras from every point of view.

The true folding camera is a masterpiece of camera design. It combines the speed and compactness of a *miniature* with the versatility and smoothness of operation of a *view* camera. Such a camera is the Linhof Technika. It has three interchangeable lenses and a multifocus rangefinder that couples to all of them. The lenses are all mounted in fully-synchronized

EVENING MIST, by John W. Doscher of Vermont. Taken with a folding camera in New York on a rainy night.

Compur Rapid shutters. Other features include a revolving, interchange-able back; the use of sheet film and film pack in the 2¼ x 3¼ size; and roll film in the 120 size.

A FOLDING
CAMERA
The Linhof
Super
Technika
23

ANOTHER
FOLDING
CAMERA
The Zeiss
Super
Ikonta
III

Another folding camera worth considering is the Plaubel Makina. Though it doesn't have a revolving back or any swings and tilts, it does have interchangeable lenses, a focal-plane shutter, an electromagnetic flash shutter release, and a rangefinder that couples to the normal lens (the others having to be focused by scale or ground glass). It uses 2½ x 3½ plate-holders interchangeably with 120 roll film and 35-mm. film.

### PRESS AND VIEW CAMERAS

The press camera is a rugged folding camera with the maneuverability of a view camera wedded to the speed and compactness of a miniature. The basic film size, because of newspaper requirements, is 4 x 5 inches, though there are press cameras for other film sizes, ranging from 2¼ x 2¾ to 2¼ x 3¼ and 3¼ x 4¼.

Most press cameras have coupled rangefinders, fully synchronized focal-plane and between-the-lens shutters, interchangeable lenses, tilts, swings, and interchangeable backs. Most of them use sheet film or film packs, though a few use 120 roll film in the 2¼ x 2¾ or 2¼ x 3¼ size.

The press camera is used mostly for sports, candids, portraits, records, street scenes and interiors. *It suffers from four troubles:* shallow depth of field, because of the focal length of the lens (usually 127 to 135 mm.); the danger of double exposure; the too-few exposures possible at one loading (though with film packs and sheet film magazines this can be overcome); and the fact that it costs more to run (in the 4 x 5 size). Balancing these is the fact that the pictures are *sharper* and that it can be used as a hand camera in almost any field of photography, color or black-and-white.

The archetype press camera is, of course, the Speed Graphic, which is still one of the best on the market. It comes in three sizes ($2\frac{1}{4}$ x $3\frac{1}{4}$, $3\frac{1}{4}$ x $4\frac{1}{4}$, and 4 x 5); uses sheet film, film packs or roll film; has interchangeable lens boards; focal-plane as well as between-the-lens shutters; built-in synchronization and a selector switch to set body release to either shutter; dual-control rack-and-pinion focusing; tilting and rising front with vertical and lateral shifts; drop bed for wide-angle use; double-extension bellows; folding infinity stops; choice of Graflex or Graflock backs; Ektalite field lens; built-in range light for night focusing; and a parallax-correcting viewfinder that accepts interchangeable cams for other lenses. It can, of course, be focused by scale. A wire sports finder is also supplied. A solenoid synchronizer for flash can be attached to the lens board; some news photographers prefer the action of such an electrical shutter release to that of one operated manually.

THE SPEED GRAPHIC. The press camera supreme. Without it, American newspapers and magazines might just as well shut up shop. As fast as a candid miniature, as talented as a view camera, it is a man's machine with a woman's touch.

A VIEW CAMERA, the Graphic View. There isn't anything this camera can't do (except be carried easily).

A PRESS CAMERA. The Simmon Omega 120. Fully synchronized and with coupled rangefinder and many unusual features that should delight the heart of a news photographer (see text). New version is Koni/Omega.

*An unusual camera* that was obviously designed with the press photographer in mind is the Omega 120. Everything about it suggests speed and ease of handling. The picture size is $2\frac{1}{4}$ x $2\frac{3}{4}$ for 9 exposures on 120 film. This strange size was chosen to match the proportions of standard enlarging papers (4 x 5 and 8 x 10). The body design makes a firm steady grip possible, to prevent jarring: *the left hand* grips and balances the camera by means of the molded handle, while the forefinger of that hand pulls the long-stroke trigger which automatically pushes the pressure plate against the film (to insure absolute flatness under all weather conditions) and then makes the exposure; *the right hand* turns the oversize focusing knob which automatically adjusts the view finder for parallax correction and, after exposure, pulls the plunger just below the focusing knob, which changes film, counts exposures, and cocks the shutter. The shutter is fully synchronized, and there is a 6-bulb rotary flash attachment, the Omegaflash, which brings a new bulb into position by the action of the film-advance plunger. Extra lamp turrets can be preloaded for instant use.

Whether or not this odd-shaped camera wins any popularity polls (a new, redesigned model appeared in 1965 as the Koni/Omega), it certainly has given other manufacturers plenty to think about. Rudolph Simmon, who designed it, was a technician and idea man in the Rolleiflex plant when that camera was first being produced, so he knows what he's doing. The lens is a specially designed four-element Wollensak anastigmat, one element of which is made of rare-earth high-index glass. It is magnificently sharp, as you can see from the view of New York on page 91.

Other good press cameras are made by Burke & James (Speed Press 4 x 5), Busch (Pressman 4 x 5), Deardoff (Universal Triamapro 4 x 5) and Linhof (Technika Press 23).

*The view camera* is the perfect camera for studio and tripod use. Though it has no portability, very shallow depth of field, is slow in operation, and shows the image upside down, it is nevertheless the ideal camera for portraits, still life, texture, detail, landscapes, architecture, and interiors. Where action isn't a factor, it is also wonderful for color. The work of Ansel Adams, Edward Weston, Samuel Chamberlain, and Edward Steichen attests to the supremacy of the view camera as the instrument of pure photography. If photography as an art form is to record detail and texture, a field in which it has no competition, there is no better camera for this purpose than the view camera. The Graphic View, shown here, is a good example of what a view camera should be. It has about every contortion and body movement a photographer would ever need, yet it is rock-rigid in each position.

Other good view cameras: Grover Universal View 4 x 5, and the Rembrandt Master Pictorialist (available in many sizes, 4 x 5 to 11 x 14).

## THE POLAROID CAMERAS

The basic feature of Dr. Land's series of cameras is the production of a dry print *within seconds* after you have snapped the shutter (see p. 11). The original model 95 was an exciting camera, but it had many design faults, the main trouble having to do with the peculiar lens-exposure system which gave the photographer a slow lens, medium-speed film, and no choice of iris openings (substituting an arbitrary single dial key-and-number system that was quite awkward). The new films and models have corrected this. As the film speeds have jumped to an incredible ASA 3000, the developing times have dropped from one minute to *10 seconds!* The new models, such as the Electric Eye 900, have range-finders, are light-sealed for the fastest film, and are fully automatic (the electric eye operating the shutter and controlling the aperture, even for films with speeds as high as ASA 6000). Film sizes start at 2¾ x 3½ and go to 4 x 5.

The new Type 55 P/N film supplies a permanent negative and a print simultaneously in 15 seconds (ASA 64), and other wonders are coming.[1]

Among the supplementary Polaroid accessories now available, there is a photoelectric shutter that can be attached to the older models to convert them to automatic electric eye operation; a Print Copier that can make exact duplicates of your originals, using your own camera as part of the set-up; close-up kits for portrait photography; and a Wink-light strobe unit that operates on a single battery for 1000 shots.

*A logical extension* of this picture-in-a-minute system is the Polaroid Land Projection Film, which has a speed of ASA 1000, produces grainless images for projection in *two minutes,* and can be used in existing Polaroid cameras. Along with this sensational panchromatic film, Polaroid has released the following accessories: the leakproof Dippit, for hardening the transparency surface and protecting it against fading and discoloration (it squeegees the transparency as it is removed); the Polaroid plastic Slide Mount #630 (for 2¼ x 2¼ transparencies) which snaps together and is so cleverly designed that you will always have your transparency right side up; the Polaroid Projector Model 610 (for the #630 transparencies); and the Polaroid Copymaker Model 208, with which you can photograph charts, maps, titles, small objects (in fact, anything that can fit into an 11 x 14 inch space).

*Polaroid instant color* (Polacolor) finally made its appearance in 1963. By 1965 a whole battery of cameras and accessories were available, for either the older roll-film or the new flat-pack type of films. The exposure time is 60 seconds (as against the 10–15 seconds for the black and white) but no swabbing is needed to make the color prints permanent. It takes some patience to get the best results from Polacolor, but it's well worth the effort. The use of the UV filter helps remove excess blue from shadows in your outdoor color pictures, and the manufacturer is so anxious for you to get good results that he supplies all sorts of booklets and instruction sheets to guide you. Furthermore, the entire process is undergoing ceaseless improvement. The latest cameras (which include automatic electronic eye shutter operation) are inexpensive and a delight to use.

[1] In 1965 Polaroid released their Infrared film (Type 413), which has a speed equivalent to ASA 800, develops in 15 seconds, and can be used in most standard Polaroid cameras.

# 7

# Introducing Your First Camera

Let us suppose that you have just bought your first camera and a roll of film. The clerk will have given you a few directions, but the camera—if you have never owned one before—is bound to seem as unfamiliar as a pair of new shoes. And if you are eager to take pictures of practically everything the minute you get home, you are certainly to be excused. The first roll of film is not exactly the most successful, but there are very few that are more exciting.

## LOADING THE CAMERA

The film, let us assume, is one commonly used, such as Kodak Verichrome Pan; the size #120, which provides for eight pictures measuring 2½ x 3¼ inches or twelve measuring 2¼ x 2¼ inches. When you open the package you find that the cartridge inside is snugly wrapped in tinfoil. This protects it against any reasonable amount of moisture; if you are in a tropical country, you will find it wrapped not in tinfoil, but sealed within a thin metal container. (I always tear these open with my teeth, which is probably not a very good idea. They cannot be opened otherwise without some sharp instrument.) Most people throw the little carton and the foil away, but if you happen to be off on a canoe trip or some kind of an expedition and the chances are that the exposed roll must be carried for some days before development, it is not a bad idea to keep both wrappings with which to protect the exposed but undeveloped film. (The wrappings from the new one quite naturally are used for the old one, when the change is made.)

So as to avoid any danger of fogging the film, you have chosen some spot away from strong sunlight. (Almost everyone has had to change films in a howling wind or in the middle of snow-covered pastures, but it is a good plan to take as few chances as possible.) You notice that the spool has at one end a small hole; at the other a similar hole, but with a slot, too.[1] It is plain that the winding key will fit into this slot. For the present, this new spool will be held in place inside the camera at the *opposite side* or end from the winding key. In fact, when you have removed the back from the camera, you find at one end of the camera itself two pins which clamp down against this full reel, at the other end an empty spool which the manufacturer has supplied for your use. If it is not, shift it or get an empty spool to put there. The dealer will let you have one if you ask him. When loading, the empty spool must always be locked in with the winding key. Of course the winding key clamps into the slot at one end of the spool; a pin into the hole at the other. It is an easy matter to break the seal of the film itself (do this *after* the roll is in the camera; it's easier and safer that way) and slip into place between the two movable pins, then draw the paper slowly as it unwinds to the empty spool and introduce the fold into the opening of the spindle (wider side, of course). Make a few turns to be sure that the paper is centered and will not climb up the side, and put the camera back together again. Then wind to the first number, as you watch anxiously through the little window.

Occasionally people start the films the wrong way, but this will not happen to you if you visualize what is going on inside. It is probably not necessary to explain that we don't see the film itself at all: We see only a strip of paper, usually red on the outside and black inside. Behind this is attached the long piece of sensitized emulsion which the light activates in order to record the so-called *latent image* which later produces the picture. Just remember to keep the red side or outside of the film out (away from the inside of the lens) and you won't be putting any film in hind-side-to. Some manufacturers mark the winding side "Top," which also helps to keep things straight.

## USING A BOX CAMERA

For the sake of simplicity let us now assume that this new camera is a so-called *box camera*. (Before its design was modernized, this type certainly looked like a black box, and nothing else.) Whatever its size or make, it will have two things which you use simultaneously whenever you make a picture: the finder, and the shutter release. Possibly it will also have a device for setting the shutter, in order to take *time exposures* (when you control the shutter opening and closing by hand instead of automatically through the spring mechanism, measuring out an exposure of perhaps several seconds). Such exposures are usually made indoors, and you will probably not take one-tenth as many of these as you will of snapshots

[1] The smallest size of film is an exception: It has a projection at either end of the spool, in one of which there is a slot.

(or more properly, *instantaneous exposures*), *i.e.*, when there is a click of the shutter and that's all.

Theoretically, in order to take a snapshot with a box camera, all you need to do is to look through the finder at your dog or your garden or whatever you are photographing and trip the shutter, but there are a few little matters that you may know about but which we are going to mention just the same. First, there is no escaping the fact that the camera must be held still. Not only must you not be moving the camera about, but it is wise to guard against *any* tremors. You may find that you can steady your hands by holding your elbows tight against the body and holding your breath. Years ago I formed the habit of holding my breath every time I made a picture without a tripod: which often is entirely unnecessary, but is always safest. I do know that there is nothing more annoying than to have all the makings of a good photograph and then find that somehow the camera moved. It makes the print look as though you were seeing it through someone's else glasses.

Then there is the very embarrassing matter of keeping the lens unobstructed. Incredible as it may sound, people sometimes cover up the aperture at the moment they are making the exposure. I had a friend who exposed an entire roll in this way, without getting a single print. Somehow, he had always managed to seal the lens up with the end of at least one of his ten fingers. An unusual demand to place on any lens.

Another troublesome thing which spoils many a picture is the tendency to tip the camera. We have all seen those landscape photographs spoiled by weirdly slanting skylines. Frequently this happens because the photographer looked into the finder carefully enough, *then* stared at the view again *while* he was actuating the shutter. Above all else, keep your eye on the ball—in this case the finder—or you will see one thing; the lens another. We have also seen those vertical pictures of lighthouses which leaned backwards, their widths diminishing alarmingly in the shape of an ice-cream cone. This kind of focusing is a great temptation. The man with the camera realized he could not get the top in unless he tilted the camera back. So get it all he did. Tipping the camera, he clicked the shutter and hoped for the best—but he might just as well have saved the film. With the ordinary, inexpensive camera, there is only one way to avoid that fault: Simply stand off at a greater distance—at a point where everything you are aiming at can be included *without tipping*. Sometimes this will mean a very small image, invariably more foreground than you want. But you must not mind. Except in the case of angle shots, where this kind of focusing is intentional, backward-leaning pictures are worthless. In the case of a picture that is straight and square, you can later crop off any excessive foreground.

You may have been wondering about distance, in relation to the box camera. Can it take pictures at any distance? Yes, almost. In other words it has been adjusted to handle anything from infinity down to five feet. (At less than five feet an object is bound to be out of focus.) In other words, within this extremely wide range everything will be *more or less* in focus, although perfect focus, or extreme sharpness, is hardly possible. Most box cameras will give sharpest pictures of objects between fifteen and twenty-five feet away from the camera. This may sound as if the box camera had few limitations, but of course it has, and especially in regard to the adjustment for varying light conditions. That is where this type of camera really must take last place. Occasionally you may hear a person stoutly insist, "With a box camera that I bought in 1920 I can take pictures that are just as good as those the high-class cameras will do." Of course, what he means is that if conditions are just about perfect, and circumstances are just right, he can take some photos that at first glance seem to compare favorably. And the perfect conditions and circumstances for snapshots with ordinary film would have to include: bright sunlight (from several hours after sunrise, until several hours before sunset); still or slow-moving objects only; no objects too close to the camera; no too-distant views. At the same time we should all be glad to agree with him that many, many times these ideal circumstances do present themselves and in its limited way the box camera does its work well. He on his part would be obliged to admit that it would be risky for him to use his camera near dawn or dusk, to photograph objects in very heavy shade, to attempt pictures on a rainy day; quite fatal to try to snap objects that were moving swiftly by. (Head-on, he might in some cases get away with it.)

One other thing which is, to be sure, rather common knowledge: No picture taking against the sun. If the lens can be placed in the shadow of a tree or perhaps your own hat, this crude way of preventing glare will often make a picture possible, but any light streaming down directly from the sun into the lens will be enough for disaster.

And finally: *Be sure to wind the film after each exposure!* This may sound like needless advice, but I suppose that everyone of us has at one time or another forgotten to wind in a fresh portion of the film—to find later that he has taken what is known as a double exposure—one picture on top of another. Nothing is more humiliating. Some photographers prefer to wind the film just *before* each exposure, claiming the film is more apt to lie flat when unrolled fresh. What ever method you use, however, adhere to it inflexibly and get the habit of doing that thing *every* time.

When you come to the last number, by the way, which in this case is 8, just keep turning the key until all the paper is wound onto the full spool (and don't open the camera until this has been done). You will have no trouble in removing this reel of exposed film from between the two catches, and sealing it up to slip in your pocket. Now change the empty spindle over to the end where you just took out the full spindle, and you will be all ready to reload the camera with a new film.

## USING A SIMPLE FOLDING CAMERA

As we have already noticed, there is not much adjusting to do with the ordinary box camera. The shutter speed is already fixed (at about 1/30 second); there is no adjustment for distance; and the largest diaphragm opening is so small (usually about $f$ 16), that even if there is a series of still smaller stops we ordinarily have very little occasion to use them.

Even an inexpensive folding camera, however, is likely to have three features which need adjustment with each new picture: distance scale, variable diaphragm openings and variable shutter speeds. It is plain to be seen that these make this type of camera ever so much more adaptable for different conditions of light, and different circumstances. (Also, you have probably noticed, they comprise three more things to remember.)

The distance scale is perfectly simple. On it are marked the number of feet away that the principal object will be, as 6, 8, 10, 15, 25, etc. You adjust it accordingly. Better measure anything less than 25 feet, as that will make a difference. If you are a fair guesser you can come close enough to any distance that is greater. Usually a hundred feet does for any distance approximating that figure, and all distances beyond, up to infinity.

Now the adjustment of shutter and diaphragm requires some judgment, and often considerable care. The whole question of exposure—how much light gets through the lens—hangs upon the stop and the shutter adjustments. Furthermore these two always depend upon each other. When one changes (and the light condition remains the same), the other is bound to change.

There are probably at least four different stops on this camera of yours, ranging from the largest, $f$ 7.7, through $f$ 11, $f$ 16 to $f$ 22 (and perhaps smaller).

Examine the shutter, if you will. Here there are two, or more likely three different instantaneous shutter speeds: 1/25, 1/50 and—in the latter instance—1/100. (These are marked simply 25, 50 and 100, but it is clear enough what is meant.) It goes without saying that if you place the indicator at 25, for example, your shutter will be set for a snapshot at 1/25 of a second. If you wanted to take a long time exposure, you would push the indicator to "T." Then, actuating the shutter release

*Upper left*: Home life in Haiti—but the camera moved at the crucial moment. *Upper right*: Lightstruck—an all too familiar sight. This happened to be the result of a hole in the bellows, easily enough detected by later opening the camera and placing a lighted bulb behind the bellows. *Below*: He tried to "get in" the top of the tree.

would open it; pressing it again would close it. You may have been puzzled by still another adjustment, namely, "B." This is for taking short time exposures. Suppose, for instance, you wanted to make an exposure of less than two seconds. At "T" you would scarcely have time to open the shutter and close it without awkwardness. At "B," however, (which stands for "bulb") you have only to press the cable release to open; release it to close.

Let us imagine that you have discovered a herd of goats cropping the grass in a pasture through which runs a brook. The sky is clear and forms part of the background. It would make a grand picture. What is still more fortunate, you happen to have your camera with you. It is loaded with Verichrome Pan, or a similar film suitable for general conditions. Since the goats are about two hundred feet away, you set the distance scale at 100 feet (or infinity). Now the question is: What exposure? What combination of shutter and diaphragm? The best combination for this picture is stop $f$ 16, shutter 1/25. This is borne out by consulting an exposure table, or even a light meter.

You may accept this statement without hesitation and then pause, remembering that according to the progression of diaphragm openings one could get precisely the same amount of light by opening the stop wider and cutting down on the exposure. You would say, "Could I not open the stop 'a notch' and halve the exposure? Could I not place the diaphragm at $f$ 11; the shutter 50?" You would be right. This combination would admit precisely the same amount of light. And so would $f$ 7.7 with a shutter speed of 1/100. "Then why," you naturally ask, "pick $f$ 16 at 1/25? Does 1/25 of a second have any special advantages?"

No, the shutter speed of 1/25 of a second has no special advantages in itself, in fact it is the slowest speed we can use (or should use) without a tripod, but the diaphragm opening $f$ 16 *does* have some important advantages. For one thing, it provides greater depth of focus. Only by using shutter speed 1/25 can we use that stop. That's the reason.

From the discussion of lenses and their faults earlier in the book you will at once recall that the more we have to open the diaphragm the more the lens is at a disadvantage, for its weaknesses begin to show up. Hence, to play as safe as we possibly can, we stop the lens down, realizing that the picture will be sharper for our precaution.

Now if the goats had been gamboling around at quite a clip, we should have *had* to use 1/50 second in order that they might not blur the picture. Then it would have been a case of using stop $f$ 11, to correspond. If we had decided to catch a glimpse of one goat at somewhat close range, jumping from one rock to another, we should have used the very fastest shutter speed of all, 1/100, and the corresponding stop, $f$ 7.7. Here we had to sacrifice everything for speed. The background and foreground would be out of focus, but that was necessary to catch the goat's motion, without blur.

If it had been a dull day, we should have had to use $f$ 7.7 and 1/25 to get any picture at all of the goats grazing. How good a picture would depend largely on how dull the day. Under such circumstances the exposure could be determined only by a meter or a very practiced eye. All you can do if you must take a picture on an overcast day with a limited camera and no exposure meter is to use the largest stop, the slowest shutter speed and a prayer for the best.

On the other hand, if it were winter and this same pasture—probably minus the goats—were covered with snow, what exposure then? If there were a dull December sun, it would be $f$ 22 with 1/25. If the sun were pouring down, as it sometimes does even in winter, a stop of $f$ 32 would be required.

Please stretch your imagination to the breaking point and imagine that now skiers are coming down the hill over the frozen stream. At a distance you would not even take a chance with the faithful shutter speed of 1/25 and you would not dare to open the diaphragm too far, because you want as much as possible of the tree-dotted background to be in focus. You would steer a middle course and use 1/50. Assuming that it is a day with plenty of snow and a bright December sun—calling for $f$ 22 at 1/25 under ordinary circumstances, as above—you would, having picked the next faster shutter speed, select the next larger stop, $f$ 16. If you decided to try to catch a skier part way down the hill (not very close, or you'd never stop the motion with this particular camera) you would without hesitation take the very fastest shutter speed, 1/100, and the next larger stop, $f$ 11.

This Goat Pasture Sequence, then, has brought into play many of the possible combinations, but we might as well admit that the stop you are bound to use most is $f$ 16 (because under ordinary conditions it is the smallest you can get away with). The shutter speed that you are bound to use most is 1/25 (because you always use the smallest stop that is feasible, and the smaller the stop, the slower the shutter speed). The standard or normal, you might say, is $f$ 16 at 1/25. Deviations from this are occasioned by "extra" light (glaring snow, etc.); reduced light (cloudy weather, etc.); by different circumstances surrounding the picture—more exposure for near-by objects, less for distant ones, etc.

As time goes on you will get to have a feeling for 1/25 as the "old faithful" speed; 1/100 as the action speed; 1/50 as the middle speed. In spite of the numerous possible combinations you will come to think of your different stops for different occasions: $f$ 7.7, the "rainy-day stop";

*f* 11, for street scenes; *f* 16, the "everyday" stop; *f* 22 for use at the beach or when there is snow on the ground.

Of course, we should emphasize that this relation holds only for film of ASA 64-80 (Verichrome Pan, Ansco All-Weather Pan, and others); time—between 2½ hours after sunrise and 2½ hours before sunset; place —temperate zones. If you live in the deep tropics, or if you use a film of special qualities, you will formulate an entirely different set of values.[2]

Exposure tables are only approximate, but this brief one tends to sum up what we have already said:

| | SHUTTER SPEED | *f* STOP |
|---|---|---|
| Water, beach, sea ..................... | 1/50 | 22 |
| Landscapes with some sky. Not too distant . | 1/50 | 16 |
| Close-ups, streets ..................... | 1/50 | 11 |
| Shaded close-ups, landscapes with veiled sun | 1/50 | 7.7[3] |

If at first this question of exposure seems to be very perplexing and you would like to get used to the camera before bothering with it as you will later, keep the camera set at 1/50, *f* 16. This corresponds roughly to the adjustment of a box camera, and you may enjoy experimenting first this way. (Incidentally, it is not such a bad idea always to leave the camera at this adjustment, *just in case* you should forget to check things up the next time you take it out in a hurry.)[4]

And speaking of check-ups; for a long time I always managed to forget something when I first used my new folding camera. So at last I had to ask myself four questions concerning each exposure:

1. Did I adjust the *S*top?
2. Did I adjust the *S*hutter?
3. Did I set the *D*istance?
4. Did I turn the *F*ilm?

("*Some Select Different Films*," just in case you might forget the four points.) It may sound unnecessary to you, but has saved me a good many failures.

[2] When you begin to use *panchromatic* film, like Plus X or Supreme, increase your shutter speed two times. That is, shift from 1/25 to 1/50, or from 1/50 to 1/100.

[3] Some cameras use *f* 8 or *f* 5.6 instead of this stop. If *f* 8, use 1/50 shutter speed as indicated; if *f* 5.6, use 1/100.

[4] If, after trying a few rolls, you find that your film is consistently *over*- or *under*-exposed, make the necessary adjustments.

# 8

# *Film and Exposure*

## SOME SECRETS OF EXPOSURE

To reproduce a scene accurately, the perfect negative has to show all the tones the way the eye sees them, with exactly the same relative contrasts between the light and dark areas, and with the color hues converted to the correct shades of black, gray and white. Though negative contrast is determined by development, and not by exposure, nevertheless the exposure *must* be correct or the tonal relations of the subject may be falsified in the negative. You will see why, in a moment.

### WHAT IS CORRECT EXPOSURE?

The average negative emulsion is so made that it can reproduce, without any loss of tones, a scene with the brightness range of 1 to 128. This means that if the brightest object is 128 times as bright as the darkest object, both can still be photographed in their true tones on a film with this latitude, and there will be full detail visible in the shadows as well as in the highlights. Now when the scene itself has a brightness range of

FIG. 46. ILLUSTRATING CORRECT EXPOSURE

128 to 1, there can only be *one* correct exposure if the tones of the subject are to match exactly the tones of the negative. Look at the sleeping gentlemen in *Fig. 46*. The one in the middle fits his bed perfectly; he

represents a scene brightness range of 128 on a film with a latitude of 128. If he were to move up or down in the bed, either his head would be lifted up at one end or his feet would dangle over the other. The effect on a film, if the exposure were *under* or *over,* would be somewhat similar; either the shadows would lose detail and go dense black or the highlights would jam up and go chalky white. In either case the reproduction would be false.

Now, if the scene has a brightness range of only 32, whereas the film latitude is still 128, we can see at once that a considerable variation in *correct exposure* is possible. See the little fellow in the big bed at the left in *Fig. 46.* He could move up or down in the bed quite a bit, and still be on the bed *in toto.* Just so, the correct exposure for a scene with a brightness range of 32 on a film with a possible range of 128 would give us an exposure *latitude* of 4 to 1. Negatives exposed at shutter speeds of 1/25, 1/50, 1/75, or 1/100, though they would vary in density, would all reproduce the scene in exactly the same way.

Finally, if the scene has a brightness range of 256 as against the film range of 128, it would be possible to record accurately only half of the scene's tones; either the highlights and/or the shadows would be lost. See *Fig. 46* again. The big sleeper with his feet dangling over the bed represents our scene with a brightness range of 256; there's too much contrast in the scene for the film, just as there is too much man for the bed. See the three photographic reproductions on pages 126 and 127 which show how this works out in practice.

## MEASURING THE EXPOSURE

The brightness of a scene or object depends not on how much light it *receives,* but on how much it *reflects.* To measure this light you need a meter, either photoelectric, visual, or comparison. The visual (like the *Leudi*) are inexpensive but inaccurate; the comparison (like the *SEI Exposure Photometer*) are extremely accurate but quite expensive. The best compromise is the photoelectric, of which there are now two types.

The conventional photoelectric meters (*Weston, GE, Sekonic*) use a selenium cell which produces current when light hits it, activating the needle. The greater the light, the more the current, and the higher the reading. The new meters (*Lunasix, Microlite,* even the Polaroid *Electric Eye*) work on a revolutionary new principle. The cadmium sulphide cell which they use acts as a light-controlled resistor to a tiny mercury battery. With light, cell resistance *decreases* and current *increases.* Hence their sensitivity is extremely high; high enough to read moonlight!

With any type of meter, it is a good idea to check your use of it against the actual results obtained and then to make the necessary adjustments. If your readings are consistently too high or too low, for example, simply give the film a different speed rating to compensate for this error.

## FILM-SPEED RATINGS

Since the various types of available films have emulsions whose response to light differs, it is necessary to know the speed rating of each in order to operate an exposure meter. All meters are calibrated to conform to a system of speed ratings. Before the war the most widely recognized standard for films was that developed by the manufacturer of the Weston meters, but there were others, notably the General Electric system devised especially for use with the GE exposure meter. Most film manufacturers designated both Weston and GE ratings in their instruction sheets.

In 1943, however, the American Standards Association arrived at a method of film rating which ultimately will become *the* American Standard to be used by all exposure meter, film and flashbulb manufacturers. The figure designated for a given film is known as the *ASA Exposure Index*. Already GE has abandoned its own system and is calibrating all new meters on the ASA system. Eastman Kodak and Ansco, too, are adopting the *ASA Exposure Index* in conjunction with their films.

Meanwhile, as in all periods of transition from one set of rules to another, there will likely be some confusion, particularly for owners of meters calibrated on the older systems. There need be no real difficulty, however, since the ASA index numbers are only slightly different from those of the exposure meter systems previously published, so that the ASA number in a given instance may be used on both GE meters and those calibrated according to the *old* Weston system (Weston went ASA in 1957). This is practical because of the exposure latitude afforded by modern films. We can make this clear with an example:

The daylight Weston rating assigned to Plus X film is 80, while the corresponding GE rating is 100. The new ASA Exposure Index for this film is 80.[1] Obviously the owners of Weston meters have all the best of it in this instance. The new ASA figures are closer to old Weston ratings than they are to the GE. So what happens if you have an old GE meter? You use the ASA figure just the same, and you'll get a printable negative. If too dense, close down an extra stop; if too thin, open up a stop.

Remember that film ratings always were approximations and that the Weston system took the variables into account when it assigned a given

[1] In 1961, Kodak adopted new ASA speeds with *reduced safety factor* for most black-and-white films: Tri-X Pan and Royal Pan, ASA 400; Royal-X Pan, ASA 1250. But in 1965 Panatomic-X (a *new* emulsion) was dropped from 40 to ASA 32, and Plus-X Pan was officially set at ASA 125.

These are three exposures of the same scene, photographed on Ansco film. The one at the top, left, is a print from a negative that was *underexposed*. The lower one on the page is a print from an *overexposed* negative. The one directly above is from a negative that was *correctly exposed*. Notice how the shadow detail has been lost in the first one, and the highlight detail lost in the one below it.

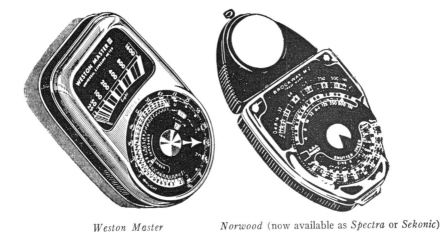

*Weston Master*       *Norwood* (now available as *Spectra* or *Sekonic*)

TWO POPULAR EXPOSURE METERS

number to a film. All Weston rating figures represented a range of three exposures. In the case of Plus X, the assigned figure, 80, represented a group of three possible speeds. Thus: 64-80-100, any one of which would yield a good negative. (In 1961 this figure, with reduced safety factor, became 160).

So you might as well get used to the new ASA system now because it won't be long before the old systems will disappear. For this reason all references to film speeds in this book are expressed according to the ASA Exposure Index, with the exception of color films, for which both old Weston and ASA ratings are given. Until all meters are accurately calibrated to the ASA system it is safer to stick to the old rating system on which your meter is calibrated, since color film has so much less latitude.

### EXPOSURE TABLES

For outdoor use, the printed exposure tables supplied for the camera you are using are a fairly reliable makeshift if you do not have a meter or if you have forgotten to take it with you. Exposure tables are only about 50 per cent accurate, but a little study of light conditions, and considerable practice, can make them very valuable tools indeed. Here is a simplified exposure table that has been found helpful by many:

| *SUBJECT:* HALF LIGHT AND HALF SHADOW | | |
|---|---|---|
| FROM 10 A.M. TO 2 P.M. (ASA 32 FILM) | | |
| SET CAMERA AT 1/50 | | |
| JUNE | 0 | BRILLIANT SUN |
| APR., MAY, JULY, AUG. | 1 | SOFT SUNLIGHT |
| MAR., SEPT. | 2 | HAZY |
| FEB., OCT. | 3 | DULL |
| NOV., DEC., JAN. | 4 | OVERCAST |
| Deduct sum of both factors from 11 | | |
| Subtract 1 for *each* hour before 10 A.M. and *after* 2 P.M. | | |
| Result will be *f* number. | | |

This can be inked in on the reverse side of a regular business card and kept with you at all times. Here's how it works. Suppose you are using Panatomic X (ASA 32) on a *soft sunlit* day in *September*. You add 1 and 2 and deduct the sum from 11. The result is 8, therefore you set the shutter at 1/50 as suggested, and the aperture at *f* 8. If the film you're using has a rating of ASA 50–80, set shutter at 1/100–1/125.

The following exposure table for indoor pictures is worked out for supersensitive pan film (like Plus X, Supreme, or Verichrome Pan) and use of a Kodaflector unit with two photoflood lamps. When using Panatomic X, Adox KB17, Finopan, Plenachrome, Isopan F, Pergrano, or Ilford Pan F, double the exposure.

## INDOOR EXPOSURE TABLE

| DISTANCE LAMPS TO SUBJECT | DIAPHRAGM OR STOP OPENING | EXPOSURE IN SECONDS | |
|---|---|---|---|
| | | No. 1 Photoflood Lamps without Adapter | No. 2 Photoflood Lamps with Adapter |
| 4 feet | f 4.5 | 1/50 | 1/100 |
| " | f 6.3 | 1/25 | 1/50 |
| " | f 11 | 1/10 | 1/25 |
| " | f 16 | 1/5 | 1/10 |
| 6 feet | f 4.5 | 1/25 | 1/50 |
| " | f 6.3 | 1/10 | 1/25 |
| " | f 11 | 1/5 | 1/10 |
| " | f 16 | 1/2 | 1/5 |
| 10 feet | f 4.5 | 1/10 | 1/25 |
| " | f 6.3 | 1/5 | 1/10 |
| " | f 11 | 1/2 | 1/5 |
| " | f 16 | 1 | 1/2 |

This table is for portraits and light-colored interiors. For dark-colored interiors without people, double the above exposures. For instance, if 1/10 second is given, using 1/5 second will double the exposure time.

Doubling the number of lamps will halve the exposure.

When the lamps are used for general illumination to make a picture of a room, use stop $f$ 16 to get sufficient depth of focus or range of sharpness.

With box, single lens, or doublet lens cameras, use the largest stop opening and use the exposures shown above for $f$ 16 or $f$ 11.

If the camera has a shutter marked with the U. S. system, use U. S. 8 instead of $f$ 11 in the above table.

The camera must be placed on a tripod or other firm support for shutter speeds slower than 1/25 second.

## A TABLE OF RELATIVE LIGHT VALUES

With the gracious permission of the editor, Henry M. Lester, we are able to reprint here the complete table of relative values of lens stops which appears in *The Photo-Lab-Index,* published by Morgan and Morgan.

# A TABLE OF RELATIVE *f* VALUES

| Lens Stop f: \\ Lens Stop f: | 1.5 | 2.0 | 2.8 | 3.2 | 3.5 | 4 | 4.5 | 5.6 | 6.3 | 8 | 9 | 11 | 12.7 | 16 | 18 | 22 | 25 | 32 |
|---|---|---|---|---|---|---|---|---|---|---|---|---|---|---|---|---|---|---|
| f² | 2.25 | 4 | 7.5 | 10 | 12 | 16 | 20 | 31 | 40 | 64 | 81 | 121 | 160 | 256 | 324 | 484 | 625 | 1024 |
| 1.5 | 1 | 2 | 3 | 4 | 5 | 7 | 9 | 14 | 18 | 28 | 36 | 54 | 71 | 114 | 144 | 215 | 280 | 455 |
| 2.0 | .5 | 1 | 2 | 2.5 | 3 | 4 | 5 | 8 | 10 | 16 | 20 | 30 | 40 | 64 | 81 | 121 | 156 | 256 |
| 2.8 | .3 | .5 | 1 | 1.3 | 1.6 | 2 | 2.7 | 4 | 5.3 | 8.5 | 11 | 16 | 21 | 34 | 43 | 65 | 83 | 137 |
| 3.2 | .22 | .4 | .75 | 1 | 1.2 | 1.6 | 2 | 3 | 4 | 6.5 | 8 | 12 | 16 | 26 | 32 | 48 | 62 | 102 |
| 3.5 | .2 | .33 | .6 | .83 | 1 | 1.3 | 1.7 | 2.6 | 3.3 | 5.5 | 7 | 10 | 13 | 21 | 27 | 40 | 52 | 85 |
| 4 | .14 | .25 | .5 | .6 | .75 | 1 | 1.2 | 2 | 2.5 | 4 | 5 | 7.5 | 10 | 16 | 20 | 30 | 39 | 64 |
| 4.5 | .11 | .2 | .37 | .5 | .6 | .8 | 1 | 1.5 | 2 | 3 | 4 | 6 | 8 | 13 | 16 | 24 | 32 | 51 |
| 5.6 | .07 | .13 | .25 | .3 | .4 | .5 | .7 | 1 | 1.3 | 2 | 2.5 | 4 | 5 | 8 | 10 | 16 | 20 | 32 |
| 6.3 | .06 | .1 | .2 | .25 | .3 | .4 | .5 | .8 | 1 | 1.6 | 2 | 3 | 4 | 6.5 | 8 | 12 | 16 | 25 |
| 8 | .04 | .06 | .12 | .16 | .2 | .25 | .3 | .5 | .6 | 1 | 1.3 | 2 | 2.5 | 4 | 5 | 7.5 | 10 | 16 |
| 9 | .03 | .05 | .1 | .12 | .15 | .2 | .25 | .4 | .5 | .8 | 1 | 1.5 | 2 | 3 | 4 | 6 | 8 | 13 |
| 11 | .019 | .033 | .06 | .08 | .1 | .13 | .16 | .25 | .3 | .5 | .7 | 1 | 1.3 | 2 | 2.7 | 4 | 5 | 8.5 |
| 12.7 | .014 | .025 | .05 | .06 | .08 | .1 | .12 | .2 | .25 | .4 | .5 | .75 | 1 | 1.6 | 2 | 3 | 4 | 6.4 |
| 16 | .009 | .016 | .03 | .04 | .05 | .06 | .08 | .12 | .16 | .25 | .3 | .5 | .6 | 1 | 1.3 | 2 | 2.5 | 4 |
| 18 | .007 | .012 | .023 | .03 | .037 | .05 | .06 | .1 | .12 | .2 | .25 | .4 | .5 | .8 | 1 | 1.5 | 2 | 3 |
| 22 | .005 | .008 | .015 | .02 | .025 | .033 | .04 | .06 | .08 | .13 | .17 | .25 | .3 | .5 | .7 | 1 | 1.3 | 2 |
| 25 | .004 | .006 | .012 | .016 | .02 | .025 | .03 | .05 | .06 | .1 | .13 | .2 | .25 | .4 | .5 | .8 | 1 | 1.6 |
| 32 | .002 | .004 | .007 | .01 | .012 | .016 | .02 | .03 | .04 | .06 | .08 | .12 | .16 | .25 | .3 | .5 | .6 | 1 |

Reprinted from *The Photo-Lab-Index*, by Henry M. Lester, Copyright 1939—Morgan & Morgan.

130

This table, as Mr. Lester points out, answers more than 324 questions which usually require a slide rule or elaborate calculations. The factors given in the table are similar to those you met in the chapter THE MYSTERY OF $f$, and they can be used in the same way.

*Directions.* The lens apertures ($f$ stops) are shown in two places—horizontally across the top, and vertically at the extreme left. They are set in a type slightly bolder than that used elsewhere in the table. Directly below the horizontal row of lens stops, and set in *italics,* you will find their respective squares (rounded off for convenience).

The relation of any two lens stops will be found at the intersection of the horizontal and vertical rows identified by their $f$ numbers. Thus to find out how much more exposure is needed when we stop down from $f$ 4 to, say, $f$ 22, just find $f$ 4 in the left column and $f$ 22 in the top row. Where these two rows join you'll find the number 30. That's your *relative light factor.* It means that you need 30 times as much exposure at $f$ 22 as at $f$ 4, or 30 times as much light. It also means, of course, that a lens at $f$ 4 transmits 30 times as much light as at $f$ 22.

If you already know the correct exposure, which, say, is 1/100 of a second at $f$ 3.5, and you want to convert this to $f$ 22, there are two methods, both simple, by which you can do this:

1. Find $f$ 3.5 in the left column, $f$ 22 at the top and where the two rows cross you'll find the number 40. Multiply your exposure by this factor and you'll get 40/100 or 2/5 of a second.

2. Find $f$ 3.5 in the *top* row, follow this down until you are on a row opposite $f$ 22 at the extreme left. You'll find the factor .025. Divide 1/100 by .025 and you'll get the same result, 2/5 of a second.

There is still a third way to use the table. Suppose you know the exposure is 1 second at $f$ 22, but there's action to be stopped and you need a shutter speed of 1/100 second. Look down the column of lens stops at the extreme left until you reach 22, follow this across *horizontally* until you get to the figure nearest to .01 (1/100 of 1 second). That figure is .008. Now follow this up *vertically* until you reach the top and you'll find that this calls for a lens stop of $f$ 2.

Though this table is not absolutely exact mathematically (round figures have been used to make calculations less cumbersome) the ratios nevertheless exceed the limits of accuracy needed for most amateur photography.[1a]

[1a] The *Photo-Lab-Index,* by the way, is a *must* item for any serious amateur. It is the most comprehensive cyclopedia of photographic facts, tables, formulas and procedures that has ever been compiled. It consists of a buckram binder and a series of self-perpetuating, loose-leaf pages, sectioned off by index cards, which are supplemented at regular intervals by additional pages of new and revised material. In its present form it runs to over 350 solidly printed pages and needs two binders. If you are at all serious about your photography, the *Index* is well worth investigating.

## THE CAMERA AS ITS OWN METER

In dim light, indoors, neither the photoelectric meter nor any chart or table is much help in calculating the correct exposure. The best method is the one devised by the oldtime commercial photographers. It is used with any camera that has a ground-glass back.

The camera is set up, the picture composed, and then the diaphragm is closed down until details in the shadows disappear. (A black focusing cloth is used to cover head and camera.) The lens aperture is now checked. Then the diaphragm is closed all the way and slowly opened until details in the shadows *just* begin to appear. The lens aperture is checked again. The first and second aperture numbers should be the same; average them if they're not. Using this *f* number now, refer to the following table, find the fadeout stop and ASA Exposure Index that apply

### EXPOSURE DETERMINATION BY FADEOUT STOP

| FADEOUT STOP | EXPOSURES AT *f* 16 IN MINUTES | | | | | | |
|---|---|---|---|---|---|---|---|
| | ASA 4 | 8 | 16 | 25 | 32 | 40 | 64 |
| *f* 4 | 224 | 112 | 56 | 28 | 14 | 7 | 3½ |
| *f* 5.6 | 112 | 56 | 28 | 14 | 7 | 3½ | 1¾ |
| *f* 8 | 56 | 28 | 14 | 7 | 3½ | 1¾ | 52″ |
| *f* 11 | 28 | 14 | 7 | 3½ | 1¾ | 52″ | 26″ |
| *f* 16 | 14 | 7 | 3½ | 1¾ | 52″ | 26″ | 13″ |
| *f* 22 | 7 | 3½ | 1¾ | 52″ | 26″ | 13″ | 7″ |
| *f* 32 | 3½ | 1¾ | 52″ | 26″ | 13″ | 7″ | 3½″ |
| *f* 45 | 1¾ | 52″ | 26″ | 13″ | 7″ | 3½″ | 1¾″ |
| *f* 64 | 52″ | 26″ | 13″ | 7″ | 3½″ | 1¾″ | ⅞″ |

in your case, and where the respective horizontal and vertical columns cross you'll find a number which will indicate exposure (in *minutes* at *f* 16, except where marked in *seconds*).

## OUTDOOR EXPOSURES AT NIGHT

Another useful table for estimating exposures under difficult conditions is the one on page 133. It is used whenever the light outdoors at night is poor.

EXPOSURES AT NIGHT WITH POOR LIGHTING

| STOP | ASA 32 (Panchromatic) | ASA 64 | ASA 16 (Orthochromatic) |
|---|---|---|---|
| f 4 | 2 min | 1 | 6 |
| f 5.6 | 4 min | 2 | 12 |
| f 8 | 8 min | 4 | 24 |
| f 11 | 16 min | 8 | 48 |
| f 16 | 32 min | 16 | |

FACTORS AFFECTING EXPOSURE

Here is a list of some factors, other than basic lighting, which may affect the exposure:

1. *The shutter.* Are its markings accurate? Is it an iris or focal plane? (The focal plane delivers 30 per cent *more* light.)

2. *The color of the light.* Morning, afternoon and tungsten light is red and yellowish; noon light is blue. Exposure should be increased when light is yellow if *ortho* film is used; decreased if type C *pan* is used (see section on "The Choice of Film" in this chapter).

3. *Temperature.* When the weather is cold, shutter mechanisms are likely to work more slowly.

4. *Focal length.* Have you allowed for this? The *f* marking is accurate only at infinity; at twice the focal length the light is cut by 1/4, or the *f* stop should be doubled.

5. *Meter.* Have you tested the film-speed rating for *your* conditions?

6. *Developer.* Some increase shadow detail; others cut it down. *Make tests!*

7. *Color of object.* Those colored green or red affect film less than those colored blue and yellow.

8. *Position of camera.* Close-ups require more exposure than land-scapes.

9. *Subject contrast.* Flat scenes require less exposure than contrasty ones. Photoelectric meters are integrated for an even distribution of light and shade. Where this condition does not hold, adjustments should be made.

10. *Kind of subject.* Seascapes, beach scenes and distant landscapes with lots of sky require 1/2 exposure indicated by the exposure meter; objects with shadows in foreground require 2 x exposure; portraits and groups, not in direct sun, require 4 x exposure; against the sun pictures

require 4 x exposure. An excellent way of checking the exposure of *against the sun* pictures is to turn around and take a reading of the cast shadow.

### USING A METER IN DIM LIGHT

If the reflected light from the object is so weak that a reading cannot be made in the regular way, try either of these supplementary methods of getting a reading:

1. Point the meter *at* the light *from* the subject, and multiply the reading by 30. Use twice the daylight reading in artificial light.

2. Place the meter at the subject position and point it halfway between the camera and the light source. Multiply the reading by 10.

### SOME METER TECHNIQUES

There are many ways of using a photoelectric meter. Here are a few suggestions:

1. *Exposing for the darkest object.* Read the shadow or darkest part of the subject and set the "U" position on the dial (Weston) to the measured light value. Every part of the scene, from the darkest object to the brightest high light, will now be correctly exposed; provided, of course, the high lights do not extend beyond the range of the film (128 to 1). This span is shown by the distance between the "U" and "O" positions on the dial, so no calculation is needed to check this point. Simply read the highlight and check to see that it does not exceed the reading at "O."

2. *Exposing for the brightest object.* This method is good for dark subjects, poorly lit interiors, outdoor scenes where the sky is an essential part of the picture. Take a meter reading of the brightest object (the sky if it's outdoors; a white handkerchief or a piece of white paper placed near the brightest object if the object itself isn't bright enough to give a reading). Set the "O" position on the dial to this light value and read off the aperture and shutter settings.

3. *Exposing for the average.* Take a high-light and a shadow reading and average the two, placing the *arrow* at this measured value. These readings will also indicate, to some extent, the contrast range of your subject.

4. *Exposing for different lenses.* Use the meter at the camera position for the normal lens; behind the camera for a wide-angle lens; in front of the camera for the telephoto lens.

5. *When only part of a scene is important,* read that part of it by moving up as close to it as you can so that the meter reads just that portion.

Roughly, the distance to the object should equal the diameter of an imaginary circle which encompasses it.

6. When exposed to bright light for any considerable time the cell of the exposure meter becomes fatigued (loses sensitivity). It recovers its power when it is kept in the dark for a while, but that's time consuming. To avoid this, *keep the meter in a case* (the ever-ready type is best) and always see that it's covered when you're not using it.

7. *Incident light.* Most exposure meters measure only the reflected light from a scene in order to determine the intensity of illumination. There are disadvantages to this method of approximating exposure. If you're trying to photograph a light object against a dark background, your meter reading will throw your exposure off, unless you make a reading of the light object close up, or unless you compensate in some way for the dark background. Another, and possibly more accurate, method of measuring the light has become very popular lately . . . the incident light method. This measures the light actually falling directly on the subject. To measure incident light, you hold the meter in front of the subject and point it directly at the camera so that it's affected by the same light that falls on the subject. In that way, the meter measures *all* the light, that bouncing off walls and ceilings as well as the direct light from the lamps.

There are several meters on the market which can be used to measure incident light as well as reflected light. Among them are the General Electric and the De Jur. One of the most interesting meters incorporating this new principle of incident light measurement (actually a variation or adaptation of the old *actinometer* principle) is the Norwood Director, and it has been adopted by many professional photographers in color work because its measurements are said to be more exact. By means of a spherical light collector called a *photosphere,* this meter is designed especially for reading incident light, rather than reflected light. The swivel-top Photosphere is pointed toward the camera instead of at the subject, thus recording exactly the light intensity as it *falls on the subject.* Accessory attachments extend the use of the meter for lighting contrast and brightness-range control. Weston has also made an incident light adapter for its Master Universal meters called the *Invercone.* This consists of an Integrating Cone and Auxiliary Multiplier which snaps into position when the baffle is swung back. This makes it possible to use the Weston for metering incident as well as reflected light.

8. *Gray card.* The electric exposure meter is more susceptible to certain colors than to others. This presents an almost insoluble problem in the response of exposure meters to colored subjects. Professional photographers solve this problem simply by the ingenious use of a neutral gray card about a foot square. They place this card in front of, or near,

the subject to be photographed, and they hold the meter at such a distance (around a foot away is about right) that it reads only the card. Kodak sells four such *Neutral Test Cards* and an instruction sheet for one dollar.

## SOME EXPOSURE HINTS

**1.** Expose for shadow detail. In case of doubt, overexpose rather than underexpose. If you make several exposures, increase each new one by at least 50 per cent. The eye can't distinguish less of a difference. Besides, a good film will stand about 200 times as much exposure as is needed to produce the first faint veil of silver and still show all tones in correct proportion. Since average scenes are rarely more than 30 to 1, this gives plenty of leeway.

**3.** Remember that it is *contrast* between light and shade that makes the picture. Avoid flat lighting. Use shadows to lend interest to the scene, to model it, give it emphasis.

**4.** Flat lighting requires a short exposure and increased developing time. If the normal exposure is 1/50 or 1/60 for example, use 1/100 and increase development by 25 per cent.

**5.** Use the monotone viewing filter for outdoor as well as indoor photography. Outdoors it will tell you whether the scene is worth taking at all; indoors it will guide you in rearranging your lights to get more luminous shadows, avoid chalky white highlights.

**6.** Contrasty subjects, or those that are lighted with harsh, strong light (as in summer sunlight) require slight overexposure and less developing time. If the normal exposure is 1/50 second, use 1/25 or 1/10 and decrease development by 10 to 25 per cent, depending on contrast desired.

**7.** Expose for weak lighting and for haze as for flat subjects. That is, underexpose a bit and increase the time of development.

**8.** *Check the speed ratings of your shutter!* You can do this by making a series of tests on an evenly lighted wall, using each shutter speed and adjusting the diaphragm openings to give you matched *thin* exposures (one stop below normal).

**9.** Do not use a larger or smaller stop than is absolutely necessary. The middle stops are the best for almost any kind of lens; at the larger stops the lens may still have some *uncorrected aberrations,* at the smaller stops it may suffer from *diffraction.*

**10.** To reduce contrast, make use of the principle of *less* light. All other things being equal, the less light on a subject the less contrast there will be. Consider the case of a white cube on a piece of black velvet. No matter how much light you use, the cube remains white and the velvet, black. Though the velvet cannot be made lighter, the cube *can* be made darker, by *reducing* the amount of light. Outdoors, the same principle applies. We can use haze, clouds, morning and afternoon light.

11. If you use a Weston meter, be sure to send for a copy of *Exposure with the Zone System,* by Minor White (published at $1.25 by Morgan & Morgan, 101 Park Ave., New York 17, N.Y.). This is a brilliant condensation of the famous Ansel Adams system of "planned photography" (*Basic Photo Series,* Morgan & Morgan).

12. *How to tell whether a picture is underexposed or overexposed.* You can't tell by looking at the print. Examine the negative before a soft or reflected light. If it's *underexposed* it will look pale, with no detail in the light parts. If it's *overexposed* it will look dark, with all detail in the darkest parts obliterated. If the negative is flat but retains all shadow detail, it is *underdeveloped.* If the negative is dense *and* contrasty, it's *overdeveloped* (and probably overexposed as well). Underexposure cannot be remedied; what isn't there, isn't. For safety, overexpose. (See 13.)

*A simple test for the perfect negative:* Place negative flat on this page. If you can't see the type through the darkest portions, your print will be a "soot and whitewash" mess. Your gamma (see page 254) is probably about 1.2 to 1.7, when it should be .6 to .8. Blocked highlights and blank shadows—avoid them!

13. *How to overexpose and underdevelop.* When you're told to give ample exposure and brief development, do this: First divide the normal developing time by 2 (half is needed to register all the picture on the film, the balance is needed to build up contrast). Take half the developing time and multiply it by the reciprocal of the exposure increase ($\frac{1}{2}$ for 2 x, $\frac{1}{3}$ for 3 x, $\frac{1}{4}$ for 4 x). Add this sum to half the normal developing time, and that will give you the new developing time. For example: suppose the regular developing time is 20 minutes and the film was overexposed 2 x. Add to 20/2, or 10, $\frac{1}{2}$ of 10, or 5. The new developing time is 15 minutes. Similarly, 15 minutes normal developing time for 3 x overexposure = 10 minutes new developing time.

14. *Mixing daylight and tungsten by meter.* To get meter reading for mixture of daylight and lamplight, use the following formula: $A / B \times D + (B–A) / B \times T$ = combination light speed. $A$ = daylight; $B$ = total light; $D$ = daylight film value; $B–A$ = lamplight; $T$ = tungsten value.

15. *Correcting exposure for bellows extension.* The formula is $A^2/B^2$ = correction factor (multiply exposure by this number). $A$ is the bellows extension in use; $B$, the bellows extension for infinity. If a 6-inch lens, for example, is extended to 9 inches, we divide 81 by 36 to get $2\frac{1}{4}$. We then multiply the exposure by $2\frac{1}{4}$.

16. If filter factors bother you, try placing your filter over your meter

(provided it's larger than the window). Your meter reading will then be automatically corrected for that filter.

17. Outdoor color pictures are usually improved by the use of supplementary flash to lighten (soften) shadow detail. This reduces contrast and enables narrow-range of film to get all of the picture. For bright sunlight, with front or side lighting, and the shutter set at 1/50 of a second, the following lens openings are recommended: for Kodachrome, daylight type, between $f$ 5.6 and $f$ 8; for Ektachrome, daylight type, between $f$ 8 and $f$ 11; for Kodacolor, $f$ 11. This presupposes the use of one No. 5B photoflash lamp at 8 feet or one No. 22B photoflash lamp at 12 feet. Adjustments in lens opening will have to be made if the distance from lamp to subject is changed. Beyond 12 feet, additional lamps are needed to reduce contrast. Strobe light is better, but since units vary in power and reflectors vary in throw, testing is necessary.

18. For taking sunsets in color, on daylight Kodachrome, best results for both sky and sun are produced by ignoring foreground landscape as well as sun and concentrating on the sky brightness. Point the meter at the sky just north or south of the sun (whichever portion is most like the picture you're planning) but be sure to shade the meter so that no direct sunlight hits it. To avoid flare, wait until sun is hidden by clouds, or place the sun out of lens range by interposing some object in the foreground.

19. Television screens can be photographed by using panchromatic film similar to Eastman Tri-X or Ansco Superpan Press at speeds of 1/5 to 1/10 of a second at $f$ 3.5. Don't try to take faster exposures because the picture is composed of lines of light which scan the face of the viewing tube at intervals of 1/30 of a second. Put your camera on a tripod, set it as close to the screen as your camera permits (using bellows extension or a supplementary lens), focus the television set for maximum brilliance and contrast, and shoot as you would for stage shots (when there's a pause in the action). For meter readings of the screen, turn all other room lights off, take your reading, but remember to keep the shutter range between 1/5 and 1/10 of a second, adjusting the lens opening to match the meter reading at those shutter speeds.

20. Here's a simple way to *adjust exposure to bellows extension* (in copying) by using the dial of a Weston meter as your calculator. This is what you do: 1. Set your emulsion speed. 2. Take a reading. 3. Set the arrow at that reading, but note where the $f$ number falls which is *closest to the bellows extension* in inches. 4. Now set the $f$ number corresponding to the focal length of the lens in inches at the point previously noted for the $f$ number corresponding to the bellows extension. This lines up your $f$ numbers and shutter speeds. 5. Now read off the combination

## FOREIGN FILMS

Travel may be broadening, but it can also be frustrating—especially if you get used to one American film and then find yourself abroad without a continuing supply of this favorite emulsion. Here are some pointers on what to buy when your regular supply of film has been used up and you can't get any more, or when the excessive duty makes it wiser to use whatever you can get.

You can find good film almost anywhere in Europe, but you have to know your way around among the unfamiliar brands. The films listed below are all excellent in quality, and can be relied on.

*Just a word of caution:* If you buy foreign *color* film, have it processed where you buy it. You may save yourself some heartaches that way. But test the processing by letting them develop *one* roll at first.

## BLACK-AND-WHITE FILM

### IN ENGLAND

| | ASA EXPOSURE INDEX |
|---|---|
| *Ilford:* | |
| HPS (sheet film, roll, 35-mm.).... | 800 |
| HP3 (sheet film, roll, 35-mm.).... | 400 |
| FP3 (sheet film, roll, 35-mm.)..... | 125 |
| Pan F (35-mm.)................. | 25 |
| *Kodak Ltd.:* | |
| Tri-X Pan (35-mm., roll)........ | 400 |
| Tri-X Pan (sheet).............. | 320 |
| Panatomic X (sheet film)........ | 64 |
| Panatomic X (35-mm.).......... | 32 |
| Plus X (roll film, 35-mm.)....... | 125 |
| Verichome Pan (roll film)........ | 125 |

### IN BELGIUM

| | ASA EXPOSURE INDEX |
|---|---|
| *Gevaert:* | |
| Gevapan 36 (35-mm.)........... | 500 |
| Gevapan 33 (sheet film, roll, 35-mm.) .................... | 250 |
| Panchromosa (Gevapan 30; sheet film, roll, 35-mm.)........ | 125 |
| Gevachrome 32 (sheet film and plates) ................... | 200 |
| Gevapan 27 (35-mm.)........... | 64 |

### IN FRANCE

| | ASA EXPOSURE INDEX |
|---|---|
| *Lumière:* | |
| Altipan (sheet film, roll, 35-mm.) ................ | 100/80 |
| Super Lumichrome (roll film). | 50/32 |
| Altipan GF (fine grain; roll film, 35-mm.)............. | 50/32 |
| *Guilleminot:* | |
| Guilipan (roll film).......... | 64/50 |
| Panchro 55 GF (fine grain; roll film)................ | 50/32 |
| Super 44 (ortho; roll film).... | 50/25 |

### IN GERMANY

| | ASA EXPOSURE INDEX |
|---|---|
| *Adox:* | |
| R18P (roll film)............. | 50/32 |
| R215 (roll film)............. | 100/80 |
| R180 (ortho; roll film)....... | 50/32 |
| KB14 (35-mm.)............. | 80/40 |
| KB17 (35-mm.)............. | 160/80 |
| KB21 (35-mm.)............. | 200/100 |
| *Agfa:* | |
| Isopan IF (35-mm.)......... | 100 |
| Isopan IFF (35-mm.)........ | 25 |
| Isopan ISS (roll film, 35-mm.) | 200 |
| Isopan Ultra (35-mm.)....... | 500 |
| Isopan Record (35-mm., roll film)................ | 1250 |

*Hauff:*

| | ASA EXPOSURE INDEX |
|---|---|
| Portrait (sheet film) | 100 |
| Pancola S-25 (roll film, 35-mm.) | 400 |
| Pancola 21 (roll film) | 160 |
| Ulchroma (ortho; roll film) | 64 |
| Leica Pancola 17 (35-mm.) | 64 |
| Leica Granex 14 (35-mm.) | 32 |

*Perutz:*

| | |
|---|---|
| Superomnia (sheet film) | 100 |
| Peromnia 21 (roll film, 35-mm.) | 100 |
| Perpantic 17 (roll film, 35-mm.) | 40 |
| Persenso 20 (ortho; roll film) | 80 |
| Peromnia 25 (roll film, 35-mm.) | 250 |
| Pergrano 14 (35-mm.) | 20 |

*Zeiss* distributes Gevaert films in Germany under its own brand names.

### IN ITALY

*Ferrania:*

| | |
|---|---|
| Super Panchro 32 (sheet film, roll) | 100/80 |

| | ASA EXPOSURE INDEX |
|---|---|
| Super Panchro 28 (sheet film, roll) | 40/32 |
| Ultrachromatic 30 (ortho; sheet film, roll) | 64/32 |
| Super Panchro S2 (35-mm.) | 100/80 |

### IN JAPAN

*Fuji:*

| | |
|---|---|
| Neopan SSS (film pack, sheet, roll, 35-mm.) | 200/160 |
| Neopan SS (film pack, sheet, roll, 35-mm.) | 100/80 |
| Neopan S (film pack, sheet, roll, 35-mm.) | 50/32 |

### IN OTHER COUNTRIES

You'll probably find one or more of the above (or one of the American films) available wherever you go. If you stick to these you'll avoid losing those precious pictures for which you've traveled thousands of miles.

## COLOR FILM

### IN ENGLAND

*Ilford:*

| | |
|---|---|
| Ilfachrome 32 (35-mm.) | 32/— |
| Ilfacolor (roll film) | 32/— |

*Kodak Ltd.:*

| | |
|---|---|
| Ektachrome Daylight (sheet film, roll, 35-mm.) | 8/— |
| Ektachrome Type B (sheet film, roll) | —/10 |
| Kodachrome Daylight (35-mm.) | 10/— |
| Kodachrome Type A (35-mm.) | —/16 |

### IN BELGIUM

*Gevaert* (distributed in Germany by Zeiss):

| | |
|---|---|
| Gevacolor Negative (roll film, 35-mm.) | 16/— |
| Gevacolor Reversal (roll film, 35-mm.) | 12/— |

### IN GERMANY

*Agfa:*

| | |
|---|---|
| Agfacolor Negative T (sheet film, roll, 35-mm.) | 16/— |

| | |
|---|---|
| Agfacolor Negative CN 17 (sheet film, roll, 35-mm) | 32/— |
| Agfacolor Reversal CU 18 (3200° K; roll film, 33-mm.) | 40/— |

### IN ITALY

*Ferrania:*

| | |
|---|---|
| Ferraniacolor Negative D (sheet film, roll, 35-mm.) | 12/— |
| Ferraniacolor T (sheet film, roll, 35-mm.) | —/12 |
| Ferraniacolor Reversal (sheet film, roll, 35-mm.) | 20/— |

### IN JAPAN

*Fuji:*

| | |
|---|---|
| Fuji Color (roll film, 35-mm.) | 10/— |

### IN OTHER COUNTRIES

Check with the consular agent in the States before you start, to find out how much film you can take in and what films are on sale there. If photographic supplies are available at all, you should be able to get one of the above, or an equivalent American film.

## HINTS FOR TRAVELERS

For best results have Kodachrome film processed by a Kodak house, and as soon after exposure as possible. There are five processing laboratories for Kodachrome still film in Europe—but do not have your film mailed across borders if you can help it. International mails are slow and uncertain, and you may lose your film.

If you plan to bring more film into a country than is allowed duty-free, and you expect to visit other countries, have the customs authorities seal up part of your supply in units of 5 or 10 rolls. You will thus avoid paying duty on the unused film, unless you break the seal.

To avoid paying duty at the borders, film should be processed in the country where you buy it. *There is no duty on processed film.*

Before you leave the United States, get a bill of sale, a copy of an insurance policy, or a notarized document, listing all your photographic equipment and supplies. This will come in handy at all borders to prove ownership for import and export.

Film sent to the States for processing should be accompanied by a declaration stating the pictures are for personal, not commercial use; otherwise duty will be imposed.

For information about allowances and duties abroad, get in touch with the nearest Field Service Office of the U.S. Department of Commerce.

Insure your equipment before your start out. The insurance is cheap, but absolutely essential.

## SOME RECOMMENDED FILM-DEVELOPER COMBINATIONS

*Small roll-film tanks; agitation 5 seconds every minute; * 68° F.*

| FILM | ASA** | DEVELOPER | MINUTES |
|---|---|---|---|
| PLUS X | 100/80 | Neofin Blue | 24 |
| PLUS X | 100/80 | Neofin Red | 18 |
| PLUS X | 80/64 | Microdol | 11–13 |
| PLUS X | 125–160D | D 76 | 10–12 |
| PLUS X | 125–160D | D 23 | 12–13 |
| PLUS X | 80–100D | P 60 | 10–12 |
| PLUS X | 125–160D | Promicrol | 7–10 |
| PLUS X | 160–200T | D 23 | 12–13 |
| PLUS X | 200–250T | D 76 | 12 |
| PLUS X | 320–400 | Promicrol | 12–14 |
| PLUS X | 320–400 | Microphen | 13–16 |
| SUPREME | 50/32 | P 60 | 6–9 |
| SUPREME | 50/32 | Finex L | 15 |
| SUPREME | 50/32 | X-33B | 12½ |
| SUPREME | 50/32 | Panthermic 777 | 9 |
| SUPREME | 100/64[a] | X-500 (1:10) | 10–12 |

| FILM | ASA** | DEVELOPER | MINUTES |
|---|---|---|---|
| SUPREME | 80/64 | Neofin$^c$ Red | 24 |
| SUPERPAN PRESS (R) | 250/160$^a$ | X-500 (10:1) | 10–12 |
| ADOX KB 14 | 25/20 | Microdol | 8–10 |
| ADOX KB 14 | 25/20 | D 23 | 8 |
| ADOX KB 14 | 25/20 | Neofin Blue | 12–14 |
| ADOX KB 14 | 25/20 | Finex L | 8 |
| ADOX KB 14 | 25/20 | P 60 | 6–8 |
| ADOX KB 14 | 25/20 | Panthermic 777 | 8½ |
| ADOX KB 14 | 25/20 | D 76 | 7–9 |
| ADOX KB 14 | 25/20 | Promicrol | 7–9 |
| ADOX KB 17 | 80/64 | Neofin Blue | 18–20 |
| ADOX KB 17 | 80/64 | Microdol | 9–11 |
| ADOX KB 17 | 80/64 | Finex L | 7½ |
| ADOX KB 17 | 80/64 | D 76 | 6–8 |
| ADOX KB 17 | 64/40 | P 60 | 8 |
| ADOX KB 17 | 50/32 | P 60 | 7 |
| ADOX KB 21 | 160/125 | Neofin Red | 16 |
| ADOX KB 21 | 160/125 | Neofin Blue | 24 |
| SUPERIOR | 64/40 | Panthermic 777 | 10 |
| ILFORD PAN F | 16/10 | D 76 | 8–9 |
| ILFORD PAN F | 16/10 | Promicrol | 7–9 |
| ILFORD PAN F | 16/10 | P 60 | 6–8 |
| ILFORD PAN F | 16/10 | Neofin Blue | 12–18 |
| ILFORD PAN F | 16/10 | Minicol | 6–8 |
| ILFORD PAN F | 16/10 | Microdol | 8–10 |
| ILFORD FP 3 | 125/100$^a$ | X-500 (1:10) | 10–12 |
| ILFORD FP 3 | 80/64 | Neofin Blue | 25 |
| ILFORD FP 3 | 80/64 | Neofin Red | 16 |
| ILFORD HP 3 | 200/125 | Microdol | 11 |
| ILFORD HP 3 | 200/125 | X-33B | 11 |
| ILFORD HP 3 | 200/125 | Neofin Red | 20 |
| AGFA ISOPAN F (35) | 32/24 | MCM 100 | 10–12 |
| AGFA ISOPAN F (R) | 32/24 | MCM 100 | 12–14 |
| AGFA ISOPAN FF (35) | 12/10 | Promicrol | 7–9 |
| TRI-X | 200/160 | Microdol | 11 |
| TRI-X | 200/160$^b$ | D 76 | 11–13 |
| TRI-X | 200/160 | X-33B | 11 |
| TRI-X | 650–800 | Promicrol | 10–15 |
| TRI-X | 650–800 | Microphen | 12–15 |
| TRI-X | 400–500 | D 23 | 12–13 |
| TRI-X | 400–500 | Clayton P 60 | 12–13 |
| TRI-X (pack) | 200/160 | D 76 (revised time) | 11 |
| TRI-X (pack) | 200/160 | Microdol (revised time) | 11 |
| SX PAN | 650–1000 | D 76 | 12–14 |
| SX PAN | 650–1000 | Promicrol | 12–16 |
| SX PAN | 650–800 | Microphen | 14–16 |
| SX PAN | 400–650 | D 23 | 12–15 |
| SX PAN | 400–500 | Clayton P 60 | 12–14 |
| VERICHROME PAN (828) | 80/64 | Microdol | 10 |
| VERICHROME PAN (828) | 80/64 | D 76 | 8 |
| VERICHROME PAN (R) | 80/64$^b$ | D 76 | 12 |
| VERICHROME PAN (R) | 80/64 | Microdol | 12 |
| VERICHROME PAN (R) | 80/64 | Versatol (1:15) | 9 |

| FILM | ASA** | DEVELOPER | MINUTES |
|---|---|---|---|
| VERICHROME PAN (R) ........ | 100/80 | ....Neofin Blue ............ | 20 |
| VERICHROME PAN (pack) ...... | 80/64 | ....D 76 ................ | 12 |
| VERICHROME PAN (pack) ...... | 80/64 | ....Microdol .............. | 12 |
| VERICHROME PAN (pack) ...... | 80/64 | ....Versatol (1:15) ........ | 10 |
| PANATOMIC X (35) ............ | 40/32 | ....Neofin Blue ............ | 12 |
| PANATOMIC X (35) ............ | 25/20 | ....Microdol .. ............ | 6 |
| PANATOMIC X (35) ............ | 25/20 | ....D 76 (dilute 1:1) ........ | 7 |
| PANATOMIC X (R) ............ | 25/20[b] | ....D 76 ................ | 7 |
| PANATOMIC X (R) ............ | 25/20 | ....P 60 ................ | 5 |
| PANATOMIC X (R) ............ | 40/32 | ...Neofin Red ............ | 18 |
| ROYAL X PAN (sheet, roll film)... | 800/650 | ...DK 50 ................ | 6–8 |
| TRI-X (sheet film) .............. | 200/160 | ...DK 50 ................ | 7 |
| PANATOMIC X (35) ............ | 50–64 | ....X-22[d] ................ | 8–12 |
| ILFORD PAN F ................ | 25–32 | ....X-22[d] ................ | 9–13 |
| ADOX KB 14 .................. | 25–32 | ....X-22[d] ................ | 9–13 |
| PERGRANO ................... | 25–32 | ....X-22[d] ................ | 9–13 |
| ADOX KB 17 .................. | 50–64 | ....X-22[d] ................ | 8–12 |
| PERPANTIC ................... | 50–64 | ....X-22[d] ................ | 8–12 |
| ADOX KB 21 .................. | 160–200 | ...X-22[d] ................ | 13 |

* Except Plux X, Panatomic X, Verichrome Pan, and Tri-X, which should be agitated 5 seconds every 30 seconds.

** These emulsion speeds are not always those suggested by the manufacturer. In some cases they make use of the safety factor provided in the original ASA rating (usually $2\frac{1}{2}$ X); in others, they recognize the emulsion speed increase produced by the developer. The times given are for *normal* contrast.

[a] Read shadow detail, agitate 10 seconds each minute, develop at 70°F.

[b] Fritz Henle suggests doubling this ASA rating to improve quality.

[c] Neofin was originally called *Neodyn* and *Neodin*.

[d] Dilute according to manufacturer's instructions; agitate 10 seconds each minute.

## NEGATIVE CONTRAST CONTROL

*How to get an "ideal" negative with a contrast of 1:30 for normal or No. 2 paper*

| IF SUBJECT CONTRAST IS | READ HIGH LIGHT BY METER, THEN EXPOSE | AND DEVELOP TO GAMMA |
|---|---|---|
| **1:500**<br>Architectural interiors; night scenes | 3-4 times normal | **0.5**<br>Shorten development by 10-25 per cent |
| **1:200**<br>Street scenes; back-lit subjects in daylight | normal | **0.7**<br>Normal development |
| **1:30**<br>Open landscape; front-lit architecture | $\frac{1}{3}$ normal | **0.9**<br>Add $\frac{1}{3}$ to development time |

This table was originally worked out by the Tetenal plant for Neofin and Adox film, based on recommendations by Willi Beutler, inventor of Neofin. It was reprinted, in revised form, by the *Leica News,* and is further revised here for use with other film-developer combinations.

# 9

# *The Picture*

## SEEING IT

There are pictures everywhere. Can you learn to see them, or will you, like Peary's cook, be searching forever for a point of view? The explorer's cook is so perfect a symbol of the unseeing eye, that his story is worth repeating for that reason.

I first heard about him from Ruth Seinfel and her husband Gerald Goode. It seems that a well-meaning friend stumbled on the cook one day and decided that there was a "marvelous story in the man." He had been with Peary through all of his historic adventures—and his point of view was *so* different; he saw it all against the background of food and hungry men. There was at least a *book* in the man, if not a whole series of magazine articles. And since Ruth and Gerald were "literary people" (they wrote stories and got them published), the friend insisted that they must do something about his "find." Ruth was skeptical (she had once been a book-review editor) but out of courtesy to the friend she invited Peary's cook to visit them at Croton.

He came with what he explained were "all his notes." Ruth and Gerald decided that perhaps they had been wrong about the man, invited him to stay for supper, and then took him out to see the local sights. One of these, of course, was the Croton Reservoir. When they got there, they found some other people looking around. This seemed to trouble the cook very much. No sooner did Ruth or Gerry maneuver him over to one interesting vantage point than the cook noticed some people elsewhere looking at something else, and he had to be taken *there* at once to see what the others were seeing. When he got there, the others had in the meantime moved on; so the cook lost interest in that place, wondered out loud about what the others had seen, and then noticed some people off in the distance pointing at something else. Which meant that Ruth and Gerry had to take him there, too. This kept on until Gerry got bored and Ruth got tired; so they took their guest home.

After supper they started checking through his notes. Have you guessed? Yes, his notes *were* complete. On the day, for instance, that the North Pole was discovered, his records showed that he had prepared and the men had eaten "so many pounds of *this* and so many pounds of *that.*" How did the men feel about the discovery, what did they do, what did Peary say? Oh, he wouldn't know about that. *He was just the cook!*

Most of us are "just cooks" when it comes to seeing things around us. We need distant pastures to prove that grass is green; we need far horizons to prove that skylines have beauty; we must travel before we can shake our "picture blindness." But our picture sense *can* be developed, in two ways: (1) by looking at pictures made by others, and (2) by making an imaginative effort to create pictures of our own.

### STUDY PICTURES MADE BY OTHERS

Pore over such picture collections as *U.S. Camera Annual, Photography Annual, International Photography Year Book, British Journal Photographic Almanac,* the *German Photographic Annual,* such magazines as *Photography* of London, *Camera* of Switzerland, *Aperture* of San Francisco, *Photo Magazin* of Germany, *Photorama* of Belgium, *Camera World* and *Modern Camera Magazine* of London, *Leica Fotografie* of Germany, and of course those wonderful American magazines *Popular Photography, U. S. Camera, Camera 35,* and *Modern Photography.* That's one of the best and easiest ways of improving your own picture sense. As you look at each picture try to visualize where the photographer stood, where the light came from, how the picture would have changed if either the camera position or light angle had been altered. Only by making a definite effort to visualize such changes can you begin to learn how to take pictures yourself.[1]

### IMAGINE OBJECTS AS PICTURES

Let your mind create the picture before the camera does. Learn to see every object around you as part of a picture. Place it and light it (in your mind) to best advantage. This exercise in picture control will help you recognize the right conditions when you meet them. It is the most valuable practice you can get as a photographer. And don't worry about whether or not the picture is technically or artistically possible. After you've snapped a couple of dozen *impossible* shots you'll begin to recognize the possible ones on sight. The important thing is to get the practice, mentally and actually. In other words, the best way to learn to take pictures is to take them.

[1] For information about foreign photo magazines write to Rayelle Publications, 76 West Chelten Ave., Philadelphia 44, Pa.

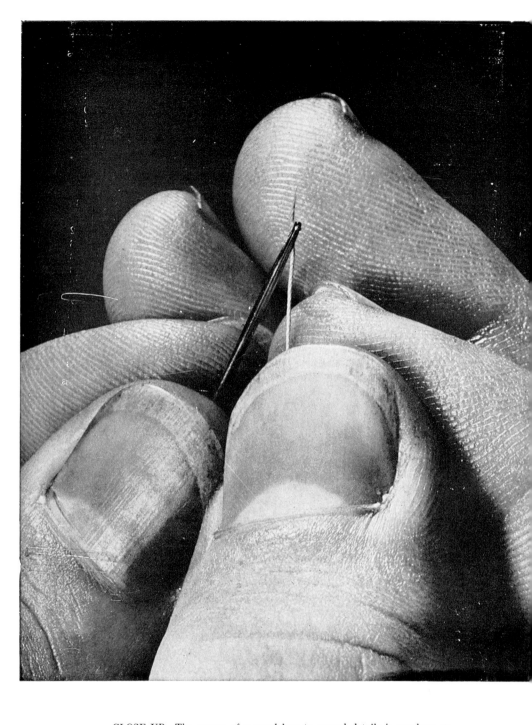

CLOSE-UP. The power of a good lens to record details is nowhere so evident as in a good close-up. This one, by Robert Comport, won first prize in the Industrial and Scientific Class in the 1946 Graflex Photo Contest. Made with 4 x 5 Speed Graphic with three flash bulbs synchronized. Exposure 1/25 second at *f* 32.

ODD ANGLE. This picture taken at Radio City shows how an odd camera angle can be used to achieve striking composition. Such angles, however, should be used only when justified, not just for the sake of distortion without purpose. Made with Rolleiflex, 1/50 at ƒ 16 with yellow filter on Supersensitive Panchromatic film.

**PATTERN.** The most familiar example of this type of picture is the country fence photographed when the shadows are long. Our sample shows a snow-covered waterfront fence and stairway in strong contrasts. Made with Graflex B on Plus X film with G filter, exposure at 1/30, ƒ 11.

**TEXTURE.** The surfaces of objects are often of unusual interest, if properly lighted. The shot below illustrates the effect of sunlight on the side of an old unpainted barn. Rolleicord, at ƒ 16, 1/10, Finopan, developed in MCM 100.

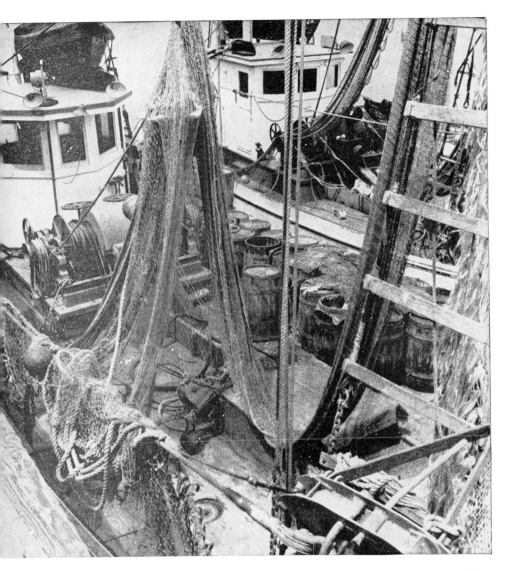

DETAIL. If you can't make an interesting picture of the whole object, let a small part of it symbolize the rest. Our photograph of a scene at Cape Cod illustrates this simple method. Rolleiflex, Plus X, 1/10 at f 16 (faint sun). Film developed in Microdol.

HUMOR. Genuinely humorous photographs are rare and opportunities for taking them do not occur often. But a quick eye and trigger finger can get pictures like this one by Lou Gardner who took it with a 4 x 5 Speed Graphic equipped with a 6-inch, $f$ 3.5 Zeiss Tessar lens stopped down to $f$ 16. He shot at 1/100 second, using a $K^2$ filter.

PEOPLE. Almost any *unposed* photograph of people doing something, or watching things, makes a good picture. Leon Arden made these two. The one above, in Manhattan's Central Park, using a Leica and Plux X film. Exposure was 1/100 at *f* 11. Film developed in Microdol. *Below:* Also a Leica shot, made on Supreme developed in Finex. Exposure was 1/100 at *f* 8. Light yellow filter used each time.

WATER is the most prolific producer of pictures in the world. Whether it's the restless movement of the sea, or the sleek motion of sailing ships, whether it's a busy harbor scene or a sunlit seascape, or a beach and a girl, as in this one by Bruce Downes, you can always be sure of a picture if you're near the water. Made with a Rolleiflex, a yellow-green filter, and Super XX film. Exposure was at 1/100 and $f$ 22, and the film was developed in Microdol.

MOOD. Any arrangement of objects, natural or otherwise, which evokes an emotion (hate, love, joy, fear) or a mood (nostalgia, wanderlust, reverie) is good for a picture. Certainly Leo Mindlin caught a mood in this shot of a man shoveling snow on his sidewalk at night. He used a 3¼ x 4¼ Speed Graphic with a Zeiss Tessar 5¼-inch, ƒ 4.5 lens. The Eastman Ortho film was exposed at 1/5 second with the lens at ƒ 8.

THE SEASONS, I. Take a familiar scene under all sorts of conditions during the year . . . summer, autumn, winter, spring, morning, noon, afternoon, in bright sun, on cloudy days, during rain. This series is titled "Through Four Generations." Taken by Joe Wiener, A.R.P.S., with a Super Ikonta B at ƒ 12, 1/10, with a GR⁵ filter, on Superpan film.

THE SEASONS, II. This is a winter version of "Through Four Generations." The result of this type of photography, if taken from approximately the same point of view each time, will make an extremely interesting series of pictures. Data: Same as I, but taken at $f$ 11, 1/10, with a G$^4$ filter.

THE SEASONS, III. This is a third version of "Through Four Generations." Same as I but taken on Panatomic at $f$ 18, ½, with a GR⁵ filter.

THE SEASONS, IV. This is the last in the series. Same as I, but taken at $f$ 11, 1/2, with a red filter, on Superpan. All four were taken by Joe Wiener, A.R.P.S., from 1937 to 1939, and illustrate perfectly how effective this type of photography can be.

FRAME. The success of many pictures depends on the way they are framed. Arches, doorways, branches, windows—these are just a few ways to enclose a scene to make a picture. This one appeared in the Rolleiflex Annual. Super XX film, K² filter, 1/100 at ƒ 16.

## HOW TO RECOGNIZE A PICTURE

Almost anything which makes you want to stop and look has the makings of a picture. It may be the representation of a person, a place, or an object. Whether it's a good picture or a bad one depends, of course, on what you do with it. The secret of most successful pictures is *simplicity*—the shearing away of everything that does not help the mood or idea you're trying to convey. We'll go into this, later, when we take up *the arrangement* of the picture. The difference between a *snapshot* and a *picture* is that one is of interest only to ourselves, as a simple record of experience, while the other serves to recreate in others the feeling or sensation we had when we took it. In other words, the snapshot is *personal;* the picture, *universal.* Take, for instance, the snapshot of some rowboats (see page 169) that helps *me* remember a certain lake which I visited one summer. It has no meaning for anyone but myself. Those rowboats, however, could be made into a *picture,* if taken in another way.

Here are some other types of photographs that have good picture quality (see pages 150-162):

1. *Close-up.* The power of a good lens to record details is nowhere so evident as in a close-up. This one won first prize in the Industrial and Scientific Class in the 1946 Graflex Photo Contest.

2. *Odd angle.* This picture taken at Radio City shows how an odd camera angle can be used to achieve striking composition. Such angles should be used only when justified, not just for the sake of distortion without purpose.

3. *Pattern.* The most familiar example of this type of picture is the country fence photographed when the shadows are long. Our sample shows a snow-covered waterfront fence and stairway in strong contrasts.

4. *Texture.* The surface of objects are of unusual interest, if properly lighted. Our illustration shows the effect of sunlight on an old barn.

5. *Detail.* If you can't make an interesting picture out of the whole object, let a small part of it symbolize the rest. Here we show a waterfront scene on one of the wharves in Provincetown at Cape Cod.

6. *Humor.* Genuinely humorous photographs are rare and opportunities for taking them do not occur often. But a quick eye and trigger finger can get pictures like this of baby and intruder.

7. *People.* Almost any *unposed* photograph of people doing something, or watching things, makes a good picture. Two are shown on page 155.

8. *Water* is the most prolific producer of pictures in the world. Whether it's the restless movement of the sea, or the sleek motion of sailing ships, whether it's a busy harbor scene or sunlit seascape, or a beach and a girl,

you can always be sure of a picture if you are anywhere near the water.

9. *Mood*. Any arrangement of objects, natural or otherwise, which evokes an emotion (hate, love, joy, fear) or a mood (nostalgia, wanderlust, revery) is good for a picture. The photograph of the man shoveling snow on a winter's night is an example of such a picture.

10. *The seasons*. Take a familiar scene under all sorts of conditions during the year: summer, autumn, winter, spring, morning, noon, afternoon, in bright sun, on cloudy days, during rain. The result, if taken from approximately the same point of view each time, will make an extraordinarily interesting series of pictures. The photographs taken by Joe Wiener, A.R.P.S., illustrate perfectly how effective this can be.

11. *Frame*. The success of many pictures depends on the way they are framed. Arches, doorways, branches, window frames—these are just a few ways to enclose our scene to make a picture. Here we show a youngster playing hide-and-seek at the base of Triborough Bridge in New York.

## WHEN THERE AREN'T ANY PICTURES

The usual complaint of most amateurs is that there are no pictures around where they happen to be. The pictures, according to them, are where the other fellows are. This is nonsense. There are pictures everywhere. But you've got to open your eyes and look. I was discussing this with a young photographer one Saturday afternoon at Jones Beach and a remark he made led to a bet, the results of which I'll show you in just a moment. He said: "Aw, that's a lot of bunk. How are you going to make a picture out of a sandy waste like this?" I bet him that I could take at least five pictures within twenty-five feet of where we sat. I took a set of five. Turn to pages 166-167 where four of the pictures are reproduced; I don't claim that these are works of art. They're far from that. But they *are* pictures, and he saw absolutely none.

## ARRANGING IT

The planning and placing of the various parts of a picture in such a way that they satisfy the eye is the function of *composition*. Some amateurs think they can do without it, but what they get instead is merely *bad composition*. While a picture may accidentally happen to be well composed though the photographer has given its composition no thought at all, it is dangerous (provided, of course, you care about the impression your picture makes on others) to let things take their course in that way.

The rules of composition are the *fruit* of all the good pictures that have ever been created. In other words, the pictures came first and then the rules were devised to explain why the pictures were good to look at. If we once realize this simple fact we can use the rules without getting hurt, or without tying ourselves up in knots. One of the rules, for instance, says that we must never place the main object of interest in the dead center of the picture space. It's a good rule most of the time. But there are many, many exceptions. Some of the most exquisite pictures ever made by Alfred Stieglitz flout this law entirely. The eye, Mr. Stieglitz pointed out, sees everything in dead center. Why, he asked, shouldn't the camera?

## A PICTURE OF WHAT?

A large proportion of the photographs taken by amateurs fail because they forget one thing. That thing is expressed in the question above. Every picture, if it really be one, must be a representation of *something*. Does this sound too simple and elementary? Does it seem too obvious to be worth mentioning? It's nothing of the kind! The fact is that this rule, one of the most important, is a rule honored more often in the breach than in the observance. The *something* may be an *egg* or a *crowd*, a *boy* or a *box;* it may even be an abstract like *jealousy*, or *romance*, or *power*. The subject doesn't matter. What *is* important, though, is that the picture has to show that thing, whether it's an idea, an object, or an emotion. If it's power you're trying to express, don't clutter up the picture with fine samples of *texture* which steal the show and make you forget all about the idea of power. If it's *boy* you're showing, make sure that the things in back of him aren't more attractive, larger, clearer.

## KEEP IT SIMPLE

No picture should have more than one subject. If it's *tree* you want to show, be sure that it doesn't unintentionally become *landscape with heavy clouds and little barn plus tree*. If it's *dog* you want to show, be sure it doesn't turn out to be *two people talking, with dog on leash held by man*.

## GET CLOSER

The difference between a picture and a snapshot is often no more than the distance between the camera and the object. See the two views shown on page 168.

## FIND THE BEST POINT OF VIEW

The position from which you see a thing is often as important as the thing itself. The rowboats on page 169, for instance, looked like noth-

WHERE THERE AREN'T ANY PICTURES, I and II. The four in this series were all taken, incidentally, with the Contax and Sonnar $f$ 1.5 at $f$ 8 to $f$ 11, 1/125 to 1/250 with a light green filter, on Superpan Supreme developed in Edwal 12.

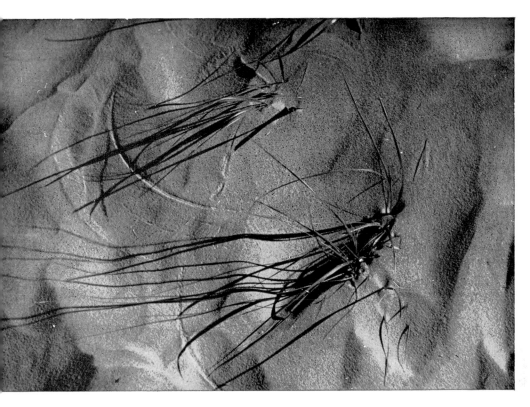

WHERE THERE AREN'T ANY PICTURES, III and IV.

Illustrating "Get Closer." The shot at the right shows the entire scene as most probably saw it; the one at the bottom is a picture of the same and shows what can be done to improve the picture quality of the scene by moving in toward the object, angling it a bit differently, and trimming away all extraneous matter. Both taken with Speed Graphic, 4 x 5, and Plasmat lens at $f$ 8, 1/100, with $K^2$ filter, on Isopan developed in Glycin.

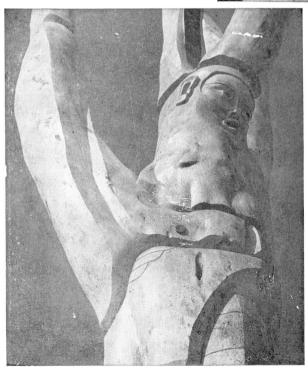

THE SAME PLACE; THE SAME TIME. *Above*: A snapshot of a vacation memory, which has no meaning for anyone but myself. *Below*: a *picture* of the same. Both taken with Contax, Elmar wide-angle lens, at f 11, 1/25, on Plenachrome, developed in Ansco 17.

ing at all when seen from shore; looked at from above or from the dock they make a real picture. The moral is to move around and about your subject, look at it from every conceivable angle until you find an arrangement of object-against-background that looks pleasing. This is illustrated in the four reproductions of the lighthouse at Digby, Nova Scotia, on page 171.

## BALANCE

Large and small objects can be balanced in a picture by use of the principle of the fulcrum. A large object in the foreground, for instance, can be balanced by a small object in the distance, just as a see-saw can be evened up if two children of unequal weights are so placed that the heavier child is nearer the fulcrum, and the lighter child is moved further out. In perspective this balancing is simple, since it means that the heavier objects are placed nearer the viewer and the lighter objects farther away. At other times it must be remembered that the nearer an object is to the picture edge, the more weight it carries; thus a comparatively small object near the right or left edge can balance quite a large object near the center.

## LINE

Every line in a picture has a special meaning. *Straight lines,* for instance, suggest solidity, strength, vigor; *curved lines* suggest beauty, softness, grace. Every good picture contains a blend of both straight and curved lines, with one definitely predominating. *Vertical lines* suggest power, hope, courage; *horizontal lines* suggest quietude, balance, rest. *Diagonal lines* suggest speed, motion, activity. *Zigzag lines* are the most active; *S-shaped curves* the most graceful. Two lines *crossing* each other suggest violent action; two lines running parallel to each other (one repeating the pattern of the other) suggest sympathy, understanding, acceptance. Such lines are often used to emphasize the main line form.

## A FEW HINTS ON COMPOSITION

Here are a few *do's* and *don'ts* culled from the words of the masters, the men and women whose work has consistently "crashed" the big salons, and who have in lectures, in conversation, or in print, tried to reveal the secrets of how they do it. Just as every good photographer has a pet developer formula, so he has a set of rules which help him arrange his pictures. At least that's what they all say. I suspect, myself, that most of them invent the rules to explain the miracle of their good pictures. However, since they all feel that these rules have really helped them, here

THE LIGHTHOUSE AT DIGBY, NOVA SCOTIA. Illustrating "Point of View." These shots illustrate the importance of searching out the best point of view. The print at the lower right is the one finally used; it was the last negative taken. Taken with a Rolleicord, at $f$ 16, 1/25, with green filter, on Finopan developed in Edwal 12. Data the same for the other prints.

they are for what they are worth. My advice is to take them or leave them alone without feeling virtuous or guilty no matter which you decide to do.

1. Don't place the main object at dead center. (Unless you're a genius, that is, as Alfred Stieglitz was.)

2. Keep the main object away from the outside edges of the picture area.

3. Arrange your light and shade so that the greatest contrast falls at the point of greatest interest.

4. Divide the picture space into thirds, horizontally and vertically, draw imaginary lines separating these portions. Where the lines cross are four magical points near which the main or subsidiary objects should be placed.

5. The closer an object is to dead center, the less it catches the eye; the nearer the edge, the more it attracts.

6. Lines intersecting at angles draw the eye; the nearer the angle is to a right angle, the stronger the pull.

7. Parallel lines that run across a picture area tend to carry the eye right out of the picture.

8. For greatest interest divide the picture area into *unequal* divisions; do the same with the area around the main object.

9. Don't include too much in the picture. Artists rarely show more on a canvas than can be seen from an angle of view of about 30 to 40 degrees. Wide-angle pictures, with an angle of view of between 80 to 100 degrees seem unreal for that reason. The eye has an angle of view of about 50 degrees.

10. If the object doesn't look interesting when photographed head on, try taking it from an angle. This applies to buildings as well as people, or to objects as well as subjects.

11. Everything in the picture must be in some sort of harmony with the main idea or object. A vase of flowers and a kippered herring, for example, would not be in harmony.

12. Never let a line cut your picture exactly in half, either horizontally or vertically.

13. Never let an uninterrupted line run parallel to any side of your picture.

14. Eliminate useless foreground or sky.

15. Remember that every spot in the picture attracts the eye; the force of this attraction depends on the size of the spot, its shape, its position. and the contrast it creates with its surroundings.

16. The main object should be the most conspicuous by size, contrast, or position.

17. The various elements of a picture should be so arranged that the eye is led in orderly progression from one element to another, resting longest on the principal object.

18. The skyline should never be in the center of the picture; place it about a third of the way from either the top or bottom.

19. The eye naturally follows light. Glancing across a picture it goes from the dark areas to the light ones. A white spot on a black background pulls the eye more than a black spot on a white background. And a *small* white spot on a dark background pulls more than a large white spot on the same background.

20. If there are people in the picture, give them plenty of room to move about in, or they will seem cramped.

21. If the picture shows people moving, leave more space in front than behind them. Similarly, leave more room in the direction in which people are facing or looking.

22. If the picture seems spotty, cover each spot in turn with a finger and notice what this does to the picture. If this improves it, remove or subdue the spot. Do this to all the offending spots.

23. Light and dark masses in a picture should always be unequal.

24. A continuous series of spots acts like a line.

25. Small spots, either light or dark, away from the principal object, only tend to distract the eye. The same is true for spots of unusual shape, or those placed in corners.

26. Long lines that run right out of the picture should be interrupted before they leave the picture area. This will help to keep the eye within the picture.

27. Arrange the pattern of the picture so that the eye enters from the lower left or right hand corner.

28. To test the composition of any picture, turn it upside down.

29. Finally, keep in mind what St. Exupéry, that extraordinary author-artist-aviator said in *Wind, Sand and Stars:* "It seems that perfection is attained not when there is nothing more to add, but when there is nothing more to take away."

## OUTDOORS

There are three things to watch out for: *bald skies, flat lighting,* and *incorrect exposure.* (1) Bald skies are easily corrected by the use of an appropriate filter, (see ALL ABOUT FILTERS) or by the use of one of the new films (like Dupont Superior I) which darken the skies *without* the use of any filter. Don't forget that overexposure will cancel out the effect of a filter, while a slight underexposure will take the place of one. (2)

CANDLE PATH, I. On this page and on the next are two of Joe
Wiener's pictures. The one above shows the scene as he originally
saw it. He liked the general arrangement of the objects, but was
disappointed in the lighting. Taken with Super Ikomat B at $f$ 8,
1/25, on Panatomic X developed in X 33. An orange filter was used.

CANDLE PATH, II. This is what Joe Wiener saw when he came back later. Taken at *f* 14, 1/10, using a green filter, on Panatomic X developed in X 33.

Flat lighting can be overcome by avoiding the middle of the day for photography. Sometimes we can't wait all day to find out when, or if, the light will be better, and the Sun Direction Indicator, shown in *Fig. 47,*

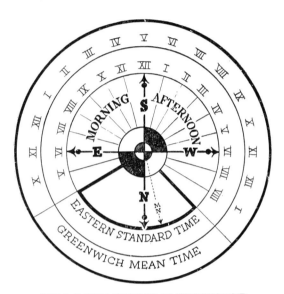

## SUN DIRECTION INDICATOR

FIG. 47. AN AID TO OUTDOOR PHOTOGRAPHY

is a simple device which helps to shorten this waiting time by indicating the position of the sun, hour by hour, in advance. We are indebted for the idea to Mr. George H. Sewell, A. R. P. S., and to the *Miniature Camera World* of London.

The directions for its use are very simple. Place it horizontally with the line marked S facing *true south.* The *direction* of sunlight at any other hour can now be predicted. At 6 P.M., Eastern Standard Time, for instance, the sun will be shining from due west, while at 9 A.M., it will be shining from the southeast.

To find true south hold the disc horizontally and place a match or toothpick vertically with its foot resting on the figure which represents the hour at that time. Move the dial until the shadow of the match falls along the radial line which joins the hour and the center of the dial. XII noon will then be facing due south.

If the sun is not out when you make the reading, you can orientate the dial with a compass, but remember that the needle points to the *magnetic* north and must be corrected. The line marked MN should be placed parallel with the needle.

Since the noon sun is directly overhead, calculating the *height* of the sun at other times of the day should present no problem to anyone familiar with the use of a protractor. *Fig. 10* would also be helpful in this connection.

One other point. The differences in standard time across the country have to be taken into account. Eastern Standard and Greenwich Times are shown on the dial. Daylight Saving Time is one hour more advanced than Eastern Standard; Central Standard, six hours less advanced than Greenwich; Mountain Standard, seven hours less advanced than Greenwich; and, Pacific Standard, eight hours less advanced than Greenwich.

(3) The *best* way to avoid incorrect exposure is to use an electric exposure meter like the Weston or the General Electric. See FILM AND EXPOSURE. The danger with most outdoor shots, especially landscapes and distant shots, is *overexposure*. For distant scenes, Weston recommends that you give one half the regular exposure. For a normal-speed film like Plus X, used outdoors in bright sun during midsummer, the exposure would be about $f$ 16, 1/100, with a light yellow ($K^1$) filter or no filter at all. For close-ups under the same conditions, the exposure might be $f$ 11, 1/100.

## A VITAL ACCESSORY

If you really want your lens to produce sharp, brilliant pictures, it is absolutely necessary for you to get a good *sunshade*. If you doubt this, stand near a window with the light coming from your left or right side and look at the opposite wall. Now cup your eye with your hand and notice the difference it makes. Your lens reacts in the same way. For better pictures, use a sunshade to cut out all stray light and haze. With a sunshade you can safely take pictures with the light almost at an angle of 30 degrees facing the camera. You can thus get all the interesting effects produced by side and front lighting, without any of the attendant dangers. Be sure the shade is large enough for your particular lens; if it isn't, the corners of the picture will be cut off, especially when you use the sunshade *over* a filter. If you're worried about the space it will take up, get one of those that folds flat. Most photographic dealers stock a variety of sunshades at prices to suit any purse.

## MOUNTAIN SCENES

There's always more light than you think, with overexposure almost inevitably the result. Distant views, above sea level, usually require only about 1/4 as much exposure as the average, normal subject. When you get to about 5000 feet you can cut this down to 1/8 as much exposure. Another reason to cut exposure for such scenes is that they are usually flat

and therefore need more developing time to bolster contrast. To increase
developing time we must cut down on the exposure.

The best time to take mountain scenes is when the shadows are long.
When there are clouds, or if there is haze, shoot across the direction of
the sunlight and you'll get some excellent pictures. Panchromatic film
and either the Aero or K series of filters are recommended for this use.
The orange (G) filter can also be used if a darker sky is wanted. If rocks
are an important part of the picture, use a light green filter such as the
$X^1$. This restrains the reds and makes the rocks print darker. With
Plus X and an ultraviolet or light yellow filter, the correct exposure for
a mountain scene on a bright summer day would be about $f$ 11, 1/300. If
the foreground were important the exposure would be about $f$ 8, 1/50 or
1/100.

### LANDSCAPES

Besides the flat skies mentioned above, another important factor in
pictures of this type is the matter of *scale* or relative size. The introduction of a foreground object, such as a person, a tree or a house, will help
establish the scale while it enhances the effect of perspective.

Don't try to get *everything* sharp in your landscapes. The eye doesn't
see things that way so there's no need to force the camera to do it. Distant objects should look somewhat softer than foreground objects. And
watch the foreground particularly: It should be somewhat dark, and not
too fussed up with eye-catching details.

*Fig. 48* illustrates various positions of camera and sun with respect to
the landscape. The heavy horizontal lines in the diagrams represent the

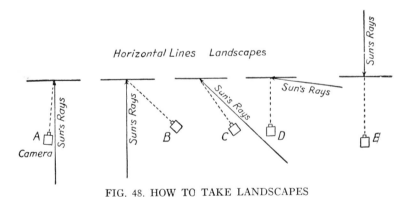

FIG. 48. HOW TO TAKE LANDSCAPES

landscape or view, the arrows the rays from the sun and the broken lines
the direction in which the camera is pointing. In the position shown at *A*
the sun will pass over your head or shoulder in the same direction that

you are pointing your camera, and this will tend to give you a rather flat picture. If you will stand in the position shown at *B* or *C* you will get one that has considerably more *snap* in it.

By standing in the position shown at *D* so that the sun shines on the view from one side, especially when it is low and near its setting time, you can get some very soft, pleasing effects. It is never good practice for a beginner to stand at the point shown at *E,* with the sun shining from the opposite side, for while some striking effects can be got in this way, unless you are an expert you will more than likely *fog the film.*

There are two other things for you to remember when you are taking a landscape, especially if there is a road or a building in it, and that is (1) not to take a direct front view of it as shown by *A* in *Fig. 49,* or your pic-

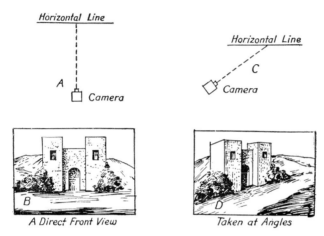

FIG. 49. HOW TO GET LINEAR PERSPECTIVE

ture will look like *B*; instead take it at an angle as shown by *C* when your picture will look like *D.*

When you stand directly in front of the view, the lines of the road will run parallel with the bottom of the picture, which will give it a mathematical appearance that is not at all pleasing to the eye. On the other hand, when you take the picture at an angle to the view, the road shows *linear perspective,* as it is called; the effect of distance is improved; and the result takes on the aspect of a work of art. And (2) do not have the building, or other chief object in the view, come right in the center of the film but to one side or the other of it, as this also tends to enhance its artistic effect.

## ARCHITECTURE

The main problem here is what to do about those *converging verticals* (they make tall buildings topple or look like pyramids) which appear whenever we tilt the camera up to include all of a structure. To make a picture of a high building, or other architectural or engineering work, and keep the vertical lines straight, that is to have the *plane perspective* of it true, you must use a view camera with a swing-back; if you have to take it in a place where you must stand up close to it, which frequently happens where it is hemmed in by other buildings, you will have to use a wide-angle lens.

To understand how the *swing-back* of a camera keeps the vertical lines of a building straight on a plate, or film, let us first see how a camera whose front and back are fixed parallel with each other acts when it is held in a horizontal position, as shown by *A* in *Fig. 50*. In this case, the upper part of the building will be cut off, as the diagram *B* clearly shows.

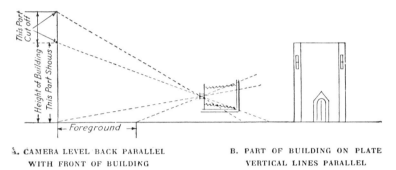

A. CAMERA LEVEL BACK PARALLEL          B. PART OF BUILDING ON PLATE
   WITH FRONT OF BUILDING               VERTICAL LINES PARALLEL

FIG. 50. WHEN THE CAMERA HAS NO SWING-BACK

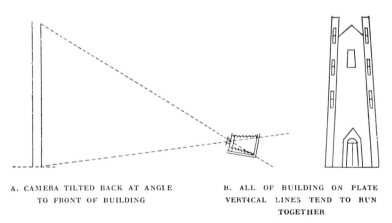

A. CAMERA TILTED BACK AT ANGLE          B. ALL OF BUILDING ON PLATE
   TO FRONT OF BUILDING                  VERTICAL LINES TEND TO RUN
                                          TOGETHER

FIG. 51. WHEN THE CAMERA HAS NO SWING-BACK

Now if you tilt the camera up, as shown at *A* in *Fig. 51*, so that all of the building comes on the screen, as the diagram *B* shows, then the vertical lines will converge at the top. To get all of the building to show on the screen and still keep the vertical lines of it parallel with each other.

the front of the camera must be tilted up and the back of it to which the screen is fixed must remain in a vertical plane as shown at *A* in *Fig. 52.* The diagram *B* shows how the rays of light pass from the building to the screen.

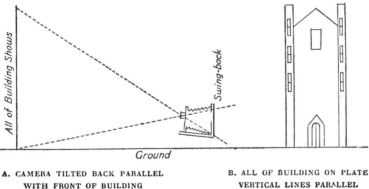

A. CAMERA TILTED BACK PARALLEL
WITH FRONT OF BUILDING

B. ALL OF BUILDING ON PLATE
VERTICAL LINES PARALLEL

FIG. 52. WHEN THE SWING-BACK IS USED

The reason a *wide-angle lens* must be used when you stand close to a building to take a picture of it is (as its name indicates) that it covers a wider angle of the view than an ordinary lens, and, in consequence, has a shorter focal length.

As explained in ALL ABOUT THE LENS, the components of a wide-angle lens have a greater curvature than those of the regulation rectilinear or anastigmat view lens and, further, they are set closer together. This allows more rays of light that are at a wider angle from the optic axis of

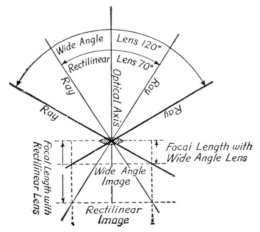

FIG. 53. WHY A WIDE-ANGLE LENS IS USED

Broken lines show camera; light lines show angle and focus with rectilinear lens; heavy lines, angle and focus with wide-angle lens.

the lens to pass through it than through the other kind, as the diagram in *Fig. 53* shows, and it also shows at a glance why a wide-angle lens has a shorter focal length than the regulation lens that covers the same size plate. It is not wise, however, to use a wide-angle lens where one of ordinary focus will do the work.

## About the Lighting

In taking a picture of a building, you should have either a bright sunny day when the play of light on it and the shadows cast by parts of it make it stand out boldly in relief, or else you should have a bright day when the sky is full of silvery clouds which diffuse the light, as this gives a softer and more artistic effect without sacrificing any of the sharp detail. The best lighting is from the side; front lighting is too flat.

## About the Best Position

Of course, the best position from which to take a picture is one that shows the interesting sides of the subject; but the exact position you choose depends chiefly on (1) the proximity of the other structures that surround it, (2) the angle that shows it to the best advantage, and (3) your conception of what will make the most interesting picture.

The first feature is the one that very often dominates the other two, but assuming that you can take the picture from whatever angle you desire, then, in general, it is better not to make a direct front view of it, but to take it so that the front and a side are both included, as this gives it a sense of perspective that makes for solidity. Usually, the best angle at which to place the camera is about thirty degrees from the longitudinal axis of the structure, since this shows a little more of the front and a little less of the side than one made at forty-five degrees. If the position taken is less than thirty degrees, the foreshortening of the side causes a more or less squatty appearance. The diagram shown in *Fig. 54* clearly indicates the meaning of this.

Many photographers point out that the picture should be taken on a level with that of the eye, that is to say, at a height of about five feet, for the reason that architects design their works to be viewed normally from this point. But it seems to me that this does not by any means always follow, and pictures taken from considerably higher levels often show up much better than those made at normal levels, and still have a perfectly natural look.

Now one more thing before we leave the question of position, and that is, get, if you possibly can, the same amount of foreground, or nearly so, in the picture as you would have if you were simply looking at it. When you look at a building, as for instance an old-world cathedral, to see the beauty of it, you have to stand some little distance away and this gives

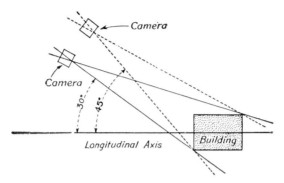

FIG. 54. HOW POSITION AFFECTS THE VIEW

enough foreground to show it up to the best advantage; and because the eye is accustomed to looking at architectural subjects in this way you should have it in the picture for the same reason.

## Focusing the Image

When you have set up the camera in the position where it shows the building the way you want it both from the lighting and perspective points of view, the next thing is to focus the image. A view camera that focuses either from the front or back is the best for architectural subjects, and it must have a very fine ground-glass screen so that you can see just what you are getting in.

Use the largest size of stop, and focus the image on the screen as sharp as you can get it; when you have done this, use a smaller stop and then make a properly timed exposure. And don't forget that where you have to use the swing-back, the farther the camera is tilted up the smaller the stop must be to make all of the parts of it sharp.

### SNOW SCENES

If shadow detail is important, always give twice the exposure indicated by a photoelectric exposure meter. The light is tricky, and the tendency is to underexpose when using a meter. However, if the highlights are what you are most interested in, expose just for them in the usual way. The shadows will go black, of course, but you'll get what you want in the print. Remember that snow shadows are blue. To darken them use a yellow filter. The best snow pictures are made in bright sunlight early in the morning or late in the afternoon. Ortho film (such as Verichrome or Plenachrome) is recommended. For unusual effects try an orange or red filter with pan film.

Before putting the camera away, after you've been out on a snow-picture binge, be sure to let the moisture caused by condensation evaporate from the lens as well as the camera body. Let the camera stand awhile indoors before you pack it up.

### SEASCAPES

The best shutter speed, to prevent blur without freezing all movement, is 1/100 second. To capture interesting wave patterns it is necessary that the photographer be above beach level. He can accomplish this from the deck of a boat or from the end of a pier.

### CLOUD STUDIES

Stop down to $f$ 11 or $f$ 16, use a yellow-green $(K^2)$ or orange $(G)$ filter, a shutter speed of between 1/50 and 1/100, and a film with an ASA Index rating of between 25 and 64. Do not overdevelop the film and print it on a normal paper.

## INDOORS

You can, of course, take *interiors,* which means the views of rooms and halls of buildings, with a box or folding camera fitted with an ordinary lens, by mounting it on a tripod and exposing the film for the necessary length of time, but you will probably not be able to get much more than a wall, or a corner, unless the room is a very long one; or you may have to take it from an adjoining room, as the lens has too long a focal length.

This untoward condition of affairs can be bettered to a considerable extent by slipping a *supplementary wide-angle lens* on the end of the barrel of the lens of your folding camera. To make interiors to the best advantage, however, you must have a view camera with a *drop-bed,* if it focuses in front, and then use a wide-angle lens with it.

### WHAT TO GET IN

A picture of a room, or the rooms, of a home, be it in a log cabin or in a mansion, makes the strongest kind of an appeal to the emotions, but most beginners spoil the "homey" atmosphere by trying to show too much furniture. The first thing to do is to look the room over and see from just what position it will make the best picture, and in doing this you will be guided to a very considerable extent by the windows that light it.

Now instead of putting in more pieces of furniture and the like, take away all you can without making it lose its homey aspect; this done, have some one object as the point of interest, such as an armchair, a table, or a fireplace, but be careful not to get the movable pieces of furniture too close to the camera or they will take on a distorted perspective. Finally have a smaller object or two, such as a book, or a mandolin, or a vase of flowers, or a statuette, on the table to lend a personal touch, and you are ready then to look after the lighting of the subject.

Since interiors usually require time exposures, it is better not to try to have persons or animals in the room. The better way to get a picture with life in it, is to take it by artificial light (either *flood* or *flash*). An inexpensive lighting unit to use for this purpose (or for any other purpose where artificial light is required) is the Eastman Kodaflector. It consists of one folding collapsible stand, with a combination clamp and swivel top, two special reflectors and angled rods, two connecting electric cords attached to sockets. All this folds flat into one easy-to-carry cardboard box. Normally this unit is designed for use with No. 1 photoflood lamps. However, by the use of a pair of inexpensive adaptors, the No. 2 photofloods can also be used. There are also photoflood bulbs with built-in reflectors.

In photographing the interiors of public buildings, churches, etc., never have the end of an arch, or the base of a pillar, cut off if you can possibly help it. The artistic effect is very much brightened by having a pillar come close to the edge of the picture. In taking a picture of a long hall, it is better to set the camera a little out of the middle, as looking down it at a slight angle increases the sense of perspective.

## HOW TO CONTROL THE LIGHTING

The difference between a good and a poor picture of an interior is largely a matter of the way it is lighted. Since rooms and other interiors are usually lighted by windows, it is often quite difficult to take pictures of them from the exact position you would like. Always try to have the windows either at the back or at the side of your camera, for if they are directly in front, *halation,* that is, the spreading of the high lights into the shadows, is almost bound to occur, and, of course, this spoils the effect of the picture.

Where windows at the side of the camera are to show in the picture, they should be screened with muslin, and by resorting to this expedient and raising or lowering the shades of other windows you can control the lighting within certain limits. Where there are windows directly in front

of the camera, you can get much better results by taking the picture **on**
**a** bright day when the sun is shaded by clouds.

### HOW TO FOCUS INTERIORS

In taking interiors it is usually quite difficult to see the image on the
ground glass bright enough to focus it sharply. There are two ways to get
around this difficulty. First, keep your head under the focusing cloth long
enough so that you can see the object you are focusing on; or, second,
light a lamp and stand it on, or in a line with, the object you want to focus
sharply and then focus on that. In either case, after you have focused the
image as sharply as you can with the largest stop, use a smaller stop to
make the exposure, then everything in the view will be sharp. It is not,
however, good practice to use too small a stop (*diffraction!*).

A simple but effective technique for taking interiors is to focus at about
$\frac{1}{3}$ of the total distance to be covered with the lens wide open (if farthest
spot is 25 feet, focus at 8 feet). Then stop lens down to about $f\,32$.

### ABOUT MAKING THE EXPOSURE

While it is not absolutely necessary to use superspeed plates or films
for taking pictures of interiors, still it is a good scheme to do so, as it cuts
down the time of exposure somewhat. The films recommended are Tri-X,
Super Hypan, Isopan Record, Plus X, Royal X Pan, or Ilford HPS
and HP3.

The exact time of exposure, of course, depends on the way the room is
lighted. Shadows in interior views usually come out very much deeper
in the finished picture than they appear on the ground glass, so that, in
the last analysis, the only sure guide to the time to give it is the exposure
meter. In using it for interior work, take the deepest shadow as the place
to test the time, if there is detail there that you want to show. (See FILM
AND EXPOSURE for a simple method of using the diaphragm in conjunction with the ground glass as an exposure meter for indoor pictures.)

*Painting with light.* A useful technique for illuminating interiors. The
flood light is held in the hand and either swung in a circle (which tends to
produce a shadowless light) or moved around to even out the dark and
light areas or produce accents.

### THE KIND OF LIGHT TO USE

Besides the Kodaflector unit described above, you can get some
clamp-on reflectors as shown in *Fig. 55*. These sell for two or three dollars

and can be had with either a 10-inch aluminum reflector for the No. 1 photofloods, or an 11-inch reflector for the No. 2 photofloods.

FIG. 55. A CLAMP-ON REFLECTOR FOR PHOTOFLOODS

Another very useful light source is the spotlight. *Fig. 56,* below, shows a new type spot designed for amateur use. It is sturdily and scientifically built (in America); is equipped with a Fresnel lens.

FIG. 56. THE F.R. SPOTLIGHT

Later you might investigate the combinations that use the famous T20 projection bulbs. These are much better than photofloods, last longer (avoiding the nuisance of frequent burn-outs) give a more constant light of better color, but cost more than photofloods and must be burned base down in special reflectors. The reflectors for the 500-watt T20 bulbs *can* be used for photofloods, but not vice versa.

## NIGHT PHOTOGRAPHY

Outdoors at night you need a good strong tripod as well as a cable release for your camera. These are necessary to avoid vibration, since night exposures are usually long ones. With super-sensitive panchromatic films like Superpan Press, or Tri-X, the following suggested exposures will serve as a starting point for testing: with the diaphragm open to about ƒ 4, a reasonably well-lit scene should be given about 10 seconds (if you can't see your watch in the dark count rapidly to 30); poorly lighted street scenes get about 20 seconds (or count rapidly to 60); badly lighted scenes get anywhere from 35 seconds to 5 minutes (or count from 100 to whatever time span you guess is right). Since an exposure meter is useless under such conditions, you'll simply have to try out about a dozen shots to get the hang of it. With Plus X, Supreme, or Verichrome Pan the above exposures should be doubled.

Some of the best night scenes outdoors, in the autumn and fall, are taken during those few minutes between dusk and night when the shapes of things are still illuminated by a sort of faint afterglow. The impression made on the negative at this time is just strong enough to capture the full beauty of the large masses. Then the artificial lights begin to go on, adding a sparkle to the scene. Paul J. Woolf uses this method to produce his remarkable night shots. He has developed an uncanny ability to judge the precise moment when to start his exposures so that he registers both the shapes and the lights. His picture, *Skyscrapers by Night* (page 189) is an excellent example of this technique. He uses a view camera and a Dagor lens for most of his pictures. Sometimes he will also use his Rolleiflex for this purpose. He prefers supersensitive panchromatic films, and the developing technique recommended by the manufacturer.

## CAUTIONS

(1) Use a lens hood at all times to keep stray light out of the lens. (2) Protect the lens against any naked lights that happen to be within range. (3) Use the cable release instead of the finger release and avoid jarring the camera. (4) Make sure your tripod is sturdy and reliable. (5) Shield the lens from car headlights or roving spotlights by covering the lens with your hand or a card until the light has moved on, and then continue with your exposure. (6) It's a good idea to have a little pocket flashlight with you to check adjustments. (7) If there's a strong wind shield the camera with your body.

## DEVELOPING AND PRINTING OUTDOOR NIGHT PICTURES

Since contrast is extreme, use a soft working developer like Ansco 17 or D-76; or you might try that excellent developer for night work devised by M. U. Wallach, author of *How to Take Pictures at Night.* You'll find this formula (W 80) in the chapter on developing. Also good for this purpose is the Windisch formula for a Compensating Developer given later in the section, *Halation and How to Prevent It,* of chapter 14.

Paul J. Woolf's picture, SKYSCRAPERS BY NIGHT, is an excellent example of a techniq
based on taking pictures at just the right moment between dusk and night. Notice how t
sky silhouettes the buildings and how the sky light separates the buildings from one anoth

### A VALUABLE HINT

Sometimes in taking outdoor night pictures we are bothered by objects moving back and forth in front of the camera. By using a small opening, such as $f$ 16 to $f$ 32, these moving objects will not show up at all, unless they are strong light sources, in which case you simply cover the lens as suggested above. In making these intermittent exposures, the interruptions and smaller $f$ opening must be compensated for.

### IN THEATERS

To take movie scenes in a theater use fast pan film, a lens opening of $f$ 2 or $f$ 3.5 and a shutter speed of between 1/10 and 1/25 second. Stage action should also be taken with a fast film such as Tri-X, Arrow Pan, or Superpan Press; the exposure will depend, of course, on the quality and quantity of the light, but a safe trial exposure is about $f$ 3.5, 1/25 or 1/50 of a second. An example of a stage-action shot is reproduced on page 191.

## SOME FOCUSING HINTS

By this time, no doubt, you are sufficiently impressed with the reasons for focusing carefully. Here are some suggestions on the technique for doing it:

1. You can increase the sharpness of ground-glass focusing by smearing a thin uniform layer of vaseline or glycerin over the coarse surface of the ground glass. This has the effect of making it more transparent and less grainy.

2. Another way of accomplishing this is by the use of a *clear spot* on the ground glass. Mark a cross in the center of the ground glass with a sharply pointed pencil and cover this with a square piece of microscopic slide cemented (to the ground glass side) with balsam. Let it dry thoroughly. Focus in the usual way, then examine the cross with a magnifier. If the image and the cross are not displaced when you move your eye, everything is in sharp focus. However, if the cross moves in the direction of the eye, the lens is racked out too far; if the cross moves in the opposite direction, the lens hasn't been racked out far enough.

3. In examining the edges of a ground-glass image, do so at an angle, in the direction of the lens center.

4. If you are working at close range on a subject that has a troublesome depth, and it all has to be sharp, use this method for determining

A THEATER SHOT. Taken with a Leica, Summitar lens at
ƒ2, 1/40, on Plus X developed in Microdol.

TEXTURE as recorded by a view camera.

the best point on which to focus: Let A represent the distance of the point closest to the camera and B the distance of the point farthest away. Then,

$$\text{the focusing point} = \frac{2(A \times B)}{A + B} \text{ or,}$$

if $A = 8$ feet and $B = 24$ feet then the point $= \dfrac{2 \ (8 \times 24)}{8 + 24} = 12$

feet which means that the lens should be focused on a point about 12 feet away. Do this with the lens at its widest aperture, and then stop down to get the increased depth necessary to bring it all into focus.

5. However, for best results on other subjects, focus the way the eye does, on the principal object (the subject of greatest interest) and let the diaphragm bring the rest into focus.

6. When you are taking a picture in a mirror, your focus will be the sum of the distances from camera to mirror and from mirror to subject. Thus, if your subject is 5 feet away from the mirror and the camera is 10 feet away, set the focus for 15 feet.

7. To find the *hyperfocal distance* (infinity near point) at any given *f* stop, square the focal length of the lens in inches (multiply it by itself), then multiply it by the reciprocal of the *circle of confusion* of the lens in inches (usually supplied by the lens maker on request; for most miniature camera lenses this figure is 500). Now divide this by the *f* stop multiplied by 12 and you will have your answer in feet. Focus on this distance and everything from about half this distance to infinity will be in apparent focus.

8. If your camera has a synchronized range finder and a ground glass, be sure to check one against the other, for infinity as well as for close-ups. Though I have never been able to understand why, the men who put the range finders on cameras at the factory are not very fussy about whether the infinity stops are set right for the particular lens in hand. Their work of adjustment is a sheer waste of time unless this basic detail is taken care of, so be sure that it is. Check on the ground glass with a focusing magnifier.

9. *Learn how to use your range finder.* Each person has a different way of making the images merge. Check your method against the ground glass, to be sure that bringing the movable image *down,* for example, to meet the other is (or isn't) better than bringing it *up* (or *sideways* if you have a Leica or Contax). This small difference in direction may be the difference between razor-sharp pictures and pictures not so sharp.

# 10

# *People and Close-Ups*

PORTRAITS, TEXTURE, STILL LIFE, GLASSWARE, COPYING

Portrait photography can be the most rewarding as well as the most thankless job in the world. As a general rule, people rarely like the way the camera sees them. Usually the portrait is something of a shock. Though the skillful, and kind, photographer can do many things to soften this blow, by artful posing and lighting, he must be prepared for the kind of reaction that makes him wonder why he *ever* bothers to take pictures of people anyway, especially friends.

This has been summed up very cleverly by two talented amateur photographers (Nina Bourne and Thomas Collins) who worked out their despair in what they have named the Collins-Bourne Law of Portrait Photography. Unfortunately, there isn't room here to reproduce the document in its original calligraphic form. What follows is the bare text, minus the handsome penmanship:

The Photographee is never more, and usually less, than one-half so pleased with any given photograph as the Photographer. I. The Photographer is: (a) Surprised to find that there is an Image on the Negative, (b) Pleased if the Image appears to be of reasonable sharpness, Density & Contrast, (c) Delighted if it bears a resemblance to any Human Being, and (d) Overjoyed if it is recognizable as a Portrait of the Photographee. II. CONTRARIWISE, the Photographee (a) Remembers the tortures of Posing, (b) Knows that he or she is Beautiful, III. THEREFORE, If he does not look Beautiful in the Photograph, it is *only because* the Photographer is Fuzzy, Under-developed & Dense.

## LIGHTING THE SUBJECT

Your first attempts at taking portraits should be made out of doors. After you have selected your subject make the sitting in the shade somewhere where the light is diffused, for direct sunlight produces altogether too much contrast. To get a good lighting effect, take the picture on the side of the house opposite to that on which the sun is shining or, better yet, on the north side of it where the light is even more diffused; or you can get under a tree if the sun is screened by white, fleecy clouds.

To make a good portrait, you do not want too much light; you need it soft and diffused, particularly where it falls on the top and the sides of the subject. To do this, you can very often use a screen made of cheese-cloth tacked to a wood frame to tone down the light where it is too strong.

### THE REFLECTOR

A very handy gadget for use outdoors is a folding reflector. The one I have is made of three pieces of three-ply cardboard, about 10 inches wide by 14 inches across, taped together so that the outside leaves fold in on one another. The taping should be done inside and out along both folding edges. Make sure you allow folding room or the top leaf won't close. After you've finished the taping and are satisfied that both leaves will lie flat, cover the inside surface of all three cards with some crumpled and flattened tin foil, the kind they wrap around film to protect it. I used rubber cement to do the job and haven't had any pieces come off in three years. The trick is to cement both the card and the foil separately, let them dry, and then bring them together. It will take a bit of yanking to separate them if you do it that way.

Use the reflector to soften harsh contrasts in outdoor portraits. You will be amazed at what a difference it will make. Those dark, unpleasant shadows that usually spoil sunlit portraits will take on a luminous quality you've only seen in the work of professionals. And a secret: *that's just how they do it!* I place it on the ground, or a rock, over a fence, stand it on end, or raise it up at an angle using one leaf as a support. There are innumerable ways of putting it to good use. It's definitely worth the effort of lugging it along if you expect to take pictures of people.

If you haven't any tin foil, a good makeshift reflector can be made out of some white showcards, newspaper, bedsheets, towels, even the side of a white house.

## A WORD ABOUT BACKGROUNDS

Next to the proper lighting of the subject is the matter of a suitable background. A natural background such as the wall of a house or a garden, provided it is not covered with vines or ramblers, can be used, but you must place the subject far enough away from the background so that the latter will be out of focus. Very few natural backgrounds are really suitable for taking bust portraits, but for three-quarter and full-

### THE SECRET OF PORTRAITURE

You don't need a photogenic model to be able to produce elegant portraits. If you doubt this, look carefully at the five on this page and then turn to page 200 to see some "bad" photographs of the same model, taken within a few minutes of the shots shown here. A model is as photogenic as you make her. Leon Arden did these fine portraits with simple equipment: A Leica fitted with an Elmar, a dark gray blanket as a backdrop, a shawl, a couple of floodlights, and one small spot. The film was Plus X, exposure at $f$ 3.5 and 1/30, and developed in Finex.

length figures they are extremely good. A prepared background five feet wide and six feet long will prove very useful for bust portraits both out-of-doors and indoors.

## AVAILABLE LIGHT

The latest vogue in photographic lighting is the use of whatever natural daylight, or skylight (as distinguished from sunlight), happens to be available. Sometimes a reflector (a wall, a sheet, a card) is used to soften shadows, but otherwise the light is nothing more than that which comes from the sky or through a door or window. Among the modern photographers who have made this "existing light" photography the rage are such men as Richard Avedon, Eugene Smith, John Rawlings, Bill Ward, Henri Cartier-Bresson, Leonard McCombe and, of course, that amazing Frenchman who prefers to be known only as Izis. The result of this lighting technique is that everything and everybody in a picture looks *real*. The impact of such photography is overwhelming. The pictures haunt you; you can't forget them.

However, there's nothing new about available light as a technique. It's a return to the luminous lighting of such masters as Alfred Stieglitz, Eugene Atget, David Hill, Lewis Carroll, Matthew Brady, and Fox Talbot We could do worse, in these days of flash and strobe, than to relearn some of the simple methods that made these masters. And you don't need a garret skylight, either.

An important thing to remember when using natural light is that the contrast is usually weak. Therefore, the exposure, especially if done by meter, should be a bit less than normal; and the development should be ample (about 25 per cent more). However, if the light is strong only on one side, be sure to give ample exposure (metering the important shadow areas, if there's time) and use normal to brief development (about 20 per cent less).

## BOUNCE LIGHT

A variation of available light, using artificial light sources, is that which has come to be known as *bounce light* or *ceiling light*. The effect is very much the same as available light: soft, natural pictures that make no harsh shadows. The technique is quite simple. What you do is bounce the light off the ceiling at an angle—the sharper the angle, the more overhead the light will seem to be. Same thing applies to walls. Experiment first with *floodlight* before you tackle *flash* or *strobe,* to become familiar with the effect of bounce light on the object or the model. Exposure and development are the same as for available light.

graphed. You can learn more about lighting by sitting through a double feature plus Bingo, than by reading all the books in the world about it. Watch especially for those photographed by that amazing Chinese genius, James Wong Howe. He has made motion picture photography a great art.

### TEXTURE

All you need to know about it, despite all the books and articles on the subject, is that *texture is produced by strong shadows,* and strong shadows require contrasty lighting. Bring your light close (use a spotlight if you have one, but it isn't necessary) and place it so that the light glances across the surface at an extreme angle (but not so much that the long shadows obliterate detail). Flat, head-on lighting is death on texture; avoid it. Also, *one* light is better than two; the second light may cancel out the very effect you are trying to achieve. Another thing, *be sure your image is in sharp focus all over* (stop down to *f* 16 or smaller to *make* sure); the sharper the negative, the better the rendering of texture will be. *One more hint:* underexpose slightly and develop a minute or two more than normal; the extra contrast you'll get that way will help out. Fine-grain panchromatic film is the best for this purpose.

### GLASSWARE

Reflected backlighting is best for this kind of subject, with no *direct* light reaching the glass at all. The light should be fairly uniform and somewhat soft. Interesting effects can be gotten by placing the glassware on a glass plate supported at both ends, and lighting it at an angle from above or below. Panchromatic film is recommended for this use.

### COPYING

The problem in this kind of photography is the balancing of the light. *The solution:* center a pin or tack just above the top edge of the copy and at right angles to the surface, and watch the shadows made by the light. When the shadows are of equal intensity, length, or angle, the lights are balanced. You'll find this easier than it sounds. The eye notes small discrepancies of lighting very quickly by means of these shadows.

## CLOSE-RANGE WORK

For near close-ups it is very important to give increased exposures when the lens is racked out more than half again its focal length. The amount of extra exposure depends on the inverse square law. You simply find out how many times the old distance goes into the new, and square that number. That will be your new exposure factor. For example, if you're using a 6-inch lens focused at 10 inches, you divide 10 by 6, which gives you 1.7; you multiply that by itself, and your answer will be 2.89 which. technically, is the *exact* multiplication factor. But in this case, you can increase your exposure either 2½ or 3 times and be near enough correct for all practical purposes.

## SOME HINTS ON PORTRAITURE

Here boiled down to just a few sentences is the result of years of experience on the part of hundreds of photographers:

1. To minimize face lines and shadow hollows in portraits of women use plenty of flat, front lighting.

2. Use the monotone filter to test the lighting set up. If the shadows are too dark, or the highlights too strong, this will tell you the story at a glance.

3. Portraits of women should be so lighted that a meter reading from each side of the face shows a proportion of 2 to 1; men, 3 to 1.

4. Place lens of camera at height of eyes for true "drawing" or perspective.

5. Pointing camera down makes forehead large, nose long, chin small.

6. Pointing camera up makes jaw large, nose short, forehead small, neck long.

7. To lengthen the legs of women, use a low camera angle.

8. To see how position changes and distorts the face look in a mirror as you move your head around and notice what this does to your features.

9. When you notice flesh tones on your ground glass you'll get good tones in your picture (provided you expose correctly); however, if the shadows are grayish, not flesh colored, your light is unbalanced and you will lose detail in either highlights or shadows.

10. Don't light the face so that the shadows distort the features; the shadows are intended only to model the face.

11. Don't use too much light in portraiture, and don't have the lights too close. Chalky faces and black shadows will be the result if you disregard this warning. Try one light only, with a reflector to illuminate the shadows. Rightly used, this combination should give you almost everything you need in the way of normal lighting.

12. Unless you want to have large hands and big noses in your portraits, don't bring your camera too close to the model. A good rule is to include at least a half-length image in the picture area; if only the head is wanted, enlarge the negative.

13. If your model has blonde hair, you can avoid a chalky mess around the head by diffusing the light.

14. To get good expression, pretend to snap one picture after warning the model you're ready; when she's relaxed take the actual picture.

15. Shadows thrown by vertical lines (arms, legs, etc.) should never show vertically. Place the lights so that the shadows are at a slant.

16. Top lighting helps give depth to the head and form to the hair.

17. Watch carefully what the lights do to the nose and the eyes. Bad lighting can ruin an otherwise good expression.

18. The 500-watt T20 projection lamps are recommended for portraiture because they give better flesh tones and crisper high lights.

19. Do your men always look unshaven? Avoid the superspeed films and keep contrast down. The blue tone of the skin which shows up as a heavy beard is due to the darkening caused by the red in the photoflood light. Use the green photofloods, or tint the skin with a pure red make-up and then use white talcum over a powder base.

20. Keep the hands of your model edgewise toward the lens if you don't want them to look like pile drivers. Don't tell your model to do this; arrange the hands for her after she has assumed a natural position. Just tilt the hands a bit so they face the lens edgewise without bothering to explain; it will only confuse her if you try.

21. The best portrait lighting is the kind that simulates sunlight.

22. High lights should be prominent on forehead, nose, cheeks and chin.

23. *Stout people* should never be photographed in full front view. This makes them seem larger than they are, especially if they wear light clothes.

24. To focus attention on the face have the model wear dark clothes, and use a dark background.

25. The most pleasing pose is oblique, with one shoulder pointing towards the camera.

26. Sleeveless dresses make arms appear too prominent.

27. If your model has a double chin, turn her head so that she looks over one shoulder: the second chin will disappear.

28. If your model is too thin, photograph her full front view; have her wear light clothes and place her against a dark background. A dress material that has large patterns will also help to make her look plumper.

29. To get accurate meter reading of the highlights on the face, place a white card in front of the face and read that. Set the "O" position (on the Weston meter) to the high-light reading and use the exposure indicated. This will give you the minimum correct exposure for portraits.

# 11

# Action, Flash, and Strobe Photography

## ACTION PICTURES

Strictly speaking, there is no such thing as an absolutely instantaneous exposure, for however small the fraction of a second may be that the shutter is open, the element of time is present. The term, *instantaneous exposure*, as it is used in the language of photographers means that the shutter is open for an interval of time that is very small, compared to the speed at which the object is moving, and so the picture shows the latter as being perfectly motionless. In other words, taking instantaneous pictures is merely a simple case of "relativity."

### MOVING OBJECTS CLASSIFIED

For the purposes of photography, moving objects can be divided into two general classes: (1) those that are at a considerable distance from the camera, and (2) those that are quite close to the camera. Further, moving objects can again be divided into two groups according to whether (*A*) they are moving along the axis of the lens, that is directly toward or away from the camera, or (*B*) whether they are moving at right angles to it, that is broadside or in front of it.

The next classification relates to the speed of the moving object and includes (*a*) objects that move slowly, say at from four to twenty miles an hour, and (*b*) objects that move swiftly, say at from twenty to one hundred miles per hour. Finally the latter can be subdivided into those objects that move rapidly as a whole, as described above, and those that do not move to any extent as a whole but whose parts are in rapid motion.

*Classes (1) and (2) Defined.* Where a moving object is at a considerable distance from the camera, the image on the film or plate will be quite small, and it follows that its motion will likewise be relatively quite small, hence, an extremely short exposure is not needed to get a sharp picture.

ACTION is often best expressed by shooting a little slower than would be necessary to stop the action perfectly. A little blur sometimes helps as in the case of Wayne Bell's shot of a close play. (*left*), in which his Home Portrait Graflex with 28-inch Zeiss Tessar lens was used at a shutter speed of 1/500, showing just enough blur to heighten the action. Glen Fishback, on the other hand. Shot at 1/1000 and *f* 8 with his 3¼ x 4¼ Speed Graphic to stop the kids perfectly in mid-air (*above*). Take your choice but use your judgment.

Conversely, the closer the moving object is to the camera the greater will be its apparent speed, and the shorter the exposure will have to be.

*Classes (A) and (B) Defined.* Where an object is moving directly toward or directly away from the camera along the axial line of the lens, the increasing or decreasing size on the film, or plate, takes place so slowly that it can be taken with a slow-speed shutter, that is, one which gives an exposure of 1/25 of a second. But where the object moves across the axial line of the lens, and especially if it is near to the camera, a high-speed shutter, that is, one which gives an exposure of from 1/100 to 1/1000 of a second, will be needed in order to get a sharp picture.

*Classes (a) and (b) Defined.* Objects that move slowly, such as people, vehicles, etc., in the street, can be taken at fairly close range with an exposure of 1/25 of a second, but railway trains, racing motorcars, running and jumping horses, and the like, especially if these are close to the camera, need an exposure of about 1/1000 of a second, and a *focal-plane shutter* is needed to get good results.

Class (b) also includes people in action: athletics, dancing, running, jumping, swimming, etc. Such subjects require shutter speeds of at least 1/100 to 1/1000 of a second. *To avoid blur, however, never use less than 1/100 of a second for any hand-held shot.*

### SLOW-SPEED INSTANTANEOUS EXPOSURES

With a stop of ƒ 11 and a shutter working at 1/25 of a second, the exposure is short enough to arrest the motion of people who are walking, provided that (1) they are in the bright sunlight, (2) you use the size of stop given above, and (3) the camera is not closer than twenty-five feet to them. This assumes the use of a film like Panatomic X (ASA 25) with a K² yellow filter; for Verichrome Pan (ASA 80) use ƒ 11 at 1/100.

Where the lens can be used with a larger stop, naturally shorter exposures can be made and better definition can be had of moving objects; thus with a lens working at ƒ 8, the exposure can be cut down to 1/50 of a second; and with a stop of ƒ 5.6 lens the exposure can be further reduced to 1/100 of a second; while with special, large-aperture lenses, shutter speeds ten times as short, or even shorter, can be used. Where vehicles are in motion on a street, a shutter speed of at least 1/50 of a second should be used, and 1/100 of a second will give a far better picture.

With a shutter speed of 1/25 of a second, you can, however, make some extremely interesting pictures, as, for instance, a train just pulling out of the station, a steamer leaving her dock, and numerous other objects in slow motion. In making slow-speed instantaneous exposures the best results are had by taking the picture at an angle to the moving object instead of broadside on, as this not only cuts down the apparent speed at which it is moving but also gives a pleasing perspective to the picture.

## HIGH-SPEED EXPOSURES

To take pictures of objects and subjects in which all or parts of them are moving swiftly at close range and often broadside on (as for newspaper work) requires not only a camera in which the operator can see the image full size and exactly as it will appear on the film or plate at the instant that he snaps the shutter, but a lens which will work at a speed of at least *f* 4.5 and a shutter that has a speed of 1/1000 of a second or less. Recommended cameras for this type of work: Speed Graphic, Graflex, Leica, Contax, Nikon, Canon, Hasselblad, Exakta.

## FORMULA FOR FINDING THE EXPOSURE FOR AN OBJECT MOVING ACROSS THE FIELD

Let $D$ = the distance of the object in feet from the camera, $F$ = the focal length of the lens, $S$ = the speed of the object in feet per second, and $E$ = the exposure for the object which is moving across the field of view, then

$$E = \frac{D}{100 \, F \times S}$$

## TABLE OF SHUTTER SPEEDS FOR VARIOUS MOVING OBJECTS

The following table gives, roughly, the shutter speeds necessary for various moving objects, using a lens with a focus of about five inches. For lenses of other focal lengths, multiply by the reciprocal. For example: to find the speed for a 2-inch lens, multiply by ⅖. Photographing a foot race with a 2-inch lens, we would only need a speed of 1/200 in column B instead of the 1/500 required for the 5-inch lens. Column A is for objects moving directly toward the camera; column B for objects moving obliquely toward or from the camera; and column C is for objects moving directly across the field of view, that is broadside on.

## SHUTTER SPEEDS FOR ENLARGING

The formula and table given below show the shutter speeds that must be used to make negatives which will be sharp enough for *direct*, or *contact*, printing. For enlarging give at least one-half to one-fifth these exposures, or take the picture further from the object. For a 2 x enlargement give ½ the time; for a 3 x enlargement give ⅓ the time, etc. The figures are not a guide to exposure; this can be found with a meter.

## SHUTTER SPEEDS FOR MOVING OBJECTS

| DISTANCE OF OBJECT 25 FEET, UNLESS OTHERWISE STATED | A ↓ | B ↗ | C → |
|---|---|---|---|
| | FRACTIONS OF A SECOND | | |
| Street groups (no rapid motion) .......................... | 1/5 | 1/10 | 1/20 |
| Pedestrians (2 miles per hour) ......................... | 1/20 | 1/40 | 1/60 |
| Animals grazing ............................. ............ | | | |
| Pedestrians (3 miles per hour) ...................... | 1/30 | 1/60 | 1/90 |
| Pedestrians (4 miles per hour) ...................... | 1/40 | 1/80 | 1/120 |
| Vehicles (6 miles per hour) ...................... ... | 1/60 | 1/120 | 1/180 |
| Vehicles (8 miles per hour) ......................... | 1/80 | 1/150 | 1/280 |
| Cyclists and trotting horses .......... .............. | 1/160 | 1/300 | 1/500 |
| Foot races and sports .............................. | 1/240 | 1/500 | 1/700 |
| Divers ..................................'........... | 1/300 | 1/600 | 1/800 |
| Cycle races; horse galloping ................ ............ | 1/300 | 1/750 | 1/900 |
| Yachts (10 knots) at 50 feet .................. | 1/60 | 1/120 | 1/180 |
| Steamers (20 knots) at 50 feet .. .......... .......... | 1/120 | 1/240 | 1/360 |
| Trains (30 miles per hour) at 50 ft. .. ............. | 1/150 | 1/300 | 1/450 |
| Trains (60 miles per hour) at 50 ft. ......... .......... | 1/300 | 1/600 | 1/900 |
| Racing motor cars (90 miles per hour) at 50 feet ....... | 1/600 | 1/900 | 1/1200 |

At 25 feet the exposure may be half of that at 50 feet.
At 100 feet the exposure may be double that at 50 feet.

## THE DISTORTION CAUSED BY THE FOCAL-PLANE SHUTTER

Since the focal-plane shutter exposes only a part of the film or plate at a time, the picture of the object thus taken, if the slit in the curtain of the shutter is very narrow and the object is moving ahead fast enough, will be distorted. As an illustration, suppose that a cyclist is moving broadside or across the axial line of the lens and that the narrow slit in the curtain moves across the film or plate from the top to the bottom. Now since the image of the cyclist is inverted and the slit in the curtain moves down, it is easy to see that the lower part of the cyclist will be impressed on the film or plate first and the upper part will be exposed last. The result is that in the interval of time which elapses between the exposure of the lower part and that of the upper part of the cyclist, he has moved forward in space an appreciable distance, and this makes the upper part project unduly too far ahead; thus the picture is distorted and even to the untrained eye it looks a little queer.

Another instance of the distortion caused by the focal-plane shutter is often seen in the pictures taken of a racing motorcar, and in this case the latter looks as if it were getting ahead of itself. This curious effect is due to the same cause as explained above, but the distortion is even more obvious because the speed at which it is moving is greater. This defect does not, as a rule, detract in the least from the value of the pictures for newspaper work, but it has undoubtedly caused no little wonder among those who have seen them and who are "not in the know."

### HOW TO PREVENT SHUTTER DISTORTION

There are two ways by which the distortion caused by the focal-plane shutter can be overcome, and these are (1) by increasing the width of the slit in the curtain and at the same time increasing the speed, and (2) by making the slit in the curtain move in the opposite direction to that in which the image is moving across the film or plate.

### SOME HINTS ON HOW TO TAKE ACTION PICTURES

1. Press the shutter release *just* before the action culminates to allow for time lag between the eye seeing it and the brain sending an impulse to the muscle.

2. Outdoors in bright sunlight, Ivan Dmitri uses the exposure $f$ 4.5, 1/500, for action pictures on Dupont Superior. His action shots of horses are good so you might like to try this.

3. To express action in a picture, the exposure should be made just at the beginning or the end of the action. See illustration on page 207.

4. The best shutter speed for pictures of the sea is 1/50 of a second. A slower speed would ruin definition; a faster speed would freeze the action.

5. Compur shutters are capable of giving speeds that are intermediate to those marked, except between 1/10 and 1/25 and between 1/100 and 1/250.

6. To catch rapid subjects at slow speeds, follow the action with the camera. The background will be blurred, but the subject will be clear.

7. The trick in taking all moving subjects is to avoid stopping motion too much, otherwise the moving object will seem to be standing still.

## FLASH PHOTOGRAPHY

When the first edition of this book was published, more than 25 years ago, the chapter on artificial lighting had quite a section on magnesium flash lamps. What a devilish device these were! A spark would ignite the magnesium, which would then explode with a blinding flash, after which a dense, acrid, white smoke would fill the air. We have traveled a long way since then. The invention of the flashbulb has made it possible to take pictures at any time and under the most adverse conditions, and today you can stuff a handful of peanut bulbs into a pocket and have enough bottled sunlight to take a dozen pictures no matter what the light.

The appearance of these midget bulbs (Nos. 5, 25) was a great advance in flash photography. You can now carry two dozen of these mighty midgets easily in a coat pocket—and they pack enough light for almost any photographic need. This was followed by the still smaller Bantam 8 bulb, which is half the size of the No. 5 but needs only half an $f$ stop more.

In January 1956, General Electric brought out the tiny but powerful Powermite M2. This bulb was designed for the nonadjustable cameras and for all those having X or F synchronizer settings. Giving about half the light of a No. 5, though only $\frac{1}{4}$ the size, it is ideal for close-ups and for medium-distance shots. It requires a special 3" reflector, for contrasty directional light, or an almost flat reflector for softer results. In 1965 GE offered the M3 with a *rhenium* igniter.

Another improvement in flashbulbs was the importation by Amplex, in November 1956, of the PF1 baseless bulb (similar to the GE Powersprite AG-1). This reduced the cost of flashbulbs by half. A permanent adapter base fits into your flashgun. A pair of exposed wires, one on each side of the all-glass bulb, assures positive contact as the bulb is seated.

A further improvement in flash photography was the introduction by Kodak, in April 1957, of their amazingly inexpensive Rotary Flasholder, which holds six M2 bulbs at one loading, all of which can be fired in rapid sequence as fast as you can rewind and set the shutter. The 6 bulbs are held in a plastic disk which is placed on the spring-loaded carrier and moved into position by pulling the rotary magazine back, revolving it until the next bulb is in position and then letting it snap back into position. It is of course wired safely so that only the exposed bulb flashes.

A wide variety of flash synchronizers is now available to meet almost every purse, and more and more cameras—even cheap ones—are appearing on the market equipped with built-in synchronizers which require only the simple connection of a battery case and reflector.

Flash photography today is practically a necessity. Without it, it is impossible to make certain kinds of action shots. Also, it is often the only way to get natural, unposed pictures.

Flash is also ideal for photographing children and animals, whose unpredictable activity makes the problem of shooting them with ordinary photoflood lamps very difficult. Flashbulbs do away with the uncomfortable heat and glare of photofloods which frequently cause squint and other evidences of strain in the expressions of babies and children.

Flashbulbs have still another valuable use: to fill in shadows in outdoor photography. In photographing people in direct sunlight we are

...dak Standard Flasholder (for ...lget bulbs) is typical of modern ...edguns. It can be quickly con...ted to a low-cost B-C outfit by ...ng a B-C Flashpack instead of the ... "C" cells. Similar guns are made ...Ansco, Kalart, Graflex (Graflite ...) and others.

...e Amplex *baseless flashbulb* PFl ...ich has strikingly reduced cost of ...sh photography by eliminating the ...d for a metal base. It can be ...ed to any bayonet-base flashgun ... means of an inexpensive adapter ...se. New flashguns are being de...ned to take these bulbs directly.

This shot by Richard K. Wood shows how you can shoot against the sun and get full illumination by means of a single flashbulb on the camera. Note luminous quality of the lighting. Made with Speed Graphic and Kalart synchronizer at 1/50 and *f* 11.

often confronted with the problem of extreme contrast. Such lighting usually casts large shadow areas over the faces. A flashbulb, properly placed, will throw enough light into these areas to counteract the shadows.

For softer results and better flash quality indoors, try *bounce flash* (see page 196). To calculate exposure, measure the distance to the ceiling or wall *and back*, then divide your normal guide number by this figure, but open up 2 *f* stops to compensate for light loss. Another useful technique for soft results is *bare-bulb* flash, if you can remove reflector from gun and *hold gun away from the camera*. As in bounce flash, open up one to two lens stops, depending on size and color of room. *Caution:* Never use bare-bulb flash at the camera.

People with cameras not equipped for synchronized flash can make flash pictures of portraits, groups, or still lifes without much difficulty. All that is needed is an inexpensive hand-battery case and reflector, which can be purchased for a few dollars. The procedure is called *open flash,* and it works this way: You place the camera on a tripod or other support, set the shutter on time or bulb, open the shutter, fire the bulb (an M2 or 5, SF, SM, or 25), then close the shutter again. The flash itself, which has a duration of about 1/50 to 1/200 second, acts like a shutter.

To get the effect of a speed flash without synchronizer equipment *for action pictures,* use open flash, as above, but substitute an SM or SF bulb. The flash of these bulbs is equivalent to 1/200 second synchronized flash. Where the action requires more speed, a flash synchronizer must be used. The following are recommended: Jen Flash, Heiland Foto-Mite, Zeiss Foldfan Ikoblitz, Kodak Rotary Flasholder (holds 6 M2 bulbs), Graflite, Ansco, Leitz, Linhof, Nikon, and Kalart.

While flash photography may seem complicated, it isn't really. In its simplest form, one bulb is used, usually clamped to the camera, but best results are obtained with two or more bulbs just as in the case of making pictures indoors with flood lamps. It goes without saying that one should learn the principles of lighting by using photoflood lamps before going on to flash. By practicing with photofloods one can see exactly what effect a lamp at a certain position has on the subject.

*Caution:* Don't keep the flashgun *on* the camera unless you want washed-out, contrasty faces. Leave that to the news photographer. Hold the light above and to the side of the camera, at arm's length, and pointed down at about a 45° angle. A fill-in on the shadow side (either by supplementary flash or a reflector) will improve modeling and quality.

### CALCULATING EXPOSURE WITH FLASH

The problem of determining correct exposure with flashbulbs has been greatly simplified in recent years as a result of a simple discovery by Percy W. Harris, editor of *Miniature Camera Magazine,* who found that with a given flashbulb and a given emulsion speed, the distance in feet (from object to flash) multiplied by the stop number equaled a constant factor. This does away with complicated calculations, for once you have this flash factor for any given flashbulb, the correct stop for any distance (from object to flash) is determined by dividing the factor by the distance in feet. Conversely, if you wish to determine at what distance the flash bulb should be placed from the object for a predetermined stop, you divide the flash factor by the stop.

This factor system has been worked out by the manufacturers of flashbulbs, who in their exposure guides provide the factor numbers (usually referred to as *Guide Numbers* or *Flash Numbers*) for all bulbs and all films. A consolidated table giving the guide numbers for both between-the-lens and focal-plane shutters, will be found on page 216.

This table gives the guide number of each bulb for the film and shutter speed used. As an example of how to use it, let us assume that you have decided to use a Press 25 (No. 5) bulb with Verichrome Pan film (which has an ASA tungsten rating of 125), in your camera. You have decided to make your exposure at 1/100 second. In the table you find that for this bulb, shutter speed and film combination the guide number is 250. If you have placed your flashbulb 13 feet from your subject, you divide the guide number, 250, by the distance, 13, which gives you 19. This is your $f$ stop. You set your diaphragm at about $f$ 19 and shoot.

If you should decide to use a second bulb at approximately the same distance at an angle of from 0° to 10° from camera to subject, one full $f$ stop smaller should be used. Additional bulbs placed at wider angles from camera to subject for use as side or backlighting may be ignored. There are inexpensive dial guides to simplify these calculations.

*How to synchronize flash (or strobe) and sunlight.* For flash fill-in to soften shadows, set exposure ($f$ stop) as for sun, and use just enough flash or strobe to lighten shadow by adjusting distance of bulb. Shutter speed is then determined as explained on page 95.

## ELECTRONIC FLASH (STROBE)

The flashbulb did away with the smoke and hazards of the old magnesium flash powder, but it did not do away with the necessity of using a new bulb or bulbs with each shot made. So for years photographers hoped for and demanded a repeating flashbulb—a bulb that would flash over and over again without the necessity and cost of using a fresh one for each exposure. Along came Dr. Harold E. Edgerton with his so-called "stroboscopic" lamp, which started a new photographic cycle. Today the market is flooded with "Strobe lights," "Speedlights," and "Electronic Flash."

Your camera must have provision for "X" synchronization before you can use a strobe light—but this is becoming standard, even in the less expensive cameras. You usually have a choice of three power supplies: 1. the *A.C.*, which connects to your house current, is compact and economical, but limits your freedom of movement; 2. the *wet-cell,* which is powerful, rechargeable, but is heavy; 3. the *dry-cell,* which can deliver a flash of 1/500 second (as contrasted with the usual 1/2000 or higher), is more portable, but is expensive when you consider the cost of battery replacement (though recent models have begun to use flashlight batteries). Possibly the ideal power supply for strobe is the *nickel-cadmium battery,* with an A.C. converter for recharging. This new type of storage battery has an extremely long life, holds its charge well, weighs no more than the lead acid battery, but gives twice the energy and number of flashes. Since it has no acid, it does not corrode. The fact that the manufacturers guarantee its life from 5 to 10 years speaks well for its ruggedness. **Graflex** and **Dormitzer** make excellent units of this type.

## FLASHBULB GUIDE NUMBERS

### FOR BETWEEN-THE LENS (*AND FOCAL-PLANE* *) SHUTTERS

*(For explanation of this table see page 214.)*

| CLASS | FLASHBULB SIZE | SHUTTER SPEED (seconds) | FILM SPEEDS (ASA Exposure Index) | | | | |
|---|---|---|---|---|---|---|---|
| | | | 10-16 | 20-32 | 40-64 | 80-125 | 160-250 |
| X F | M2 POWERMITE M2 7,000 LS [a] | Up to 1/50 3" polished refl. 4" satin refl. | 60 50 | 90 70 | 130 195 | 180 140 | 250 190 |
| M X F | AG-1 POWERSPRITE AG-1 [b] 7,000 LS [a] | M to 1/50 X-F 1/100 2"-3" 1/200 reflectors 1/400 | 40 35 25 20 | 55 48 34 28 | 70 60 44 36 | 100 85 80 50 | 150 130 100 75 |
| F | SF [c] SM [c] 4,800 LS [a] | Up to 1/100 1/200 | 80 60 | 110 85 | 155 120 | 210 165 | 300 220 |
| M | 5 [d] PRESS 25 [d] 16,500 LS [a] | Up to 1/50 1/100 1/200 1/500 | 125 100 75 50 | 200 150 100 75 | 250 200 150 100 | 300 250 210 150 | 425 350 300 200 |
| FP * | Focal Plane 6 FP 26 17,500 LS [a] | Up to 1/50 1/100 1/200 1/400 | 80 55 38 26 | 110 80 55 40 | 150 100 75 50 | 190 175 110 75 | 250 200 150 100 |
| M | 22 [e] 65,000 LS [a] | Up to 1/50 1/100 1/200 | 165 130 100 | 200 160 130 | 275 225 180 | 400 300 250 | 510 420 325 |
| S | 50 PRESS 50 100,000 LS [a] | Up to 1/50 1/100 1/200 1/500 | 190 130 95 80 | 260 190 130 110 | 370 270 190 160 | 480 360 270 230 | 680 510 360 300 |

* Use only #6 or FP 26 bulbs with focal-plane shutters.

[a] Indicates approximate Lumen Seconds, which is the relative amount of light delivered by each bulb. Some deliver this light spread out over the full time of flash (as in SF or SM type); others pack a light punch at the peak (as in the #5 and #2).

[b] About half the size of the M2 bulb, easier to carry, but gives as much light.

[c] For use in midget reflectors; provides quick-freeze flash of between 1/100 and 1/200 seconds, even with open flash (for nonsynchronized cameras). Needs 1 *f* stop more than #5 bulb.

[d] For use in midget reflectors specially designed for these bulbs.

[e] For extra light and wider coverage; used in large reflectors.

Pictures made with speedlights, because of the split second duration of the flash, freeze action completely, which is not always desirable. The slight blur of motion recorded with the slower shutter speeds used with flashbulbs gives a more realistic portrayal of action. Speedlight pictures

Nothing like synchronized flash for making pictures of children. Esther Bubley made this one for Standard Oil Company (N.J.), using an Ikoflex with a peanut GE No. 5 bulb in fireplace and a second on the camera. Exposure at 1/100 and *f* 11, Super XX film developed in Microdol.

of boxers, basketball players or dancers give the subjects more the appearance of statues than of real people in motion.

Speedlights certainly widen the range of photography and for certain specialized purposes are definitely a boon. Press photographers are making extensive use of them in sports coverage where it is practical to carry the power pack, and studios specializing in baby and child portraiture find them a godsend. As the size and price of strobe units come down, the amateur use of these portable suns will increase. The light is soft (needs extra developing time) but matches sunlight in sharpness and color. Perfect for color fill-in outdoors, they are also ideal for simulating sunlight indoors when your camera is loaded with outdoor color film. No conversion filters are required under these conditions, which is a comfort to the gadget-ridden photographer.

Films exposed with speedlight require longer development than those made with flashbulbs or photoflood lamps. Whether because of the color of the light or its brief duration, the negatives tend toward "softness" and so require from 50 to 100 per cent longer development to build up normal contrast.

BRAUN HOBBY *AUTOMATIC* ELECTRONIC FLASH UNIT (Leitz)

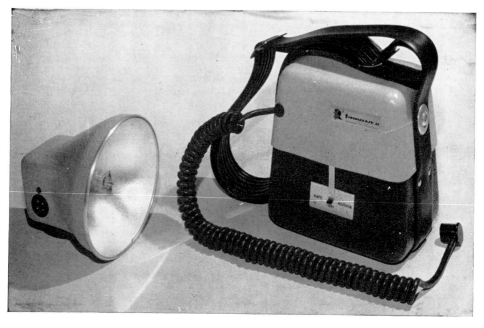

STROBOFLASH II FITTED WITH *NICKEL-CADMIUM STORAGE BATTERY* (Graflex)

## B-C (BATTERY-CONDENSER) FLASH

This new battery-condenser (or *capacitor*) system of flash (introduced by Busch, Jen, and Kodak in 1951) has revolutionized flash photography. It not only gives the photographer more power (as many as seven bulbs can be *perfectly* flashed on 100 feet of cord, provided they're wired in series), but it also makes him practically independent of such uncertain factors as age of battery, condition of metal contacts, and temperature. Besides, the peaking time of flash lamps fired by a B-C circuit is much more uniform.

Ordinary flash works on a direct circuit between batteries, bulb, and solenoid; that's why the batteries have to be at peak strength for efficient operation. B-C, on the other hand, works this way: A small 22.5 volt B battery (the kind they use in hearing aids) feeds power to a condenser which stores the power until you're ready to make the exposure. The circuit is so ingeniously wired that no current flows between battery and condenser until a flashbulb is inserted into the flashgun socket. Then the condenser begins to fill up (it takes no more than two seconds!) and you are ready to flash. Though the small B battery replaces the three large batteries normally used, it delivers fifteen times the voltage wallop of those regular 1.5-volt flashlight batteries. Long life (up to two years and thousands of shots) and consistent synchronization are among the advantages of this new power supply. You can buy either a complete B-C flashgun unit (such as the Busch, Kalart, Polaroid, Jen, Kodak, Standard) or you can buy B-C cartridges which, with a B battery, will convert your present gun to a B-C unit. Heiland, Kodak, Shureflash, and Linhof manufacture these inexpensive conversion cartridges. Almost all the new flash units are now made B-C. For carefree flashing, go B-C.

Some recommended books on flash photography:

*Flash Technique* (Kodak Data Book), Eastman Kodak Co., Rochester 4, N.Y., 50¢.

*Flash in Modern Photography,* by William Mortenson. Camera Craft Publishing Co., San Francisco, Cal.

Booklets: *How to Take Speed Flash Pictures of Baby,* and *How to Take Synchro-Sunlight Pictures,* both published by The Kalart Company, Plainville, Conn., 10 cents each. *Photolamp and Lighting Data,* General Electric Photolamp Department, Nela Park, Cleveland 12, Ohio, 10¢.

# All About Filters

The first thing you ought to know about them, and the most important fact to remember, is that a filter is exactly what its name indicates, a *screen*. It *sifts* light rays. Secondly, it would be well to keep in mind that *a filter adds absolutely nothing to a picture.* I know this may sound strange to some of you, but it's about the only positive thing one can say about filters. The function, you see, of every filter is negative; it *subtracts* a part of the light, holds back certain of the rays in the rainbow of colors. All that a filter does is to convert a part of the object light to image shadow. It does this *selectively,* and that's why filters are so useful in photography.

The unfortunate thing about the *filter fetish,* as some have called it, is that it leads either to hysteria ("I never take a picture without one") or to bitter disappointment ("I wouldn't trade a plugged nickel for the best filter; they're a racket"). It's just as silly to say that a filter can solve all your picture problems as it is to say that it can solve none of them. Many weird notions have been traded back and forth about filters. One of the hardiest of these is that quaint one that "all filters require a doubling of the exposure." Try a red filter on some orthochromatic film the next sunny afternoon and you'll see what I mean.

To use filters effectively it is not necessary to dive into a lot of technical charts and sensitivity curves. Let the experts have fun with those things. All we want to know about filters is why they work, what they do, the kinds there are, and how to use them.

## HOW FILTERS WORK

White light, as you may remember, is made up of seven spectral colors. (See *Fig. 62.*) When a red filter is interposed between the glass prism and a white card, certain of the colors are absorbed by the filter (green, blue, indigo, violet) and the rest are transmitted. You will notice (*A* in *Fig.*

63) that the red rays come through strongly, the orange next, and the yellow less. This is represented by the thickness of the lines in the drawing.

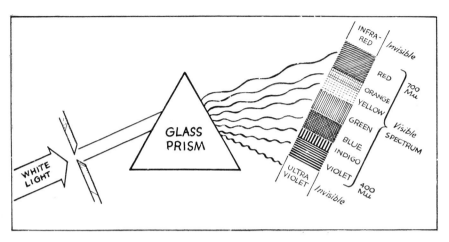

FIG. 62. THE DECOMPOSITION OF WHITE LIGHT

Next we try an orange filter (*B* in *Fig. 63*) and find that it passes all the red and orange, most of the yellow, and none of the green, blue, indigo, or violet.

Then we try a yellow filter (*C* in *Fig. 63*). This transmits all of the red, orange and yellow, a little of the green, and none of the blue, indigo, or violet.

Now we try a green filter (*D* in *Fig. 63*). In this case all of the green is transmitted, a little of the yellow and blue, and none of the red, orange, indigo, or violet.

Finally we try a blue filter (*E* in *Fig. 63*) and discover that it lets through all of the blue, indigo and violet, a little of the green, and none of the yellow, orange, or red.

The color of the light absorbed by any object is complementary to the color reflected or transmitted by it. We find therefore, from the action of these various filters, that

RED is complementary to GREEN-BLUE
ORANGE is complementary to BLUE-INDIGO
YELLOW is complementary to INDIGO-VIOLET
GREEN is complementary to VIOLET-ORANGE
BLUE is complementary to YELLOW-RED

The interesting thing about these complementary colors is that any pair of them (red and green-blue for instance, or yellow and indigo-violet)

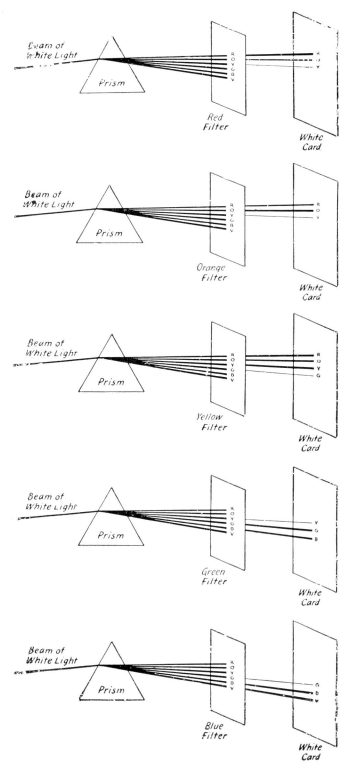

FIG. 63. HOW FILTERS SCREEN WHITE LIGHT

will create the effect of white light, or daylight. We can say, therefore, that yellow is daylight without indigo-violet; red is daylight without green-blue; orange is daylight without blue-indigo; green is daylight without violet-orange, and blue is daylight without yellow-red. All this has an important bearing on the actual use of filters.

As we can see, filters are *negative,* or *minus,* colors; they censor or destroy their complementaries. This action leaves blank patches on the negative, which in turn produce dark patches on the print. Keep this in mind when you use filters. Remember that you can't *add* anything to a scene or object by slapping a filter over the lens. Be sure that what the filter suppresses can be spared, and that its loss improves the picture.

Except for process filters and those made for scientific use and to get special effects, most of the filters used in amateur photography neither transmit all of any color nor do they block it out entirely. However, for general purposes, a good guide to filter use is the following brief summary of filter effects:

To photograph a color as *black* use a *contrasting* (complementary) filter.

To photograph a color as *white* use a *matching* (similar) filter.

## WHAT FILTERS DO

There are at least two reasons why photographers use filters: (1) to enable the emulsion to register the various colors as tones of gray more nearly the way the eye sees them, (2) to increase the contrast between these tones.

## THE VISUAL CURVE

If we placed a series of color bars vertically on a card, one next to the other in the order of their decreasing wave lengths (red, orange, yellow, green, blue, violet) and then separated them by similar bars of gray tone that shade evenly from white at the top to black at the bottom, we could indicate on such a chart by means of points the intensities of gray which match the color intensities as the eye sees them. If we connected these points to make a continuous curve we would have what is known as the *visual* (or *eye*) *curve.* This would look like the outline of a mountain with its peak over the yellow and falling away gradually towards the red on one side and towards the blue and violet on the other side. What this would indicate is that the eye is most sensitive to *yellow* and least sensitive to *violet* (that being lower on the curve than the red). Now if we took the same chart and photographed it in daylight with an *orthochromatic* film (like Verichrome, Plenachrome or Multichrome, sensitive to all colors except spectral red), matched up the color tones, and made another curve, we should find that it had flattened out, being very low in the red, lower in the orange and yellow, a little higher in the green, still higher in the blue, and highest in the violet. This would indicate that such a film was most sensitive to *blue-violet* and least sensitive to *red*. We see at once that this contrasts sharply with the way the eye sees things.

If we do the same thing with a *panchromatic* film (like Supreme or Plus X, sensitive to all colors) we find that the curve is just a little lower in the *yellow,* higher in the blue, and still higher in the violet, which indicates that the tonal sensitivity of such a film most nearly matches that of the eye. The crux of the situation, however, is that though the eye is most sensitive to the *yellow* region of the spectrum, photographic emulsions are most sensitive to the *blue-violet*. This explains why *blue* skies, uncorrected by filters, often print as blank *whites,* and why *red* lips print as *black* when photographed with *ortho* film. To make these visual and emulsion curves match, then, is one of the prime functions of filters.

We know, from the table of complementary colors above, that a yellow filter holds back the indigo-violet light and lets the yellow stream through unhampered. By placing a yellow filter over the lens when we use orthochromatic film, we *correct* the film and force it to register colors as gray tones the way the eye does.

Similarly, we know that a filter midway in color between yellow and green would hold back some of the indigo, violet and orange, in which panchromatic film is strong, while it would let through all the yellow and green, in which it is weak. A yellow-green filter, therefore, is the proper correction filter for panchromatic film.

Sometimes, however, we deliberately want to distort, emphasize, or change the contrast between colors. To do this we use *blue, green, orange* or *red* filters. We'll explain the specific uses of such filters presently.

## THE KINDS OF FILTERS

There are four general types of filters: sheets of plain gelatin film; sheets of film cemented between glass flats; dyed-in-the-mass glass; and those made of transparent plastics. The cheapest, of course, are the gelatine sheets, but they are very fragile and difficult to handle and to keep flat. The cemented filters (made by Eastman Kodak) are next in price, and they are offered in two forms: cemented in A glass which is hand ground so that the surfaces are absolutely plane parallel, and those in B glass which does not have a surface as accurately ground as that of the A-type optical flats, but is accurate enough for most purposes. The all-glass filters are dyed in the mass, are accurately ground (if made by reputable concerns like Zeiss, Lifa, Optochrom, Omag, Rolleiflex, Goerz, Ednalite, and Leitz) and are quite thin, which is an important consideration in view of the fact that heavy glass, especially if it is not absolutely plane parallel, spoils lens definition. The plastic filters are comparatively cheap, but can not be surfaced as accurately as the glass flats, nor do they absorb colors as efficiently. The recommended types are the all-glass and the cemented flats. For amateur use, the Wratten filters in B glass are excellent.

## A TABLE OF FILTER FACTS

Reproduced below is a simple, compact color reference chart for use in altering the gray tones of colored objects:

### USES OF FILTERS

| COLOR OF SUBJECT | TO LIGHTEN, Use | TO DARKEN, Use |
|---|---|---|
| Violet | Blue | Red or orange |
| Indigo | Blue or green | Orange, yellow |
| Blue | Blue or green | Red or orange |
| Blue-green | Blue or green | Red |
| Green | Green or yellow-green | Red or blue |
| Yellow | Yellow, orange or red | Blue |
| Orange | Orange or red | Blue or green |
| Red | Deep red or red | Blue or green |
| Purple | Blue | Green |
| Magenta | Red | Green |

## SOME HINTS ON THE USE OF FILTERS

Before we take up each of the filters specifically, let's jot down a few general odds and ends on the use of filters that are well worth remembering:

1. Using a yellow filter under artificial light is a waste of time. It has no effect at all because the light, being yellow, is its own filter. For the same reason yellow filters are not needed outdoors late in the afternoon. The light is weak in blue and strong in yellow at that time.

Illustrating use of the *yellow-green* filter. Made with a Rolleiflex, 1/100 second at *f* 11 on Super XX developed in Microdol. The scene is Menemsha Harbor, Martha's Vineyard.

Illustrating the use of the *red* filter. Made with a Rolleiflex and Tessar
lens on Plus X film with red filte  Exposure was 1/25 at *f*8. Developed in D-76.

2. Shadows are usually made up of bluish tones of gray. To *soften contrast* between the shadows and the object, use a green or blue filter; to *increase contrast,* use a red or orange filter.

3. Objects that are lighted by a source of their own color get more exposure and are therefore white on the print. Use a complementary filter to even things up when that happens.

4. White light is made up of the three basic colors: red, green and blue; a filter of any one of these colors will absorb the light of the other two.

5. Atmosphere haze (not to be confused with mist or fog which are white) is *blue;* it is reduced by almost all filters. Red reduces it most, green the least. The blue filter, however, increases haze. If haze adds to your picture, don't destroy it by using a filter; or, use the green or blue.

6. The sky near the sun, being brighter and having less blue in it, is less affected by filters; as you swing away from the sun the sky will gradually get darker, and it will be darkest when your back is to the sun. Similarly, a filter will not darken the sky along the horizon; the light there is weak in blue rays, strong in yellow and orange. (To understand why, refer back to *Fig. 10.*)

7. A filter will not darken a sky that is misty, overcast, grayish or whitish.

8. *Overexposure* will cancel out the effect of a filter; *underexposure* will often take the place of one.

9. If the sky is clear and blue, and you are photographing very light objects against it, on panchromatic film, you won't need any filter to darken the sky. Be sure to turn away from the sun, however, and don't overexpose.

10. Flat lighting, or a scene without contrast, needs strong filters like the red or orange; sharp lighting, or a scene of great contrast, needs the softening effect of the green or blue filters.

11. Early in the morning, and late in the afternoon, filters are needed only for *color correction* since lighting contrast is adequate; around noon however (and except for shots against the light) they are needed for *color contrast* as well.

## WHAT THE VARIOUS FILTERS DO

Actually, the amateur photographer needs at most only three filters (a *yellow-green,* an *orange,* and a *red*) and he can even do without the orange or red. However, there may be occasions when other filters are called for. To help you recognize these, as well as to give you some additional clues on the use of the filters you already have, here is a description of what the basic filters can do and how to use them. After each one (in parentheses) you'll find listed one or more examples of this type of filter. We have not tried to list all the good filters of this kind now being offered. Check with your dealer to find out what others are available, and at what price, before you buy.

*Yellow* (Zeiss G² or Lifa Y²). The only kind of filter to use with ortho film, which it corrects completely. Though it can also be used with pan film, it is not so effective in adjusting the visual curve differences. Absorbs ultraviolet light and some of the blue-violet. Lightens reds and pinks too much and is therefore not suitable for portraits. Good for landscapes and snow scenes and for cloud photography.

*Yellow-green* (Wratten K² or Aero²). Can be used for both *ortho* and *pan* film. It corrects type B pan completely in daylight. Absorbs ultraviolet and some blue light. Useful in darkening skies, emphasizing clouds, reducing haze, increasing contrast. Good for outdoor portraits (it darkens lips and cheeks) landscapes, distant views, water scenes, snow scenes, mountain scenes, sunsets, and for the photography of architecture. Adds brilliance to a scene of normal color distribution.

*Green* (Wratten X¹ or Lifa Green). For types B and C pan film. Absorbs ultraviolet, violet, some blue, and some deep red. Corrects type C pan in daylight; type B in tungsten. Though it tends to soften *light contrast,* it increases *color contrast.* Good for pictures against the light, snow scenes, portraits outdoors.

*Blue* (Wratten C⁵ or Zeiss B⁴⁰). For ortho and pan films. Absorbs red, yellow, green, and ultraviolet. Used for color separation with tungsten light. Makes an emulsion color blind (blue registers as white, other colors as dark gray or black). Increases the effect of haze outdoors. Indoors, the effect of this filter can be produced (more easily and more cheaply) by using blue photo floods. Good for copying, especially where yellows or reds have to be separated, and for photographing white objects against snow (most white objects have some yellow in them, and snow is bluish; by darkening the yellow the filter produces crisp separation).

*Orange* (Zeiss G⁴, Lifa RO, Wratten G). Absorbs ultraviolet, violet, and most of the blue rays. For pan and ortho film. Excellent for increasing contrast between colors. Lightens flesh tones and therefore good for suntanned subjects. Makes blue sky (and water surface reflecting skylight) quite dark. Improves rendition of texture outdoors in sunlight under a blue sky (by suppressing the blue shadows which create texture). Hence, ideal for rendering texture of architectural stones, sand, fabrics, outdoors. Penetrates haze beyond the eye. Good for mountain and airplane photography, for contrast emphasis in studio work, and for bringing out the grain in wood furniture.

Illustrating the use of the *graduated sky* filter (yellow). This filter works best when used in front of the sunshade, as in the case of the Rollei cameras. Taken with a Rolleiflex at *f* 16, 1/10 second, Finopan developed in Edwal 12.

Illustrating the use of an *orange* filter. Made with a Rolleiflex, Plus X film, orange filter. Exposure was 1/2 second at *f* 16. The scene is Pilgrim Heights at North Truro, looking toward the Provincetown tip of Cape Cod.

*Red* (Wratten A, Lifa Red, Zeiss R$^{10}$). Absorbs ultraviolet, violet, blue, and green rays. For pan film. Darkens blue skies almost to black, producing spectacular cloud effects. Ideal for photographing light-colored buildings, statues, shiny metallic structures, faces against a dark sky; creates exquisite landscapes and airplane studies. Increases over-all contrast considerably, cuts haze entirely; good therefore for landscapes with distance where it penetrates mist and makes the invisible clear. Not good for shots of green vegetation, dark buildings, portraits (lips and cheeks go ghastly white), artificial light (the source usually has red in it and cancels out effect of filter). Slight underexposure with this filter produces night effects. Indoors it is useful for increasing contrast between colors (see color separation chart) as in photographing blue handwriting. It is also useful in photographing furniture (mahogany, for instance) where it helps bring out detail of the grain.

*Graduated Sky* (Rolleiflex Graduated, Zeiss VG$^{6}$). For pan or ortho film. A yellow-green filter which is split so that only about half of it has color, the balance being clear glass. It is used mostly to compensate for contrast between sky and landscape, or foreground and background. Useful in photographing seascapes and landscapes. Requires no additional exposure. For best effect, however, it should be held about one focal length away from the lens (as in the Rolleicord and Rolleiflex, where it is designed to be placed over the sunshade at the proper distance from the lens).

*Ultraviolet* (Lifa Haze, Zeiss G$^{0}$). For pan or ortho film. Absorbs only ultraviolet rays, which do not focus on the same plane as the other rays and therefore blur the image. At sea level, these rays have been filtered out, to a great extent, by the atmosphere and are not much of a problem; at high altitudes, however, they become very troublesome. Requires no additional exposure. Useful for mountain scenes and snow scenes.

*Polarizing* (Kodak Pola-Screen, Polaroid Filter). Absorbs ultraviolet rays; transmits plane polarized rays of all visible colors. For pan, ortho, or kodachrome. Good for darkening blue skies without distorting color rendering of foreground objects; the only filter that can be so used in color photography. Greatest effect occurs when you're photographing almost at right angles to the sun. By placing the filter over your eye and rotating it, you can tell easily which indicator position is best for the conditions at that time. When photographing through glass or water at an angle, surface reflections interfere with the visibility of detail below the surface; the polarizing screen subdues the reflections and shows the detail. It can also be used in the same way to bring out texture in such nonmetallic objects as grained wood, linoleum, tile, lacquered or varnished objects, glass, leather, etc. The most effective camera angle for its use is about 35 degrees to the surface. The polarizing screen at the lens only will not subdue reflections from metal surfaces; the light source would also have to be polarized. The polarizing screen is especially effective in photographing sunsets. The Pioneer Scientific Corporation now manufactures a Polaroid yellow polarizing filter which combines the features of a standard yellow filter and a light-polarizing filter in a single unit.

## COLOR SEPARATION CHART

Where two colors have to be separated, as in copy work, it is important to know what filters can accomplish this without upsetting, too much, the entire color balance of the subject. This chart will be of help if you find yourself in such a dilemma.

### COLOR SEPARATION CHART

| COLOR I | COLOR II | FILM | FILTER | EFFECT |
|---------|----------|------|--------|--------|
| WHITE | BLACK | pan or ortho | none | — |
|  | RED | ortho | yellow-green or green | — |
|  | YELLOW | ortho | blue | — |
|  | GREEN | pan | red | — |
|  | BLUE | ortho | dark yellow or orange | — |
|  |  | pan | red, orange or dark yellow |  |
| BLUE | BLACK | ortho | Blue | Blue goes white |
|  | RED | ortho | yellow-green, green or blue | Red goes dark |
|  | RED | pan | red, orange, dark yellow | Red goes light |
|  | YELLOW | ortho | orange, or dark yellow | Yellow goes light |
|  | YELLOW | pan | red, orange or dark yellow | Yellow goes light |
|  | GREEN | ortho | dark yellow, yellow-green, green | Green goes light |
| GREEN | BLACK | ortho | yellow, orange, green | — |
|  | RED | ortho | yellow, green, yellow-green | Red goes dark |
|  | RED | pan | red | Red goes light |
|  | YELLOW | pan | red | Yellow goes light |
| YELLOW | BLACK | ortho | orange, yellow | — |
|  | BLACK | pan | red, orange, yellow | — |
|  | RED | ortho | green, d. yellow, yellow g. | Red goes dark |
| RED | BLACK | pan | red, orange | Red goes light |

## THE VIEWING (OR MONOTONE) FILTER

This one is not used over the lens but over the eye, so that you can tell approximately how any scene will look in shades of gray on the final print. It can be used indoors or outdoors. Originally made in only a deep blue color, for orthochromatic film, it is now also colored yellow, purplish-green, or green for panchromatic film. The most valuable use of the monotone filter is in conjunction with the regular lens filters. We can try out the effect of any filter by first looking through the monotone filter (which shows us how the film will see it) and then by placing the lens filter in front of the monotone and looking through both. You can eliminate a lot of time-consuming and expensive guessing that way. These filters used to be expensive, prohibitively so. But you can get a good one now for a dollar (there are three or four excellent ones available at this price); so there's really no excuse for not having one. It can become one of your most valuable accessories if you learn to use it right.

### FILTER FACTORS

Since every filter cuts out part of the available light, we necessarily have to increase the exposure to compensate for this loss. One of the tough problems in photography is determining how much this increase should be. Filter factors, as given usually (*yellow* 2 x, *orange* 3 x, *red* 6 x, *green* 3 x, etc.), are not much help because they may not apply at all to the conditions under which we happen to be working. The factor depends on the quality (spectral composition) of the light, on the color sensitivity of the film (whether it's ortho or pan; and if it's pan, whether it's type B or C) and on the reflection and absorption characteristics of the object (a blue object will photograph lighter outdoors than a green one on type B pan, for instance). With all these complications entering into the seemingly simple problem of photographing a sky with clouds in it, it's no wonder that most amateurs throw in the sponge at this point and simply double or triple the exposure when using a filter and trust to luck.

There's an easier and more practical method. Use a test chart (such as those described on page 333); photograph it indoors and outdoors, with and without filters; with normal, half and double your *guess* exposures; develop the film. If you have three filters to test you can do this all on one roll of 35-mm. film, two rolls of the 120 size, or two film packs. This may sound like a waste, but it isn't. Provided you don't change your filters, and use the same type film, you'll have to do this only once in your entire career as a photographer. Then you'll know once and for all what the factors are for each filter under all your special conditions. The only variants (and they are constant variants which you can adjust for) will be the changes in light outdoors from morning to evening. If you make your test at about noon when the light is normal, you need only multiply the noon factor by 1½ before 11 A.M. and after 2 P.M.; and by 2 before 9 and after 4 P.M. And that is all the calculating of filter factors you'll ever have to do.

APERTURE COMPENSATION TABLE

Once you know your filter factor, you'll want to know how to adjust your exposure, if and when you alter your $f$ stop. The following lens aperture table will tell you what stop to use at a glance.

LENS STOP TABLE

| WITHOUT FILTER | FILTER FACTORS | | | | | | | | | |
|---|---|---|---|---|---|---|---|---|---|---|
| | 1.25x | 1.5x | 2x | 2.5x | 3x | 4x | 5x | 6x | 8x | 10x |
| $f$ 16 | 14.3 | 13.1 | 11.3 | 10.1 | 9.2 | 8 | 7.2 | 6.5 | 5.6 | 5.1 |
| $f$ 12.7 | 11 | 10 | 9 | 8 | 7 | 6.3 | 5.6 | 5 | 4.5 | 4 |
| $f$ 11 | 10 | 9 | 8 | 7 | 6.5 | 5.6 | 5 | 4.5 | 4 | 3.5 |
| $f$ 9 | 8 | 7.5 | 6.3 | 5.6 | 5.1 | 4.5 | 4 | 3.7 | 3.2 | 2.8 |
| $f$ 8 | 7.2 | 6.5 | 5.6 | 5.1 | 4.5 | 4 | 3.6 | 3.2 | 2.9 | 2.5 |
| $f$ 6.3 | 5.6 | 5.1 | 4.5 | 4 | 3.6 | 3.2 | 2.9 | 2.6 | 2.3 | 2 |
| $f$ 5.6 | 5.1 | 4.5 | 4 | 3.6 | 3.2 | 2.8 | 2.5 | 2.3 | 2 | 1.8 |
| $f$ 4 | 3.5 | 3.3 | 2.8 | 2.5 | 2.3 | 2 | 1.8 | 1.6 | 1.4 | .. |
| $f$ 3.5 | 3 | 2.7 | 2.4 | 2.2 | 2 | 1.7 | 1.5 | .. | .. | .. |
| $f$ 2.8 | 2.5 | 2.3 | 2 | 1.8 | 1.5 | .. | .. | .. | .. | .. |
| $f$ 2 | 1.9 | 1.7 | 1.5 | .. | .. | .. | .. | .. | .. | .. |

## FILTER MOUNTS

Be sure that your filter mount enables the filter to attach firmly to the lens and to lie parallel to the image or lens plane. The screw-in or bayonet type mounts are the most precise; the type that places the filter between the elements of the sunshade is most practical and least expensive (the Hollywood Camera Exchange sunshades and those made by Eastman Kodak are excellent examples of this type). With care, and if properly made, any one of these types will serve equally well. Sometimes, when the photographer is careless, the bayonet filter is mounted on the lens slightly askew; when that happens the image will be slightly distorted.

## FILTERING FOR SHADOW DETAIL

An interesting method for improving detail, brilliance and tone renderings in shadows was suggested by Marshall Perham in *The Camera* magazine for February 1939. The method, briefly, is as follows:
1. Take a light reading of the scene from the camera position.
2. Multiply that by *one-half* the factor of the proposed filter.
3. Take a direct reading from the shadow.
4. Multiply that by the factor of the proposed filter.
Readings 2 and 4 should equal each other, approximately.
A. If shadow reading is greater, *filter is too dense.*
B. If general reading is greater, *filter is too pale.*
This method is based on the principle that filters tend to lighten objects of similar color and darken objects of a complementary color. The color selection of the filter will depend, naturally, on the color contrast between object and background. The method works best with reddish objects.

## FILTERING FOR INTENSE LIGHT

Two polaroid filters used together but rotating independently of one another, make one of the most useful accessories for your gadget bag. They form a neutral density filter which is ideal for recording full detail when shooting directly into any strong light source (such as the sun, arc lights, fires, etc.). Also useful as a variable density filter if you're caught with fast film, a speed lens that can't be stopped down enough, and an intensely lighted picture that won't wait. The density varies from light gray (when the axes of both filters are parallel) to almost black (when the axes are at right angles). The amazing thing is that no increase of exposure is necessary. You look through both filters to give you the scene density you want, set them that way in front of your lens, then expose normally, disregarding the filters in your calculations.

## DESERT EXPOSURES

To subdue desert contrast, use a light yellow filter. It holds back the ultraviolet rays in the highlights. But be sure to double your normal exposure for that particular filter, and underdevelop somewhat, using D-76. Don't trust your eye on desert light, especially for color shots. Use an exposure meter at all times.

# 13

# How to Take Pictures of Children

It takes a mean man to resist the appeal of a child; which probably explains why there are more pictures taken of baby than of any other one subject in the world. The drugstore photo-finishers, who are certainly in a position to know, claim that the three most popular snapshot subjects, in order, are: (1) baby; (2) the girl friend; (3) the dog. But baby leads the others by a good margin.

And yet the snapshots of baby, too often, are as distressing to the child as they are exasperating to the parent. Usually, after a picture session, both parent and child are exhausted.

To make things easier for you, *and* for the child, here are a few pointers on what to do and what to avoid the next time you start to take some pictures of the youngster. If you follow these suggestions, what has usually been a *trying* time may become a *pleasant* one, for both of you.

## WHAT YOU NEED

1. A camera with a lens speed of about $f$ 4.5 and a shutter speed of about 1/500; you can get along with less, but you may lose some pictures when the light is dim, or when you want to stop fast action with a high shutter speed. Good baby pictures have been taken with a box camera, so don't weep if you can't get this equipment at once. The best cameras for this kind of work are the twin-lens reflex type (Rolleiflex, Ikoflex, Argoflex, Graflex 22, Yashica, Minolta Autocord, Kalloflex). Also good are the Leica, Contax, Nikon, Konica, Hasselblad, Exakta, Contaflex, Canon.

2. A tripod and a long cable release. With these you can move around as easily as the baby does. Of course, you'll have to stop down to about $f$ 11, to be sure of enough depth of focus should the subject begin to move out of range. Some photographers prefer to move around with the camera, snapping when the best point of view and the most appealing expression coincide. But this is a matter of taste. If you find it more convenient to

carry the camera with you, do so; if you're the lazy type, set the machine on a stand, focus on the place where the baby is most likely to be, stop down to $f$ 8 or $f$ 11—and use that long cable release to capture the expression you want.

3. For indoor shots, two No. 1 photofloods, in reflectors, or a flash synchronizer for those tiny GE 5 or Wabash Press 25 bulbs, with which you can shoot at $f$ 11 and 1/200, at a distance of about 6 feet.

4. Some rolls of fast panchromatic film—preferably Superpan Press or Tri-X—or, if you use smaller sizes, Ultra Pan or Ilford HPS or HP3.

5. A $K^2$ filter if you want to soften the effect of skin blemishes, bruises, freckles, etc. Use the *outdoor* factor for the film and filter combination you choose. With Tri-X this factor is approximately 2, which means that using this combination indoors, you expose for twice the indicated exposure, whatever that happens to be; $f$ 11, 1/200 would, for instance, become $f$ 11 1/100 or $f$ 8 1/100.

6. A lens hood to keep out stray light.

7. An exposure meter like the Weston or General Electric, if you can afford it.

## WHAT YOU DO

Have your camera loaded, set and prefocused before you bother the baby. Don't fuss with lights and gadgets on his time. It will make him cranky.

Choose a spot that gives the child room to wander, and still makes it possible for you to gauge your focusing distance accurately. With the lens set at $f$ 11 and focused on 25 feet, the depth of field for a lens of about 2 or 3 inch focal length extends from about 12 feet to infinity. For close-ups set your distance at 10 feet, and your range is from about 6½ feet to 18 feet. With this much depth to work in you should have no trouble keeping baby in focus. A simple trick used by Burt Martinson, is to anchor the child in a rocking or high chair. One of his pictures is on page 239.

## SOME TEMPER-SAVING PRECAUTIONS

### PLAN EVERYTHING IN ADVANCE

Arrange the camera, lighting, backgrounds before you call the model. Have everything ready; don't tire the child by making him wait while you focus, rearrange, adjust. When you have everything in order, relax and get acquainted with the model. Play with him; talk to him; make him feel that you're someone to have fun with, not just a fussy man with a lot of lights. When you're all through taking pictures, finish any game

Burt Martinson took this one with a studio camera, a couple of photofloods, and one spotlight
The exposure was *f* 6.3, 1/50. Note especially the effect of the low camera position.

you've started; otherwise the child may not let you take pictures of him again.

## DON'T HAVE TOO MANY PEOPLE IN THE ROOM

Things get too noisy and distracting. The child tires quickly when there are a lot of faces poking around, raising bedlam. Grownups know this feeling when they shop in the department stores; the mere pressure of people seems to drain you of all energy. At the end of a good shopping spree, you really *are* spent, both ways. Children are even more sensitive to crowds than grownups are. Besides, a gang of people around a photographer is dangerous. Someone is liable to get hurt, if someone else doesn't, in the meantime, ruin your equipment. A wire tripped over, or a tripod leg accidentally kicked, can do terrible things to your poise and pleasant manner. If people will just not stay out of the room, save your film, *don't take any pictures.* The results would have been terrible anyway.

## DON'T HURRY

If you're tense and sudden in your movements, the child will be nervous, and show it. *Easy does it.* Work slowly, carefully. Have patience. The child will feel more at ease, and so will you. Don't start snapping the moment the light goes on; let the child get accustomed to the light.

## WATCH THOSE BACKGROUNDS

This seems to be about the most difficult thing in the world to learn. We get used to the presence of objects so quickly that we forget they're there almost as soon as we see them. Haven't you often been shocked when someone else pointed out something that you've seen twice a day for ten years and didn't notice at all? It's such blindness that makes it impossible for most of us to see backgrounds until the final print is in our hand. The only way to protect yourself against backgrounds is deliberately to search them out. Check the background each time just before you shoot. You'll have to make a real effort every time, because your mind will continue to play tricks unless you're on guard.

The background, generally, should be as simple as possible—neutral in shade, contrasting with the subject, but without any strong, striped or fussy pattern. Remember that your lens records everything it sees. Watch out for telegraph poles, cans, cows, fences, branches of trees, other people's feet. The best background for indoor shots is a plain wall; outdoors, a filtered or gray sky.

For the tiny infant, a blanket or pillow makes a good background.

PORTRAIT OF A VERY YOUNG LADY (*right*). Stairs running up, rails moving out, flowers growing out of head—and a stray foot in sharp black and white. And that's not all: notice the expression. Otherwise it's pretty bad, technically, if you want to get technical. Rolleicord, *f* 11 1/100, Supreme developed in Harvey's Panthermic 777.

GET THEM WHILE THEY'RE BUSY (*below*). Taken by Robert Berson with Rolleicord, *f* 11, 1/200, Super-XX developed in D-76.

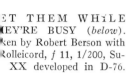

Don't lay him down on a large flat surface; it looks hard and unpleasant An older baby can be placed in a chair, or on a blanket spread out on the floor.

Bring attention to the child in your picture by throwing the background out of focus (with a large lens stop). Professional portrait photographers use lens stops of $f$ 4.5 and $f$ 5.6 for this reason.

Place the camera low, on a line with the child's head. A point of view as low as this seems more natural for pictures of children.

### GET THEM WHILE THEY'RE BUSY

The best pictures of children are made when they're not aware of what you're doing—when they're not bothering about you but are doing something they like—playing a game with a friend, reading the funnies, building sand structures, digging a hole, filling a pail, eating some ice cream, putting a doll to sleep. It doesn't matter what they're really doing, as long as it holds their attention and leaves you free to take pictures. In other words, if you want a good picture of a child, your problem isn't the camera and how to operate it, but finding something pleasant for the child to do. Incidentally, be sure (this can't be repeated too often) to let him get used to you being around with the camera before you actually start taking any pictures.

### LIGHT ON THE SUBJECT

Though we can't control the sun, we can still exercise plenty of control over the lighting of our picture outdoors. We can choose a time when the light is soft and diffused—in the mornings and late afternoon. And we can place our subject in the shade, away from the harsh glare of direct sunlight. Keeping the light soft avoids those black shadows which spoil so many pictures taken outdoors. A simple way to soften harsh shadows, by the way, is to use a folding reflector—a piece of white cardboard, or a large handkerchief, held a few feet from the subject. Watch the shadows under the nose and the eyes; avoid ugly shapes and dark sockets. Outdoors, let the light come from the side; indoors use a flat front light for general illumination and to soften shadows, and model the face with a stronger side light.

1. *An effective arrangement for two photofloods in reflectors:* place one 6 feet from subject and to the left; place the other 4 feet from subject and to the right. An additional overhead light is useful, sometimes, to add sparkle to dull hair.

2. *Another good arrangement for two photofloods in reflectors:* place

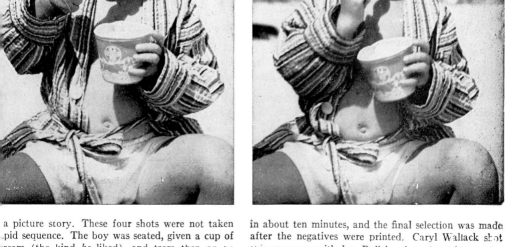

a picture story. These four shots were not taken
.pid sequence. The boy was seated, given a cup of
ream (the kind *he* liked), and from then on he
lost to everything. A dozen pictures were snapped

in about ten minutes, and the final selection was made
after the negatives were printed. Caryl Wallack shot
this sequence with her Rolleicord at *f*8, 1/100, using
Panatomic film developed in D-76.

one 2 feet in back and to the left; the other 3 feet in front and to the right. Place a reflector to prevent stray light, from the lamp facing the camera, hitting the lens.

Much can be done with only a single light source, using a reflector to soften the shadows.

### WHEN THEY WON'T SIT STILL

To get sharp pictures of children in action, use the fastest shutter speed your camera offers. This applies, of course, not to the miniature cameras with ƒ 1.5 lenses and 1/1000 shutters, but to the ordinary cameras with more modest equipment. The following table, calculated for moving objects in sunlight, may help you decide which shutter speed to use, depend-

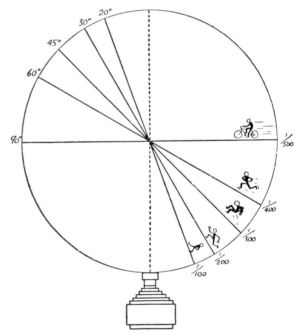

FIG. 64. SHUTTER-SPEED TABLE

ing on which angle of action you are photographing. Remember that distance also alters your shutter speed requirement. The greater the distance between object and lens, the less speed you need. A boy running toward you can be sharply photographed at, let's say, 30 feet, with a shutter speed of 1/200; at 15 feet you'll need 1/400. Under the same conditions, a boy moving horizontally across the field of view will need a shutter speed of 1/500 to stop motion.

IF HE WANTS TO TRAVEL

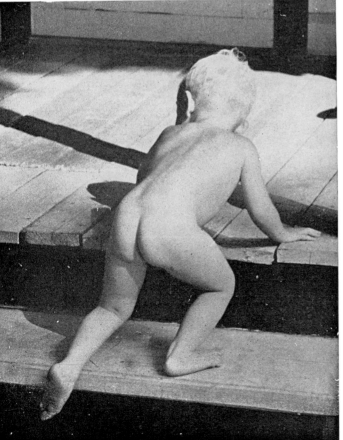

. . . LET HIM. Taken by Lawrence Ferguson with a Contax, Sonnar $f$ 2 lens, at $f$ 8, 1/250 second on Plus X, developed in Edwal 12.

Indoors, where the action is necessarily more restricted, a shutter speed of 1/200 or even 1/100, will prevent blur.

If your shutter does not have sufficient speed, you can still get sharp pictures of moving objects by adopting a device used by news photographers: *follow the action with your cameras.* The background will be blurred of course, but your subject will be sharp.

### GO WHERE HE GOES

If the child won't stay where you put him, if he feels like traveling, let him alone; just follow him. He'll undoubtedly head for some nice spot where he feels at home—and if you don't like it there, why that's just too bad. But as a matter of fact, you'll probably find this spot as suitable for your use as any other. So whenever you start taking pictures don't drag baby places. If you do, he won't stay there; and if you fight him about it he'll start to cry; and if he cries, where are you? Let *him* decide where the photographing is to take place. It'll be simpler that way.

### DON'T FORCE HIM

It's not a good idea to make the child do anything he doesn't want to do. Don't *make* him pose, or perform, or play with others, or act like a grownup (except in fun). Don't dress him up in fancy (but uncomfortable) clothes; you'll get better pictures if he's wearing his ordinary ones. Don't take pictures of him in hot weather, if he doesn't feel like it. And don't use make-up on a child at all, whether boy or girl. Avoid such blighting expressions as *Stand still for a moment, Put your hands down, Raise your head a little;* they simply petrify your subject.

### BE YOUR AGE

Don't try to amuse the baby by making funny faces or funnier sounds, hopping up and down, waving a newspaper, or rattling keys. Let him amuse *himself.* He's much better at it anyway.

### DON'T SKIMP ON FILM

Always have plenty of it with you, and use it freely. Your best pictures will happen suddenly; be ready for them. The cost of an extra negative is only a couple of cents, at most—so it's very poor economy to save on film when there's a priceless gesture or expression you want to capture. Two examples of what I mean are on page 247.

I had already wasted quite a bit of film on this little fellow playing at the water's edge and had almost given up hope of getting a real picture . . .

when suddenly he reached up—a man-sized stretch that said, "Isn't everything just wonderful!"

I had been snapping this young lady as she walked back and forth very busily, but caught nothing that looked like a picture . . .

when she suddenly stopped to examine something in the sand. The lighting was better, and that forefinger gesture was perfect.

All pictures taken with the Contax and Sonnar $f$ 1.5 at $f$ 8, 1/250, on Dupont Superior I, developed in Harold Harvey's Panthermic 777.

## BE CAREFUL

Especially indoors, where hot photoflood bulbs, trailing wires and clumsy tripod legs always seem to be getting in the way.

If you want to avoid hurting the child, perhaps seriously, take steps to prevent accidents, *before they happen.* Don't leave things lying around; be neat. And don't let other people clutter up the scenery. The best place for people who aren't really helping you is on the other side of a closed door.

## JUST TO REMIND YOU

1. Have everything ready before you call the child.
2. Use low camera angle.
3. Use small lens openings for depth of focus ($f$ 8 to $f$ 16).
4. Use fast shutter speeds to avoid blurring (1/100 or faster).
5. Watch those backgrounds.
6. Have light come from side or rear; avoid strong front light or direct sunlight.
7. Don't tell the child to smile or to look at the birdy.
8. Don't make him do anything he doesn't want to do.
9. Don't take pictures of him in hot weather if he doesn't feel like it.
10. Have patience, don't hurry!
11. Use plenty of film, preferably panchromatic.
12. Don't make the child pose or perform.
13. Snap him while he's busy.
14. Finish a game if you've started one; don't let the child suspect you weren't really playing.
15. Don't dress him up for the occasion; his regular clothes are more comfortable.
16. The best time to take pictures of any baby is after he's rested or had a nap.
17. Let the child go where *he* wants to; you follow him.
18. Don't start snapping as soon as the lights go on; let the child get used to the lights and to you.
19. Don't use make-up on children at any time.
20. Be careful.

# 14

# *Developing*

The making of a photograph can be as simple or as intricate a process as you wish. If you're only interested in *taking* snapshots, and don't want to be bothered with anything else, just "press the button" and let the corner drugstore do the rest. Your results will not be as good, but you'll never know the difference anyway, so it won't matter. If you want to have some *control* over your picture taking, and want the fun, too, of doing your own printing, developing and enlarging, you'll find this chapter and the next one helpful.

The technique of the darkroom deals with the selection and use of the following:

1. A *developer* that will bring out the latent image and create a negative of correct contrast and fine grain.

2. A *fixer* that will keep the negative from fading or spoiling.

3. A *print* or *enlargement* that will reproduce it as a positive, after it has been exposed, developed, and fixed.

Though none of these things presents any difficulty, especially with modern methods and materials, they nevertheless all require some attention to detail, some care in the choice of materials, and some skill in the use of equipment. The purpose of this chapter is to give you the basic essentials of good technique—the technical details (and some shortcuts) that will make it easier for you to take better pictures. No attempt will be made to cover the ground completely. Confusion would only be the result of trying to include *all* the soups, films, papers and devices that are on the market or are being whispered about in the darkrooms.

Of the materials and methods recommended here, only two things need be said: (1) *they work;* and (2) *they are easy to get and to use.* If, however, you prefer fancier folderol, you'll find thousands of glib amateurs, with secret formulas bulging out of all pockets, ready and willing to oblige. Remember, though, that most secret formulas lead nowhere. They usually waste time and money, and they serve only to prove that the standard formulas are better after all. If it's *pictures* you want, don't get cluttered up with experimental chemistry. As we said before, earlier in this book, the manufacturer of a photographic product usually knows how to use it to best advantage. That's his job. What he recommends is certainly worth trying before you go on to something else. And when you do try something new, be sure to compare the new results, critically, with the old. Only in that way will you learn *where* you're going and *what* you're doing in photography, and so profit from experience.

## THE CHOICE OF A DEVELOPER

### HOW A DEVELOPER WORKS

Photographic films and papers are coated with a gelatine emulsion that holds in suspension minute grains of a chemical salt of silver (*bromide* in the case of films, *bromide* and/or *chloride* in the case of papers). When light strikes these grains, a mysterious change takes place; the light forms what is known as a *latent* image. Certain chemicals have the property of breaking down these light-affected particles into their molecular constituents (*reducing* the so-called halides of silver to the pure metal, which looks black in its naked form, and releasing the bromine or chlorine as a gas). This process, as you might guess, is called *reduction;* and a developer is therefore nothing more than a *reducer.*

Most of the chemicals used to do this work do not function well alone; they are either too slow in getting started, or too fast once they have started. To balance the activity of a developer, therefore, we use an *accelerator* (like borax, carbonate, tribasic sodium phosphate, or Kodalk) and a *restrainer* (like potassium bromide). To preserve the solution (prevent it from oxidizing too rapidly) we also add sodium sulphite. This snares the dangerous oxygen before it can harm the developer and so converts the *sulphite* to *sulphate.* Some reducers work only on the high lights, producing negatives of great contrast; others work on the shadows almost as much as on the highlights, producing *flat* negatives. The perfect developer adjusts these chemical peculiarities so that normal contrast is produced by normal use.

Another important property of a developer is its power to cut down the *clumping* of grain. No negative is grainless. What we object to as "grain" is the bunching of silver particles that produces a mottled effect on the print. When these bunches are small and evenly distributed we have a negative of *fine grain;* when the bunches are large and spotted, the negative is *coarse grained.* Grain is affected by the type of emulsion, the amount of exposure, the temperature and time of development, the kind of reducer (paraphenylene diamine produces finer grain than most), the speed of drying. The developer, you see, is only *one* of many factors in the production of grain.

## RECOMMENDED DEVELOPERS

The easiest to use are those that are already made up in powder or liquid form. The powders should be dissolved, as directed, in distilled water (or in filtered rain water, or boiled and filtered tap water). These are all good:

| | |
|---|---|
| EASTMAN'S | D-76 (powder) |
| ANSCO'S | 17 (powder), Hyfinol (liquid), and Normadol (liquid)[a] |
| EDWAL'S | 12 and 20 (powder or liquid) |
| HARVEY'S | Panthermic 777 (powder or liquid)[a] |
| F-R'S | X-33 (liquid)[a] or X-22 [b] and X-44 [a] (1-shot liquid packets) |
| EASTMAN'S | Microdol (powder or liquid)[a] and Microdol-X [a, b] |
| EASTMAN'S | Versatol (concentrated liquid)[a] |
| TETENAL'S | Neofin (concentrated liquid)[a, b] |
| MAY & BAKER'S | Promicrol (powder or liquid)[a] |
| EDWAL'S | Minicol (powder or liquid)[a] |
| ANSCO'S | Finex-L (liquid)[a] |
| CLAYTON'S | P-60 (liquid)[a] |
| ILFORD'S | Microphen (powder or liquid)[a] |

[a] These developers are available *only* in prepared form. Manufacturers have not made formulas public.
[b] For new thin-layer emulsions such as KB-14, KB-17, Panatomic X, Isopan F, FF.

## HOW TO DEVELOP THE FILM

The easiest way is in a tank (either the plastic, adjustable-reel type, or the stainless-steel type). In either case, the film has to be loaded in a darkroom or in a changing bag (which is virtually a *pocket darkroom,* and one of the most useful photographic gadgets you can get). Follow the simple instructions supplied by the manufacturer of the tank, and you'll have no trouble. Be sure the reel is dry, or the film will stick. Hold the film by the edges as you move it into the grooves of the reel; avoid touching the emulsion surface. If the film sticks, cut the corners a bit and the film will move more easily. After the reel is loaded and the cover replaced, you can take the tank out of the changing bag or darkroom and do everything else with the lights on.

When you first buy your tank, find out, by experimenting, how much liquid it needs to cover your size film. Too much solution is as bad as too little. Measure out the amount needed each time *exactly;* otherwise you'll have parts of your film undeveloped (if there's not enough solution) or drooling all over the place when you start twirling the reel (if there's too much). Another important thing to find out, once and for all (and you can do this with plain water as well as developer), is just how long it takes to fill and empty the tank. You'll have to know this later in order to make allowances in your developing time. It's a good idea to learn how to fill the tank rapidly. The faster you do it, the more evenly will your film be developed. There's a knack in pouring the developer evenly so that you avoid splashing and making air bubbles which clog the spout. Practice this a few times before you actually load the tank with film.

*Highly recommended:* Paterson tanks (self-feeding, three-way agitation, adjustable). For 35-mm. and roll film. Can be imported from Wallace Heaton, Ltd., 127 New Bond Street, London, W.1.

A few other things you'll need:

1. A cellulose sponge or a piece of chamois. Both should be kept in jars filled with water and squeezed out (*not by twisting!*) just before using.

2. A pair of clips with which to hang up the film when drying it. Find a place where this drying can be done. It should be some dust-free corner, away from drafts and human traffic. A closet is a good place.

3. Two graduates, a four-ounce and a quart size. The larger one can be a pyrex beaker marked off in *cc.* and/or *ounces.*

4. An interval timer to check your processing along the way.

5. A reliable thermometer. Eimer and Amend, New York, offer an inexpensive glass-mercury type, packed in a wooden tube. Or you can get the all-metal Weston with its handy dial at top. Eastman and Ansco also make excellent thermometers. Be sure to say you want it for "round tank" use; there's another type made for tray use (when printing).

Have everything ready before you start. Cool the developer to the required temperature (if you're bothered much by the problem of high temperature, use Harold Harvey's Panthermic 777 which was compounded for just that purpose); make up the short stop (1 ounce of Kodak Liquid Hardener or 28 per cent *acetic acid* in each 16 ounces of water) and the hypo (4 ounces of *plain* hypo crystals in each 16 ounces of water, with 1 ounce of Kodak Liquid Hardener added. This is the best and least expensive way of making up a hypo solution. You can buy plain hypo for a few cents a pound; why pay more for the packaged kind?) Both the short stop and the hypo should be made the same temperature as the developer. One way to do this is to keep the glass containers for all three solutions in a large tray of iced water.

Now proceed as follows (*time and temperature* method):

1. Load the tank in the darkroom, or in a changing bag.

2. Fill the tank with water. Some amateurs prefer to dispense with this step. If you want to save time, you may do so, though it's really worth the effort. This preliminary water rinse gets rid of air bubbles, prevents streaky development, and removes the backing dye which interferes with the action of certain developers. It also reduces the temperature of the film (which is usually warmer than the developer) making it possible for the developer temperature to remain constant.

3. Pour out the water after 2 minutes and pour in the developer. *Start the interval timer when you start pouring the developer.*

4. Agitate the film *gently*, rotating spiral half a turn backwards and forwards (by means of center rod) at intervals of 30 seconds for the new thin films, and of one minute for the others. If it's a stainless-steel Nikor tank, or one of the three-way Paterson Adjustable tanks, it can be turned upside down at the above intervals without losing any liquid.

*The important thing is to keep this agitation uniform and gentle* (about 5 seconds each time); otherwise streaks and uneven development may ruin your film.

5. At the end of the development time (*and not before* . . . that's why, in 3, we started the timer when we did) start pouring out the developer. Don't try to pour it from the tank right into the bottle; use an intermediate beaker.

6. Pour in the short stop and agitate thoroughly.

7. At the end of three minutes *discard* the short stop.

8. Pour in the hypo solution.

9. At the end of ten minutes, pour out the hypo. You can use this hypo later to fix prints, so store it in a large (half-gallon) bottle. However, see caution on page 310.

10. Remove the cover of the tank, fill it with water and empty it again three or four times, and then set it under the faucet, with the stream playing on the center of the reel.

11. After fifteen minutes, remove the film, hang it up to dry (using a clip at each end, the lower clip serving to weight the film) and wipe off the surplus moisture on both sides with the sponge or chamois. Don't *rub* the emulsion side. To avoid using sponges or chamois, dip film for 30 seconds in dilute *Photoflo,* or similar *Aerosol* compound (follow manufacturer's directions). Result: *no scratches!*

12. Leave film to dry.

The process of developing film packs or cut films is no different from the method described above, for roll films, when you use the Nikor adjustable cut film tank. This tank (for all sizes up to 4 x 5) is fool-proof and easy to use. It is recommended highly.

The only difference between the development of cut films or film packs and roll films is in the loading of the tank. Just follow the instructions supplied by the manufacturer. For the rest, follow the procedure outlined above. For *development by inspection* see page 276.

## GAMMA

Messrs. Hurter and Driffield, who first used this term in explaining their *time-and-temperature* method of development, would be shocked, I'm sure, if they could hear the way it is now thrown carelessly about. Gamma is nothing more mysterious than the measure of negative contrast. Though it is useful in the laboratory, where controls can be enforced to give it meaning, it has no value to amateurs except in a rough sort of way. Unless we know what the contrasts were in the original subject as well as the characteristics of the printing medium to be used, the gamma of the negative is a meaningless bit of information. All you have to know about gamma is that it indicates the contrast relations between the original subject and the negative image. A gamma of 1, for instance, means that the contrast in the negative is just like the contrast of the original subject; a gamma of less or more than 1 indicates that the negative contrast is less or more than that of the original subject. Negatives for amateur use are developed to a gamma of about .8. Since contrast is usually *increased* by printing (or enlarging) the negative, this reduced gamma makes it possible to produce a print that seems to have normal contrast. Specimens of *underdeveloped, normal,* and *overdeveloped* negatives are on page 255.

The term *gamma infinity*, refers to the maximum amount of contrast that can be obtained with any given emulsion when developed to its fullest extent short of fog.

Speaking in less technical terms, I should advise you to follow this principle:

Develop for contrast; that is, develop for the time required to bring out correct contrasts between shadows and highlights. Usually that means developing for *less* time than is normally recommended. The negative will thus be a little softer (less contrasty) and will seem to have more quality. Most amateur negatives are frightfully overdeveloped: hard as nails. Cut down your developing time until you reach a point where the contrast of your negatives is right for the kind of prints you like. Don't be afraid to abbreviate developing time in this way (unless, of course, the developer is old and weak, in which case the best thing to do is to throw it out and start with a fresh batch).

An underdeveloped negative.          A normally developed negative.

An overdeveloped negative.

The respective gammas of these negatives would be about .4, .8, and 1.3. These negatives were made with Ansco film.

### HOW TO DRY A NEGATIVE QUICKLY

*Formalin* can harden the wet film of a negative so that heat will not melt it. If you're in a hurry, therefore, wash your negative thoroughly and use the following:

#### DRYING SOLUTION

|                    | AVOIRDUPOIS |        | METRIC |       |
| ------------------ | ----------- | ------ | ------ | ----- |
| Sodium bisulphite  | 2¼          | ounces | 63.6   | grams |
| Formalin           | 6           | ounces | 170    | grams |
| Water              | 32          | ounces | 1000   | cc.   |

Leave the negative in the tank, pour in the solution, and let it stand for five minutes. Then wash it, remove from tank, and heat gently. The solution can be kept and reused.

*Alternate method:* Remove surface water, dip negative in alcohol bath (90% alcohol, 10% water). Hang up to dry. *Do not use rubbing alcohol;* it leaves an opalescent deposit.

## THE BUGABOO OF GRAIN

Ever since the miniature camera came into vogue, we've heard a lot about that photographer's headache called grain. Strangely enough, and despite all the squawking, no picture can be made without it. Grain is the positive image of the spaces between the clumps of silver that make up the negative. You can't eliminate it; only minimize its troubles.

*For grainless negatives:* Use a fine-grain emulsion (the slower the film, the finer the grain). New emulsions released in 1956, such as Plus X and Verichrome Pan, are less grainy than the old films of equal speed. *Do not overexpose.* Use a fine-grain developer such as D-76, D-23, D-25, Microdol, MCM 100, Edwal 12, Promicrol, Microphen, X-33, Clayton P-60, or Ethol UFG. *Keep all solution temperatures uniform.* For *best* results try the wonderful new thin-emulsion films (Panatomic X, Adox KB-14, KB-17, Adox R18P, Isopan F and FF, Ilford Pan F). These give spectacular results when developed in Neofin Blue, FRX-22, Clayton P-60, D-76, Windisch 665, or Willi Beutler's Developer.

*For grainless prints:* avoid hard, glossy paper, condenser enlargers, concentrated paper developers; use matte surface paper or soft or diluted developers. Some amateurs minimize grain by throwing the enlarged image slightly out of focus, or by enlarging through a mesh screen or a silk stocking stretched taut over a sewing hoop.

## HALATION AND HOW TO PREVENT IT

Halation—that is, the halo of light that is formed around the edge of a brightly illuminated surface and which cuts into the shadows—is often found in landscape and other kinds of photography, but it is particularly troublesome in interior views, especially around the windows. The cause of halation is easily traced to the rays of bright light which strike the sensitized surface and pass on through it and the plate, or film, that supports it. When the rays reach the other side they are reflected back, and so act again on the sensitized surface, and this fogs the plate or film all around the brightly-lighted area.

Films are not subject to halation as much as plates are, because they are thinner; in any case, most modern films and plates are already coated with a non-halation backing which is satisfactory protection for most purposes. For still greater protection it is better to develop the film in a *compensating developer* (one that acts on the *surface,* does not penetrate to the bottom of the emulsion). Such a developer (recommended by Hans Windisch, author of *The New Photo School*) is given below. The virtues of this developer are that it equalizes extreme light contrasts, requires no extra exposure, and produces fairly fine grain. The developer consists of two stock solutions, which are mixed in certain proportions and diluted for use.

### COMPENSATING DEVELOPER FOR EXTREME CONTRASTS

WINDISCH

*A*

| | | |
|---|---|---|
| Water (boiled) | 100 | cc. |
| Pyrocatechin | 8 | grams |
| Sodium sulphite (cryst) | 2.5 | grams |

This solution can be stored in a brown bottle if filled almost to the brim.

*B*

10 per cent caustic soda solution (made by dissolving 10 grams of caustic soda in about 75 cc. of *cold* water and then adding enough cold water to make 100 cc.)

This solution can also be stored for about 2 months if kept in an ordinary bottle filled almost to the brim.

*Directions for use.* For tank development take 500 cc. of water plus 12 cc. of solution *A* plus 7 cc. of solution *B*. Development time is 15 to 20 minutes.

For contrasty negative material take 500 cc. of water, 20 cc. of solution *A*, 5 cc. of solution *B*. Develop for 18 to 20 minutes.

*The developer should be used only once.*

For still softer negatives curtail the development time; for more contrast, increase time.

For tray development of large negatives, development can be stopped after 12 to 14 minutes. The best concentration for this purpose is 100 cc. water, 4 cc. of solution *A* plus 3 cc. of solution *B*.

## THE AFTER TREATMENT OF NEGATIVES

A negative that is too thin will make a flat print, and one that is too dense will not show the proper gradation in the finished print. There are two ways in which these defects can be rectified, namely, (1) by using the proper paper for making the print, and (2) by *intensifying* or *reducing* the negative as the case may be. It has to be a pretty poor negative that will not make a fair to middling print if you use the right kind of paper. If it is too thin, try intensifying it; if too dense, try reducing.

### HOW TO INTENSIFY A NEGATIVE

A negative that is too thin can be considerably bettered by intensification, but you must not be led to believe that this treatment will improve the detail for all it can do is to strengthen that which is already present in the negative. Now there are two reasons why a negative may be thin and these are because (*a*) the plate was underexposed, or (*b*) it was underdeveloped, or it may be due to both of these faults.

(*a*) Where the negative was *underexposed,* fix and wash it thoroughly and then immerse it in the following intensifier:

### CHROMIUM INTENSIFIER

STOCK SOLUTION

|  | METRIC | AVOIRDUPOIS |
|---|---|---|
| Potassium bichromate | 90 grams | 3 ounces |
| Hydrochloric acid | 64 cc. | 2 ounces |
| Water to make | 1000 cc. | 32 ounces |

For use, take one part of stock solution to 10 parts of water. Bleach thoroughly, then wash five minutes and redevelop fully (about 5 minutes) in artificial light or daylight in any quick-acting, non-staining developer (such as D-72 diluted 1:3). Then wash thoroughly and dry. Greater intensification can be secured by repeating the process. The degree of intensification can be controlled by varying the time of redevelopment. This treatment, of course, does not produce detail that was lost through underexposure; it only increases contrast in the existing weak detail.

*Warning.* Developers containing a high concentration of sulphite such as D-76 or DK-76 are not suitable for redevelopment since the sulphite tends to dissolve the silver chloride before the developing agents have time to act on it. However, films developed in D-76 or DK-76 can be intensified in the mercury bleacher and ammonia blackener given below and next page, or in the prepared intensifier sold in photo-supply stores.

The Eastman chromium intensifier powders are as satisfactory as the above formula, and are supplied in prepared form ready to use simply by dissolving in water.

Stains are sometimes produced during intensification or reduction unless the following precautions are observed: (1) The negative should be fixed and washed thoroughly before treatment and be free of scum or stain. (2) It should be hardened in the formalin hardener given below before reducing or intensifying. (3) Only one negative should be handled at a time and it should be agitated thoroughly during the treatment; then washed thoroughly and wiped off carefully before drying.

### FORMALIN HARDENER

|  | METRIC | AVOIRDUPOIS |  |
|---|---|---|---|
| Water | 500 cc. | 16 | ounces |
| Formalin (40 per cent |  |  |  |
| Formaldehyde sol.) | 10 cc. | 2½ | drams |
| Sodium carbonate (dry) | 5 grams | 73 | grams |
| Water to make | 1000 cc. | 32 | ounces |

This formula is recommended for the treatment of negatives which would normally be softened considerably by intensification or reduction.

After hardening for three minutes, rinse the negative and immerse it for five minutes in a fresh acid fixing bath. Wash well.

(*b*) If the negative has been *underdeveloped*, then make up the following solutions which may be used over and over again. These solutions are called the *bleacher* and the *blackener* respectively.

### MERCURY BLEACHER

|  | METRIC | AVOIRDUPOIS |  |
|---|---|---|---|
| Mercury bichloride (*poison!*) | 30 grams | 1 | ounce |
| Hot water | 500 cc. | 16 | ounces |

When this solution is cool, pour it off from the white feathery crystals that are thrown down and then add

| Hydrochloric acid | 2 cc. | ½ dram |

Now put the negative in this solution and rock the tray until it has turned a creamy color all the way through. Then wash the bleached negative thoroughly and immerse it in the following solution for about one minute when it will be greatly intensified and of a good black color.

## AMMONIA BLACKENER

|                    | METRIC    | AVOIRDUPOIS |
|--------------------|-----------|-------------|
| Ammonia (0.880)    | 30 grams  | 1 ounce     |
| Water              | 1000 cc.  | 32 ounces   |

### HOW TO REDUCE A NEGATIVE

A negative that is too dense will not only take a long time to print, but it will make a picture which is too full of contrasts. This contrast may be so great that the thinner parts will print up before the light will make any impression through the darker parts, and there will be neither detail nor gradation; hence a reducer must be used to improve it. The cause of dense negatives is (*a*) either overexposure, or (*b*) overdevelopment. It can be remedied very considerably by immersing it in the following reducer which greatly decreases the contrast by lighting up the shadows and leaving the high lights as they are.

### FARMER'S REDUCER

|                                                    | METRIC   | AVOIRDUPOIS |
|----------------------------------------------------|----------|-------------|
| Hypo solution (1 part hypo to 5 parts water)       | 226 cc.  | 8 ounces    |
| Potassium ferricyanide (10 per cent solution)      | Q. S.    | Q. S.       |

To add Q. S. means a sufficient quantity of the ferricyanide to the hypo solution to make it a light lemon color. Now immerse the negative in this solution and rock the tray; if the negative does not get thinner add more ferricyanide until it has the desired action. When the negative is reduced as much as you want it, take it out and wash it *quickly* or the reducing action may go on and spoil the negative.

See the supplemental glossary, under "reducer," for further notes on cutting, flattening, and proportional reducers.

## HOW TO REMOVE FOG

A fogged negative is one that looks as if it were covered with a thick layer of smoke. Fog is often caused by white light striking the plate and this may occur (*a*) while the plate or film is being put in the holder or the camera, (*b*) while it is in the camera, or (*c*) while it is being developed. It can also be caused (*d*) by developer itself. If the fog is slight, it can be cleared away by immersing the negative in the following solution:

### FOG REMOVER

|  | METRIC | AVOIRDUPOIS |
|---|---|---|
| Alum | 42.4 gr. | 1½ ounces |
| Citric acid | 42.4 gr. | 1½ ounces |
| Ferrous sulphate | 113 gr. | 4 ounces |
| Water | 1000 cc. | 32 ounces |

As this solution does not deteriorate, you can pour it back in the bottle after you have used it and keep it for the next time you have a fogged plate. After the negative has been fixed and washed put it in the solution and rock the tray until the fog disappears. If the fog is very bad it should be put in a weak solution of Farmer's Reducer, previously described, but you must be careful not to leave it too long or there will be nothing left to tell the story except the blank film.

## HOW TO GET RID OF BLEMISHES

First, be sure your negative is spotlessly clean. Use carbon tetrachloride, or Edwal Film Cleaner (removes dirt *and* eliminates static). Then, use any of the following: (1) Retouch negative (see page 262). (2) Make soft-focus prints by interposing something like a gauze, a screen, or a silk stocking stretched over a hoop. (3) Use rough, matte instead of smooth, glossy papers. (4) Use a cold-light enlarger instead of the condenser type. (5) Throw your enlarger lens slightly out of focus. (6) Subdue lips, freckles, blemishes by using *pan*chromatic film, instead of *ortho*. (7) Clean film with ammonia. See also pages 265 and 266.

## HOW TO SPOT A NEGATIVE

You will very often find after you have made a negative that the film has transparent spots and pinholes in it. These must be painted over or filled in, or *spotted out* as it is called. To spot a negative you can use a little India ink or you can buy a cake of *opaque,* and this you put on with a No. 3 red sable brush that has a fine point. An improvement over India ink or opaque are the recently perfected dye retouching mediums: Spotone, Dyene, Dyacol; and the reducers, Spotoff and Etchadine. They are easy to use and easy to control. You can get full information about them, and instructions for their use, free, by writing to Retouch Methods Co., Chatham, N. J. (for *Spotone* and *Spotoff*); to Dyacol Products Laboratory, P.O. Box 192, San Francisco, California (for Dyacol and Dyene); and to Jamieson Products Co., 9341 Peninsula Drive, Dallas, Texas (for Etchadine). The manufacturer of Etchadine will also send you, free (as long as the supply lasts), a plastic mixing tray if you write for it. Also ask for the Etchadine Instruction Booklet, *Liquid Light* (20 pp.).

### HOW TO RETOUCH A NEGATIVE

You need: (1) a retouching desk, (2) a medium soft lead pencil, (3) a retouching knife, and (4) a bottle of retouching medium (which gives the polished side of the negative a surface that takes pencil). The tools of a

FIG. 65. A CHEAP RETOUCHING DESK (*left*) AND A
PROFESSIONAL RETOUCHING DESK

FIG. 66. A HOLDER FOR RETOUCHING LEADS (*left*) AND
A RETOUCHING KNIFE

retouching outfit are shown in *Figs. 65* and *66.* The retouching desk is used to support the negative and allow light to pass through it. It has either a fixed or pivoted reflector at the back, and the upper board serves to shade the negative.

The first thing to do, when you start to retouch a negative, is to clean the polished side of it (see item 38, page 377), then make a little pad of a soft, old cotton rag and moisten it with a little retouching medium, which you can buy ready to use. Rub the negative with the pad, giving it a rotary motion; this will produce a surface with a "bite," so that the pencil marks can take hold.

Having prepared the negative, set it on the frame of the desk which should stand in front of a window or near some other light source; then put a medium-soft lead with a very sharp point in the pencil holder and touch out blemishes first. This you do by beginning at the center of each light spot and make little marks on it with your pencil like a lot of commas, gradually easing off as you get to the edge. This done, work over the other parts, giving your pencil a rotary motion until you have produced a stipple effect. Where the negative is too dense you can lighten it by using your retouching knife (but be very careful not to scrape through the film). A better way to reduce those areas is to use Spotoff, Etchadine, or Dyene (see page 262).

## HOW TO VARNISH A NEGATIVE

When you are going to make only a few prints from a negative, it is not at all necessary to varnish it, but a coat of varnish will give it an extremely hard surface that will protect it for all time against wear. Negative varnish can be bought (as in Kodalak Clear) or you can make it up:

### COLD NEGATIVE VARNISH

| Celluloid | $\frac{1}{8}$ | ounce |
| Amyl acetate | 6 | ounces |
| Oil of lavender | 3 | drops |

The amyl acetate gives off a sickly odor and the oil of lavender is put in to kill it. This varnish can be poured on the negative and flowed over it, or it can be put on with a brush while both are cold. To retouch a varnished negative, use retouching medium as before.

## NEGATIVE FAULTS

Here are the most common negative defects and a few ideas on things you can do to avoid or overcome them.

### STREAKS OR OTHER IRREGULARITIES

1. *Cause:* Insufficient or improper agitation. *Cure:* Constant agitation during development, changing motion at frequent and regular intervals.

## AIR BELLS

2. *Cause:* Air bubbles clinging to emulsion surface and preventing action of developer. *Cure:* Place film *into* solution instead of pouring solution into tank. Agitate. Knock tank against table to dislodge bubbles.

## BLACK SPOTS

3. *Cause:* Undissolved developing agent particles settling on emulsion surface. *Cure:* Better preparation of solution, and filtering.

## UNEVEN DEVELOPMENT

4. *Cause:* Developer poured into tank too slowly. *Cure:* Pour solution into tank quickly and continuously.

## PINHOLES

5. *Cause:* Gas bubbles formed when film is placed in acid rinse or acid hypo baths. *Cure:* Avoid strongly acid afterbaths. Agitate. Avoid developer with carbonate; use those which contain borax or sodium metaborate, neither of which produces a gas on contact with acid.

## RETICULATION

6. *Cause:* Sudden *drop* in temperature between developing and fixing, or the use of an exhausted fixing bath. *Cure:* Avoid both causes.

## FOG

7. *Cause:* If margins are clear, fog was produced in camera; if margins are also fogged, fogging occurred while loading or developing and may have been caused by light leaks, unsafe safelight, high temperature, over-developing or old film. *Cure:* Obvious precautions.

## WATER SPOTS

8. *Cause:* Uneven drying, or failure to remove all excess water. *Cure:* Wipe film carefully after washing. Water spots can usually be removed by soaking film in water, wiping and drying. If this doesn't work, try softening the film with weak ammonia water or a solution of sodium carbonate. Then refix, wash, and dry.

## BLUE OR RED STAINS

9. *Cause:* Halation backing not completely dissolved. *Cure:* Bathe in a weak solution of ammonia, or a ten per cent solution of sodium sulphite.

## THIN

10. *Cause:* If shadow detail is lacking, it was *underexposed;* if the negative is flat, but with shadow detail, it was *underdeveloped.* *Cure:* Underexposure cannot be remedied; you can only improve what detail there is by intensification with chromium intensifier, which at the same time increases contrast. Underdevelopment can be corrected by *intensification.*

## DENSE

11. *Cause:* If the negative is flat, fogged, with too much shadow detail, it was *overexposed.* If it is contrasty, it was *overdeveloped.* *Cure:* chemical reduction.

## MILKY

12. *Cause:* Incomplete fixation. *Cure:* Replace negative in fixing bath, then wash and dry.

### GREEN STAINS

13. *Cause:* Too high a concentration of chrome alum in hardening bath. *Cure:* Use more dilute solution or less alum.

## YELLOW STAINS

14. *Cause:* Dichroic chemical fog. *Cure:* Wash in a dilute solution (.25 per cent) of potassium permanganate. If brown stain results, wash in a ten per cent solution of sodium bisulphite.

## HOW TO AVOID AND OVERCOME SPOTS AND SCRATCHES

Keep dust out of camera; blow it out with a rubber ear syringe. Keep tanks clean. Filter all solutions. Don't cinch the film by pulling it too tight. Avoid the felt-mouthed film cassettes. Harden the film after development. View with suspicion all sponges and chamois. If you do swab the film after washing, do so very gently. Make sure that the pressure plate in your camera is absolutely smooth and *clean;* if there's any

grease on it, it will become a dust trap. Use reloadable cassettes in preference to the daylight-loading cartridges; film with paper leaders is best
of all. See item 40, page 377.

Here's a simple technique for overcoming pinholes and scratches:

1. Place the negative in the enlarger. With orange filter in place, project the image on the paper. Scratches and pinholes will show up clearly.

2. Fill in blemishes *on the paper* with medium-soft lead pencil.

3. Swing filter out of the way and make the exposure.

4. The pencil marks on the printing will protect the emulsion from the
light that streams through the pinholes or scratches.

5. Erase pencil marks, before developing.

6. Retouch after drying.

John Adam Knight suggests this way to get rid of scratches:

1. Make a solution of 1 part glycerin to 6 parts water (70° F.).

2. Soak the scratched film in this bath until it becomes damp.

3. Very gently wipe *across* the scratch with a wet chamois squeezed
almost dry. Do this once only. Then hang up to dry.

Three other ways to overcome scratches:

1. Make a sandwich of negative in *glycerin* or *carbon tetrachloride* [1]
between two thin glass slides. Eliminate air bubbles before removing
sandwich from liquid. Wipe edges and both faces and enlarge at once.

2. Place a bit of Vaseline between thumb and forefinger, then spread
thinly on both sides of negative before enlarging. Works like magic!

3. Use *Refractasil,* a unique silicone compound produced by General
Electric. It hides scratches because it has the same refractive index as
film. It cannot be absorbed by the emulsion, is easily wiped off with clean
chamois or tissue.

### NEWTON'S RINGS

These troublesome color rings may appear when the film touches a glass
surface in the enlarger. Suggested cure: After the film is developed and
dry, roll the film backwards (reversing its natural curve). Let it stay that
way about 12 hours. Clean pressure plate with slightly damp cloth (not
*chamois*). Pass cloth over glossy side of film.

## FORMULAS

You'll need an accurate pair of scales, preferably *metric,* a quart pyrex
beaker, an asbestos coated screen to place over the raw flame when you

---

[1] *Dangerous!* See item 38, page 377.

heat the solutions, a fluted funnel (liter size), filter paper (preferably the gray Prat-Dumas No. 33), a good thermometer, another pyrex beaker or two for transfer of solutions, a stirring rod, some brown bottles (liter size, with bakelite-type screw caps).

## 1. FINE GRAIN, SOFT WORKING (SAME AS D-76)

For maximum emulsion speed and fine grain. Use without dilution except where noted.

| Dissolve chemicals in this order: | METRIC | AVOIRDUPOIS |
|---|---|---|
| Water, about 125° F. (52° C.) | 750 cc. | 24 ounces |
| Elon (Metol) | 2 grams | 29 grains |
| Sodium sulphite, dry | 100 grams | 3 oz. 145 grains |
| Hydroquinone | 5 grams | 73 grains |
| Borax, granular | 2 grams | 29 grains |
| Cold water to make | 1 liter | 32 ounces |

Average time of tank development at 68° F., intermittent agitation (5 seconds every 30 seconds): Panatomic X (35-mm., *thin* emulsion), dilute 1-1, 7 minutes; Panatomix X (roll film), 7 minutes; Plus X (35-mm., *fast* emulsion) and Verichrome Pan (828), 7 minutes; Isopan FF and Adox KB 14, 7 minutes; Isopan F and Adox KB 17, 9 minutes; Verichrome Pan (roll film and pack), agitate 5 seconds every minute, 12 minutes; Tri-X (roll film and pack, revised time), agitate 5 seconds every minute, 11 minutes.

Contrast can be altered by varying development times.

## 2. FINE GRAIN, METABORATE (SAME AS DK-76)

For greatest shadow detail on fine-grain film.

|  | METRIC | AVOIRDUPOIS |
|---|---|---|
| Water, about 125° F. (52° C.) | 750 cc. | 24 ounces |
| Elon (Metol) | 2 grams | 29 grains |
| Sodium sulphite, dry | 100 grams | 3 oz., 145 grains |
| Hydroquinone | 5 grams | 73 grains |
| Kodalk (sodium metaborate) | 2 grams | 29 grains |
| Water to make | 1 liter | 32 ounces |

Development times at 68° F., one minute more than for D-76.

If the Kodalk concentration is increased to 5 grams (2½ times normal) reduce developing time to ½; if Kodalk is increased to 10 grams (5 times normal), reduce development to ⅜; if Kodalk is increased to 20 grams (10 times normal), reduce development to ¼.

### 3. FINE GRAIN, SUPERB GRADATION (SAME AS D-25)

|  | METRIC | | AVOIRDUPOIS | |
|---|---|---|---|---|
| Hot water (125° F. or 52° C.) | 750 | cc. | 24 | ounces |
| Elon (Metol) | 7.5 | grams | ¼ | ounce |
| Sodium sulphite, dry | 100 | grams | 3 | oz., 145 grains |
| Sodium bisulphite | 15 | grams | ½ | ounce |
| Cold water to make | 1 | liter | 32 | ounces |

Dissolve chemicals in order given. Do not dilute for use.

Average developing time for roll film: 18 minutes in a tank at 77° F. (25° C.). *Temperature is important.* This is one of the best of the fine-grain developers. It is nontoxic and nonstaining, and gives beautiful gradations. Introduced by Kodak in 1944, it has become an international favorite. It was worked out by R. W. Henn and J. I. Crabtree.

For Panatomic X, Plus X, Verichrome Pan, Adox KB 17, and Isopan F, Kodak has not released revised developing times. Try 8-10 minutes at 77° F.

For replenishment, add DK-25R (see below) at the rate of 45 cc. (1½ ounces) per roll for the first 12 rolls per liter (or 50 rolls per gallon) and thereafter 22 cc. (¾ ounce) per roll for the next 12 rolls per liter (or 50 rolls per gallon). The developer should then be discarded and replaced with fresh solution.

#### REPLENISHER FOR D-25 (DK-25R)

|  | METRIC | AVOIRDUPOIS |
|---|---|---|
| Hot water (125° F. or 52° C.) | 750 cc. | ?4 ounces |
| Elon (Metol) | 10 grams | 145 grains |
| Sodium sulphite, dry | 100 grams | 3 oz., 145 grains |
| Kodalk | 20 grams | 290 grains |
| Cold water to make | 1 liter | 32 ounces |

### 4. FINE GRAIN, FOR LONG SCALE SUBJECTS (SAME AS D-23)

|  | METRIC | | AVOIRDUPOIS | |
|---|---|---|---|---|
| Hot water (125° F. or 52° C.) | 750 | cc. | 24 | ounces |
| Elon (Metol) | 7.5 | grams | ¼ | ounce |
| Sodium sulphite, dry | 100 | grams | 3 | oz., 145 grains |
| Cold water to make | 1 | liter | 32 | ounces |

Dissolve chemicals in order given. Do not dilute for use.

Average developing time about 19 minutes in a tank or 15 minutes in a tray at 68° F. (20° C.). For thin-emulsion films (Panatomic X, Adox KB 14 and KB 17, Isopan F and FF) and for Plus X and Verichrome Pan, try 8-10 minutes at 68° F.

Replenish with DK-25R at the rate of 22 cc. (¾ ounce) per roll. Discard after 25 rolls per liter (32 ounces).

### 5. METOL SULPHITE (WINDISCH)

This is a compensating, fine-grain developer that acts without an alkali.

|  | METRIC | | AVOIRDUPOIS | |
|---|---|---|---|---|
| Water, boiled | 500 | cc. | 16 | ounces |
| Metol | 2.5 | grams | 38.5 | grains |
| Sodium sulphite, cryst | 50 | grams | 1¾ | ounces |
| Water to make | 1000 | cc. | 32 | ounces |

Dissolve the metol in warm water, then add the sulphite. If the anhydrous (dry) form of the sulphite is used, only half the above quantities should be used. Average tank developing time, 18-25 minutes at 68° F. For thin emulsions try 10-15 minutes at 68° F.

### 6. SEASE ND 3 (FINE GRAIN, GOOD CONTRAST)

This developer requires 50 to 100 per cent more than normal exposure.

|  | METRIC | | AVOIRDUPOIS | |
|---|---|---|---|---|
| Water (125° F.) | 975 | cc. | 31 | ounces |
| Sodium sulphite, dry | 90 | grams | 3 | ounces |
| Paraphenylenediamine (base) | 10 | grams | 146 | grains |
| Glycin | 2 | grams | 29 | grains |
| Water to make | 1000 | cc. | 32 | ounces |

For tank use develop fast emulsions at 68° about 25 minutes. For Panatomic X, Plus X, and Adox KB 17, try 15-20 minutes at 68° F.

### 7. WINDISCH 665 (FINE GRAIN)

This superb developer requires 2X normal exposure, gives very fine grain, full shadow detail, highlight compensation. Also from Perutz.[2]

|  | METRIC | | AVOIRDUPOIS | |
|---|---|---|---|---|
| Water (boiled) | 500 | cc. | 16 | ounces |
| Sodium sulphite, dry [3] | 90 | grams | 3 | ounces |
| Orthophenylenediamine | 12 | grams | 180 | grains |
| Metol | 12 | grams | 180 | grains |
| Potassium metabisulphite | 10 | grams | 150 | grains |
| Water to make | 1000 | cc. | 32 | ounces |

[2] Available from Studiophot Corporation, Cleveland, Ohio.   [3] See next page.

*Do not dissolve the sulphite in hot water.* Dissolve all chemicals separately. The metol and orthophenylenediamine dissolve completely only after the two solutions have been mixed. Add the sulphite solution, then the bisulphite to the developer solutions. Stir until clear, then filter.

Average developing time for medium-speed film, 13 minutes at 68° F. For thin-emulsion films, 8-9 minutes at 68° F.

### 8. WILLI BEUTLER'S FINE-GRAIN DEVELOPER
#### (FOR MAXIMUM EMULSION SPEED AND SHARPNESS)

Yields delicate, fully graded negatives, high emulsion speed, and exceptional resolution. Willi Beutler is also the inventor of Neodyn, renamed Neofin (a surface developer that hardens the emulsion), which is said to be a variation of this formula. Make two stock solutions:

*A*

| Water | 1000 cc. |
|---|---|
| Metol | 10 grams |
| Sodium sulphite | 50 grams |

*B*

| Water | 1000 cc. |
|---|---|
| Sodium carbonate (dry) | 50 grams |

To mix, add 50 cc. of *A* and 50 cc. of *B* to 500 cc. of pure water.

Develop slow emulsions (Panatomic X, Adox KB 14, Isopan FF) 7 to 10 minutes at 65° F.; medium-speed emulsions (Plus X, Isopan F, Adox KB 17) 8 to 12 minutes at 65°. *Do not use higher temperatures.*

### 9. PHENIDONE FINE GRAIN (HIGH EMULSION SPEED)

Phenidone (or 1-phenyl-3-pyrazolidone, as the chemists know it) was first compounded in 1890, but it wasn't until 1940, when Drs. J. D. Kendall and A. J. Axford of Ilford, Ltd., rediscovered it as a possible substitute for metol that it began to have its present vogue. It was first marketed in 1952, has since become a vital ingredient in many excellent fine-grain developers, notably Microphen and Clayton P60. Among its many remarkable properties: it is nontoxic, gives very fine grain and increases speed of film.

Here is a fine-grain, high-emulsion-speed formula using Phenidone that shows little change of activity in use. It resembles Microphen in action.

| *Dissolve in this order:* | METRIC | |
|---|---|---|
| Sodium sulphite, dry | 100 | grams |
| Hydroquinone | 5.0 | grams |
| Borax | 3.0 | grams |
| Boric acid | 3.5 | grams |
| Phenidone | 0.2 | grams |
| Potassium bromide | 1 | gram |
| Water to make | 1000 | cc. |

This developer is used undiluted. Average developing time for medium-speed film is 7-11 minutes at 68° F.

Another interesting formula for the use of Phenidone, this time as a stock solution, is the following. It was suggested by Ilford and is reprinted from *The British Journal of Photography*, February 8, 1957. The advantages of a stock-solution developer are many: you are using fresh developer each time; and it resists oxidation.

### STOCK SOLUTION

| *Dissolve in this order:* | METRIC | |
|---|---|---|
| 1. Potassium sulphite, dry | 297.2 | grams |
| (in 400 cc. warm water) | | |

2. *Then add to 500 cc. water (plus a pinch of potassium sulphite):*

| | | |
|---|---|---|
| Glycin | 50 | grams |
| Phenidone | 1.75 | grams |
| Potassium bromide | 8 | grams |

*Mix 1 and 2, then add:*

| | | |
|---|---|---|
| 3. Potassium hydroxide | 34 | grams |

Finally add enough water to make total volume 1000 cc.

This concentrated stock solution is diluted 1:7 for use.

Average developing time for medium speed film is 7 minutes at 20°C. (68°F.) for a gamma of 0.7. For the new thin emulsions (Panatomic-X, KB 17, Isopan F) try 5 minutes.

One of the special characteristics of all Phenidone developer formulas is their unusually long life. This is due to four unique properties of Phenidone. It resists oxidation and exhaustion, can activate other chemicals at low concentrations, it can produce active developers at lower pH's (measure of acidity), and it is unlikely to cause dermatitis.

When a PQ developer (Phenidone-Hydroquinone) finally oxidizes, which it does slowly, the oxidation product is colorless, so it doesn't stain

### 10. SUPERFINE GRAIN W 80 (M. U. WALLACH)

This developer was originally designed for use in photographing night scenes or scenes of extreme contrast. It can, however, also be used for other scenes with good results. Complete details for its use may be found in Mr. Wallach's booklet, *How to Take Pictures at Night*. It produces very fine grain without any appreciable loss of speed.

|  | METRIC | | AVOIRDUPOIS | |
|---|---|---|---|---|
| Water (about 100°) | 600 | cc. | 24 | ounces |
| Metol | 10 | grams | 155 | grains |
| Sodium sulphite, dry | 125 | grams | 4½ | ounces |
| Paraphenylenediamine | | | | |
|    hydrochloride | 16.6 | grams | 257.3 | grains |
| Glycin | 8.3 | grams | 128.6 | grains |
| Pyro (or rubinol) | 1.6 | grams | 24.8 | grains |
| Trisodium phosphate, | | | | |
|    monohydrate | 3.3 | grams | 51 | grains |
| Water to make | 1000 | cc. | 32 | ounces |

Develop all types of films at 70°, from 17 to 28 minutes, depending on gamma desired. For thin emulsions (Plus X, Verichrome Pan, Panatomic X, Adox KB 17) try 8 to 15 minutes at 70°.

### 11. EDWAL 12 (FINE GRAIN)

For maximum emulsion speed and enlargements to 15 or 20 diameters.

|  | METRIC | | AVOIRDUPOIS | |
|---|---|---|---|---|
| Water (125° F.) | 600 | cc. | 20 | ounces |
| Metol | 6 | grams | 90 | grains |
| Sodium sulphite, dry | 90 | grams | 3 | ounces |
| Paraphenylenediamine | 10 | grams | 150 | grains |
| Glycin | 5 | grams | 75 | grains |
| Water to make | 1000 | cc. | 32 | ounces |

Average developing times at 70°: 12½ to 18 minutes.

For more recent and thin emulsions (Panatomic X, Plus X, Verichrome Pan, Adox KB 17), developing times of 7 to 11 minutes are suggested for testing. *Cut developing time 20 per cent on first roll of film.* Roll film should be developed 10 per cent longer than 35-mm. film; cut film and film pack should be developed 20 per cent longer than 35-mm. film.

For best results add 20 per cent of old used Edwal 12 to each new batch. If the developer is stored in a quart bottle, 6 ounces of fresh solution can be kept aside in a small bottle when the developer is made up, and 6 ounces of old solution added to the remaining 26 ounces of fresh developer. Then, as a little solution is lost each time a roll is developed,

the loss is made up from the 6 ounces of fresh solution in the small bottle.
There are three other ways of using Edwal 12:

1. *Replenishment method.* Develop 4 rolls of film in a quart of fresh
solution (or 2 rolls in a quart that has 20 per cent of old Edwal added),
discard enough solution so that 29 ounces remain and add 3 ounces of
fresh developer from another bottle. From this point on, repeat the replenishment *after every roll,* discarding enough solution so that 3 ounces
of fresh solution can be added. A quart of the developer will last indefinitely when used this way, provided the solution is not exposed too much
to air. If the developer begins to get weak, discard 6 ounces instead of
the usual 3 and it will be brought back to full strength. After developing
about 25 rolls let the precipitate settle and pour off the clear solution.
Filter after every forty rolls.

2. *Dilution method.* Dilute one part of *fresh* developer with 9 parts of
water (for instance, 50 cc. of unused Edwal 12 with 450 cc. of water);
develop one roll of film in this solution for *twice* the developing time of
the regular concentrated developer, and then discard the solution.

3. *Thiocyanate method.* This is simply a variation of method 2. Add
½ gram (7½ grains) of potassium thiocyanate to each liter (quart) of
diluted developer. Since this amount is hard to weigh accurately, it is
better to add 5 grams (75 grains) of potassium thiocyanate direct to the
liter (quart) of concentrated Edwal 12. *Do not use with thin emulsions!*

### 12. GLYCIN FINE GRAIN, STOCK

For clear, clean negatives with very fine grain.

|  | METRIC | AVOIRDUPOIS | |
| --- | --- | --- | --- |
| Hot water (125° F.) | 750 cc. | 24 | ounces |
| Sodium sulphite, dry | 125 grams | 4¼ | ounces |
| Potassium carbonate | 250 grams | 8½ | ounces |
| Glycin | 50 grams | 1½ oz. 80 gr. | |
| Water to make | 1000 cc. | 32 | ounces |

For tank development take one part stock solution, fifteen parts water,
and develop 13 to 22 minutes at 68° F. For more recent and thin emulsions (Plus X, Panatomic X, Verichrome Pan, Adox KB 17), try 7 to
12 minutes at 68° F.

### 13. MCM 100

This developer does not require any increase of exposure, gives very
fine grain, superb tonal gradations, and produces some of the best-looking

negatives you've ever seen. The emulsion side has so high a polish that it
will be difficult to distinguish it from the other side.

|  | METRIC | | AVOIRDUPOIS |
|---|---|---|---|
| Water (125°) | 750 | cc. | 20 oz. |
| Sodium sulphite, dry | 88 | grams | 2 oz., 360 grains |
| Meritol [a] | 16 | grams | 224 grains |
| Borax | 2.3 | grams | 32 grains |
| Tri-sodium phosphate, *crystalline* | | | |
| (*not* the monohydrate) [b] | 6.9 | grams | 96 grains |
| 10 per cent potassium bromide | 2 | cc. | 32 minims |
| Water to make | 1000 | cc. | 32 oz. |

*Use weak acid short stop* (15 gm. citric in 1000 cc. water plus 5 drops
Aerosol).

For tank use at 70° F.: 8-20′ (minutes); Adox KB 14, 8′; KB 17, 9′;
Isopan F, 10-12′; Plus X and Verichrome Pan, try 10-12′; Panatomic X,
try 9-11′; Tri-X, 18-20′. After first two films add 10 per cent to each film
up to 6. If used infrequently, add 20 per cent to the above times. Reasonable agitation. *Presoak roll film in plain water or a 5 per cent sulphite
solution for 2-3 minutes* (to remove soluble backing material which restrains developing action). If *crystalline* sulphite is used, double the
quantity.

## 14. CHAMPLIN 15 (FINE GRAIN)

This still is the best and most dependable of the Champlin formulas.

|  | METRIC | | AVOIRDUPOIS | |
|---|---|---|---|---|
| Water (125° F.) | 600 | cc. | 12 | ounces |
| Rubinol or pyro | 3.5 | grams | 32 | grains |
| Sodium sulphite, dry | 60 | grams | 1½ | ounces |
| Benzoic acid | 1.2 | grams | 12 | grains |
| Salicylic acid | 0.5 | grams | 4 | grains |
| Boric acid | 2.5 | grams | 25 | grains |
| Tannic acid | 1 | gram | 9 | grains |
| Glycin | 11.5 | grams | ¼ | ounce |
| Paraphenylenediamine | 11.5 | grams | ¼ | ounce |
| Isopropyl alcohol | | | | |
| (97 per cent) | 50 | cc. | 1 | ounce |
| Nickel ammonium sulphate | 1 | gram | 10 | grains |
| Water to make | 1000 | cc. | 20 | ounces |

If Meritol is not available, use 7 grams of *paraphenylenediamine* together with 9 grams
of *catechol* to replace the 16 grams of Meritol.
[b] If *monohydrate*, use 3.5 grams; if *dry* (anhydrous) use 2.9 grams.

Dissolve the nickel ammonium sulphate in a small quantity of water and add *slowly* to developer after it has *cooled* to 70°. A precipitate may form. *Whether it does or not, filter the solution!*

For tank use at 70°: 16-20 minutes. For more recent and thin-emulsion films (Panatomic X, Plus X, Verichrome Pan, Adox KB 17, Isopan F, Pergrano), try 8-12 minutes. You can alter these times if you prefer more or less contrast. Increase developing time 2 minutes for each additional roll of film. Champlin can also be used by the dilution method described under Edwal 12, but the developing time has to be tripled. Champlin 15 can also be used by the replenishment method, adding 3 ounces of fresh developer after each roll of film.

## 15. CHAMPLIN 16 (FINE GRAIN, STOCK)

The advantage of this developer is in its method of use. One part of the stock solution is diluted with 9 parts of a 10 per cent sodium sulphite solution, and the working solution is thrown out after use. Negatives developed in fresh solutions of this sort are, naturally, much more uniform.

|  | METRIC | | AVOIRDUPOIS | |
|---|---|---|---|---|
| Water (cold) | 300 cc. | | 10 | ounces |
| Sodium sulphite, dry | 50 grams | | $1\frac{2}{3}$ | ounces |
| Chlorhydroquinone | 25 grams | | $\frac{3}{4}$ | ounce |
| Tironamin C [a] | 30 cc. | | 1 | ounce |
| Water, to make | 500 cc. | | 16 | ounces |

For tank use at 75° (the recommended temperature): Plenachrome, $6\frac{1}{4}$ minutes; Finopan, $6\frac{1}{4}$ minutes; Superpan Press, $8\frac{1}{2}$ minutes; Verichrome roll film or film pack, 8 minutes; Panatomic X roll film or film pack, $6\frac{1}{4}$ minutes; 35-mm. Supreme, 8 minutes; 35-mm. Superior, 8 minutes; 35-mm. Panatomic X, $6\frac{1}{4}$ minutes; Super XX, 8 minutes; Plus X, $6\frac{1}{4}$ minutes, Tri-X, $8\frac{1}{2}$ minutes.

*Do not use chrome rinse or sodium bisulphite with this developer.*

*Method of use:* Take $1\frac{1}{2}$ ounces (45 cc.) of stock solution and add enough 10 per cent sulphite solution (3 ounces of sulphite in 32 ounces of water) to make 16 ounces (500 cc.) of working solution. *Agitate constantly.* For rinse, Kodak Liquid Hardener or formula bottom p. 309.

---

[a] Dr. Edmund W. Lowe, in his book *What You Want to Know About Developers*, suggests that this can be replaced with 11 cc. of *triethanolamine* (the commercial 90 per cent product) to give somewhat finer grain. *Mix without heat.*

## 16. LEICA TWO-BATH FORMULA

For greatest possible sharpness without loss of speed, and for un-blocked highlights. The first bath develops out the highlights, hardly affecting the shadows; the second solution brings out all the detail in the shadows without blocking up the highlights. Both solutions can be used about four times for full-length films, though an increase of 5 per cent in developing time is required for each successive film.

Solution *A* contains 5 grams metol and 100 grams sodium sulphite (dry) in 1000 cc. of water; solution *B* contains 6 grams sodium sulphite (dry) and 15 grams sodium carbonate (dry) in 1000 cc. of water. Develop films 2-5 minutes at 68° F. in solution *A*, followed by 3 minutes in solution *B*. *Don't rinse films between baths.*

## DEVELOPMENT BY INSPECTION

The time-and-temperature method of development is fine if there are no special problems of *under-* or *over-*exposure, and if you are quite sure that your meter and shutter are working perfectly. But if you've taken a problem shot that you must desperately get right, especially if a retake is impossible and time is urgent, you can protect yourself against disaster by using one of the oldest methods of development known to photography: *inspection development.*

In the early days of orthochromatic film it was easier than it is now because a red safelight (Wratten Series 2) made it possible for you to inspect the progress of development to your heart's content, without endangering the film. Now, in these days of fast panchromatic film, you have to use a dark green safelight (Wratten Series 3), with a bulb no larger than 25 watts, and placed about 2-3 feet from the tank.

You start developing as if for time-and-temperature (page 253). When you reach item 4, and have completed *half* the indicated time, turn out all other lights, turn on the green safelight, and wait until your eyes have become accustomed to the dark. Now open the tank and, pulling out a bit of the film, glance at the *emulsion* side to see how it's coming. Look *at* the film, not through it, and remember that the smaller the film size, the darker it will look under the green light. (You'll have to try this out on a test film once or twice to get the hang of it and to learn how a good negative should look under the safelight.) Don't expose the film to the green light for more than a few seconds each time. When you think development is done, recap the tank, turn on your white light, and proceed with items 5 to 12 on page 253.

*George Jewell Baker,* an instructor at the Fred Archer School of Photography, suggests this clever way to tell when your negative is ready: place a finger between the safelight and the film, letting it cast an opaque shadow with which you can compare the dark highlight areas. At first the image will seem flat and fogged. But soon the outlines will become clear. When the finger shadow matches your highlight density, development is done.

## DEVELOPING TIME AT VARIOUS TEMPERATURES

| t | 64° | 65° | 66° | 67° | 68° | 69° | 70° | 71° | 72° | 73° | 74° | 75° | 76° | 77° |
|---|-----|-----|-----|-----|-----|-----|-----|-----|-----|-----|-----|-----|-----|-----|
| T | 1.23 | 1.16 | 1.10 | 1.05 | 1.00 | .95 | .90 | .85 | .81 | .78 | .75 | .72 | .69 | .66 |

This table gives the *ratio* of the developing time for any desired temperature (indicated by top line *t*) to that at 68° F. Given the developing time at 68°, you convert to the time at any other temperature by *multiplying* the given time by the *desired* temperature factor *T*. To convert from the time at any temperature other than 68° to any other temperature, you *divide* the time of the *given* temperature by its own factor and then *multiply* by the factor of the *desired* temperature.

*Example:* Film develops in 9 minutes at 68°; what time at 65°? *Answer:* Multiply 9 by factor 1.16. Result is 10.44, or about 10½ minutes. *Example:* Film develops in 14 minutes at 65°; what time at 68°? *Answer:* Divide 14 by factor 1.16. Result is 12 minutes. *Example:* Film develops in 10½ minutes at 65°; what time at 75°? *Answer:* Divide 10½ by 1.16 (factor at 65°) and multiply by .72 (factor at 75°). Result is 6½ minutes.

These new times are not always the ones specifically recommended for certain formulas, but they are close enough to be workable. If precise results are necessary, test first or keep to the original time and temperature. If more than one reducing agent is included in a developer, changes of time will not compensate for changes of temperature since it is more than likely that the reducing agents will have unequal temperature coefficients, one being affected more than the other and thus altering the final result.

## SOME DEVELOPING HINTS

1. Check your timer and thermometer for accuracy.

2. *Caution:* change of time does not compensate for *all* chemical changes caused by change of temperature!

3. Bakelite tanks are not so susceptible to temperature changes; stain-

less-steel tanks are more durable. Avoid tanks with celluloid aprons.

4. For a free *Handy Dilution Formula Chart* printed on stiff cardboard, ready for hanging in your darkroom, send to Mallinckrodt Chemical Works, Photo Department, 72 Gold St., New York 8, N. Y.

5. To bring the temperature of the film to the working temperature of the developer, give it a preliminary soak in water of that temperature.

6. Always dissolve chemicals *completely,* in order given in formula; otherwise some may not dissolve at all.

7. For best results, dissolve all chemical solutions in distilled water; if that isn't possible, use filtered rain water; if rain water isn't available, use boiled and filtered tap water (and add a pinch of *Calgon,* 1 gm. in 1000 cc., or 1/2 gm. of Kodak *Anti-Cal* in 1000 cc.).

8. See pages 290 and 373 for more developing hints.

9. Take the advice of famous Leica expert Anton Baumann and filter *all* your solutions *before* use. That's the best way to prevent spots on your negatives and so avoid tedious retouching on your prints. You can filter with cotton or gauze if you don't have filter paper. Some developers, like Microdol, precipitate a dark sludge of free silver; it's a good idea to filter it out.

10. Never dissolve developing agents in water hotter than 125° F.

11. Never use a developing solution immediately after it is prepared. Let it stand an hour or two before using.

12. *Acetic acid substitutes* (in case there's a shortage): *Short stop for paper or negatives:* 3% solution of sodium bisulphite or sodium metabisulphite, 30 gm. in 1000 cc. of water (1 oz. in 32 oz.); citric acid, 15 gm. (1/2 oz.) in 1000 cc. (32 oz.) of water (see also item 26, page 375). *Short stop for negatives only:* potassium chrome alum, 20 gm. (290 gr.) in 1000 cc. (32 oz.) of water. Use immediately (for 5 minutes at 68° F.) as it will not keep. *Fix negatives or prints* in F-24: water, (125° F.) 16 oz.; hypo, 8 oz.; sodium sulphite, *dry,* 145 gr.; sodium bisulphite or metabisulphite, 365 gr.; cold water to make 32 oz. Regular fixing baths such as F-1 (see p. 297) can be made with citric or tartaric acids in place of acetic. For each 1 1/2 fluid ounces (48 cc.) of 28% acetic, replace with 3/4 ounce (21.3 gm.) of citric or tartaric acid. Or, use white vinegar.

13. Keep all developing solutions at the same temperature.

14. Where several temperatures are offered for a developer, use 70°.

15. A 28 per cent acetic acid is made up by dissolving 3 parts of glacial acetic acid with 8 parts water.

16. To remove color backing from film, and to prevent opalescence, soak films after fixing and before washing in dilute solutions of sodium carbonate, ammonia, or even plain sodium sulphite.

17. See pages 309-311 for some hints on the use of hypo.

# 15

# *Printing and Enlarging*

To make a *positive* from a *negative,* you must use paper that has been specially sensitized so that it will react to light. The process by which this positive is made is called *printing* (*contact* printing if there is no increase in size) or *enlarging* (if the picture is reproduced larger in size, by projection). The resultant picture is sometimes called a *contact print* or an *enlargement,* but most often it is simply referred to as a *print.*

## KINDS OF PRINTING PAPERS

There are two types of photographic papers used for making prints. These are: (1) *Printing-out,* or *solio,* paper, and (2) *developing-out* paper. The printing-out paper is so called because the image appears when it is printed out in the sun (this takes from five to thirty minutes, depending on the density of the negative) and its progress can be seen by lifting up a corner of the print as it rests in one of the split-back printing frames especially made for this purpose. Printing-out papers are rarely used by amateurs; their chief use is by professional portrait photographers who submit them as *proofs* to clients. These proofs are not *fixed;* so they darken after a few days' exposure to light. However, they *can* be fixed and made permanent by placing them in a regular hypo bath.

The developing-out paper (unlike the printing-out paper, which needs only strong daylight or sunlight) must be chemically treated (as was the negative) to bring out the latent image.

### KINDS OF DEVELOPING-OUT PAPERS

There are three types of developing-out papers: (1) *chloride;* (2) *bromide;* and (3) *chlorobromide.* Chloride papers, so called because they are coated with a silver chloride emulsion, are slow (not very sensitive to light) and are therefore used mostly for making *contact* prints; that is, prints made by placing the paper directly on the negative and exposing to daylight or artificial light. They are ideal for subjects with strong contrasts; are poor in their ability to reproduce delicate gradations. Their contrast cannot be changed by varying the time of development without degrading the print.

Bromide papers (silver bromide emulsions) are *fast,* and are therefore used mostly for making *enlargements,* where increased sensitivity of the paper is essential to avoid overlong exposures to the inherently weak light of *projection* printing (law of inverse squares). They are about one hundred times as fast as chloride papers. They reproduce middle tones superbly, but the blacks are usually dingy. Their contrast cannot be controlled in developing.

Chlorobromide papers, coated with an emulsion that combines the chloride and bromide salts of silver, are medium fast and can be used either for contact printing or enlarging. They can produce beautiful prints with good tones and rich, lustrous blacks; they are also better in rendering shadow detail. They are twenty times faster than chlorides.

The slower chlorobromides are made in only one grade of contrast, for *normal* negatives. All the other papers are made in three or more grades (*soft, medium* and *hard*) for hard, medium, and soft negatives, respectively. There is also a large choice of surfaces, which may be roughly classified as (1) *glossy* (for detail and brilliance), (2) *semi-matte* (a compromise surface with a slight sheen), and (3) *matte* (with a dull surface).

All papers are usually supplied in two weights: *single weight* and *double weight.* Though the single-weight papers are less expensive, they are more likely to curl.

A new type of enlarging paper that provides *variable contrast* control in *one* contrast grade by the use of intermediate filters has now been placed on the market. The secret of this unusual paper is in the split-sensitivity of the emulsion. With a blue filter over the lens maximum contrast is produced; with a yellow filter maximum softness is produced. By varying the exposure between the blue and yellow filters, almost any range of contrast is possible. This paper, marketed as Dupont's *Varigam* or Kodak's *Polycontrast,* requires a special safelight (the S 55X or Kodak OC), but otherwise it is treated like any other *chlorobromide* paper. The necessary gelatine filters are supplied with each package. It is best to mount them between cardboard to avoid touching them by hand; or buy sets of mounted filters for this purpose. See also pages 288-289.

WHY VARIOUS CONTRASTS?

All other things being equal, the best print (full scale from white to black, with rich contrasts) can be produced only by a normal negative

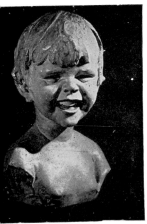
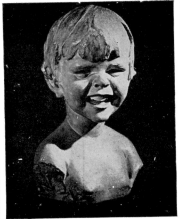

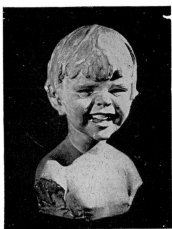

TROLLING CONTRAST. For best results, match the negative
printing paper. Only that way is it possible to get a rich, bril-
full-scale print. If the negative is soft, a hard paper is called
nd vice versa. Here we show the effect of various paper con-
on a normal negative. Azo glossy was used, in contrast grades
5, corresponding to prints A to E. Print B, printed on Azo 2, is
al. If too hard a paper is used, print E is the result; all the mid-
nes have been lost. If too soft a paper is used, all the tones tend
tten out and there are no strong blacks and no brilliant whites.

*ead of child was sculptured by Helen Webster Jensen of Santa
Monica, California.*

*A.* AZO 1

*B.* AZO 2

*C.* AZO 3

*D.* AZO 4

*E.* AZO 5

→ *A B C*
*D*
*E*

and a normal paper. Hard or soft papers are only compensating devices, at best, but very useful ones sometimes. Test strips *A* to *E* on page 281 show the effect of printing a uniform step-wedge negative on papers of various contrasts. The practical result of this is shown in prints *A* to *E*. In both cases Azo paper (glossy), in contrasts 1 to 5, was used.

The trick in printing, to produce a full-scale print, is to match the negative to the paper. If it is a *soft* negative, a *hard* paper is called for, and vice versa. What this does is to expand or contract the image tones in such a way that they produce a print of approximately normal tone range. However, there is one other factor affecting contrast which we should not overlook. It is paper *surface*.

Depending on the surface chosen, a full-scale normal negative printed on a full-scale normal paper will reflect, roughly, the following scale of tones:

| | |
|---|---|
| Glossy | 1 to 50 |
| Semi-matte | 1 to 30 |
| Matte | 1 to 15 |

The loss of tones then, as you can see, may be due as much to the paper *surface* as to the paper *contrast*. If a long range of tones is called for, it is best to use a glossy paper, or one with a smooth surface like Illustrator's Special.

## HOW TO MAKE CONTACT PRINTS

You'll need the following materials and equipment: (1) A safelight, with filters for prints and negatives. (And be sure it is *safe*. Test it by placing a coin over a piece of print paper and leave it as close to the light as you expect to be working. After five minutes, develop the print in the usual way. If the outline of the coin is visible on the paper, the light is *not* safe.) (2) A printing *frame* or a contact printing *box*. (3) Four trays (the hard-rubber kind are best; they are light in weight, will not chip or crack, and are quieter in use). (4) A four-ounce graduate (if possible, get one that is marked for metric as well as ounce measure; if you can't, just remember that 1 ounce is approximately 30 cc.). (5) A package of printing paper. (6) A developer. (7) An acid rinse bath. (8) A fixing bath. (9) Three pairs of tongs (the wooden ones put out by Burke & James are far from ideal, but they are still the best). (10) Some ferrotype tins (if you plan to make glossies). (11) A print roller. (12) A stirring rod. (13) A thermometer. (14) An interval timer or a wall clock with a sweep second hand. (15) A sponge (the Dupont cellulose variety is good). (16) Weighing scales (if you're going to make up your own developer).

Arrange your trays in such a way that your print can be carried in orderly progression from developer to acid rinse to hypo to water bath. Fill each tray to within a half or three-quarters of an inch from the top.

## THE PRINTING FRAME

A printing-frame is a wooden frame with a hinged back to it, as shown in *Fig. 67.* The back can be taken out by releasing the springs. If you use a *film* negative (instead of a *plate,* the emulsion of which is already mounted on glass) you must put a sheet of clean glass in the frame first (they are usually supplied with such glass) and lay the film on top of this

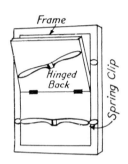

FIG. 67. PRINTING FRAME

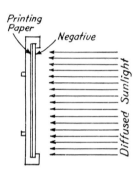

FIG. 68. HOW THE PRINT-
ING FRAME WORKS

with the emulsion side away from the glass. This done, lay the paper on top of the negative with the emulsion surface facing that of the negative; finally put the back in and slip the springs under the clips. The negative and the paper will now be held in close contact, as shown in the cross section view in *Fig. 68.*

Since some parts of the negative are transparent and other parts of it are opaque, it must be clear that when the rays strike it, they will pass through the transparent parts and darken the paper. Where the opaque parts prevent them from passing through, the paper remains white. In this way, then, the picture printed on the paper is just the reverse of that which is on the negative. Hence, it looks like the original scene, object or subject which was photographed in so far as the gradations of light and shade, outline and contour are concerned.

## MAKING THE PRINT

First put the negative in the printing frame and the paper in contact with it in the way described above. You can then hold the frame up before a tungsten electric lamp as shown in *Fig. 69.*

The length of exposure depends on a number of factors which include (1) the kind of paper that you use, (2) the density of the negative, (3) the kind and strength of the light you are using, and, finally, (4) the dis-

*Frosted Bulb*

FIG. 69. MAKING A PRINT BY HAND

tance you hold the frame from the light. The exact distance does not matter, but ten inches is about right for 4 x 5 negatives and smaller ones, while larger negatives must be held farther away so that the light will strike all parts of it equally. Here's a table to guide you on exposures.

TABLE OF APPROXIMATE EXPOSURES

| Size of Negative | Distance from Light | 25 Watt Electric Lamp | 40 Watt Lamp | 60 Watt Lamp | 100 Watt Lamp | 200 Watt Lamp |
|---|---|---|---|---|---|---|
| 4 x 5 and smaller | 10 inches | 12 seconds | 6 seconds | 4 seconds | 2 seconds | 1 second |

You can find the exact length of time required for the exposure by cutting a sheet of the kind of paper you are going to use into strips about one inch wide, placing a strip under a part of the negative with lots of detail in it, then making a test exposure, noting the exact time and precise distance, and developing it. By exposing two or three strips and giving them slightly different exposures, you can easily find out what the proper time is; this done, you can duplicate prints by repeating same time and distance. *An alternate method:* Place printing frame on a table, face up, and rig up the bulb so it can be raised or lowered. You then vary exposure by changing distance, leaving the time constant at, say, 10 seconds.

## THE PRINTING BOX

The most satisfactory contact printing method is by the use of a *printing box*. This is an oblong box made of wood or metal. Inside the box are one or more bulbs (usually 40 to 60 watts each) as well as a small ruby bulb. The hinged cover is connected with a switch so that when the cover is pressed down, the exposing lamps are turned on and the ruby lamp is turned off; when the cover is raised, the reverse happens. The inside of the box is usually coated white or silvered to give maximum even illumination, and in the better quality boxes there is an intermediate diffusing screen (a piece of ground glass or milk glass) to even out the light and eliminate hot spots. If the hot spots persist, there are two ways of dealing with them: (1) place a piece of heavy white bond paper over the intermediate screen, so marked with pencil or crayon that the hot spots are toned down and the lighting is even over the entire area. This requires a few trials until you get it just right, and the best way to test the result is to expose a piece of contrasty *chloride* paper (Azo No. 5, for instance) on the upper glass *without* a negative, expose for a very brief time, and develop fully. If the lighting is uneven, this test will show it at once. (2) Paint the upper portion of the lamps so that only *reflected* (instead of *direct*) light reaches the negatives. This method, also, requires some testing. And since it is a fussier procedure, the first method is preferred. Once this adjustment has been made, the printing box is ready for use and will need no further adjustment.

A modified kind of dodging, or retarding the printing of certain parts of a negative, is possible with a printing box by using white paper on the diffusing screen. If the negative, for instance, has a very dense sky, simply place an extra piece of tissue (tracing paper or bond paper will do) over the corrective tissue described above, and darken this supplementary tissue on one side, grading it evenly so that a sharp separation doesn't show. The darkened side should be placed, of course, so that the foreground is held back, permitting the sky to print through.

With a printing frame, dodging is accomplished by tilting the frame so that one portion of it is nearer the light than the other, or by interposing a card or any other opaque material between the light and the loaded frame.

Contact printing is the only method to use if you want the *ultimate* in sharpness of detail. However, for most practical purposes, and provided the final print does not exceed a 10 x enlargement (1 inch of the negative blown up to 10 inches on the print), printing by projection furnishes prints of sufficient crispness to look sharp when viewed at a *normal* viewing distance. Very roughly calculated, this normal viewing distance should *exceed* the diagonal of the picture size. For a print that is 11 by 14 inches in size, the viewing distance should therefore not be less than 18 inches. At this viewing distance (which will seem unfair to the picture *sniffers*) grain will also seem less of a problem.

## PROJECTION PRINTING

If the print is to be made larger (or smaller) than the size of the original negative, projection printing (by means of a lens) must be used. If your camera has a detachable back and a bellows extension front, you can use that as your projector. However, you will have to rig up a holder for the negative, a firm support for the camera, and a light-proof cooling system for the light source. When you get through, the result will be almost as expensive, but not quite so good, as one of the excellent enlargers now on the market; so our advice is to save up for a good enlarger and be content with contact printing until you can afford the other.

### THE KINDS OF ENLARGERS

There are two kinds: the *fixed-focus type* which furnishes only a single size of enlargement and the *variable-focus* style, which is more versatile

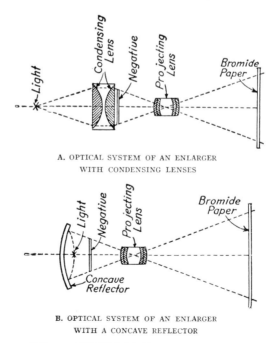

A. OPTICAL SYSTEM OF AN ENLARGER
WITH CONDENSING LENSES

B. OPTICAL SYSTEM OF AN ENLARGER
WITH A CONCAVE REFLECTOR

FIG. 70. ENLARGER OPTICAL SYSTEMS

and therefore more practical. The latter type is also available with *condensing lenses, concave reflectors, diffusing screens* (see *Fig. 70*), and cold-light lampheads. The best type for amateur use is the variable-focus condenser or cold-light system, as in the Omega, the Leitz Valoy and Focomat, the Beseler, and the Exact 35 and 66. These are *vertical* enlargers, which are preferred for amateur use.

A good enlarger provides the following:

1. Focusing adjustments that are precise and easy to use.

2. A tall, *rigid* support for big enlargements.

3. A simple method for changing lenses.

4. A negative carrier that holds the film flat without resorting to glass plates.

5. Adequate heat control that does not leak light.

6. Adequate balance or control for ease in raising and lowering the lamphouse.

7. If possible, some method for compensating for distortion of perspective. This is done by tilting the negative, or by turning the enlarger head on a swivel joint.

8. A heavy, well-seasoned, plywood baseboard.

9. Adequate, convenient, well-insulated electrical connections.

10. A red or orange filter that can be swung under the lens while composing the picture.

In the long run, a *good* enlarger is a wise investment. A faulty machine will not only spoil your pictures, but it will destroy your interest in photography and ruin your disposition.

The Omega enlargers, manufactured by Simmon Brothers, Long Island City, New York, are unquestionably the best in the field. They are scientifically designed, precisely manufactured to rigid standards, are really inexpensive for the materials and workmaship involved, and are certain to produce superb pictures if intelligently handled. There are supplementary accessories now available for making color separations from Kodachrome originals, and for other uses.

Other recommended enlargers are:

The Automega
The Dejur Versatile
The Unomat
The Duomat Super
The Micromat
The Graflarger Back (which converts a Speed Graphic to a vertical enlarger (cold-light) by means of a special stand.

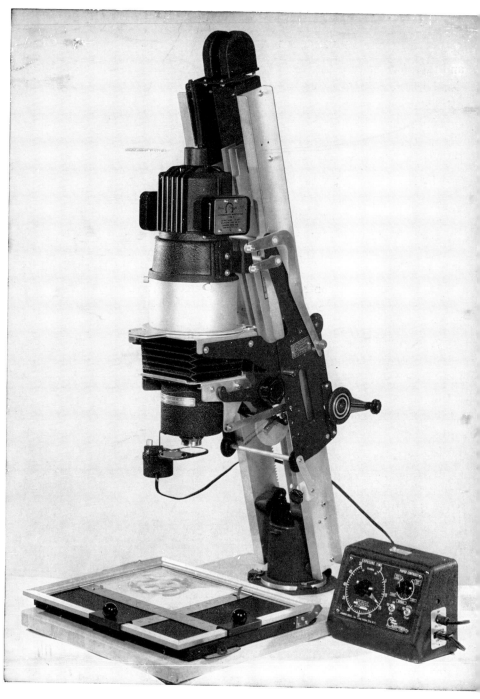

The Automega D, a condenser type vertical enlarger with tilting and rotary negative holder, automatic focusing, and color head for use in making color or monochrome prints from color negative-positive and reversal films.

The control box on the table near the enlarger is the Omega Electronic Contrast Timer for multiple-contrast paper. This "brain box" activates the filter shift unit seen directly below the enlarger lens, by means of a solenoid. This automatically moves the yellow or blue filters into position for the exact times needed to give the contrast and exposure desired.

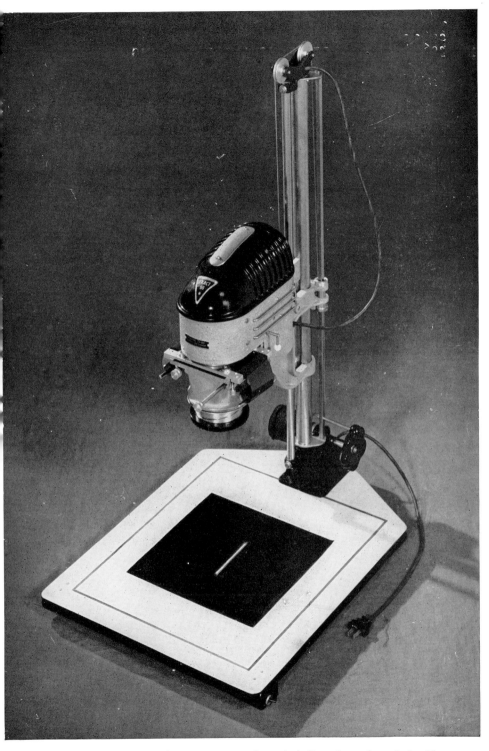

The Exact 66 enlarger, for 2¼-inch-square negatives. A similar enlarger is made for 35-mm. negatives, the Exact 35. Both use range-finder focusing for maximum image sharpness.

## HOW TO MAKE AN ENLARGEMENT

As all the operations for making an enlargement are carried out in a darkroom, you can use an orange light for bromide paper and a green-yellow (Wratten OA filtered) light for chlorobromide paper. Having placed the negative in its holder, focused the image, stopped the lens down to about $f$ 8 or $f$ 11, turned off the switch, you are ready to make the exposure. But first you will want to check the exposure.

You can do this in one of three ways: (1) use an oil-spot *print meter* (*MCM Photometer, Spotomatic*). (2) Use a Kodak Projection Print Scale by placing the scale over a sheet of print paper; with the negative in the enlarger expose through the scale for one minute and develop in the usual way; the correct exposure time can then be read directly from the

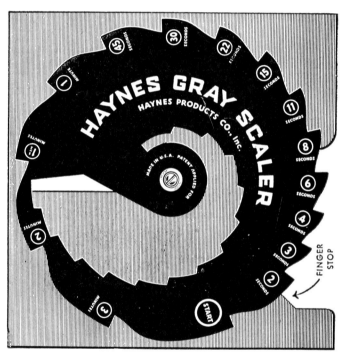

FIG. 71. THE HAYNES GRAY SCALER
(Indicates exposure and contrast)

best-appearing sector in the enlargement. Or (3) make one or more *test exposures*. To do this, tear a small sheet of paper into strips about an inch wide and five or six inches long; then lay one of them directly across the center of the image on the easel or table and lay a ruler on each edge to hold it down flat. You can also use a sheet of glass if you prefer.

The range of exposures should bracket what you consider to be the correct exposure. For example, if you guess (from previous experience) that 20-25 seconds would be right, make this series of exposures: 5, 10, 20, 40, and 80 seconds. You do this by covering the entire sheet first with a piece of cardboard or black paper and then uncovering inch segments in this order: 40 seconds for the first, then 20 more for the second, 10 more for the third, 5 more for the fourth, and finally 5 for the last. When you develop, fix and wash this test sheet, you will find that you have a series of exposures, each step of which is double or half that of the one next to it: 80, 40, 20, 10 and 5 seconds. It shouldn't be difficult to gauge the correct exposure from this sample. *Caution:* Develop and fix the test sheet in exactly the same way as your final print; and judge the exposure (after fixing and washing) under *white* light, not the safelight.

An easier way is to use the *Photo-Genie Enlarging Meter* (Ideax Corp.).

### CONTRAST AND HOW TO CONTROL IT

One of the most serious problems in photography is the difficult one of adjusting the contrast of the scene to the contrast of the negative, and then to the contrast of the print. The scene contrast (or brightness) range may vary from 2 to 1, for landscapes in misty weather, to as much as 1000 to 1, for an interior with windows showing a sunlit landscape. The negative emulsion, however, can record a range (by *transmitted* light) of only 130 to 1. The print, to add to our woes, can record a maximum brightness range, by *reflected* light, of only about 30 to 1 (see paper tone scales p. 282). The main technical effort of amateurs and professionals alike is to capture the scene on paper, just as it is, without losing highlights or shadows. Actually, that's impossible. But practically, it is possible by exposure-development manipulation, and by using special developers, enlargers, papers, and printing techniques, to expand or contract the range of the scene and the range of the negative until it precisely fits the range of the paper. When the scene range and the negative range are the same, we say the negative has a gamma of 1 (see page 254), but it is not always necessary, or even desirable, to print the scene as you see it. You may want to lighten, darken, or emphasize parts of it. Here are some of the controls, to use as you see fit:

### The Negative

*Exposure.* In general, if the scene is long range, *underexpose;* if short range, *overexpose* (see item 13, page 137; and reverse the procedure for underexposure). You can also *filter* for shadows and bright lights (see page 236). About 15 years ago, William A. Oberlin tried an unorthodox way to adjust exposure to planned development. Assuming that a scene range of 1-200 is normal and gets normal exposure and development, he found the following variations worked for other scene ranges: scene range 1-90, exposure 85% normal, development 125% normal; scene range 1-400, exposure 115% normal, development 75% normal; scene range 1-850, exposure 133% normal, development 62% normal; scene range 1-1700, exposure 180% normal, development 50% normal. He used Superpan Press and Ansco 17 (similar to D-76). But these figures will be useful as a starting point for testing other combinations. Another method (*for extreme contrast* only) suggested by Joseph Foldes in *The Camera:* Meter the darkest part of the scene where details are important (disregard highlights entirely), give 10 times that exposure (yes, 5 seconds if your meter said ½), then develop your *pan* film in fresh Microdol, diluted 1 to 10 (one part developer to 10 parts water) for 1 hour at 68° F., agitating (important!) at least 5 seconds every 2 minutes. See also item 10, page 142, for some expert advice on how to use your meter for special conditions; and page 147 for a *Negative Contrast Control* table.

*Development.* Use *compensating* formulas for excessive contrast. See the Windisch formula on page 257, also D-76 (page 267), D-23 and D-25 (page 268), the metol-sulphite formula (page 269), W-80 (page 271), and the Leica two-bath formula (page 276).

Rudolph Simmon suggests a new and better way to use Microdol: Dissolve ½ gallon of the developer and condition it (to reduce contrast and grain) by developing 6 rolls of 120 film or 36-exposure 35-mm. film *without adding anything.* This is your *stock solution.* Now dissolve some more Microdol (*not* the replenisher) and store in 32-ounce bottles. This is your *replenisher.* Add 8 ounces to your stock solution each time while you are developing the film. When development is complete, pour the tank developer into the stock solution bottle until full and discard the rest. Develop Plus X, Supreme, and Verichrome Pan about 11 minutes at 70° F.; Tri-X and Superpan Press about 16 minutes at 70° F. Another good developer for contrasty subjects is Edwal's Minicol.

### The Print

*Paper.* The easiest way to control contrast is by using *Varigam* or *Polycontrast* and their various filters (see page 280). For the treatment of other papers, see below.

*Exposure.* To determine normal exposure, see page 290; for the probable effect of under- and over-exposure, see page 295.

*Enlarger.* Condenser enlargers give more contrast, so do coated lenses. For softer results remove the lower condenser lens and replace with a disc of diffusing opal glass (but remember that this reduces your light intensity). A better way is to use a cold-light enlarger, or get an Aristo cold-light unit for your own enlarger. To increase contrast, replace the opal lamp in your condenser enlarger with a regular (sandblasted or etched) household lamp of 25-40 watts. (Exposure is shorter, but it *increases grain!*)

*Development.* For soft enlargements use Ansco 120 (page 296), or Selectol Soft (packaged by Kodak), or Mark Shaw's water-bath method for high-key prints (page 317), or try the bichromate *pre*-rinse (item 29, page 376). To increase contrast, use your developer without dilution.

*Other Techniques.* This is a variation of an old method called *visible enlarging.* You soak your print in the developer (under darkroom light, of course) for about half a minute, lift by one corner and place it on a sheet of glass, remove surplus developer, and place in position under your enlarger lens (having prefocused your enlarger on the back of an old print). Now make your exposure for the shadows (about $\frac{1}{2}$ to $\frac{1}{10}$ of the normal time indicated by your print meter). Turn the enlarger light off and watch the image come up by safelight. After the developer is exhausted, give another exposure for the highlights and then back into the developer. Fix and wash as usual. The first exposure creates a mask which keeps the dark areas from being overexposed. Another unusual method (for softening a contrasty negative (even on hard paper) is called *flashing.* First find out by testing what exposure is best for the shadows (leave highlights white). Then give the new print a pre-exposure flash, without the negative, of about $\frac{1}{2}$ second or less (stopping the lens way down). Now replace the negative, expose for the time previously indicated, develop, fix, and wash.

### DEVELOPING THE PRINT

After the exposure has been made, remove the paper from the printing frame or enlarging easel and slide it quickly, edgewise, into the tray of developer. Sliding the paper into the solution prevents the formation of air bells—bubbles of air that cling to the paper and cause white spots on the print. To prevent streaking and uneven development it is a good idea to rock the tray gently from side to side.

For amateur use the best paper developers are Eastman's famous D-72 (formula given later in the chapter), which is really a universal developer in every sense of the term, and the two splendid Edwal developers, 102 and 111. D-72, however, in prepared form is no longer available, having been replaced by Eastman's Dektol, which comes in powder form. Also recommended: Kodak's *Versatol,* available in liquid form. The formulas for the Edwal developers are as follows:

## EDWAL 102 PRINT DEVELOPER

### FOR DELICATE GRADATIONS

|  | METRIC | AVOIRDUPOIS |
|---|---|---|
| Water | 500 cc. | 16 ounces |
| Sodium sulphite, dry | 80 grams | 2⅔ ounces |
| Trisodium phosphate, monohydrated | 120 grams | 4 ounces |
| Monazol (glycin) | 25 grams | 375 grains |
| Potassium bromide | 3 grams | 45 grains |

For use, dilute 1 part stock with 3 parts water for chloride and chloro-bromide papers; with 4 parts water for bromide papers.

Normal developing time is 3 to 6 minutes at 70° F., but it can also be used at temperatures between 50°-90° F.

Rinse prints for at least 2 minutes in a short-stop bath containing 1 ounce of citric acid per gallon of water. *Otherwise a scum of aluminum phosphate will form on the paper surface in the fixer.*

## EDWAL 111 UNIVERSAL PRINT DEVELOPER

|  | METRIC | AVOIRDUPOIS |
|---|---|---|
| Water (125° F.) | 500 cc. | 16 ounces |
| Metol | 5 grams | 75 grains |
| Sodium sulphite, dry | 80 grams | 2⅔ ounces |
| Monazol (glycin) | 6 grams | 90 grains |
| Chlor-hydroquinone (C.H.Q.) | 15 grams | 225 grains |
| Potassium carbonate (Edwal) | 120 grams | 4 ounces |
| Potassium bromide | 3 grams | 45 grains |

For use, dilute 1 part stock with 7 parts water for bromide papers; with 5 parts water for fast chlorobromides (Velour Black, Kodabromide); with 4 parts water for slow chlorobromides (Kodak Opal, Illustrator's Special) and contact papers.

Normal developing time is 1½ to 3 minutes. The best black tones are obtained with a developing time of 2 minutes or more.

*Prints should be rinsed after development as above, for Edwal 102.*

With most developers, the print will be fully developed in about 90 seconds. This means that, normally, the print should not be removed from the solution before that time. It is always better to leave the print in the solution for 2 to 3 minutes. By doing that you make it possible for the developer to penetrate to the full depth of the emulsion and so produce rich, lustrous blacks and full detail in the highlights.

If the print gets too dark when you develop it for more than 90 seconds, you've overexposed it. Cut down the exposure and try again. By using a photometer you can reduce these wasteful trials and errors to a minimum. The temperature of the developing solution should be 70 degrees F. If you find it hard to keep the developer at that temperature, place the tray in a large container of water of the correct temperature.

Small changes in contrast can be effected by over- or underexposing and over- or underdeveloping the print. However, these changes are slight and will never equal the difference in contrast between two contrast grades of the same paper. It is best to stick to the latter method and use the developer according to the manufacturers' directions. If you want brilliance and good black tones use D-72 or the new Dektol. If you are using a warm tone paper such as Kodak Opal and you want the tones warm and the gradation soft as with portraits, then Eastman's D-52 or the new Selectol, which replaces D-52 in the prepared form, should be used.

Here are the two Eastman formulas:

### EASTMAN D-52 FOR WARM TONE PAPERS

|  | METRIC | | AVOIRDUPOIS | |
|---|---|---|---|---|
| Water, about 125° F. | 500 | cc. | 16 | ounces |
| Elon (metol) | 1.5 | grams | 22 | grains |
| Sodium sulphite, dry | 22.5 | grams | ¾ | ounce |
| Hydroquinone | 6.3 | grams | 90 | grains |
| Sodium carbonate, dry | 15.0 | grams | ½ | ounce |
| Potassium Bromide | 1.5 | grams | 22 | grains |
| Cold water to make | 1.0 | liter | 32 | ounces |

For use dilute 1 part stock solution with 1 part water. Normal developing time is about 2 minutes at 68° F.

### EASTMAN D-72 UNIVERSAL DEVELOPER

|  | METRIC | | AVOIRDUPOIS | |
|---|---|---|---|---|
| Water (about 125° F.) | 500 | cc. | 16 | ounces |
| Elon (metol) | 3.1 | grams | 45 | grains |
| Sodium sulphite, dry | 45 | grams | 1½ | ounces |
| Hydroquinone | 12 | grams | 175 | grains |
| Sodium carbonate, dry | 67.5 | grams | 2¼ | ounces |
| Potassium bromide | 1.9 | grams | 27 | grains |
| Water to make | 1000 | cc. | 32 | ounces |

For use, dilute 1 part stock solution with 2 parts water.

Normal developing time 1 to 1½ minutes at 68° F. Greater or less contrast can be obtained by varying dilution.

For Ansco papers, the two developers suggested are:

### ANSCO 120 SOFT-WORKING DEVELOPER

|  | METRIC | | AVOIRDUPOIS | | |
|---|---|---|---|---|---|
| Water (125° F.) | 750 | cc. | 24 | ounces | |
| Metol | 12.3 | grams | ¼ | oz., 70 | gr. |
| Sodium sulphite, dry | 36 | grams | 1 | oz., 88 | gr. |
| Sodium carbonate, monohydrated | 36 | grams | 1 | oz., 88 | gr. |
| Potassium bromide | 1.8 | grams | 27 | grains | |
| Water to make | 1000 | cc. | 32 | ounces | |

For use, dilute 1 part stock solution with 2 parts water.

Normal developing time, 1½ to 3 minutes at 68° F.

### ANSCO 130 UNIVERSAL PAPER DEVELOPER

|  | METRIC | | AVOIRDUPOIS | | |
|---|---|---|---|---|---|
| Water (125° F.) | 750 | cc. | 24 | ounces | |
| Metol | 2.2 | grams | 32 | grains | |
| Sodium sulphite, dry | 50 | grams | 1¾ | ounces | |
| Hydroquinone | 11 | grams | ¼ | oz., 50 | gr. |
| Sodium carbonate, monohydrated | 78 | grams | 2½ | ounces | |
| Potassium bromide | 5.5 | grams | 80 | grains | |
| Glycin | 11 | grams | ¼ | oz., 50 | gr. |
| Water to make | 1000 | cc. | 32 | ounces | |

For use, dilute 1 part stock solution with 1 part water.

Normal developing time at 68° F. for bromide papers, 2 to 6 minutes; for chlorides and chlorobromides, 1½ to 3 minutes.

Greater contrast can be obtained by using full strength; softer results, by diluting 1 part stock with 2 parts water.

### RINSING

After development, rinse prints for about 5 seconds in a short-stop bath made up with 1½ ounces (48 cc.) of 28 per cent acetic acid (made by diluting 3 parts of glacial acetic in 8 parts water) in 32 ounces (1000 cc.) of water. This does not apply, of course, to the two Edwal formulas which require a special citric rinse as explained above. This rinse stops development and neutralizes the alkali in the developer, which would otherwise spoil the hypo solution.

## HOW TO FIX PRINTS

To fix your prints so that they will not stain, blister, or mar and yet will last, you must (1) use an *acid fixing bath,* (2) use a fresh fixing bath for each new batch of pictures, (3) avoid using a fixing bath in which you have fixed films having a colored backing dye lest the backing dyes discolor the print, and (4) add a *hardening solution* to it. You can buy an acid fixing powder all ready to make into a bath by simply dissolving it in water, or you can make one yourself as follows:

### ACID HARDENING FIXING BATH (F-1)

|  | METRIC | AVOIRDUPOIS |
|---|---|---|
| Water, hot | 500 cc. | 16 ounces |
| Hypo | 240 grams | 8 ounces |
| Water to make | 1000 cc. | 32 ounces |

Dissolve completely, then add 2 ounces (64 cc.) Kodak Liquid Hardener, or the entire quantity of a hardening solution prepared as follows:

| | | |
|---|---|---|
| Water (125° F.) | 80 cc. | 2½ ounces |
| Sodium sulphite, dry | 15 grams | ½ ounce |
| Acetic acid, 28 per cent | 48 cc. | 1½ ounces |
| Potassium alum | 15 grams | ½ ounce |

Dissolve the chemicals in the order given. The sulphite should be dissolved completely before adding the acetic acid. After the sulphite-acid solution has been thoroughly mixed, add the potassium alum while stirring constantly. Cool the hardening solution and add slowly to the cool hypo solution. When the hypo is first dissolved, the temperature of the solution drops considerably.

Rapid and thorough fixing of prints can be insured by immersing prints face up in the bath, then agitating, separating, and turning them at intervals of five minutes. Normally, if the hypo solution is fresh, about 15 minutes is required for this bath.

The secret of making permanent prints lies quite as much in properly fixing them as it does in washing them well after they are fixed. After the prints have been fixed they should be rinsed in running water to remove surface hypo and then washed thoroughly to get the hypo and other salts out of them.

## HOW TO WASH PRINTS

The prints can be washed in any one of several ways: (1) by placing them in a tray of water and then constantly turning them over and changing the water at least a dozen times at five-minute intervals; (2) by using two trays of water and taking them from one and putting them in the other when the water is changed; (3) by keeping them moving in a tray in which a stream of water is running, and (4) by washing them for the same length of time in an automatic washer. Whichever way you follow, the water should be kept at as nearly the same temperature as possible all during the process of washing.

If washing is not complete the prints may later fade, darken, or stain. The Eastman Automatic Tray Syphon, the Ingento Print Washer (shown in *Fig. 72*) or the Arkay Rapid Print Washer all afford a simple, effi-

FIG. 72. THE INGENTO PRINT WASHER

cient means of washing prints thoroughly and quickly. When one of these is used, the washing time can be cut to 30 minutes without affecting the permanence of the print.

### HOW TO TELL WHEN PRINTS ARE PROPERLY WASHED

You can tell when a print is properly washed by making and applying the following simple test solution:

HYPO TEST SOLUTION

|  | METRIC | AVOIRDUPOIS |
|---|---|---|
| Potassium permanganate | 0.6 gram | 8 grains |
| Caustic soda | 0.5 gram | 7 grains |
| Distilled water | 240 cc. | 8 ounces |

To make the test put four drops of the above test solution in three-fourths of a glass of pure water; it will have a violet tint. Now take some of the prints from the water you are washing them in and let the latter drain off in the glass containing the test solution. If there is still hypo in it, the violet tint will change to a slightly greenish hue, and this is your cue to keep on washing the prints until a like test shows that all of the hypo has been removed.

For absolute print permanence, soak the prints after fixing and rinsing, and before washing, in a 1 per cent solution of sodium carbonate for 1 minute. Then each 10 minutes of washing time thereafter will be equivalent to 30 minutes for prints not so treated.

### HOW TO DRY PRINTS

After you have washed the prints lay them with the picture-side *up* on a clean blotter, and then remove the excess of water by pressing another sheet of blotting paper down on them, or better yet, by removing the surface moisture with a folded section of a paper towel.[1] When you do this, rub from the center outwards, to avoid frilling the emulsion at the edges. Then lay the prints with the picture-side *down* on a *cheesecloth stretcher,* (made by tacking the cloth over a wooden frame) or lay them face down on *dry* paper towels. Don't dry prints between blotters; they'll stick and spoil. For faster drying get yourself a Lott rotary or one of the other *electric* dryers. *Caution:* Use blotters made for photographic use.

### HOW TO KEEP PRINTS FLAT

To overcome a natural tendency to curl when drying, immerse the prints for a minute or two after washing in a bath containing 1 part glycerin to 10 parts water. This will remove all tendency to curl and will also add depth and luster to the blacks.

If the print still curls after it has dried, dampen the back with a solution of 1 part glycerin to 3 parts water and place under pressure. The old-style letter presses or some modern variant of them are best for this purpose. I have also placed prints, after they are *dry,* between the pages of an unabridged dictionary to good effect.

### HOW TO MAKE GLOSSY PRINTS

The prints have to be made, of course, on *glossy* paper; that is, paper with a special, smooth surface. After the prints are fixed and washed, slap them face down while still wet on a *ferrotype tin,* squeegee into perfect

---

[1] Some paper towels are more absorbent than others, and chemically purer. I found the Scott towels very satisfactory; some of the others only fair.

contact, let them dry (*Fig. 73*). When the print is thoroughly dry, it will peel off of its own accord with the desired luster.

After you have used the ferrotype tin for some time, the prints may have a tendency to stick to it. To prevent this, rub the surface of the

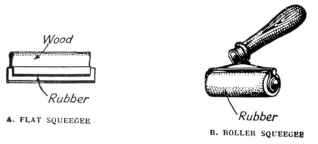

A. FLAT SQUEEGEE

B. ROLLER SQUEEGEE

FIG. 73. KINDS OF SQUEEGEES

tin with a soft piece of flannel on which you have put a few drops of ferrotype waxing solution. After you have rubbed the surface thoroughly, polish it off with a piece of dry flannel. It is also a good scheme to clean the tintype plate once in a while with hot water to remove such particles of matter as may have stuck to it from the prints you have previously glossed. Another good polisher: Sight Saver silicone tissues.

## HOW TO DIFFUSE PRINTS

For soft pictures, especially portraits of women, and for certain types of landscapes, a pleasant effect can be produced by stretching a silk stocking or some similar material over a sewing hoop and interposing this between the lens and paper during all or part of the enlarging time.

## HOW TO DODGE PRINTS

This is done by placing the hands or some other opaque object between the lens and the paper during part of the exposure. In this way a foreground or some other part of the image can be held back while the sky or a face is printed in. To avoid having the outlines of the hand or card show, it should be moved around during the exposure. A few actual trials will teach you just how to do this and what to avoid. For spot printing, which is the reverse of dodging, a card with a small hole is placed between lens and paper, to accent with additional exposure some overexposed part of the negative. In spot printing, also, it is important to keep the card moving to avoid sharp edges.

## HOW TO SPOT PRINTS

After the print has been dried and flattened, it usually needs spotting (depending on the care with which you processed and handled the negative, or the amount of dust in your darkroom). You touch up the *white* spots by dotting gently and slowly with a sharp, *soft* pencil or by dotting with a fine-pointed sable brush dipped into a spotting color that is either mixed from opaque, diluted from India ink, or worked up from a card or jar of spotting color (white, black, or brown, or the proper matching mixture of these). *Caution:* keep the brush pointed, use as little water as possible, and fill the blemish with many minute dots, rather than with one big blob of color.

But better than these spotting colors, which have the disadvantage of showing marks (especially on glossy prints) are the new *dye* products: Spotone and Dyacol (see p. 262). These sink right into the emulsion, leaving no trace on the surface. *Black* spots are removed by using iodine (see item 28, p. 375) or by reducing with Spotoff, Etchadine, or Dyacol (see p. 262).

## HOW TO MAKE WHITE MARGINS

*On contact prints:* Whether you are using a printing frame or a contact printer, first place a mask of the correct size and shape (see *Fig. 74*) next to the glass, then place the negative on top of that, with the emulsion side up, now place a sheet of printing paper against the emulsion side of

FIG. 74. PRINTING MASKS

the negative, and finally close the back and lock it. You can cut these masks yourself, from black paper or a transparent red Kodaloid, or you can buy the masks ready made.

*On enlargements:* If you use a printing frame, the method is the same as above, except be sure to use *enlarging* paper and not *contact* paper. A more convenient method is to use an enlarging easel with adjustable leaves.

*If you don't want margins:* On contact prints, simply have the negative extend slightly beyond the paper. On enlargements, to get prints that bleed to the edges, use a sheet of *spotlessly clean* plate glass to hold the paper down, or place some sticky tape triangles, face up, at the four corners of the easel, just under the leaves, so that the tape grips the underside of the paper and keeps it from curling.

## OTHER KINDS OF PRINTS

Besides the prints made on solio, bromide, chloride and chlorobromide paper, there are several other kinds. Chief among these are: *platinum prints, carbon prints,* and *bromoil prints.*

### HOW TO MAKE PLATINUM PRINTS

Platinum prints are just as easy to make as solio prints; and the *platinotype process,* as it is called, produces prints that are absolutely permanent, artistic and—costly. Platinum paper can be bought all ready to use, together with all the chemicals necessary to develop it; it is about three times as sensitive as printing-out paper and it can, therefore, be printed either by daylight or by a very strong artificial light. When the paper is printed, the image is of a pale, yellowish brown color; but when it is developed it gives a beautiful black or a soft sepia color according to the kind of paper you use. To develop the prints use the following solution:

### DEVELOPER FOR PLATINUM PRINTS

|  | METRIC | | AVOIRDUPOIS | |
|---|---|---|---|---|
| Potassium oxalate | 85 | grams | 3 | ounces |
| Potassium phosphate | 42.5 | grams | 1½ | ounces |
| Water | 1000 | cc. | 32 | ounces |

Float the prints in the developer, picture-side down, for fifteen seconds to one minute and then, without washing, place them in the following clearing bath:

### CLEARING BATH

|  | METRIC | AVOIRDUPOIS |
|---|---|---|
| Hydrochloric acid (conc.) | 22 cc. | 6 drams |
| Water | 2000 cc. | 64 ounces |

Leave them in this bath for five minutes, then put them in a second bath of the same solution for five minutes, then in a third bath for five minutes and finally wash them in running water for fifteen minutes. The whole operation should take about thirty minutes.

## HOW TO MAKE CARBON PRINTS

The *carbon* process, as it is called, has, curiously enough, nothing to do with carbon. The pictures made this way are beautiful, can be had in any color, and are permanent. But it is not an easy process to work. It is really a *gelatine-bichromate* process, and this is the way it is carried out: First of all, a paper called *tissue* (but it is not tissue paper) is bought already prepared; this has a coating on it of gelatine mixed with a pigment—usually a moist water color. This tissue, or paper, you sensitize in the dark by floating it in the following *bichromate solution:*

### SENSITIZING SOLUTION

|  | METRIC | AVOIRDUPOIS |
|---|---|---|
| Potassium bichromate | 28.4 grams | 1 ounce |
| Liquid ammonia (.880) | 4 cc. | 60 minims |
| Water | 750 cc. | 25 ounces |

After sensitizing the paper, let it dry in the dark and then contact-print it under the negative in the usual way. A red darkroom safelight can be used at this stage.

The action of light *hardens* the gelatine. To bring out the image, you must dissolve away the *soft* gelatine (which the light has not acted on) in warm water. This, however, is not so simple as it sounds. When the print is made, a thin skin of insoluble gelatine is formed all over the surface of the paper and you must transfer the whole coating to another sheet of paper. To do this, soak the print together with a sheet of paper coated with gelatine (called *transfer paper*) in cold water. Then lay the former with the picture-side down on the latter. Next squeegee them to remove all excess water. Then place them under pressure for twenty minutes, and finally put them in hot water.

In a few minutes you will be able to strip off the original paper that supports the tissue, which will leave the top, or picture side, with its skin of insoluble gelatine on the transfer paper. The image can now be brought out by placing the print in warm water for an hour or more. This dissolves away the soluble gelatine with the pigment in it, and it is now ready to be fixed (that is, *hardened*) in the following bath:

### HARDENING BATH

|  | METRIC | AVOIRDUPOIS |
|---|---|---|
| Alum | 42.5 grams | 1½ ounces |
| Water | 1000 cc. | 32 ounces |

After the prints are fixed, they are washed and dried.

## HOW TO MAKE BROMOIL PRINTS

The bromoil process is a combination of photographic printing and mechanical printing. That is, a bromide print serves as a plate which is *inked up* and from which an impression is made in the same way that an impression is made of an engraved plate in a printing press. The bromoil process is based primarily on the fact that oil and water will not mix, and secondarily on the fact that the gelatine of a bromide print which the light has not acted on remains soft and will absorb water, while those parts that the light has acted on will get hard and will not absorb water.

When such a print is dabbed over with oily ink, the ink will stick only to the hardened parts. A sheet of paper is then laid on the inked-up bromide paper and both are run through a pair of rollers. An impression is thus obtained that is quite charming and out of the ordinary. To make a bromoil print the first thing to do is to make a good bromide print, or an enlargement. You can use either an ordinary bromide paper for this or you can buy a paper that is made especially for the purpose.

After you have made the print or enlargement and developed it, fix it in a plain hypo bath made as follows:

### FIXING BATH, NO. 1

|  | METRIC | AVOIRDUPOIS |
|---|---|---|
| Hypo | 454 grams | 1 pound |
| Water | 1000 cc. | 32 ounces |

Now wash the print thoroughly and then dry it. It is now ready to be put in the hardening or *bleaching* bath, as it is called. You can get this ready-made, or make it yourself as follows:

### BLEACHING BATH

|  | METRIC | | AVOIRDUPOIS | |
|---|---|---|---|---|
| Copper sulphate | 8.5 | grams | 130 | grains |
| Sulphuric acid | 5 | cc. | 1½ | drams |
| Potassium bromide | 8.5 | grams | 130 | grains |
| Potassium bichromate | .7 | gram | 12 | grains |
| Chrome alum | 1.5 | grams | 25 | grains |
| Water | 1000 | cc. | 32 | ounces |

When placed in this bath the bromide print fades out until only a very feeble, gray-brown image is left. At this point, wash it for five minutes in the following solution:

### ACID SOLUTION

|  | METRIC | AVOIRDUPOIS |
|---|---|---|
| Strong sulphuric acid | 4 cc. | ⅛ ounce |
| Water | 500 cc. | 16 ounces |

This done, wash the print again; then fix it in a hypo bath made as follows:

### FIXING BATH, NO. 2

|  | METRIC | AVOIRDUPOIS |
|---|---|---|
| Hypo | 56.7 grams | 2 ounces |
| Sodium sulphate, dry | 7 grams | ¼ ounce |
| Water | 500 cc. | 16 ounces |

Finally wash the paper for about five minutes and you are then ready to ink it up.

To ink it up, you can use the lithographic inks of various colors or, better, you can buy inks that are ready, prepared in tubes. To put on the ink, use a brush that is made of long, fine hog's hair which has a slightly rounded end. This is held in a vertical position by the top of the handle and the ink very gently dabbed on, or *hoppered* as it is called. You can also use an *adjustable hopper*, as shown in *Fig. 75*, which holds the brush in the proper position.

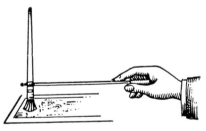

FIG. 75. AN ADJUSTABLE HOPPER

Now when you have inked up the bromoil print, or *pigmented* it, and while it is still wet, lay a sheet of any kind of good drawing paper on it and a sheet of smooth pasteboard about one-sixteenth of an inch thick on top of them both. Tighten up the screws of a wringer so that the pressure between the rubber rolls will be as great as you can make it, and then run the print, paper and cardboard through it. A steel-roll press is, of course, much better, but it is also quite expensive. Finally, strip the drawing paper from the bromoil print and you will have a picture that is distinctly different from those which are made by any other photographic or me-chanical printing process.

## HOW TO MOUNT PRINTS

The best way to mount prints is with *dry tissue*. It forms a *permanent* bond between print and mount and, most important, it *does not stain* or discolor the print. The semitransparent tissue, impregnated with wax or plastic, melts under heat and welds the print to the mount. If you can't afford a mounting press, use a flatiron, but keep it at about 140° F. (just hot enough to sizzle a wet finger), and cover the print with a sheet of heavy paper, to keep from scorching it. The tissue is first tacked to the untrimmed print at several spots, using tip of iron. Then trim print to size, arrange on mount, cover with protective paper (avoid shifting position) and smoothly, carefully iron.

## HOW TO TONE PRINTS

When bromide or chlorobromide prints are normally developed, the images are in black and white. But you can tone them *red, blue, green,* or *sepia* by simply immersing them in the following solutions:

### RED TONING SOLUTION

|  | METRIC | AVOIRDUPOIS | |
|---|---|---|---|
| Copper sulphate | 10.4 grams | 160 | grains |
| Potassium ferricyanide (*poison*) | 20.8 grams | 320 | grains |
| Ammonium carbonate | 99.2 grams | 3½ | ounces |
| Water to make | 1000 cc. | 32 | ounces |

After the prints are washed, and while they are still wet, put them in this bath until all of the shadows take on a red hue. Then wash for ten or fifteen minutes.

### BLUE TONING SOLUTION

#### BLEACHING SOLUTION

|  | METRIC | AVOIRDUPOIS | |
|---|---|---|---|
| Potassium ferricyanide (*poison*) | 21.3 grams | ¾ | ounce |
| Ammonium carbonate | 212.6 grams | 7½ | ounces |
| Water | 1000 cc. | 32 | ounces |

#### TONING SOLUTION

|  | METRIC | AVOIRDUPOIS | |
|---|---|---|---|
| Ferric chloride | 10.4 grams | 160 | grains |
| Hydrochloric acid | 85 grams | 3 | ounces |
| Water | 1000 cc. | 32 | ounces |

Put the print in the bleaching solution first, then immerse it in the toning solution until it takes on the desired color.

## GREEN TONING SOLUTION

|  | METRIC | AVOIRDUPOIS |
|---|---|---|
| Ferric chloride | 4.2 grams | 64 grains |
| Vanadium chloride | 4.2 grams | 64 grains |
| Ammonium chloride | 8.4 grams | 128 grains |
| Hydrochloric acid (10 per cent) | 85 grams | 3 ounces |
| Water | 1000 cc. | 32 ounces |

Bleach the print in the bleaching solution used for the above blue toning, then wash it thoroughly and immerse it in the following toning bath.

## SEPIA TONING SOLUTION

|  | METRIC | AVOIRDUPOIS |
|---|---|---|
| *A* Solution: |  |  |
| Alum | 28.4 grams | 1 ounce |
| Hypo | 113.5 grams | 4 ounces |
| Boiling water | 1000 cc. | 32 ounces |
| *B* Solution: |  |  |
| Silver nitrate | 1 gram | 15 grains |
| Sodium chloride | 1 gram | 15 grains |
| Water | 7 cc. | ¼ ounce |

When the *A* solution is cold, add the *B* solution. Heat the bath to 120 degrees Fahrenheit, immerse the prints in it, and they will tone to a fine sepia color in about thirty minutes. The exact time you leave the prints in the bath does not matter, for when they reach the sepia color the toning stops. Eastman and Ansco make a prepared sepia toner that can be used at room temperature.

## COLOR PRINTS FROM MONOCHROME NEGATIVES

You can make exquisite full-color prints or enlargements from your ordinary black-and-white negatives (or indirectly from your color transparencies) by using the Kodak Flexichrome process. You start from any good negative, make a straight black-and-white print on Flexichrome film, transfer the film emulsion to any paper you like, then apply colors which *physically replace* the monochrome image with a full-color image. *Sad news*: Kodak may discontinue manufacture of this useful material.

## TRIM WHEN IN DOUBT

When there's something wrong with the composition and you can't decide what it is, start trimming. Nine times out of ten that's about all that is necessary to improve your picture. The best way to do this without injury to the print itself is to make up two L-shaped pieces of card to form an adjustable frame. These can be moved around until the best composition is found, whereupon the print is trimmed accordingly. After you've found the best arrangement for a certain negative it's a good idea to make a contact print which should be marked, to indicate the way it should be trimmed, and then filed with the negative for future reference.

## PRINT FAULTS

Here are the more common print defects and some suggestions on what to do about them.

### TOO DARK

1. *Cause:* Overexposure. *Cure:* Try again, but use less exposure.

### TOO LIGHT

2. *Cause:* Underexposure. *Cure:* Make another print, but give more exposure.

### TOO FLAT

3. *Cause:* Either wrong grade of paper was used, or print was jerked from the developer too soon. *Cure:* Use a more contrasty grade of paper and leave print in developer between two to three minutes.

### TOO HARD

4. *Cause:* Wrong grade of paper. *Cure:* Use a softer grade of paper, or increase exposure and shorten period of development.

### FRILLED EDGES

5. *Cause:* Solutions or wash water too warm, or hypo or short stop too acid. *Cure:* Keep solution at seventy degrees. Replace hypo and short stop with correctly acidified solutions.

### PURPLE STAIN

6. *Cause:* Improper fixation which permitted developer to continue action, thus producing stain. *Cure:* Rinse prints quickly and thoroughly before placing in hypo, and be sure that when in the hypo they are *below* the surface of solution.

## UNEVEN DEVELOPMENT

7. *Cause:* Failure to immerse print quickly and smoothly in developer. *Cure:* Slide paper *quickly* into developer and rock tray from side to side.

### GLOSSY TROUBLES

8. *Cause:* If prints stick to ferrotype tins, the tins were not cleaned, or the gelatine was too swollen (inadequately hardened) or the wash water was too warm, or the ferrotyped prints were dried at too high a temperature. *Cure:* Clean tins with hot water and rub with ferrotype waxing solution. Avoid excess heat for washing or drying. If dull spots appear, squeegee better. Use roller squeegee.

## SOME HINTS ON THE USE OF HYPO

1. A stock solution of freshly dissolved hypo should not be used until a couple of hours after all visible particles are gone. The mixture is not fully dissolved until then. For the same reason a solution of hypo in water should stand for at least two hours before other chemicals (hardener or acid) are added.

2. The most convenient way to use hypo is as a *concentrated stock solution* made up as follows:

### HYPO STOCK SOLUTION

|                       | METRIC     | AVOIRDUPOIS |        |
|-----------------------|------------|-------------|--------|
| Water, warm           | 500 cc.    | 16          | ounces |
| Hypo                  | 800 grams  | 28          | ounces |
| Sodium sulphite, dry  | 40 grams   | 1½          | ounces |
| Water to make         | 1000 cc.   | 32          | ounces |

For use, dilute 1 part stock with 3 parts water, and add 1 part Kodak Liquid Hardener to each 15 parts of working solution, or 1 part of the following hardener to each 15 parts of working solution.

### STOCK HARDENER

|                       | METRIC      | AVOIRDUPOIS |        |
|-----------------------|-------------|-------------|--------|
| Water, warm           | 600 cc.     | 20          | ounces |
| Sodium sulphite, dry  | 85 grams    | 3           | ounces |
| Glacial acetic acid   | 66.5 cc.    | 2¼          | ounces |
| Sodium citrate        | 21.3 grams  | 328         | grains |
| Potassium alum        | 85 grams    | 3           | ounces |
| Water to make         | 1000 cc.    | 32          | ounces |

3. *Hypo becomes exhausted from use,* despite the serene faith with which amateurs continue to dump more and more prints into a single tray of the stuff. Chemists estimate that each pint (16 ounces) of fresh hypo can properly fix about 700 square inches of emulsion surface. This works out as follows for the various sizes:

67 prints, 2¼ x 3¼ inches
34 prints, 4 x 5 inches
20 prints, 5 x 7 inches
8 prints, 8 x 10 inches
4 prints, 11 x 14 inches

Since hypo is cheap, don't be a hypo miser. Above all, *use fresh hypo for all your films!* If you want to economize, store the hypo that you've used once for negatives and use it later for prints. There's a danger of staining the prints, however, if the films you use have a colored backing dye that attacks the print surface. If the margins of your prints show even the slightest stain, use *fresh* hypo thereafter.

4. Acid hypo solutions *must* include some sodium sulphite or a precipitate of sulphur will be thrown down. The sulphite redissolves the free sulphur and reforms hypo (sodium thiosulphate). Sodium bisulphite or potassium metabisulphite can also be used.

5. The temperature of hypo solutions should not exceed 70° F., or the salts will be decomposed. If an acid solution (hardener) is added to warm hypo, a white precipitate will form.

6. The concentration of the hypo solution determines the speed of fixation. A 40 per cent solution fixes the fastest. Higher concentrations, strangely enough, fix more slowly. The 25 per cent solution is the one recommended for normal use (4 ounces of hypo in 16 ounces of water).

7. *For rapid fixation, ammonium chloride* is added to the hypo in the following proportions:

2 per cent in a 40 per cent hypo solution
4 per cent in a 20 per cent hypo solution
5 per cent in a 10 per cent hypo solution

The fastest acting is the 20 per cent hypo solution with 4 per cent of ammonium chloride. Here is the formula for a *Two Minute Hypo Fixer* used by press photographers. It will clear a negative in 1 minute, fix it completely in 2 minutes:

|  | METRIC | | AVOIRDUPOIS | |
|---|---|---|---|---|
| Water, warm | 500 | cc. | 16 | ounces |
| Hypo | 200 | grams | 8 | ounces |
| Sodium bisulphite | 19.6 | grams | 322 | grains |
| Chrome alum | 19.6 | grams | 322 | grains |
| Ammonium chloride | 85 | grams | 3 | ounces |
| Cold water to make | 1000 | cc. | 32 | ounces |

8. Prints should not be left in hypo for more than fifteen minutes, provided of course that the hypo has had access to the emulsion surface (piling prints on top of one another makes this impossible). A fresh hypo bath will bleach prints if they are left in for more than that time; it will also degrade images, dissolve shadows, discolor or stain prints. This is more likely to happen where an acid rinse is used before fixing, the acid serving to soften the gelatine. The acid short stop should not be too strong (1½ per cent is about right, and that's what is usually recommended). *Caution*: Don't leave prints in *rapid* hypo solutions more than 5 minutes!

9. Hypo is at its best after it has been used a little while.

10. The addition of other chemicals to hypo will affect the color and contrast of the final print. Adding sodium chloride, for instance, gives the print a bluish tinge; adding potassium iodide gives it a warm tone (the print will turn yellow; when the tint vanishes, fixation will be complete); adding potassium iodide and silver nitrate will increase contrast and give warm tones; adding sodium chloride and silver nitrate will give blue tones and intense contrast.

11. A single print will fix completely in 30 seconds in a fresh hypo bath which has not been used previously, especially if the print is moved about or if the tray is rocked back and forth and sideways during the entire 30 seconds.

12. When compounding the hardener for a hypo bath, don't mix the sodium sulphite with the potassium alum before adding the acid; a sludge of aluminum sulphite will be the result if you disregard this warning.

13. The best way to fix prints is to use two trays of hypo, one old and one new. Transfer the prints from the short stop to the old bath for 5 minutes, and then to the new bath for another 5 minutes. Then wash. When the first tray is exhausted, dump the solution, refill with fresh hypo and shift trays.

14. The hypo can be washed out of a print faster if it is soaked for one minute in a dilute (1 per cent) solution of *sodium carbonate*. Take the print out of the hypo, rinse in plain water, soak in the carbonate, and then wash for 15 minutes. A 1 per cent solution of carbonate is made up by dissolving 10 grams of the chemical in 1000 cc. of water (⅓ ounce in 32 ounces). Don't use so-called *hypo killers;* they're a cure that's worse than the disease.

15. A simple test for determining whether the prints are washed sufficiently: drop a crystal of *potassium permanganate* in about 10 ounces (or 300 cc.) of water. Shake until water has a slightly pink tinge. Pick up a print by one corner and let some water from it drip into the solution. If the solution changes color continue washing.

# 16

# *Fun with Your Camera*

There is a difference, as Alfred A. Knopf once wisely pointed out, between *fact* and *truth*. The camera can be used to record facts, but those very facts may actually be "false," or give an impression that is false. There is danger here, as well as the possibility of innocent fun. Following are seven ways in which your camera can be used to afford amusement, surprise, or wonder by altering facts seen by the eye.

## HOW TO TAKE MOONLIGHT PICTURES

Imitation moonlight effects are easy enough to get, for all you have to do is to put a print of almost any kind of a landscape or other scene in the following solution when it will turn a blue color which makes it look as if it were taken by pale lunar light instead of by the bright light of the sun. After the print is blued, wash it until the white parts are perfectly clear.

MOONLIGHT BLUE

|  | METRIC | | AVOIRDUPOIS | |
| --- | --- | --- | --- | --- |
| Ferric ammonium citrate | 1.2 | grams | 19 | grains |
| Potassium ferricyanide | 1.2 | grams | 19 | grains |
| Nitric acid | 22 | cc. | 6 | drams |
| Water | 240 | cc. | 8 | ounces |

Another simple way to simulate moonlight effects is to take the pictures outdoors when the sky is clear and blue and use a deep red filter. Type B pan (such as Plus X, Verichrome Pan, or Supreme) is the film to use.

It is not, however, so easy to make a photograph by actual moonlight. If you will follow the method of A. W. Dryer, who has specialized in this branch of photography, you will meet with success. To take an actual moonlight picture you must have (1) a full moon, (2) a rapid lens, and (3) a moving body of water. The best time to take the picture is soon after the moon has risen but it must be high enough to be above the haze that hangs on the horizon.

The lens should be an anastigmat, and the faster it is the better, while, of course, it must be used with the full opening. The water should be preferably a running river as this will reflect the light in a broad band and this is much more effective than a thin streak such as a still lake gives. In taking the picture, set up your camera so that it includes the moon, the water in the middle ground, and a tree or a bridge in the foreground. Use an ultra-rapid film like Superpan Press, Tri-X or Ilford HPS and do not give it an exposure of more than eight seconds for otherwise the apparent movement of the moon will make it appear as a spheroid instead of a disk. The plate will, of course, be underexposed but this is required to give the appearance of moonlight. It is best to use a dilute developer and develop it very slowly.

## PHOTO DRAWING

The interesting process which goes by this name is the invention of Leonard Misonne who described it in the *American Annual of Photography*. Many variations have since been suggested, but though some of them are ingeniously different, none has improved on the simplicity of Misonne's original conception.

The process is based on the notion that an enlarged image of a negative is a reversed positive. That is, whites are where the blacks ought to be and vice versa. If you have ever placed a negative over a contact print and shifted it about a bit, you must have noticed how the image is suddenly and completely neutralized when the two match exactly. Everything looks gray or black, and there's no picture. Misonne's method is to make the matching positive by hand in pencil, by filling in the gaps or blank patches in the projected image on a sheet of white paper. If all the blank areas are filled in correctly, so that everything looks one uniform tone, the result will be a startling reproduction of the original scene, drawn by hand! The beauty of this method is that you don't even have to be able to draw to be an excellent artist—and you don't have to mess around with developers or hypo. The final result is a pencil drawing made by you, and no one who sees it will deny that it's remarkably and incredibly good.

These are the only things you have to do:

1. Project the negative image on a white sheet of paper.

2. Fill in all the white so that you see a uniform expanse of black or gray. Use a carbon pencil and whatever strokes seem easier for you to make.

You'll find that the process works best for portraits, that the negatives ought to be of average transparency, and that the image should be sharp and have some snap to it. Later, as you acquire skill, you'll be suppressing backgrounds and eliminating unwanted details. The whole operation is very swift, taking only from about 5 minutes to half an hour, depending on how carefully you want to do it.

## TWO-TONE PICTURES

A variant of Leonard Misonne's photo drawing technique is the method of converting a photograph in tone to an ink sketch in sharp *black* and *white*. The method is quite simple:

1. Make a strong bromide or chlorobromide print.

2. Bleach it until all the blacks have become a medium gray and all the lighter tones have disappeared.

3. Wash and dry.

4. Paint over all the remaining tones in India ink.

If you want to study the composition of any scene, this is an ideal method. The clutter of small details is removed at one fell swoop. Nothing but the bare bones of composition remain. An illustration is reproduced on page 315 to show the results you can get.

## PHOTOS THAT TELL FORTUNES

Pictures made by the following process were first produced by Sir John Herschel, the great astronomer, eighty-five years ago, and were called by him MAGIC PHOTOGRAPHS. These pictures have been used ever since by fortune-tellers the world over, to show a girl how her future husband looks, and a man how his future wife looks. You can do the same wherever two or more are congregated together and thereby much harmless pleasure can be got out of them. This is the effect you get:

You show a piece of perfectly blank paper about one inch square, dip it into a saucer of what appears to be pure water, and then with all the impressiveness of a master prestidigitator you press it on the forehead of the person who would pry into the future and see at any cost what his or her life partner is to be like. This done, remove it with all due solemnity when, lo and behold! a photograph has really appeared on it of a handsome youth or a beautiful maid as the exigencies of the case require.

Now the way it is done is at once simple and quite scientific. Take a little picture of a nice young man and a pretty girl and make a print of each negative on smooth solio paper (the kind professional photographers

Illustrating a simple and ingenious method for making two-tone pictures. Full directions are given on page 306. If you want to study the bare composition of any scene, this is the technique to use. No special equipment is required —and the only supplementary chemicals required are a bleach, such as Farmer's reducer, and India ink.

use for proofing portraits) in the usual way. After washing them thoroughly, fix them in a plain hypo bath made as follows:

PLAIN HYPO BATH

|  | METRIC | AVOIRDUPOIS |
|---|---|---|
| Hypo | 28.3 grams | 1 ounce |
| Water | 240 cc. | 8 ounces |

After they are fixed and washed thoroughly bleach them out in the following solution:

BLEACHING SOLUTION

|  | METRIC | AVOIRDUPOIS |
|---|---|---|
| Mercury bichloride (*Poison!*) | 14.1 grams | ½ ounce |
| Potassium bromide | 7 grams | ¼ ounce |
| Water | 240 cc. | 8 ounces |

When the salts are completely dissolved, filter the solution and pour it into a dish or tray, then put the prints into this and let them stay there until every trace of the image has disappeared; now pour the bleaching solution into its bottle again, as it can be used over and over. The next step is to wash the bleached pictures thoroughly and let them dry, when they will seem to be perfectly plain pieces of paper however closely they may be examined. To bring out the picture you need only put it in a strong solution of hypo, which seems to be just pure water to the on-looker; let it remain for a few moments, when it will reappear. But just before this happens, place it on the forehead of the curious and super-stitious fortune-seeker.

## HOW TO MAKE HIGH-KEY PICTURES

After you've learned to take and print a *full scale* picture (one that has *all* the tones from white to black—and a good print *should* have all the tones, even if only in minor accents—you may want to try your hand at some high- and low-key subjects. The photography of such subjects is not difficult, and the results are surprising and rewarding. But you will have to learn some new techniques, and may have to unlearn others.

The first thing you have to remember is that all good photographs, whether they be high, low, or medium key, use the full range of tones from white through all the thirty shades of gray to black. The difference between the various keys is merely one of *emphasis*. In every high-key picture there should be some accents of black; in every low-key picture there should be some brilliancies for contrast.

If you will glance back at the top picture on page 31, you will see three geometric shapes so lighted that practically all shadows have been eliminated. Imagine these shapes placed against a white background and you'll begin to understand some of the problems of high-key photography. While it is true you have to eliminate strong shadows, which you do by flooding the subject from all sides with soft, *feathered* (edge) light, diffused light, and/or with lots of reflected light (from walls, ceiling, or reflectors), you still have to separate the delicate tone differences which help define the subject. Your main light, by the way, should be closer to the subject than for normal-key lighting. The way to capture those subtle tone differences is not to underexpose or overexpose but to give the negative *correct* exposure. This places the gray tones in the middle of the density range, where they belong, instead of at either end, where they would be thinned out or wedged together. The method, and you will need a good exposure meter for this unless you have a lot of patience to test and try again, is to read the highlights and favor the "O" reading slightly (see page 134). Development should be *normal*. Thin, underdeveloped negatives are not true low key; they tend to create shadows without glow or detail. Overdeveloped negatives, on the other hand, increase contrast.

Now you're ready to make the print. You can, of course, use Varigam variable contrast paper and get the exact effect you're after by using one or more of the various filters, and exposing just enough to develop out in 4 or 5 minutes. But if you've ever seen one of Mark Shaw's magnificent fashion shots you may want to try his technique. He uses conventional paper. The secret is in an extra print tray which contains nothing but plain water. He uses this either to presoak the paper, which seems to soften the tones by diluting the developer upwards, or he uses it after partial development (to about when the blacks *begin* to come up strong). The print is then quickly, but *gently*, transferred from the developer tray to the water bath, and then left there to soak *undisturbed* until it looks right. *This is what happens:* while the print is soaking, the dark portions use up the developer right away and then stop, while the highlight areas continue to work. The result is a handsome print with pearly whites and glowing blacks. To *water-bath* prints successfully you have to have a full-bodied negative and give ample exposure in the enlarger. *Caution:* If, after soaking, you want to put the print back into the developer, be sure to agitate constantly *or your print will mottle.*

## HOW TO MAKE LOW-KEY PICTURES

For *low-key*, the techniques of exposure, development, and printing are exactly the same as those described above for high key. The only difference is in the choice of subject (dark instead of light) and in the lighting. Normally, only *one* light is needed. If two lights are used, the main light can be shot from the side, and the fill-in light can then be weaker than the one used for medium key. An interesting variation is to place the strong light behind the subject, and fill in from the side. It's a good idea to have shadows somewhere in each low-key picture, to accent the mood. Low key needs strong blacks, so use dark, unlit backgrounds; don't worry about printing the pictures dark if they look better that way; and, if they need it, you can even flash the corners and edges of the print with a small searchlight (making sure to protect the areas you don't want darkened). *Caution*: Don't underdevelop your prints; they'll come out gray and dull. Adjust your exposure so that you can leave the prints in the developer *at least* 2 minutes. As with high-key prints, an exposure that permits development of from 4-5 minutes usually gives better results.

Turn to page 195 to see what can be done with one model and lighting in high, medium and low key.

## HOW TO MAKE SILHOUETTES

Originally the profile view was cut out of some black silk and this was mounted on a white card. It got its name from M. de Silhouette who was the French Minister of Finance in 1759; his rigid economy in the conduct of his office caused everything that was cheap to be called by his name.

To make silhouettes with your camera is the easiest thing in photography. You can use any kind of a camera and the only other piece of

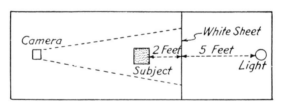

FIG. 76. HOW TO TAKE SILHOUETTES

apparatus you need is a strong light source. When you have this in readiness hang a sheet, after you have ironed the creases out of it, in an open doorway. Now place your subject in the middle of the sheet and about two feet in front of it, and set the camera in front of the subject.

These preliminaries attended to, turn his or her head so that it will be at right angles to the axis of the lens and then focus it sharp. Now place the floodlights, so that the light, the subject and the camera are all in a straight line, as shown in *Fig. 76,* and setting your shutter on *bulb* or *time,* hold it open for about as long as it takes you to say "Oh where are the circles of confusion?" Now close the shutter, turn off the floodlights, and process the film, increasing the developing time 25% to get maximum contrast.

## A NEW WAY TO PHOTOGRAPH YOUR FRIENDS

Though the effect is striking, the procedure is quite simple. It involves nothing more than the making of two negatives; one, a simple silhouette by the method described on page 318; the other, a straight portrait shot.

Illustrating
A NEW WAY
TO PHOTOGRAPH
YOUR FRIENDS

Photograph
by Leon Arden

By placing both negatives together in the carrier and enlarging through them simultaneously, you will get the effect shown here.

To be sure that the silhouette is positioned properly, set your camera on a tripod as you take both shots. A twin-lens reflex is best for this purpose, so that you can trace the outlines of head and silhouette to make sure one fits within the other. You can also combine *two* subjects this way.

CHAPTER

17

*Slides and Transparencies*

Making and projecting lantern slides was a fussy, complicated and expensive procedure until the advent of color film. The slides were monochrome glass plates (usually 3¼ x 4 inches in size) with chloride, chlorobromide and bromide emulsions. And the projectors (magic lanterns or stereopticans) were clumsy, inefficient and costly.

With the appearance of Kodachrome, followed later by Anscochrome, Ektachrome and all the other color films, a photographic revolution set in. The result was a tremendous revival of interest in the 35-mm. camera (since color film presented no processing problem—Kodak, Ansco, or their licensed processors, did all the work—and, in the miniature size, it was less expensive and easier to use). This was followed by the production of beautifully engineered, efficiently cooled, and inexpensive slide projectors—culminating in those wonderful *automatic* projectors which show 36 slides at one loading (some as many as 40) merely by turning a dial and pushing a button, *and that by remote control!*

A TYPICAL MODERN SLIDE PROJECTOR. The Argus 300 Automatic, for 35-mm. and bantam slides. Has automatic push-pull slide carrier. Can be fitted with a motorized remote-control unit with push-button operation.

We will discuss this new material and equipment later in this chapter, and in Chapter 19. But for those who still want to make *monochrome* lantern slides, here are some tested procedures. Like any other mono-chrome negatives, slides can be reduced, intensified, cleared of fog, spotted, colored by tinting (in a solution of dye so that highlights and shadows are colored), colored by toning (in which the chemical solutions replace the silver image, with the result that only the image is colored, the highlights remaining clear), or hand colored. Full instructions for these processes are available in a booklet entitled *Lantern Slides,* issued free by the Sales Service Division of the Eastman Kodak Co., Rochester, N.Y. See pages 258-263 for formulas and techniques of after-treatment of negatives.

## MONOCHROME SLIDES

Any negative that would make a good print will make a good slide. It must, however, be free from spots, scratches, and other defects, for these will be magnified on the screen.

### HOW TO PRINT MONOCHROME SLIDES

A lantern slide can be made in either of two ways: (1) *by contact,* placing the lantern slide plate directly on the negative, emulsion sides facing each other, and putting both together in a printing frame just as you would if it were a sheet of sensitized paper; and (2) printing it by *projection* with an enlarger, as you do when making an enlarged, or re-duced, print. See pages 282 and 286.

To make a lantern slide by direct contact, the portion of the negative you use must be the same size as a lantern slide plate (2 x 2, 3¼ x 3¼, or 3¼ x 4¼).

To make a slide by projection, you can use a negative of any size, pro-vided it fits your enlarger.

As it is much easier and cheaper to make slides by the *contact* method, it is best, if you plan to make many slides, to buy a camera that takes a picture which is the exact size of the slide you plan to use.

### DIRECT POSITIVES FROM NEGATIVE FILM

In the 35-mm. size, you can use Panatomic X, the negative emulsion, and convert it to a direct positive film by processing it in the Eastman Di-rect Positive Kit. When used this way, the ASA speed jumps from 25 to 80. This b/w transparency can then be mounted or bound between glass like a color transparency.

You can also use Kodak Direct Positive film to make b/w transparen-cies. It is available only in 100-foot 35-mm. bulk rolls (enough for 18 36-exposure rolls). This film has an ASA speed rating of 80 for daylight and 64 for tungsten. It can be processed in the direct-positive-film processing kit. You can also use this same film to make negatives by developing normally (9 minutes at 68° F.) in D-23. Furthermore, if you have a transparency on Direct Positive film and want to make a print from it, you can do so by using Kodak Super Speed Positive Paper, which comes in eight different sizes from 2¼ x 3¼ to 8 x 10. It is processed like the direct positive film (developed, bleached, cleared, redeveloped, and fixed).

## EXPOSURE IN CONTACT PRINTING OF MONOCHROME SLIDES

The trial-and-error method of determining exposure when making slides may be sure, but it is also time-consuming and costly. A more efficient way is to find the correct exposure for *one* negative and then to use that, with the aid of an electric exposure meter, to give you the correct exposure for other negatives.

The method is quite simple. First you place a "normal" negative in position on the contact printer, set the meter over a representative section, turn the light on and note the meter reading. Then, by trial and error, expose and develop a series of plates until you get the best result possible. The exposure time for that "normal" negative is then marked beside its meter reading. The same procedure is carried out for a "thin" negative and also for a "dense" one. With the meter readings for each of these now recorded, it should be quite easy to calibrate all the intermediate exposures for negatives of varying density.

## HOW TO DEVELOP THE SLIDES

You can use almost any of the popular negative developers to process lantern slide plates. It is best, however, to use whatever the manufacturer of the plates suggests in the instruction sheet packed with the plates. If, for any reason, that is not possible, here are some good developers you can rely on.

The most convenient one to use is Versatol solution, diluted about 1:3. The development time is from 1½ to 3 minutes at 70° F.

Another good one that you can buy already compounded is Dektol. For lantern slides it is diluted 1:2. Develop 1 to 3 minutes at 70° F. For greater or less contrast, dilute to suit.

To develop the plate pour the developer into a tray and slide the *dry* plate into it. (Your darkroom is illuminated, of course, by a green-yellow Wratten OA safelight). Don't wet the plate in advance. If any air bubbles form on the surface, you can remove them by touching them with your finger. The temperature of the developer should be 70° F. If the negative is properly exposed it will develop in from one to five minutes, depending on which developer you use. If you prefer to mix your own, try this one:

## FOR WARM BLACK TONES

### D-32

| STOCK SOLUTION *A* | METRIC | | AVOIRDUPOIS |
|---|---|---|---|
| Water (125° F.) | 500 | cc. | 16 ounces |
| Sodium sulphite, *dry* | 6.3 | grams | 90 grains |
| Hydroquinone | 7 | grams | 100 grains |
| Potassium bromide | 3.5 | grams | 50 grains |
| Citric acid | .7 | gram | 10 grains |
| Add cold water to make | 1 | liter | 32 ounces |
| STOCK SOLUTION *B* | METRIC | | AVOIRDUPOIS |
| Cold water | 1 | liter | 32 ounces |
| Sodium carbonate, *dry* | 30 | grams | 1 ounce |
| or, Sodium carbonate, *monohydrated* | 35 | grams | 1 oz., 70 gr. |
| Sodium hydroxide (caustic soda) | 4.2 | grams | 60 grains |

*Caution:* Cold water should always be used when dissolving caustic soda because it generates considerable heat; if hot water were used the solution would boil up with explosive violence and cause serious alkali burns. Stir solution *B* when adding the caustic soda, otherwise heavy caustic solution will sink to the bottom. Dissolve chemicals in the order given.

*For Use:* Take 1 part *A* and 1 part *B*. For still warmer tones, 1 part of *A* and 2 parts of *B*. Develop for 5 minutes at 70° F.

See pages 293 to 296 for other developers. Keep in mind, however, that they should be diluted when used with slides, as is Dektol, above.

## UNDEREXPOSURE AND OVEREXPOSURE

You can easily tell whether you have *under-* or *over*exposed the plate almost as soon as you have put it into the developer. If it is underexposed, the image will appear very slowly, and this is your cue to add more full-strength stock solution to the developer tray or transfer the slide carefully to a tray of more concentrated solution; on the other hand, if the image appears very quickly, add water to the developer, or slow up development by shifting the slide to another tray with plain water or dilute developer.

While underexposed slides can be intensified, and overexposed slides can be reduced, it is better to perform these operations while they are in the process of development.

## HOW TO FIX, WASH, AND DRY THE SLIDES

When the slide is fully developed, immerse it in water to rinse off the developer and then fix it in an acid fixing bath which is made up as follows:

### THE FIXING SOLUTION

|  | METRIC | AVOIRDUPOIS |
|---|---|---|
| Hypo | 240 grams | 8 ounces |
| Water to make | 1 liter | 32 ounces |

When the hypo is thoroughly dissolved then add the entire amount of the following hardening solution:

### THE HARDENING SOLUTION

|  | METRIC | AVOIRDUPOIS |
|---|---|---|
| Water (125° F.) | 160 cc. | 5 ounces |
| Sodium sulphite, *dry* | 30 grams | 1 ounce |
| Acetic acid, 28 per cent | 96 cc. | 3 ounces |
| Potassium alum | 30 grams | 1 ounce |

If you prefer a *stock* hardening solution, use the Kodak Liquid Hardener, 1 ounce in each 16 ounces of hypo solution, or make up the following, which is used in the same way:

### STOCK HARDENER

|  | METRIC | AVOIRDUPOIS |
|---|---|---|
| Sodium sulphite, *dry* | 45 grams | 1½ ounces |
| Acetic acid (28 per cent pure) | 500 cc. | 16 ounces |
| Potassium alum | 60 grams | 2 ounces |
| Water, to make | 1 liter | 32 ounces |

Add two ounces of this stock solution to the hypo solution, and then immerse the developed slide in it. You can tell when the slide is fixed by looking at the back of it and observing when the milky color disappears. The slide should be left as long again in the fixing bath to make sure that it has been permanently fixed.

After the slide is fixed, either wash it in running water for fifteen minutes or in half a dozen changes of water. Then gently wipe off the surface with a moist piece of absorbent cotton or chamois, to remove the particles of dirt and water. *Gently does it;* the emulsion side is still very tender, so take it easy when you rub; and don't leave cotton lint on it. Finally, put the slide in a rack to dry, away from any air currents that can blow dust on the vulnerable emulsion surface.

## HOW TO IMPROVE THE SLIDE

### BY INTENSIFICATION

If the slide is too thin it can be intensified with the following *acid-metol-silver* intensifier:

### DR. MEES' INTENSIFIER

| SOLUTION *A* | METRIC | | AVOIRDUPOIS | |
|---|---|---|---|---|
| Metol | 9 | grams | 140 | grains |
| Glacial acetic acid | 45 | cc. | 1½ | ounces |
| Citric acid | 18 | grams | 280 | grains |
| Water | 1 | liter | 32 | ounces |
| | | | | |
| SOLUTION *B* | | | | |
| Silver nitrate | 42.5 | grams | 1½ | ounces |
| Distilled water | 1 | liter | 32 | ounces |

When you are all ready to intensify the slide, take

| Solution *A* | 15 cc. | ½ ounce |
|---|---|---|
| Solution *B* | ± 1 cc. | 10 to 20 minims |
| Warm water (80° F.) | 15 cc. | ½ ounce |

These solutions must be mixed immediately before using and the slide put into them dry for one-fourth to one and one-half minutes. It must then be washed in running water for a minute, again put in an acid fixing bath for five minutes and washed.

### BY REDUCTION

If the slide shows too much contrast it can be reduced, and if a little fogged it can be cleared by immersing it in a weak solution of the following *hypo-ferricyanide reducer.*

### FARMER'S REDUCER

| SOLUTION *A* | METRIC | AVOIRDUPOIS |
|---|---|---|
| 10 per cent of plain hypo | 30 cc. | 1 ounce |
| SOLUTION *B* | | |
| 10 per cent solution of potassium ferricyanide | 30 cc. | 1 ounce |

Add enough of the *A* solution to the *B* solution to make it lemon-colored. Let the slide remain in the reducer for a minute or so and then wash. If any great amount of either intensification or reduction is needed it is better to discard the slide and make a new one.

## HOW TO PROTECT THE SLIDES

The slide should now be covered with a protective coating to keep it from absorbing moisture in damp weather. (This moisture is released by the heat of the projector.) Kodachrome transparencies are delivered with such a lacquer coating.

A varnish or lacquer for this purpose can be bought ready-made in any photo-supply store. Kodak makes one called Kodalak WP Clear. There is also a Kodalak Thinner, to dilute the solution when it thickens. You can also get plastic or lacquer solutions that are packaged in convenient spray cans. It's a good idea to spray the slide first with an anti-static solution like Anti-Stat 6, made by Braun Laboratories, Philadelphia 7, Pa. This eliminates static from color film, b/w film, plastics and glass—and it dries rapidly. You spray it on, and then wipe it off, thus removing dirt, dust, fingermarks, etc.

### MASKING SLIDES

The next step is to put a paper *mask* on the film side of the slide. The opening of the mask must be of the shape you want the picture to appear on the screen and this is usually rectangular, oval or round, as shown in *Fig. 77.* You can either cut your own masks out of a sheet of black paper

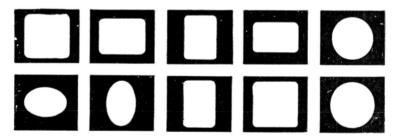

FIG. 77. MASKS FOR LANTERN SLIDES

or buy them already made. It is better to buy the ones ready-made for they are accurate and clean-cut, with the openings exactly in the center.

After you have selected the mask you want and put it on the slide, you should place a small white sticker, made for this purpose, on the lower left-hand corner so that you will know the right way to put it into the projector.

BINDING

The final operation is to put a *cover glass,* which is simply a thin sheet of perfectly clear and clean glass of the same size as the slide, on the film side over the mask. The slide and cover glass are then bound all around the edges with a strip of black tape coated with adhesive. When this is done your slide is ready for use.

## THE NEW POLAROID SLIDE SYSTEM

A revolutionary new slide system for monochrome transparencies was announced in March 1957 by Dr. Land of Polaroid. It uses a reversal film which can be exposed at a rating of 1000 ASA daylight and 700 tungsten, the fastest film on the market, and virtually grainless even when blown up to 12 feet by 12 feet. After a two-minute development in the camera in the conventional Polaroid manner, the transparency is removed from the camera and dipped into a plastic leak-proof container to harden the emulsion. The transparency can then be easily and quickly mounted in special plastic mounts. There are two sizes: 2¼ square, or 3¼ x 4. A projector of unique design is also available which makes it impossible to project slides upside down or backwards when using the Polaroid plastic mounts. The Polaroid Land Projection film can be used in any of the existing Polaroid cameras.

## SLIDES IN COLOR

As we pointed out at the beginning of this chapter, the appearance of Kodachrome in 1935 started a revolution in photography. Color slides, mounts, binders, 35-mm. cameras, projectors and screens—all suddenly became big business. This was followed by the release of Ektachrome and Anscochrome in various sizes, including the 120. Since the best projectors were those made for 35-mm. film, it was only natural that someone should eventually come up with a practical method for making slides in 120 size cameras that could also be shown in the 35-mm. projectors.

The first solution to this problem was the Rolleikin adapter for Rolleiflex and Rolleicord cameras. This permitted the use of 36-exposure cinefilm (the kind used in all 35-mm. cameras) in Rollei cameras. But this had many disadvantages, not the least of which was the fact that the resultant slides were always vertical pictures.

## SUPER-SLIDES

A better solution was the invention, by Frank Rizzatti of Burleigh Brooks, of the Super-Slide. This is a supersize color slide that can be made in any reflex using 120 size films. By using a 38 x 38 mm. film-gate and viewing-screen mask, you can make a 2 x 2 inch slide that is completely interchangeable with the standard 35-mm. slide—*and you produce it with the regular 120 size film.* The field angle for Super-Slides, if you have a 75-mm. lens (as in the Rolleiflex) is 39°, as compared with 50° for the picture area of a regular 2¼ x 2¼ inch slide. That means you get a slight telephoto effect with the Super-Slide. This, together with the fact that you get a picture that is 85% larger in area than that of a 35-mm. slide, makes the Super-Slide projections on a screen seem spectacular. See *Fig. 78.*

Placing 38 x 38 mm. mask in position over ground glass.

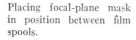

SUPER-SLIDES

Placing focal-plane mask in position between film spools.

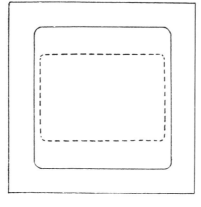

FIG. 78. Comparison of 35-mm. slide area (dotted lines) with new 38 x 38 mm. Super-Slide area (inner rectangle with rounded corners).

The success of the Super-Slide has had two other good effects: it has persuaded Kodak to release Ektachrome in the 127 size, which is the

Super-Slide size (38 x 38 mm.) without waste; and it has convinced Franke & Heidecke to reissue the 127 size "baby" Rolleiflex in a vastly improved model. This points to 127 as the film size of the future for color slides.

A kit similar to the Super-Slide is now being introduced by the FR Corporation for other cameras, notably the Minolta Autocord, Yashica, Accuraflex, Ikoflex, and others. HPI is also releasing a Master Kit for Super-Slides that can be used with either *single-* or *twin*-lens reflex cameras. For the Hasselblad single-lens reflex there is a new 16 Roll Film Magazine which produces 16 Super-Slides on a single roll of 120 film. The new magazine back actually makes an oversize Super-Slide (45 x 60 mm.), but the template of the HPI or FR kit can be used to mark and cut the Hasselblad transparencies for Super-Slide mounts. Hasselblad does not make or market any mounts of its own.

## HOW TO MAKE SURE OF GOOD COLOR SLIDES

It is no great trick to get perfect results if, like the professionals, you expose your film indoors under controlled lighting conditions and then develop it yourself under ideal darkroom conditions. But if you're an amateur, that's another story. Laboratory developing is often whimsical, if not uncertain. And the manufacturer may have altered the film a bit —not much, but just enough to confuse both the exposure and the processing. Result: no picture. Take a tip from a very successful amateur, Jack A. Goldsack, who has probably won more awards and honors in photographic contests and exhibitions than anyone else in the field. His method is quite simple. He makes at least three exposures of every color shot he feels is worth taking: one according to the meter reading; another at one stop *above* that reading; and, finally, one at a stop *below* the meter reading. This not only protects you against errors in exposure or processing, but intentional *over-* or *under*-exposure often produces a better, more dramatic slide. If the picture you're trying to capture is especially important, take five exposures; four of these can be in half-stops, two above and two below the meter reading.

## A HINT FOR TESTING COLOR EXPOSURES

By using new Panatomic X as an alternate for Ektachrome daylight, and shooting both at ASA 32, you can tell without delay whether your color exposures are going to come out all right. Panatomic X can be processed at once, and at home. One look at the negatives and you'll know whether you have to retake your color shots. This method was devised by Arthur Rothstein, Technical Director of *Look* magazine's photography department. He worked it out originally as a way of teaching photography to correspondents (*in from three days to two weeks!*). You'll find a full report in the March 1957 *Popular Photography*.

## SPOT-TINTING COLOR TRANSPARENCIES

If it becomes necessary to spot-tint your color transparency, the best method so far devised involves the use of Flexichrome Dyes diluted in an acetic acid solution (about 2 cc. of 28% acetic acid per quart of water). If you have to do this on Kodachrome, remove the lacquer first by using a 1% solution of sodium carbonate. Before you attempt this, get a copy of *Storage and Care of Kodak Color Films* from the Sales Service Division of Eastman Kodak, Rochester, N. Y. You'll find complete details there on how to remove lacquer from Kodachromes.

## HOW TO MAKE COLOR TRANSPARENCIES FROM KODACOLOR NEGATIVES

Normally, Kodacolor CU being a negative emulsion, it is used to make color *prints*. But it is easy enough to make a color transparency by using Ektacolor Print *Film*. This material was designed for use with *Type B* and *Type S* Ektacolor film, which produce negatives like Kodacolor, but excellent transparencies have been made on it with Kodacolor negatives as well. It does require care in processing, but is well worth trying.

## HOW TO MOUNT AND BIND COLOR SLIDES

The simplest way to project color slides is in the glassless cardboard mounts similar to those used by Kodak for Kodachrome 35-mm. transparencies. The trouble with these is that the slides pop or buckle in the projector, and they are not protected against dirt, dust, moisture and mishandling. There are many varieties now on the market, including the Porter Selfsealing Mount and the Kwik Mount.

You'll want to keep your best slides, however, in glass mounts. These can be bound with tape, as with the Leitz Bindomat (though you can also do this by hand), or you can use any of the many metal-and-glass or plastic-and-glass ready mounts now on the market. Two especially recommended are the Lindia all-plastic mounts and the all-metal Leitz Pro-Color push-together binders, which can be sealed with the Leitz Proloc crimping device.

### HOW TO PREVENT NEWTON RINGS

You first met these colorful little monsters when you started to enlarge your negatives and a condenser surface came into contact with the film (page 266). There are two simple and effective methods of eliminating this nuisance in glass-mounted slides: 1. Use the Leitz *Pro-Color* (or Agfa *Dia* K) mounts with their thin foil masks which keep the film from touching the glass, or 2. Use the *Lindia* mounts with the *Newlo* glass (Karl Heitz). The glass has a specially etched surface just rough enough to eliminate the rings, but the roughness does not show up on projection.

### HOW TO SHOW COLOR SLIDES

The best way, of course, is with one of the new slide projectors, of which there are many now on the market. One of the more interesting (see also p. 345) is the Kodak 35-mm. *Carousel* Projector, with a revolutionary new 80-slide round tray that fits on top of the projector, loads like a piggy bank, and changes like a record. The trays come in indexed cases that store like books. Has automatic remote control cord for reverse, forward, fine-tune focusing. Hi-lo brilliance controlled by 300-500 watt selector button on control panel. Other good projectors: *Realist 600* (for 2¼ square *and* 35-mm.), Leitz *Prado* SM300, and the Argus *Electromatic* 570 (with a 60-slide tray).

THE BELL & HOWELL ROBOMATIC, a totally automatic 35-mm. and Super Slide projector that can "run the show" by remote control for as long as 45 minutes of slides at a time, without your having to leave your chair.

# 18

## *What's Wrong?*

Sooner or later in his camera career, every amateur runs into the same ditch. When that happens he usually asks himself: "Why must this happen to *me?* One day everything seems to be going swell; the next day everything's in a mess. Why?"

It isn't always easy to answer that question. Yet it is terribly important to track the trouble to its source lest it sour your pleasure in photography. If you're bothered by film scratches, it may be the camera; but then again, it may not. Your film cartridge may be at fault. Or you may be placing an oily finger (unsuspectingly) on the emulsion (which oil gets transferred to the pressure plate and becomes a trap for stray dust or dirt).

If your pictures are not sharp, it may be the lens. But then again, it may be nothing more than hand "shake" or a badly constructed tripod. If your negatives are underexposed, especially when you use a filter, it may be the exposure meter, or the shutter, or the developer. But more than likely it's none of these. You're simply using the wrong filter factor.

If your negatives are sharp (by inspection with a 10 x or 20 x pocket magnifier) and your prints are not, it may be your enlarger, or the lens. But it probably is neither. Your negative probably buckles (from too much heat, *after* you've focused sharply) or your light source has too much red-yellow light and you're having *visual-chemical image* trouble (which can be corrected to some extent by the use of a heat-proof blue glass to intercept the heat rays). It may even be the kind of paper you are using. If you've been using a matte or semimatte paper, shift to a semi-gloss stock like Kodabromide N or Illustrator's Special and you'll note an immediate improvement.

The purpose of this chapter, then, is to point out a few of the things that may go wrong, things that you might otherwise overlook, and to give you a few ideas on how you can do your own testing all along the line.

## CHECKING YOUR CAMERA

The only piece of equipment you need for this purpose is a *test chart*. You can make one up yourself. It consists of a step wedge (made by exposing a piece of print paper in successive steps of a geometric progression such as 1 second, 2 seconds, 4 seconds, 8 seconds, etc.; this is used to check against exposure and processing, since a loss of certain of the steps in reproduction indicates a fault in exposure or development); an area ruled off with varying spaced fine pen lines; some pure color swatches of blue, red, and yellow; and some assorted curves and circles, all mounted flat on a card.

An easier way, perhaps, is to get a ready-made test chart. The plate on page 334 shows how one looks. If you can't get one of these, make up one of your own, or send $1.75 to the Superintendent of Documents, U.S. Government Printing Office, Washington, 25, D.C., and ask for NBS Circular 533 (Method for Determining the Resolving Power of Photographic Lenses). You will get an excellent 27-page explanatory booklet, well illustrated, and a supplement consisting of two sets of two resolution test charts (high and low contrast) printed from intaglio plates that are engraved and reproduced the way postage stamps are made.

This is the way you use a test chart. First hang it up somewhere as if it were a picture you were going to copy. Illuminate it evenly; place your camera about 10 to 15 feet away, on a *sturdy* tripod; load it with the finest-grain film you can get for your camera. The reason we want a fine-grain film is to be sure that any loss of definition is not due to the film. This eliminates one known factor, which makes it that much easier to track down the cause of any trouble.

Now focus sharply upon the very fine lines. Take this series of exposures:

1. Lens wide open: normal exposure (preferably by meter), then half normal, and twice normal.

2. Lens stopped down about half way (about $f 8$ for an $f 3.5$ lens): repeat normal, half-, and twice-normal exposures.

3. Lens stopped way down ($f 11$, 16, 22, or 32, depending on your lens): repeat normal, half-, and twice-normal exposures.

4. Place a filter over the lens, the one you normally use indoors. For pan film this usually is the light green, Wratten $X^1$, or perhaps the yellow-green, Wratten $K^2$. Note the filter factor you ordinarily give, then use that exposure for one shot, snap another at half, and a third at twice.

That makes 12 exposures which, if you're using a film pack or a 120

A LENS TESTING CHART. This one is no longer being made, but you can get a good one from the U.S. Government Printing Office (see p. 333) or from Morgan & Morgan, Inc, 25 Main Street, Hastings-on-Hudson, N.Y. 10706 (who publish the Photo-Lab-Index Lens

roll film, completes your exposures for the moment. Develop this film according to the directions given by the manufacturer; fix, wash, and dry it in the usual way, and then examine it carefully with a 10 x or 20 x magnifying glass, or, better still, make a series of test enlargements. These are some of the things you'll learn:

1. *Your Lens.* You'll find out if the lens works best wide open, or stopped down; whether it has astigmatism, coma, or any of the other aberrations; whether your range finder (if that's what you used to focus with) is correctly synchronized to the lens.

2. *Your Exposure.* A glance will tell you if you muffed the exposure. If you *underexposed,* two or more of the dark steps of the wedge will be merged into *black.* If you *overexposed,* the lightest parts of the step wedge will run together into *white.*

3. *Your Developing.* If you haven't developed the film long enough, you'll see each step of the wedge distinctly, but the whites will be gray and the blacks will be gray. If you've overdeveloped, the white steps of the wedge will become quite dense in the negative, though the dark ones will remain almost transparent.

4. *Your Printing.* The tests for printing and enlarging are similar to the others made above. If the negative is sharp and correctly exposed, then the cause of your bad prints can be checked right at the enlarger. In the same way you can also check your print-developing methods.

5. *The Filter.* If your factor was high, the filtered shots will be overexposed; if low, they will be underexposed. You will also be able to tell whether the filter affects the sharpness of the lens, and how it alters the color response of the film.

6. *Paper Contrast.* If the negative is normal and the print shows the wedge steps at both ends running together with almost no grays, you are using too *hard* a paper. Conversely, if there are no blacks or whites and the entire wedge is an unhappy looking series of dull grays, your paper is too *soft.*

That isn't all the test chart will reveal, of course, but this much will at least give you an idea of the technique involved. Other tests that can be made with this chart include:

1. Tests for resolving power
   a. Depth of field
   b. Effect of supplementary lenses
   c. Characteristics of emulsions
   d. Breakdown due to grain size
2. Rectilinear lens field
3. Flatness of field
4. Astigmatism

5. Chromatic aberration
6. Spherical aberration
    a. Coma
    b. Zonal aberration
7. Exposure
    a. Film sensitivity
    b. Checking exposure meter. (Send also to Kodak Sales Service Division at Rochester 4, N. Y. for a *free* leaflet on *How to Check Your Exposure Meter and Camera.*)
    c. Lens-shutter efficiency
8. Developers
    a. Optimum time and temperature
    b. Comparative *gamma* (a measure of contrast)
    c. Comparative developer tests. After checking the recommended developer, try one of your own choosing. The best way is to repeat a set of exposures *twice* on one roll, then cut the film in half and develop each section separately. What you learn from this kind of test is worth all the time, effort and materials it takes.
9. Papers
    a. Sensitivity
    b. Contrast grade
    c. Exposure
    d. Developing time

## CHECKING YOUR ENLARGER

If your prints are not as sharp and clear as your negatives indicate they should be, your enlarger lens may be suffering *chromatic aberration, curvature of field, spherical aberration,* or perhaps a few other things. Here's how you can find out. Make a negative from the diagram shown in *Fig. 79.* Try to fill as much of the negative as possible. Stop down to be sure every part of it is in focus, underexpose the negative a trifle and overdevelop it to get the maximum contrast (the fine-grain pans are better for this purpose than the others) and then fix, wash and dry it in the usual way. The result will be a projection tester, by which you can check the accuracy of your focusing. But it can also be used in other ways.

1. To check *chromatic aberration,* focus carefully, stop down to about *f* 8 or *f* 11 and make a print. If it's uniformly unsharp all over, and none of the lines or curves seem otherwise distorted, the lens probably has that fault. Try printing through a green or yellow-green filter (which will cut out some of the offending rays) or have your dealer get you a piece of that heat-resistant blue glass to fit your enlarger. It is made in two

styles: *clear* or *diffusing,* and is supplied by The Lynhoff Laboratories, Rochester, N. Y.

2. To check *curvature of field,* focus carefully in the center (with the lens wide open) and notice whether the corners are sharp. Now focus so that the corners are sharp and notice whether the center is sharp. If one or the other is unsharp in both cases your lens does not have a flat field.

FIG. 79. AN ENLARGER FOCUSING TESTER (Make a copy for your enlarger)

The worst offenders in this regard are regular camera lenses used on the enlarger; having been corrected for infinity, they do not work as well at close distances. It is better to get a regular enlarging lens (like the Componar). Such a lens has been corrected for close-ups and has a flatter field. The correction for curvature of field is to stop down until edges and center are all in focus. Make a series of tests to determine at what point this is true for your enlarger (it will vary, of course, with the distance, but since the majority of your prints are made about the same size, this variation will not be serious).

3. To check *spherical aberration,* focus carefully with the lens wide open. Assuming that your lens is otherwise okay, you will have no problem in regard to flatness of field and can therefore leave the lens open. Make a print. If all the lines have a gray edge around them, the lens has not been corrected for spherical aberration. The only cure (outside of replacing the lens with a better one) is to stop down until this fault disappears. The point at which this happens can only be determined by making some test prints at various apertures (and marking them on the back before placing them in the developer). After the prints have been fixed, washed and dried, examine them, select the one that looks best, and then use the *f* aperture indicated on the reverse side.

4. To check *vibration,* place a shallow saucer filled with some water or ink on the easel, focus on the surface of the liquid, and then watch the reflection of the image. Do all the things you ordinarily do around the enlarger when you make a print and watch what this does to the surface reflection. If there's an unusual amount of vibration you'd better do something about it. If the problem stumps you, call or write to Mr. Tuthill Doane of the Vibration Eliminator Co., Inc., 10-28 47th Ave., Long Island City, N. Y. He will probably be able to work something out for your particular case.

## CHECKING BELLOWS FOR LIGHT LEAKS

If your negatives are light-fogged, show uneven densities, have a veil or fog over the whole image area, the bellows of your camera may have begun to leak light. If it only happens occasionally it may mean that the holes are deep within the leather folds and are exposed only when the bellows are extended or pushed out of shape. Examine the outside surface carefully for obvious holes and thin spots, and if none are found remove the back and put a lighted bulb inside the bellows (with the camera in a dark closet or corner). The lamp need not be large or very bright. If you see spots of light, take the camera to your dealer for fixing. To prevent this deterioration of the leather parts of your camera use Leather

Vita (sold by Brentano's), Collectors' Book Dressing (Haas Pharmacy, New York), or any of the other preservatives mentioned on page 99. Follow directions and you can keep leather pliable miraculously for years.

## CHECKING YOUR SHUTTER

If you have, or can borrow, a phonograph turntable this test is easy. It can be used, however, only for between-the-lens shutters. Get a Haynes Shutter Checker. It costs 50 cents and is supplied with detailed instructions. You simply place the checker (shown in *Fig. 80*) on the phonograph turntable, flood light it, and shoot away at the rotating spot. Projection of your negative through your enlarger will tell you at once what the exact

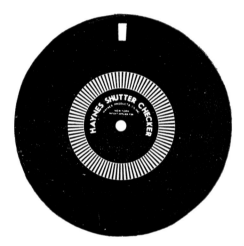

FIG. 80. THE HAYNES SHUTTER CHECKER [1]

speed of each exposure actually was by comparison with the reverse side of the checker. No calculations are needed for speeds between ½ and 1/500 second.

## CHECKING THE FILTER

Besides the color-response test which can be made with a lens testing chart, there's another important test that should be given each filter. That's the test for *distortion* or optical faults. A filter that has lumps on it will ruin the resolving power of the best lens. A filter that hasn't any lumps, but the sides of which are not plane-parallel, is just as terrible an offender, since it acts as a prism and disperses the light. The extent of

[1] If you can't find a Haynes Shutter Checker (they are no longer being manufactured) use the method suggested in exposure hint No. 8, page 136.

the damage depends on how far from parallel the plane surfaces happen to be.

There are two ways of testing the filter for these faults:

1. Hold the filter in front of your eye at an angle, look at any stationary object that has straight edges (a building, a box, a book), and jiggle the filter up and down quickly. If the object remains stationary, the filter is okay. If the object moves, return the filter and get another.

2. Hold the filter in front of your eye at an angle, but instead of looking *through* it, search out the *reflection* of some illuminated object that has a sharp edge. You will see a double image, one above or to the side of the other and one tinted the color of the filter. Now slowly turn the filter in your hand and watch carefully what this does to the *thickness* of the space between both images. If the filter is optically correct, there will be no variation. If it is not, this space will get thicker and thinner as you revolve the filter.

## CHECKING THE PRINT RINSE BATH

Dip a piece of blue *litmus paper* into the solution. If it turns *red* it's still good. You can buy the litmus paper in any drug store or chemical supply house (Eimer & Amend of New York, for example). It comes in two varieties, red and blue. Acid turns the blue to red; alkali turns the red to blue.

### CHECKING THE HYPO

Make up a 10 per cent solution of potassium iodide (10 grams in a little water and then add enough water to make 100 cc., or 1 ounce in a little water and then add water to make 10 liquid ounces). Add 3 or 4 drops of this solution to about 20 cc. (or a little more than half an ounce) of the hypo bath. If there is no precipitate, the hypo is still good. If a precipitate forms but redissolves when the mixture is shaken, the bath is still usable. If a heavy precipitate forms and does not redissolve when shaken, throw out the hypo.

## CHECKING FLASH AND STROBE SYNCHRONIZATION

Put a 2.2-volt flashlight bulb (not a *flash* bulb) into the socket of battery unit with suitable adapter. Hold on one side of lens, and watch from other side of lens as you fire. A bright light means close synchronization. Adjust until it is brightest. Start at $\frac{1}{25}$ and go higher as you make finer adjustments. To check strobe is even simpler. Just watch bulb through lens as you fire. A round hole means perfect synch; if you see shutter blades adjust until they disappear.

# 19

## *Color Photography*

Like the man who discovered to his surprise that he had been talking prose all his life, we often forget that we see the world in color. For more than a hundred years, men have tried to find some simple way to capture this color photographically on paper. The methods devised were ingenious, but difficult and expensive. In 1956, Eastman solved the problem by improving Kodacolor and releasing Type C paper for direct printing from *negative* emulsions. What had only been a dream suddenly became a photographic reality.

Now the amateur working in color has a wealth of materials and techniques at his disposal: Kodachrome, Ektachrome, and new Anscochrome, for slides; Type R and Printon papers for making color prints from transparencies; negative emulsions like Ektacolor, Kodacolor, Agfacolor CN 17, and Gevacolor, for making color prints directly on Type C paper; the Dye Transfer Process, if he has the time, the skill, and the equipment; Flexichrome, if colors need changing *after* exposure; and a Polaroid material for "color pictures in a minute." And that isn't all.

But first let's review briefly what the scientists have told us about how light produces the sensation of color.

## THE SCIENCE OF COLOR

Sir Isaac Newton, using a glass prism, split up white sunlight into seven spectral hues. He proved that these were *basic* or primary colors in that series of classic experiments that were described in the chapter, THE MAGIC OF LIGHT. Other scientists, notably Young, Helmholtz, and Maxwell, continued the experiments on color vision and discovered that the retina of the eye has three kinds of nerve ends, each sensitive to a different range of color. Arbitrarily grouped, these bands of color are *red, green* and *indigo,* or blue-violet. When spectral light of these hues is mixed in the right proportions, the eye gets the sensation of *white* light.

Further, by altering the proportions of these three spectral hues, we can produce not only the entire *seven* spectral colors but all the intermediate hues as well; red and indigo, for instance, produce *magenta;* red and green produce *yellow*; while green and indigo produce *blue-green.* This method of mixing colors is called the *additive process,* because the colors are produced by adding one to another (see *A* of *Fig. 81*).

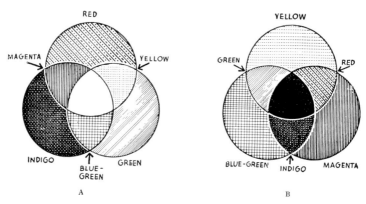

FIG. 81.  THE ADDITIVE (*A*) AND SUBTRACTIVE (*B*)
METHODS OF MIXING COLORS

Now, if instead of using green, indigo, and red light, we mixed *magenta, yellow,* and *blue-green* paint (the respective complementary colors), a strange thing would happen. Instead of the white, as before, we would create an absence of light, or the sensation of *black*. Mixing yellow and blue-green, moreover, would give us *green;* yellow and magenta would give us *red;* and magenta and blue-green would give us *indigo.* This second method of mixing colors is known as the *subtractive process* (because one color is produced by the absorption or filtering out of others), and it explains what happens when we mix pigment colors (see *B* of *Fig. 81*).

Thus mixing pigment yellow with pigment blue produces *green,* while if spectral colors of these hues were mixed a dull *white* would result. The reason for this difference in action lies in the fact that the pigment blue in the paint *absorbs* most of the yellow and red light, while the pigment yellow *absorbs* the blue and violet light, leaving only the green. You may remember that in the chapter, THE MAGIC OF LIGHT, we explained that a red safelight was red because it absorbed all the other colors, while blood was red because it absorbed green. The color of any object then depends on its *selective absorption*—its ability to filter out colors. Those colors which it does *not* absorb or filter out are the ones we see as the colors of the object.

At this point you are probably wondering what this has to do with taking photographs in color. Well, if James Clerk Maxwell hadn't proved, in 1861, that our eyes have three-color vision, other men who followed him might not have stumbled on the secret of color photography.

## SEPARATION NEGATIVES

Until recently color prints were made by exposing three separate black-and-white films through a series of red, green, and blue filters and then, by an elaborate process, converting these so-called *separation negatives* into a color print. If the object to be photographed was a still life, the regular camera could be used to expose three negatives, through each of the three filters, and adjusting the exposures to compensate for the filter factors. If the object was in motion, however, the photographer was in serious trouble. He could, of course, use Tripac film, which consists of a three-layer film sandwich so treated with backing dyes that each film is sensitive only to one of the primary colors. The image produced by this film, however, is neither sharp (since the three films can never lie in exactly the same plane), nor can one exposure produce equal densities in all three negatives. A better way of exposing these three films is in a specially designed *tricolor camera* which is so constructed that the image beam is split (by prisms and mirrors) into three parts, each part passing through an appropriate filter before it registers on one of the films. Since all three films are exposed at one time, such cameras are called *one-shot cameras*. They are not suitable for amateur use, however, since they are quite expensive, are heavy and therefore difficult to handle, and require considerable skill in manipulation both before and after exposure.

In the foregoing discussion of separation negatives it is important to remember that we were dealing with black-and-white film whose images are *afterward* converted by an elaborate and very difficult process into a single full-color print. Although this method remains the best for the making of high-quality color prints and is still used in commercial photographic studios in conjunction with the Carbro and Wash-off Relief printing processes, it is beyond the skill of even the advanced amateur. We can dismiss the whole complicated subject of separation negatives at this point and proceed to the more practical aspects of color photography and color films.

## MODERN COLOR FILMS

### KODACHROME

The problem of separation negatives, so far as the amateur was concerned, was overcome in 1935 when Eastman Kodak introduced Kodachrome film, which makes use of the subtractive process of color rendition.

In this film the color separations *are built right into the emulsion.* To make this possible the film has to be coated five times and finally resembles a three-layer cake with three coatings of emulsion separated by two of gelatine. Like the jelly fillings of a layer cake, the gelatine layers separate the first, second, and third emulsion layers and so prevent the emulsion sensitizers from spreading.

The coating of each layer of emulsion is selectively sensitized. The bottom coat, next to the film base, is *red* sensitive; the center coating is *green* sensitive; the uppermost layer is *blue* sensitive. The combined thickness of all five coatings, however, is only microscopically greater than the coating of regular black-and-white film. When finally processed, the blue sensitive layer becomes a yellow image; the green sensitive layer, a magenta image; and the red sensitive layer, a blue-green image. The separation negatives and their conversion into positive color images are thus achieved in a single process. The film is exposed in the camera like black-and-white film, and processed by Kodak or other licensed processors. What you get back is a full-color *transparency* which you look at by transmitted light. The three colored images blend to form a single image which reveals all the colors of the original subject.

Kodachrome film in its new form (sharper, better color balance, wider exposure range) is now supplied in three types: *Kodachrome II, daylight* (ASA 25), available in 35-mm. and 828; *Kodachrome II, type A,* designed for use with photofloods (ASA 40), with tungsten 3200° K lamps and 82A filter (ASA 32), and in daylight with the No. 85 filter (ASA 25), available only in 35-mm. size; and as *Kodachrome-X, daylight* (ASA 64), available in 126 cartridges and 35-mm. magazines.

### OTHER COLOR FILM

Since the advent of Kodachrome, several other color films have appeared on the market employing, for all practical picture-making purposes, the same general principle. These are: Anscochrome and Eastman's Ektachrome, both reversal films which can be processed in your own darkroom, and which, like Kodachrome, yield full-color transparencies. In addition, Eastman offers its Kodacolor which differs from the others in that processing converts the film into a *color negative* from which positive prints in color are made. These will be discussed more fully later.

Another film worth trying is *Dynachrome 25,* manufactured by a subsidiary of the 3M Corporation. Though less expensive than the standard brands, it seems to have the same high quality. The ASA rating is 25, and it is available in the 35-mm. size.

The presence of all these materials has caused considerable confusion in the minds of a large part of the public. It is surprising that so many

*(Continued on page 346)*

# AUTOMATIC COLOR SLIDE PROJECTORS

A great convenience for putting on a good show. The most popular types are, of course, designed for the 35-mm. and new Superslide sizes, but Ansco, Bell & Howell, TDC, Rollei, and others have begun to market a variety of manual, semi-automatic, combination, or fully automatic projectors for the 2¼ square sizes as well.

The most interesting is the one just announced by the Heiland division of Minneapolis Honeywell: HONEYWELL MODEL 650, which operates automatically to take all sizes from 35-mm. to 2¼ square. Slides of *any* type are floated into viewing position *magnetically,* and those that are not metallic simply have a steel clip attached to one side. To avoid the cumbersome methods previously used to adjust to the various sizes, there is an optical shift system that adjusts the distance between condenser and slide guides. Trays of both sizes can be fed from one side and, besides a choice of 300- to 500-watt illumination, there is a pushbutton remote control unit to change slides, focus, reverse slides, operate light pointer, or light up an editing panel.

*Below, A:* FRANKE & HEIDECKE'S ROLLEI PROJECTOR, the first designed to show slides of all three amateur sizes automatically and interchangeably. The projector accepts magazines on both sides, one to hold the 2¼ square size, the other to hold the 35-mm. and Superslide sizes. Has remote control cord for changing slides and shifting focus automatically.

*B:* LEITZ PRADOVIT N. The famous 35-mm. slide projector. Fully automatic. Has a 12-v. 100-watt lamp with new type of small filament and high color temperature. Remains cool, preventing card-mounted slides from "popping" out of focus. The lamp's narrow cone of light gives high depth of focus, perfect over-all definition. Has remote control cord for focusing, changing slides backward or forward. *C:* The REVERE AUTO-MAGAZINE 35-mm. slide projector. This automatically shows 36 slides in sequence, using a permanent plastic tray. Skips or selects slides at will, returning them to file in proper sequence. Supplied with 5-inch *f* 3.5 Wollensak lens and either 300- or 500-watt lamp.

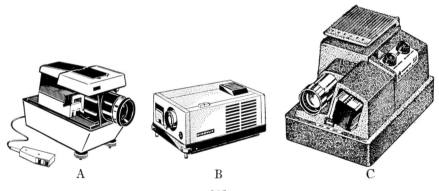

A          B          C

people with cameras are awed by color photography which they believe requires elaborate special equipment. Nothing could be further from the truth. All the films referred to in the foregoing paragraphs are made for use in cameras designed for black-and-white films and are used in the same way. There is no mystery about making pictures in color, but there are certain limitations and conditions which have led to some misunderstanding. Let us try to clear it up now.

## TRANSPARENCIES

Color photography today can be undertaken with almost any type of camera. But it is important to remember that, except for such *negative* emulsions as Ektacolor, Agfacolor CN14 and CN17, Kodacolor, modern color films are designed to produce *positive transparencies.* Unlike the black-and-white negative, the full-color transparency is *a picture complete in itself.* Its drawback is that it must be viewed by *transmitted* light, or projected on a screen.

Color prints on paper, or on opaque material, *can* be made from color transparencies, but because of limitations inherent in the process of viewing by *reflected* light, some of the color fidelity and brilliance of the original transparency are lost. The new negative emulsions, matched to Kodak's remarkable new Type C paper (renamed *Ektacolor Paper*) for making color prints, have to some extent overcome this defect.

The very drawback of reversal, or *positive,* film, however—the necessity for viewing it by transmitted light—has proved one of its greatest boons, having opened up a whole new field of photographic enjoyment. Various devices for viewing color transparencies in the smaller sizes (35-mm., Bantam, 120, and 620) have been developed and are available at reasonable prices. There are hand viewers into which transparencies mounted in the form of slides are inserted and viewed through a magnifying eyepiece. Others contain their own means of illumination, obviating the necessity for holding the device up to light. But by far the greatest pleasure is to be derived from projecting the transparencies onto a screen where they can be enjoyed by groups of spectators.

## COLOR-FILM SIZES

This form of color photography, however, may now be enjoyed by those owning roll-film cameras using film in the following sizes:

| | |
|---|---|
| 35-mm. | (Kodachrome, Ektachrome, Anscochrome, Agfacolor) |
| K-828 Bantam | (Kodachrome, Ektachrome) |

120    (Anscochrome D/50, Kodacolor, Agfacolor, and Ektachrome)
620    (Anscochrome, Agfacolor, and Ektachrome)

Though these are the only roll film sizes in which color films producing color transparencies are now available, the manufacturers promise that other film sizes will soon be ready. Until then, owners of other size *roll film* cameras will have to confine their color photography to Kodacolor, Ektacolor, Agfacolor CN 17, and Gevacolor, all of which produce color negatives from which color prints can be made on *Ektacolor Paper* (formerly Type C print material). These films are available in most of the popular roll film sizes.

Users of view and press-type cameras accommodating cut film holders or cut film magazines have practically every size of sheet film available as follows:

| | |
|---|---|
| 2¼ x 3¼ | (Ektachrome, Ektacolor, Anscochrome) |
| 2½ x 3½ | (Ektachrome) |
| 3¼ x 4¼ | (Ektachrome, Ektacolor, Anscochrome) |
| 4 x 5 | (Ektachrome, Ektacolor, Anscochrome) |
| 5 x 7 | (Ektachrome, Ektacolor, Anscochrome) |
| 8 x 10 | (Ektachrome, Ektacolor, Anscochrome) |
| 11 x 14 | (Ektachrome, Anscochrome) |
| 4.5 x 6 cm. | (Ektachrome) |
| 4.5 x 10.7 cm. | (Ektachrome) |
| 6.5 x 9 cm. | (Ektachrome) |
| 6 x 13 cm. | (Ektachrome, Anscochrome) |
| 9 x 12 cm. | (Ektachrome) |

These larger sheet film sizes yield transparencies that can be viewed by transmitted light without any need for magnification as in the smaller sizes. That's why they are preferred by magazines, advertising agencies, and calendar manufacturers; photomechanical reproduction being easier in these larger sizes. The chief drawback to sheet film in the larger sizes is its cost.

## THE ECONOMICAL WAY

From this it can be seen that the least expensive way to enjoy color photography is with the smaller cameras utilizing roll film. For those considering the purchase of a camera for purposes of color photography, and where economy is important, the small camera using 35-mm. or Bantam-size film is the logical choice for several reasons: (1) film cost is lowest, and (2) these sizes are returned to you mounted in 2 x 2 cardboard slide mounts which are accommodated by the greatest variety of available viewers and projectors. Until recently, only a few viewers or projectors were made for 120 size film. But the situation has changed, and now you can find a wide choice of models in the stores. Among them are the Realist 620 and the Opta-Vue "2¼", which accommodate all film sizes from 35-mm. to 2¼ square; the TDC, which uses interchangeable carriers; the Kimac Viewer, shown on page 349; and many others.

Up to now we have discussed color films in more or less general terms. Let us now point out the important differences in available color films. We have already described Kodachrome, which because of its intricacy is processed by Kodak or any other licensed processor. The cost of the film does not include finishing. The other films we have mentioned—Anscochrome and Ektachrome—differ essentially from Kodachrome in that they bring color processing directly into the home darkroom.

Processing your own color film, of course, is neither as simple and foolproof as developing black-and-white film, nor as inexpensive. It requires more trays or tanks for sheet film, though not for roll film, and demands far more care and accuracy with respect to time and temperature control. Nevertheless, it can be a convenience, and is worth trying.

## ANSCOCHROME

Anscochrome is used in the camera just like black-and-white film. It is supplied in 35-mm. and most roll film sizes, in three speeds and two emulsions: D-50, D-100, and D-200 for daylight with the ASA exposures of 50, 100 and 200; and T-100 for tungsten, with an exposure index of 100 when used with the recommended filters.

Although the user of Anscochrome may, if he wishes, have his film processed by his photo dealer, a local commercial laboratory, or the Ansco Color Laboratory (Building 6, Binghamton, New York), he can also, if he has the patience, is in a hurry, or just wants to enjoy the fun of developing his own film, buy a home-processing developing outfit which Ansco supplies in a 16-ounce size.

### HOW TO PROCESS ANSCOCHROME ROLL FILM

You can develop Anscochrome almost as easily and quickly as black-and-white, but there are a few important differences. Black-and-white film requires three solutions and takes about half an hour; Anscochrome uses six different baths and takes a little more than an hour. Any roll-film tank whilch has a reel that can be easily loaded is suitable, though those with the translucent or transparent reels, or the open-wire-frame type like the Nikon, can save you the messy job of unloading and reloading the film when you have to fog it by exposing it uniformly to white light (step 4).

The Twinlenz Viewer, with double lens eyepiece, produces the illusion of depth when viewing single color slides. There are many single-lens viewers on the market.

The Kimac desk viewer is made to accommodate slides from 2 x 2 up to 2¼ x 3¼. Viewer incorporates its own illumination system and magnifies the slides by means of a 3½-inch viewing lens.

(*Below*) The Kimac company also markets this slide binder set for 2¼ x 2¼ transparencies which are not mounted by the manufacturers after processing the film. Set contains cover glass and masks.

(*Below*) The Argus desk and hand viewer comes with attachments for magnification and focusing hand use.

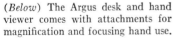

All the chemicals you need are supplied in the Anscochrome developing outfits. Just mix the chemicals in water, as directed, and you're ready.

Complete and detailed processing directions are given in the instruction sheet packed with each developing outfit. Since these recommendations are changed from time to time, make sure to follow the latest directions as packed with the outfit you buy.

For the best quality and color rendition, Anscochrome should be exposed and processed normally, according to the manufacturer's directions.

Certain techniques which you may have used successfully in developing black-and-white film may harm your processing of Anscochrome, so it is important to observe these six simple cautions:

1. Do not presoak Anscochrome film in water before processing.
2. Do not use water rinses between the two developers and the short-stop-hardeners.
3. Do not extend the washes beyond the recommended times.
4. Hold the temperatures of solutions and wash water at 75° F.
5. Use regular tap water for washing whenever possible.
6. Do not keep shortstop-hardener solutions longer than 14 days, or use them beyond the recommended number of Anscochrome rolls (as indicated in the instruction sheets supplied with each kit).

## HOW MUCH FILM CAN YOU PROCESS WITH ONE ANSCOCHROME COLOR KIT?

(This capacity table will tell you)

| | Square Inches of Film | 12 Exp. 35mm | 20 Exp. 35mm | 36 Exp. 35mm | 127 Roll | 120/620 Roll | 4 x 5 Sheet | 5 x 7 Sheet | 8 x 10 Sheet |
|---|---|---|---|---|---|---|---|---|---|
| Process this much film at the times given | 160 | 4 | 3 | 2 | 4 | 2 | 8 | 5 | 2 |
| Then increase processing times to: | | | | | | | | | |
| First developer: 13 min. | | | | | | | | | |
| Color developer: 14 min. | | | | | | | | | |
| Bleach: 6 min. All other times remain the same. | | | | | | | | | |
| Process this much additional film at these times. | 65 | 2 | 2 | 2 | 2 | 1 | 4 | 2 | 1 |
| Discard solutions after this total amount of film has been processed. | 225 | 6 | 5 | 4 | 6 | 3 | 12 | 7 | 3 |

It is always best to process Anscochrome as soon as possible after the roll is exposed. Nevertheless, if you have to keep exposed film for prolonged periods, or under unfavorable conditions of heat or moisture, you can protect the color quality of the image by running it through the first three steps of processing (*first development, short stop, wash*) then drying it. The film can then be stored indefinitely, provided it is not exposed to sunlight or strong daylight.

To finish the transparencies later, they are given normal second exposure and the rest of the processing is carried out as though uninterrupted. Such partially processed film can also be sent to the Ansco Laboratories in Binghamton, New York, for completion of processing, *but the package must be clearly marked "Department K"* or it will get full processing and be spoiled.

There are 14 steps in all. As indicated above, it is best to follow the latest directions as supplied in the kit itself. Here, in skeleton form, is an outline of the various steps and what each accomplishes. *The first two steps are carried out in total darkness,* or with the light-tight cover of the daylight tank in place. Temperature must be 75° F., and agitation, which is important, should follow the directions given in the instruction sheet.

1. *First Development.* Has the same effect as the developer in black-and-white. It develops or reduces to a metallic silver negative image, the silver halides affected by the camera exposure.
2. { *Short Stop.* Neutralizes developer and halts action, as in black-and-white.
   { *Hardener.* Conditions film for processing steps to come.
3. *Rinse.* Removes hardener and other chemicals. *Keep temperature below 70° F.*

*Following eleven steps are carried out in bright room illumination.*

4. *Second exposure.* Here film is evenly fogged in *bright* white light (flood lamp or equivalent) which exposes silver halides not previously exposed in camera.
5. *Color development.* This bath creates colored dyes and forms a metallic silver positive image in those parts of film that were exposed in step 5, above. *Caution:* Don't immerse hands in this solution; if any of it gets on you accidentally, *wash off at once!* It's a good idea to keep a tray of 2% acetic acid (or vinegar diluted with an equal amount of water) handy. Rinse hands, dip in acetic solution, and rinse again to remove all color developer.
6. *Short Stop Hardener.* Same as step 2.
7. *Rinse.* Same as step 3.
8. *Bleach.* Converts negative and positive metallic silver images formed during steps 1 and 6 to soluble compounds. (75° F.)
9. *Rinse.* Same as step 7.

10. *Fixation.* Removes compounds formed in film during bleaching, leaving only dye images which form color picture.
11. *Rinse.* Same as step 9.
12. *Stabilizer.*
13. *Rinse* in running water for 3 minutes.
14. *Final rinse,* ½ minute.

## EKTACHROME-X

Like Anscochrome, Ektachrome is a reversal color film intended for processing by the user to produce positive color transparencies. It first appeared in 1946 as a film with a daylight exposure index of 10, later corrected to 8. This has since been speeded up to 64, daylight. An improved High-Speed Ektachrome, daylight, is also available with a speed of ASA 160 (see page 356). Unlike Ansco, Kodak does not offer a processing service for Ektachrome. It must be developed by the user or by independent finishers. The film is available only in the daylight type which, however, can be used indoors at night with photoflood (at an ASA speed of 25) provided on 80B filter is added. The average exposure in bright sunlight is *f* 11 at 1/100 second. Blue flashbulbs are helpful in softening harsh shadows, a typical exposure being *f* 16 at 1/50 second with the subject about 8 to 10 feet away.

### PROCESSING EKTACHROME ROLL FILM

The developing of Ektachrome is similar to that for Anscochrome, and takes about the same time. But there are two important differences: Kodak adds a *stabilizing* bath as the final step, followed by heat drying (not over 110° F.); and the *Ektachrome color developer is nontoxic.* Each developing kit has complete instructions, which should be followed exactly.[a]

## KODACOLOR-X

When Kodacolor was first announced in 1942, it offered the simplest method of making color snapshots. There were two types of film then, one for daylight and another for flash and flood. Now there is just one *Universal Type* with a daylight exposure index of 64. It can be used for daylight *or* flash without any filter (but remember to use *clear* lamps indoors and *blue* lamps outdoors). The price of the film does not include processing. But you can buy a processing kit (C22) for use at home.

Kodacolor is as easy to use as black-and-white. The processed film

[a] *A speed increase of one full stop* can be obtained by two simple changes in processing: 1. Increase time in first developer (Process E-2) to 14 minutes; 2. Add to color developer 5 cc. per liter of 10% of sodium hydroxide. Time in modified developer remains 15 minutes, as in normal processing. Developer can be returned to normal condition by adding 3½ cc. of 10% (by volume) sulfuric acid solution per liter. *Note:* This is not recommended for the new Ektachrome-X emulsion. Check first on a test roll.

produces a strange-looking color negative in reverse from which both monochrome prints on *Panalure* photographic paper, and color prints on *Ektacolor* or *Type C* paper, can be made. The basic exposure in bright sunlight is *f* 11 at 1/100 second. It is available in most roll film sizes.

## EKTACOLOR

This latest addition to the Kodak family of color films was released in 1951. Ektacolor is a tripack emulsion (like Kodachrome and Anscochrome) consisting of red-, green-, and blue-sensitive layers coated on a single sheet of film. After processing, it looks like a Kodacolor negative (with densities inverted and colors complementary), but it's on a heavier film base. It is excellent for making dye transfer prints, since *no separation negatives are required,* and can be processed in your own darkroom.

There are two types of Ektacolor: *Type L* (Long Exposure) designed for exposure times of 1/10 second to 60 seconds with 3200° K lamps, or, with appropriate filters, by photoflood or daylight; and *Type S* (Short Exposure) for exposures of 1/25 second or less, with a daylight index of 80. Color prints can be made from the negatives on Ektacolor Paper, or by the Dye Transfer process (see page 367). Positive color transparencies can be made on Ektacolor print film. *Note:* Use filters suggested on data sheets in each box of film.

## WHICH FILM?

At this point the reader may be puzzled as to which of the available color films he should use. As in black-and-white photography that is a matter to be settled individually. All the materials discussed will do what is claimed for them if *all* the conditions of exposure and processing are carried out faithfully. Transparencies made on Kodachrome, Anscochrome, and Ektachrome are all beautiful and exciting if properly handled, but there *are* differences. Kodachrome is characterized by brilliant contrast, whereas Anscochrome is softer, its colors more delicate, its latitude somewhat greater. Ektachrome, too, is marked by greater latitude, which means that it will stand somewhat more underexposure than Kodachrome without sacrificing all shadow detail and color.

You can now make excellent color prints from transparencies, as easily as from negative materials, just by making an intermediate negative on Ektacolor or Kodacolor through your enlarger, or contact printer. Your enlarger will have to be equipped with a heat-absorbing glass, and you may need an ultraviolet absorber in the filter pack, but otherwise the processing procedures for both the negative and the print are standard. If you are interested, send for Kodak's *free* 15-page booklet, No. E 51: *Printing Color Negatives on Kodak Ektacolor Paper (Print Material Type C).* It will tell you all you need to know about how to use this remarkable new paper. Write to the Sales Service Division, Eastman Kodak Co., Rochester 4, N.Y.

Users of cut-film have the full range of choice, as between Ektachrome, Ektacolor, and Anscochrome. Those who are interested in doing their own processing may use any one of the films, though some will find it more convenient to have the processing done for them. The way to determine which of these films is best for you is to try all three; each has something to recommend it.

Costs are a factor in choice. Size for size there is little difference in the cost of color film. The smaller the size film you use obviously the less color photography will cost you. If you process your own films you reduce the cost, naturally.

## EXPOSURE FOR COLOR FILMS

The exposing of color film differs from black-and-white film in two ways. It is considerably slower and it has far less latitude. For this reason greater care is essential in determining correct exposure than is the case with black-and-white film, with which compensations in developing and printing can be made for errors of exposure. With color films exposures should be accurate within half a stop if one wants the best possible results. Errors in exposure, remember, not only affect the density of the transparency, but the color as well. *Accurate color reproduction demands accurate exposure.*

But this exposure problem is not so difficult as it might sound. A photoelectric exposure meter is, of course, an important aid, but it is not absolutely essential. Color films can be exposed very accurately with the aid of the simple directions that are packed with the film. Eastman markets the popular snapshot and flash color *Kodaguides* by which exposures are quickly and easily calculated.

### A SAFE RULE

If you ever happen to find yourself with a roll of Kodachrome II (ASA 25) film in your camera and you have lost the instruction sheet and exposure guide, fix this key exposure in your memory and you won't go very far wrong: 1/100 second at *f* 8 for use on a bright sunny day for average front lighted subjects. If the day is somewhat less than bright and sunny, try either halving the speed, 1/50 at the same stop, or 1/100 at a stop wider, *f* 5.6. If you are at the seashore where the light is brilliant, go the other way, shooting at 1/100 at *f* 11 or 1/50 at a stop smaller, *f* 16.

If this should happen to you when your camera is loaded with either Anscochrome-50, Ektachrome-X, or Kodacolor-X, just keep in mind that your basic exposure in bright sunlight is $f$ 11 at 1/100 second for all three.

Remember that no matter what method you use you will have to experiment with your own camera before you can determine correct exposure with any degree of accuracy. Camera shutters vary in their performance. An indicated speed of 1/50 in one shutter may be actually slower or faster in another. If you keep a record of everything you do with your first roll of color film, you will know whether an exposure indicated by a given exposure table or guide is correct for *your* shutter. If your results show up in transparencies that are too dark, you will know that your exposures were insufficient and that next time you will have to open up a half or full stop wider or shoot at a slower shutter speed. If they are too light and washed out, you will have to reduce the stop or use a faster shutter speed.

Here is the way Eastman returns 35-mm. and Bantam-size transparencies mounted in 2 x 2 Kodamounts ready for viewing or projection.

## USE OF AN EXPOSURE METER

These cautions are equally applicable if you are using a photoelectric exposure meter. The same factor of shutter performance enters into your calculations and another is added: Exposure meters themselves vary in accuracy of light measurement and must be used carefully. If, for instance, you hold your meter in such a way that too much direct light from the sky is allowed to enter the cell, you will get a reading that is *too high* for the subject you are photographing, and if you calculate your exposure on that reading your subject will be underexposed. *It is most important with an exposure meter to take your readings directly from the important subjects you wish to be correctly exposed in the picture.*

Recommended meter settings for all color films will be found in the table below. These have been revised in accordance with the latest information for both the Weston and ASA systems. Where the manufacturer's rating disagrees with the Weston or ASA rating, the system rating has been given, to avoid underexposure. *Caution:* Do not interchange

RECOMMENDED METER SETTINGS FOR ALL COLOR FILMS

| Film | Light | Weston | ASA | Filter |
|---|---|---|---|---|
| Kodachrome II (daylight type)[e] | Daylight | 20 | 25 | None [b] |
| *35-mm. and 828 film* | Photoflood | 10 | 12 | Wratten 80B |
| Kodachrome-X [e] | Daylight | 48 | 64 | None [b] |
| *35-mm. and 828 film* | Photoflood | 20 | 25 | 80B |
| Kodachrome II (Type A) | Daylight | 20 [a] | 25 [a] | 85 |
| *35-mm. film* | Tungsten | 24 | 32 | 82A |
| | Photoflood | 32 | 40 | None [b] |
| Ektachrome-X | Daylight | 48 | 64 | None [b] |
| *35-mm. and roll film* | Photoflood | 20 | 25 | 80B |
| High-Speed Ektachrome | Daylight | 125 | 160 | None [b] |
| High-Speed Ektachrome B | Tungsten | 100 | 125 | None [b] |
| *35-mm. and roll film* | Photoflood | 80 | 100 | 81A |
| | Daylight | 64 | 80 | 85B |
| Anscochrome 50 (daylight type) [f] [g] | Daylight | 40 | 50 | None [b] |
| *35-mm. and roll film* | Tungsten | 16 | 20 | 80B and 82 |
| | Photoflood | 20 | 25 | 80B |
| Anscochrome 100 (daylight) | Daylight | 80 | 100 | None [b] |
| *35-mm.* | Tungsten | 32 | 40 | 80B and 82A |
| | Photoflood | 40 | 50 | 80B |
| Anscochrome 200 (daylight) [g] | Daylight | 160 | 200 | None [b] |
| *35-mm.* | Tungsten | 64 | 80 | 80B and 82A |
| | Photoflood | 80 | 100 | 80B |
| Anscochrome T-100 | Daylight | 48 | 64 | 85B |
| *35-mm.* | Tungsten | 80 | 100 | None [b] |
| | Photoflood | 64 | 80 | 81A |
| Kodacolor-X | Daylight | 48 | 64 | None [b] |
| *roll film* | Tungsten | 24 | 32 | 82C [a] |
| | Photoflood | 32 | 40 | 82A [d] |
| Ektacolor (Type S)[e] | Daylight | 64 | 80 | As noted in carton |
| *roll and sheet film* | | | | |
| Ektacolor (Type L)[f] | 5 seconds | 40 | 50 | None at 3200° K |
| *sheet film only* | (3200° K) | | | 81A (photoflood) at 1 second |

[a] These film-and-filter combinations not recommended by manufacturers.

[b] No filter is needed if light of correct Kelvin temperature is used. *Daylight* emulsions are balanced for 5600° K; *tungsten,* for 3200° K floodlights; *photoflood,* for 3400° K lamps.

[c] No filter required when using clear blue lamps.

[d] Exposure must be 1/2 second or less, or color will be degraded.

[e] Exposure must be 1/10 second or less, or color will be degraded.

[f] Designed for use at 1/10 to 60 seconds. At 1 second (photoflood) ASA is 50 (with 81A filter).

[g] For information on electronic flash exposures write to Supervisor, Camera Club Service, General Aniline & Film Corporation, 140 W. 51 St., New York 10020. Ask for the data sheets on Anscochrome D/50, D/100 and T/100, or D/200.

Delicate flesh tones, colors of flowers and fabrics are reproduced faithfully in this Eastman Ektachrome (daylight type) shot. Exposure was made outdoors in strong sunlight, yet film holds fine detail in shadows. Exposure, 1/25 at f 16.

Beach scene in Ansco Color

system ratings for color film. Exposure in color *must be exact,* and it is therefore unsafe to use an ASA rating on, say, an old GE meter not calibrated on the ASA system.

## LIGHTING FOR COLOR PHOTOGRAPHY

Whereas in black-and-white photography we are concerned mainly with light intensity and contrast, another factor enters into the problem of lighting for color—*the color quality of the light source.* It is because of this factor that manufacturers have had to make color films in two basic emulsions. Light itself has color, and its degree varies from light source to light source. This aspect of light is measured as its *color temperature,* and this measurement is stated as *Kelvin temperature,* named after Lord Kelvin, the great physicist. The difference in color temperature between daylight and tungsten light is so great, daylight being toward the blue-violet end of the spectrum and tungsten light toward the yellow-orange area, that two distinct emulsions balanced for those color temperatures have been devised. Daylight film is therefore balanced for bright sunlight whose Kelvin temperature is around 5600 degrees. *It cannot be used under tungsten light* except with a special blue filter over the lens. But this filter reduces the speed of the film by a factor of about four times and so makes it impractical.

Tungsten-type color film is balanced for use with light in the yellow-orange area and should be used only with lamps of a color, or Kelvin temperature, specified by the manufacturer of the film. In the case of the Anscochrome, Ektachrome, and Kodachrome Professional films, for instance, the light source must have a rating of $3200°$ Kelvin. A specially designed filter used over the lens renders tungsten film usable in daylight. Unlike daylight-type film used with a blue filter, the tungsten-type emulsion, which is faster than the daylight type, does not in combination with the special filter lose sufficient speed to make it impractical.

Although these special filters are available to convert daylight film for use in tungsten light and tungsten film for use in daylight, *it is never advisable to do so except in cases of absolute necessity.* For best color results use film designed for the type of light under which you intend to use it.

There are many filters used in color photography for correcting the color temperature of the light. These are listed for all color films below. It need hardly be necessary to point out that filters used in black-and-white photography *should never be used with color films.*

## FILTERS FOR COLOR FILM

*(See also table on page 356.)*

| | |
|---|---|
| Wratten 1 | Used with daylight Kodachrome Professional sheet film, to reduce bluishness in (a) pictures taken on overcast days, (b) pictures taken in shade under clear blue sky, and (c) distant scenes, mountain views, aerial photography. |
| Skylight (1A) | For use with daylight type Kodachrome and Ektachrome, to reduce bluish haze in distant scenes, on cloudy days, and for snow, water scenes, mountain and aerial photography. |
| Wratten 2A | Used like Wratten 1, above, and permits use of Type B film with clear flashbulbs. |
| 78B | Permits use of Kodacolor[a] with ordinary tungsten home lighting lamps. |
| 80A | Permits use of Anscochrome and Super Anscochrome daylight type film with $3200°$ K tungsten and $3400°$ K photofloods. |
| Photoflood (80B) | Permits use of Kodak daylight color films with photofloods. |
| 80B+82A | Permit use of daylight Kodachrome and Ektachrome with $3200°$ K floodlights. |
| 81A | Permits use of Type B color films with photofloods (replaces CC13). |
| | Permits use of Anscochrome daylight type with electronic flash (interchangeable with UV15.) |
| | Permits use of Anscochrome tungsten ($3200°$ K) sheet film with ($3400°$ K) photofloods. (Interchangeable with UV15.) |
| 81C | Permits use of Type A color films with clear flash lamps, except SM, SF and M2. (No filter is needed for Type A film with SM and SF flash lamps.) |
| | Permits use of Type B color films[b] with clear flash lamps, except SM, SF and M2. *See instruction sheet packed with film.* |
| 81D | Permits use of Type A color film with new type M2 flash lamps. |
| | Permits use of Anscochrome tungsten type ($3200°$ K) film with clear flash lamps. |
| 82A | Permits use of Type A color film with $3200°$ K floodlights. |

| 82A | Permits use of Kodacolor-X color film with photofloods (3400° K). See footnote *d*, page 356. |
| 82 | Permits use of Type A color film in daylight. Reduces bluish haze in open shade or overcast, in distant scenes, mountain and aerial photography. |
| 85B | Permits use of Type B color film,[b] and Anscochrome tungsten (types 3200° K and 3400° K) in daylight.<br><br>Reduces bluish haze in open shade or overcast, for distant scenes, mountain and aerial photography. |
| 85C | Reduces bluish haze in open shade or overcast. For distant scenes, mountain and aerial photography.<br>Suggested for use with Ektacolor Type S[c] in daylight. |
| UV15 | Interchangeable with 81A.<br><br>Also used with Anscochrome daylight type for *slight* haze correction, and for electronic flash.<br><br>Used with Anscochrome T/100 (type 3200° K) for 3400° K photoflood. |
| UV16 | Used with Anscochrome daylight type for *medium* haze correction. |
| UV17 | Somewhat denser than UV16. Used with Anscochrome daylight type film for full haze correction, and for aerial photography. |

[a] Kodacolor film is balanced for daylight and clear flash lamps. No filters are required when so used.

[b] Ektachrome film, type B, is balanced for exposure with 3200° K lamps.

[c] Ektacolor film, type S (for short exposures, less than 1/10), has filter suggestions for each batch of film noted on data sheets which are packed in film carton.

## FLAT LIGHTING IS BEST

Because of its restricted latitude, color films should always be used with fairly flat lighting which means that shadows should be held to a minimum. In black-and-white photography we make our pictures effective by getting as much contrast into them as the limited scale of the printing paper will allow; hence whenever we can we use sidelighting and backlighting, working for roundness and long dramatic shadows. But in color we do the opposite. We keep shadows weak and we rely on the colors themselves to produce the effect of contrast, which would be lacking in black-and-white pictures lighted in the same way.

## OUTDOORS

The lighting problem outdoors is relatively simple. Always shoot with the sun coming from behind the camera and you'll never get into trouble with excessive contrast. If you shoot with the sun coming from an angle or overhead you'll get harsh, unpleasant black shadows which are the bane of color photography. If you do wish to have the sun coming from the side it is necessary either to place a reflector on the shadow side of your subject to reflect light back into those shadows, or to fill in the shadows with synchronized flash using a blue flashbulb designed especially for use with daylight color film. (See exposure hint 17 on page 138.)

A photoelectric meter is most helpful in keeping the range of contrast within the limits of color film, which is a ratio of 1 to 4. It is simply a matter of taking two close-up readings of the subject—the brightest area and the darkest area. If the latter is more than four times darker than the reading obtained from the brightest color, you will know that the range is too great for perfect color rendition throughout your picture. But if you are not extremely critical you will find that even if you violate this rule of contrast range you will often get pleasing pictures suitable for viewing and projection, if not for prints. Such violations should, of course, be within reason. A ratio of 1 to 8 will usually produce satisfactory exposures in which there will be some deterioration in the shadow color but not enough to be offensive. In general, though, keep the contrast within narrow limits, making sure that whenever possible everything important in the picture receives full illumination.

On overcast and hazy days and when you are photographing a subject in the shade, or for distant scenes, mountain views, high altitude aerial shots, the haze filter should be used on the lens for Kodachrome roll film, the Wratten 1 or 2A for Kodachrome Professional sheet film and Ektachrome, and the UV16 or UV17 for Ansco Color roll and sheet film (see table of Filters for Color Film). These filters reduce the excessive bluishness that is prevalent under these conditions.

## INDOORS

The same contrast principle applies to the indoor or tungsten-type films. Lighting should be relatively flat. But with artificial illumination this problem is simpler than it is in daylight since the lights are more easily controlled. The simplest setup is two lamps close to the camera, one on each side of it. If the main light is placed at the side with its light striking the subject from an angle, the shadows cast by this light must be counteracted or filled in with a light placed near the camera. The shadow areas should receive at least one-fourth (by meter reading) the illumination reaching the high-lighted areas.

It is important to remember that indoors, backgrounds require attention, too. The light striking the subject falls off by the time it reaches the background with the result that the background, although it looks all right to the eye, turns out too dark and of indeterminate color. The remedy is to provide additional illumination for the background of an intensity about equal to that reaching the subject.

Here again the photographer has a variety of lighting arrangements, dictated by his imagination, at his disposal. But no matter what the arrangement, he should see to it that the shadows receive sufficient illumination to prevent them from going harshly black. The background, remember, when it is neglected becomes in effect a large shadow area.

## IMPORTANCE OF COLOR TEMPERATURE

In photography by artificial light it is important to keep in mind the color quality of the light source. Kodachrome Type A roll film is balanced for use with photoflood lamps. It should always be used with these lamps. Kodachrome Professional and Ektachrome, Type B, sheet film on the other hand are balanced for $3200°$ K lamps, and these should always be used with it. Such lamps are available in any photo-supply store and are inexpensive. Anscochrome *tungsten type* sheet film and Ektacolor *Type B* sheet film are also balanced for $3200°$ K floodlights, though the manufacturers suggest that each can be used under $3400°$ K photofloods with an 81A filter.

Color temperature of the light source is extremely important. Except for special effects, light sources of two different temperatures should never be used at the same time. With tungsten-type film in the camera it is fatal to mix daylight with artificial light. With daylight films, however, blue photofloods may be used as fill-in lights for indoor subjects in which the main source of illumination is daylight. These blue bulbs are not recommended as the sole source of illumination with daylight-type film mainly because, as we explained awhile back, the blue dye reduces the light intensity so much that extremely long time exposures are necessary.

Thus in making color photographs indoors by artificial light tungsten-type film should be used in combination with a light source of the correct color temperature. There are exceptions to this rule and the following table shows at a glance the color films that may be used in artificial light and the filters required to adjust the color temperature to the emulsion:

| | | ILLUMINATION | |
|---|---|---|---|
| FILM | TYPE | *3200° K tungsten* | *3400° K flood* |
| Kodachrome II | Daylight | Not usable | 80B |
| Kodachrome X | Daylight | Not usable | 80B |
| Kodachrome II | A | 82A | None |
| Ektachrome-X | Daylight | — | 80B |
| High-Speed Ektachrome | Daylight | (Use 80C for clear photoflash) | |
| High-Speed Ektachrome B | Tungsten | None | 81A |
| Anscochrome-50 | Daylight | 80B and 82 | 80B |
| Anscochrome-100 | Daylight | 80B and 82A | 80B |
| Anscochrome T-100 | Tungsten | None | 81A |
| Anscochrome-200 | Daylight | 80B and 82A | 80B |
| Kodacolor X [1] | Daylight | 82C | 82A |
| Ektacolor Type S | Daylight and flash | 80B and 82A | 80B |
| Ektacolor Type L | Photoflood | 81A, 1 second, flood; 85B, 1/5 second, daylight; 85, 1/10 second, daylight | |

With this table you may quickly determine whether and how you can use 3400° K photofloods or 3200 ° floodlights with a given film.

## COLOR PHOTOGRAPHY WITH PHOTOFLASH

Because color emulsions are so slow, flashbulbs are even more valuable in color photography than in black-and-white. It is practically impossible to photograph children and pets in color by ordinary tungsten light. To stop action a shutter speed of 1/50 to 1/100 second is necessary; and, to shoot that fast, light of such intensity is needed as would cause great discomfort to the subject. Flashbulbs solve the problem. With their flash of high intensity and short duration (1/50 to 1/200 second) the sudden unpredictable movements of a child or pet can be stopped on the film without blur. The quantity of illumination is so great that quite large areas may be covered with a single flashbulb.

Here again we must observe the rule of matching color temperature of light source with the type of film we are using. The color temperature of clear flashbulbs (those of all makers) varies from the temperature required for tungsten-type films, but filters are available to bring the Kelvin temperature of the flashbulb in balance with the emulsion.[1] These are listed in the table of Flashbulb Guide Numbers in the next section. The flashbulb manufacturers make blue flashbulbs designed especially for use with *daylight*-type films. Because the color temperature of these blue bulbs is correct, you will notice in the table that they require no filter.

[1] Kodacolor requires clear flashbulbs indoors, or outdoors at night, but blue flashbulbs in daylight.

## GUIDE NUMBERS AND EXPOSURE

The use of flashbulbs in color photography is exactly the same mechanically as it is in black-and-white photography. (This was discussed on page 211.) Flashbulbs may be used with a synchronizer or by the simpler open-flash method. In either case aperture and speed settings are easily determined by means of the flash guide numbers system explained on page 214. Such information is usually supplied with the instruction sheet packed with the film, but it is more completely available in exposure guides published by the flashbulb manufacturers.

The table of flashbulb guide numbers on pages 364-365 are used the same way as the table for black and white film on page 216. The distance in feet between flashbulb and subject is divided into the guide number, the resultant figure being the $f$ stop to use.

The same principle observed for color photography in sunlight and by photoflood illumination applies also to flash. Contrast must be minimized. The simplest foolproof method of using flash is to use one bulb at the camera. This provides a direct, flat light, and a single bulb is ample to cover relatively large areas. In using a single bulb, it is important to place the subject close to the background, not farther away than one foot, in order to make certain that the single source of illumination does not fall off sufficiently to cause imperfect reproduction of the background.

## USING MORE THAN ONE BULB

In using two or more flashbulbs it is essential that these be placed so that the light from each one balances the other. If one light is placed so that it overpowers the other, thus causing deep shadows, the resulting transparency will be poor. Judgment as to the relative distances of each lamp from the subject is developed with experience, but there is a more accurate way of setting the lights correctly.

By using the regular photoflood reflectors, the lighting set-up can first be arranged with photoflood bulbs. In this way the effect can be inspected visually and the relative intensity of the light from each bulb as it falls upon the subject can be checked with the exposure meter. If the ratio is greater than 4 to 1, the lamp farthest from the subject should be brought closer until the correct ratio is established. When this is done you know that the contrast range of the lights is correct. You now remove the photoflood bulbs and replace them with flashbulbs, calculating your exposure on the basis of the distance of the main, or closest light, to the

# FLASHBULB GUIDE NUMBERS FOR COLOR FILM

## FOR CLEAR BULBS WITH TUNGSTEN FILM

| BULB | SHUTTER SPEED | KODACOLOR-X | HIGH SPEED EKTACHROME B ANSCOCHROME T/100 | KODACHROME II A KODACHROME X |
|---|---|---|---|---|
| **M3** 3–4″ polished reflector | 1/30 (X or F) 1/50 (M) 1/100 (M) 1/200 (M) Focal Plane 1/125 | 180 160 150 120  100 | 300 260 240 200  160 | 170 120 130 120  90 |
| **5 or 25** 4–6″ polished reflector | 1/25 1/50 1/100 1/200 | 170 150 130 110 | 340 300 260 220 | 130 120 100 90 |
| **SM or SF** 4″ polished reflector | 1/25 1/50 1/100 1/200 | 90 85 80 75 | 150 140 130 125 | 75 72 68 65 |
| **AG-1** 2–3″ polished reflector | 1/25 1/50 1/100 (M) 1/200 (M) | 90 70 60 44 | 130 110 90 75 | 70 55 48 34 |
| FOCAL PLANE **6 or 26** 4–5″ polished reflector | 1/25 or slower 1/50 1/75 1/100 | **170** 150 125 90 | 260 225 175 110 | 130 110 85 55 |
| **2 or 22** 6–7″ polished reflector | 1/25 1/50 1/100 1/200 | 280 220 200 100 | 450 350 300 225 | 220 170 160 130 |
| PRESS **40(M)** 6–7″ polished reflector | 1/25 1/50 1/100 1/200 | 150 130 110 90 | 300 260 220 170 | 140 125 100 85 |

(M) denotes M synchronization only.
For satin-finished reflector, use ½ lens opening larger.

## FLASHBULB GUIDE NUMBERS FOR COLOR FILM (*concluded*)

### FOR BLUE BULBS WITH DAYLIGHT FILM

| BULB | SHUTTER SPEED | KODACOLOR-X | HIGH SPEED EKTACHROME B ANSCOCHROME T/100 | KODACHROME II A KODACHROME X |
|---|---|---|---|---|
| M-2B 3″ polished reflector | 1/30 or slower X-F setting | 75 | 130 | 65 |
| M-2B 4″ polished reflector | 1/30 or slower X-F setting | 50 | 100 | 45 |
| 5B 25B 4″ polished reflector | 1/25 1/50 1/100 1/200 | 60 50 46 40 | 150 130 120 100 | 95 80 75 65 |
| 6B 4–5″ polished reflector | open 1/50 1/75 1/100 | 110 85 75 55 | 190 175 130 95 | 95 85 65 48 |
| AG-1B 2–3″ polished reflector | 1/25 1/50 1/100 1/200 | 70 55 46 36 | 130 95 80 65 | 65 48 40 32 |
| SM SF 4″ polished reflector | 1/25 1/50 1/100 1/200 | 65 65 60 55 | 50 50 45 40 | 40 40 35 32 |

Note: *No filter needed when using blue bulbs with daylight film.*

subject.[2] This distance is divided into the guide number of the flashbulbs you are using. It is essential, of course, that the photoflood bulbs you use for establishing the placement of your reflectors be of equal size, either two No. 1's or two No. 2's, and that the two flashbulbs likewise match each other. This procedure, remember, has nothing to do with *exposure;* it is merely a guide for arriving at correct *placement* of the lights.

The photoflash exposure guides, it should be remembered, are merely *guides* and cannot possibly be expected to yield accurate results in all cases. Here again one has to reckon with the variable factors of shutter behavior and individual judgment. The guide numbers have been calcu-

[2] *Caution:* Do not use house current for flashbulbs (especially midget bulbs) unless manufacturer's instructions permit. Use a B-C flash setup instead. (See page 219.)

lated for average conditions, but conditions are not always average. A white-walled room will reflect more light than one painted dark blue or brown. It should therefore be remembered that the reflecting quality of the walls as well as the size of the room affects the exposure. Dark walls *absorb* a lot of light, white walls *reflect* light, and a large white-walled room will not reflect so much light back to the subject as will a small light-walled room. Photography will never be so simple that guide numbers or gadgets will completely eliminate the factor of human judgment.

## COLOR PRINTS

There is no question that every person with a camera wishes he could make, or have made, fine color prints in which the colors are true to the original subjects and as brilliant as those he finds in his transparencies. This is the goal of color photography. Though we haven't reached this goal as yet, we have certainly made giant strides in that direction (and without having to spend a fortune, or devote a whole day to making one print, either). For instance:

1. The new, improved *Kodacolor-X,* which is faster, better color-cor-
   rected, and sharper than the old film which it replaces. It can also
   be used to make negatives from positive transparencies.
2. *Ektacolor Paper* (formerly Kodak Color Print Material Type C:
   Process P-122) for making brilliant color prints with a single exposure from Kodacolor and other *negative* color emulsions. Can be
   processed at home.
3. *Ektachrome Paper* (formerly Kodak Color Print Material Type R:
   Process P-111) for making excellent color prints with a single exposure from Kodachrome and other *positive* transparencies.
4. *Ektacolor* sheet film (Type S and L) which can be processed at
   home, and is used mainly as an intermediate in the preparation of
   color transparencies on Ektacolor Print Film.

With four such formidable color weapons in the amateur's arsenal, it will not be long before he has conquered his photographic objective. But before the amateur can get the utmost out of these wonderful materials, he has to make sure his enlarger has the proper white light, that the light remains constant by use of a suitable voltage control meter, and that he learns how to use the Color Compensating Filters made to help control color value and intensity.

## EKTACOLOR PAPER (FORMERLY TYPE C COLOR PRINT MATERIAL)

This new material is a multilayer paper which was designed for direct printing or enlarging from Kodacolor and Ektacolor negatives. It can be exposed with ordinary enlarging equipment and processed with ordinary darkroom equipment. When care is taken, the color reproduction possible with this material compares favorably with that obtainable through the Dye Transfer Process.

Ektacolor Paper (Type C) is only a sandwich of three emulsions, sensitive to blue, green and red light, coated on a medium-weight paper base. The emulsion surface has a fairly high gloss, which permits the prints to retain a long tonal range. It is available in sheets (from 8 x 10 to 30 x 40 inches in size) and in rolls (from $3\frac{1}{2}$ to 40 inches wide, and from 50 to 250 feet long). To protect it against deterioration, it should be stored in a refrigerator at 50° F. or lower. It can be handled for a limited time under a safelight fitted with a Wratten Series 10 filter.

There are two methods of exposure: by a single *white light* exposure, or by three successive exposures through tricolor (red, green, and blue) filters. Prints of excellent quality can be made by either method.

## EKTACHROME PAPER (FORMERLY TYPE R COLOR PRINT MATERIAL)

This can be used in very much the same way as Type C, above, except that it is a reversal color-print material designed to yield prints by either contact or enlargement from *positive* color transparencies. It can also be handled under a Series 10 safelight filter, with a bulb of no more than 25 watts, preferably with the light used indirectly. For full information on how to test your safelight, write to the Sales Service Division of Eastman Kodak, Rochester, N.Y., for free pamphlet K-4, *How Safe Is Your Safelight?*

### EASTMAN DYE TRANSFER PROCESS

The best and most difficult color printing process is *Carbro*, which requires about eight hours to make one print. The *Dye Transfer Process*, a simplification of wash-off-relief, shortens this time considerably, and simplifies the method. Here, briefly, is the way it works:

Three separation negatives must first be made either directly from the subject in a one-shot camera, or from a color transparency. The negatives are printed, by contact or projection, on Kodak Matrix film. Each exposed film is then processed to obtain a relief image in gelatin—the actual thickness of the gelatin varying in accordance with the density of the image. The relief films, known as matrices, are soaked in appropriate dyes. The amount of dye taken up by each matrix is proportional to the height of its relief image. The dyes are then transferred from the matrices to a sheet of Kodak Dye Transfer Paper by successively placing them, gelatin side down, in contact with the paper. Registration of the images is obtained mechanically through the use of the Kodak Dye Transfer Blanket. The three dye images combined on the paper form the final color print.

Prints resulting from this process compare favorably with Carbro. They are excellent in color fidelity and brilliance.

### ANSCO PRINTON

Ansco Printon solves the separation negative problem by incorporating the color separations in the material itself in the same way that it is done in color films. With it prints can be made by contact or enlargement with a single exposure just as in the case of black-and-white printing paper. Instead of a negative, a color transparency is placed in the negative carrier, and then is projected directly onto the sheet of Printon on the easel. Printon is processed with the chemicals supplied in the Ansco Printon Developing Outfit.

Although any ordinary enlarger or contact printer may be used without radical adaptation, the process requires the use of color filters to adjust the color quality of the exposing light. Ansco heat-absorbing glass is also necessary for enlargers not already equipped with heat-absorbing glass. There are eleven filters available and these are used at one time or another for the purpose of achieving correct color balance in the final print. It is this problem of color balance which makes the use of Printon far trickier than making black-and-white prints on ordinary sensitized papers.

In making color prints by direct exposure on Printon the worker has to contend with color temperature as he always does and always will in color photography. A tungsten enlarger or printer lamp operating at a color temperature of approximately 3000° K, such as a GE 212, is recommended. A light source that varies from this standard can be used but requires correction by means of filters.

### COMPENSATING FILTERS

Each package of Printon comes with a label which states the specific color compensating filters for that emulsion. These filters are used simultaneously with the Ansco heat-absorbing glass and the UV16P filter. This combination, says Ansco, should yield a print of *approximately* the correct color balance, and this combination is recommended as a guide for test exposures. But such are the vagaries of color that one has always to contend with such perversities as the quirks of individual optical systems, the color of condensing lenses, the fluctuations of line voltages which change the color of light, and the alterations in color which occur progressively with the aging of the lamp itself. The use of filters for these corrections is covered in Ansco's own instruction material, and although somewhat complicated, can easily be followed with a little practice.

The processing of Printon is similar to that used for Anscochrome transparencies and takes somewhat over an hour. Cleanliness and accuracy of time and temperatures are absolutely essential.

### SELECTING TRANSPARENCIES FOR PRINTING

For best results with any color printing process only accurately exposed transparencies of normal contrast should be used. Such transparencies should have no black or very dark underexposed areas, and the colors should be rich. The flesh tones should be warm. If the transparency is thin and pale it will not make a good print, which tends to wash out colors under the best circumstances. Slightly underexposed transparencies in which the contrast is not excessive, and in which there is good detail and color in the shadow areas, usually make good prints. Transparencies made in flat, evenly distributed light make better prints than those in which side lighting created strong, contrasty shadows. Shadows will always print darker than they appear in the transparency. Needless to say, good prints cannot be made from transparencies which are not sharp.

## COLOR FIDELITY

Since this chapter, of necessity, cannot be a complete treatise on color photography, much material of an advanced technical nature has been omitted. The intention in the main has been to clarify the situation, to inform the reader what materials are available and, in general, how to use them. With reasonable care existing color films are capable of yielding beautiful, natural-color transparencies, and the instructions given should prove an adequate introductory preparation for the photographer who has never attempted this fascinating new photographic field. Many, after trying color films, will want to go further into the subject. Experience usually leads to higher critical standards in any field, and color photography is no exception.

Just as in radio the practiced ear is not satisfied with radio sets of poor tonal fidelity, in color photography the practiced eye soon becomes critical of color fidelity. For such workers there is a wide field for expansion. Existing color films, for example, are inherently capable of high color fidelity, and when they fail in a given instance, assuming correct exposure, it is usually due to departures from normal in the color quality of the light under which the picture was taken. If an emulsion is balanced for light whose color temperature is 3200° K, and the light source under which it is used has a color temperature of, say, 3000° K, then the resultant transparency will be somewhat (not noticeable to the inexpert eye) warmer in color than the original subject. If the color temperature is higher than it should be, the result will be cooler or bluer in color. There is an accurate way to prevent such fluctuations from the normal.

### COLOR-TEMPERATURE METERS

It is not necessary to go deeply into the subject. Variations in light-source color temperatures can be measured with an instrument called a *color-temperature meter*. With this instrument the actual color temperature of any light source, including daylight, can be measured. Daylight itself is constantly fluctuating throughout the day. When the color temperature of the light is known, it is then a simple matter to use a filter to bring it into line with the color temperature for which the emulsion you are using is balanced.

Such meters are made by General Electric (GE Color Control Meter, type PC-1), Gossen (Sexticolor meter), Rebikoff (distributed by Karl Heitz). The Preston Miredometer (nonmechanical, inexpensive) is distributed by Weaver & Co.

Harrison also manufactures an excellent, yet inexpensive, color temperature attachment for use with GE and Weston exposure meters. For average use, however, such color meters are not essential.

## STORAGE OF COLOR FILM

The reader should be cautioned that the dyes in existing color film are not permanent. If pictures are to be made as permanent records they should be made on black-and-white film. Color films are adversely affected by heat, light, and moisture, and these factors are deleterious both before and after the film is exposed and processed. Excessive heat and humidity will deteriorate the structure of the three emulsion layers in unexposed film and so result in defective colors in the final picture. Therefore, after film is purchased *it should be stored in the coolest and dryest place in the house.* Damp cellars and other humid locations should be avoided. Home refrigerators usually have a high humidity percentage, and it is advisable, should it be necessary to store film there, to enclose it in an airtight container.

Excessive heat rather quickly affects color film. Storage places near steam pipes, in top floors of uninsulated buildings during the summer, or in automobile glove compartments should be avoided. Eastman Kodak Company recommends maintenance of the following storage temperatures:

| For storage periods up to | 2 mos. | 6 mos. | 12 mos. |
|---|---|---|---|
| Keep film below | 75° F. | 60° F. | 50° F. |

Whereas black-and-white film may usually be kept for long periods after the date of expiration stamped on the package, it is best to expose color film *before* that date if satisfactory color is to be assured.

After exposure and processing, color transparencies should likewise be kept in the coolest and driest place in the house. While the colors will maintain their richness for long periods under adverse conditions, they will last for many years if properly stored. The same conditions cautioned against for storage of unexposed film should be avoided with finished transparencies. Keep them out of the direct rays of the sun, and avoid excessive exposure to heat in viewers and projectors. Do not purchase projectors which are not equipped with heat-absorbing glass between the lamp and the slide carrier, and do not allow a slide to remain in the projector for more than a minute and a half. Excessive exposure to heat will soon cause the colors to fade.

The foregoing cautions are applicable also to Ansco Printon, prints on which should not be exposed for long periods to sunlight. If they are to be framed, hang them on a wall which is shaded from direct sunlight.

Some recommended books on color photography:

*35-mm. Color Magic,* by Walther Benser. Dr. Diener & Co., Stuttgart.

*Kodachrome and Ektachrome from All Angles,* by Fred Bond. Camera Craft Publishing Company, San Francisco, Cal.

*Photographing in Color,* by Paul Outerbridge. Random House, New York.

*The Art and Technique of Color Photography,* by the Staff Photographers of *Vogue, House and Garden, Glamour.* Simon and Schuster, New York.

*Kodak Color Handbook:* Materials, Processes, Techniques.

*Data Book on Kodak Color Films.* Eastman Kodak Company, Rochester.

*Tips on Better Color Pictures* by Ivan Dmitri. General Electric Company (Apparatus Dept.), Schenectady, N. Y.

*Derivatives from Color Photographs.* Eastman Kodak Company, Rochester, N. Y.

*Data Book on Kodak Flexichrome.* Eastman Kodak Company, Rochester, N. Y.

*How to Make Better Color Pictures with High-Speed Anscochrome.* Ansco, Binghamton, N. Y.

*Vacation with Your Color Camera.* Eastman Kodak, Rochester, N. Y.

*Let's Take Kodacolor Pictures.* Eastman Kodak, Rochester, N. Y.

*Kodak Ektachrome Film.* Eastman Kodak, Rochester, N. Y.

*How to Take Better Kodachrome Pictures.* Eastman Kodak, Rochester, N. Y.

The following pamphlets may be obtained *free* by writing to either Eastman Kodak Company in Rochester, or Ansco, Inc., in Binghamton, New York:

*Color Separation Negatives for the Kodak Dye Transfer Process,* Eastman Kodak Company.

*Color Prints with the Kodak Dye Transfer Process,* Eastman Kodak.

*Filter Data for Kodak Color Films* (Kodak Pamphlet E-23).

*Processing Ansco Color Sheet Film,* Ansco, Inc.

*Exposing and Processing Ansco Color Roll Film,* Ansco, Inc.

*Making Color Prints with Ansco Color Printon,* Ansco, Inc.

*Processing Formulas for Ansco Color Film,* Ansco, Inc.

*Prevention and Removal of Fungus Growth* (Kodak Pamphlet E-22).

# 20

# *Hints and Suggestions*

1. The average box camera has a shutter speed of 1/30 second and an aperture of about *f* 16.

2. A piece of sponge rubber such as you can get at the dime stores will make it easier for you to jiggle and bounce your tank around as you agitate it; this is a good thing to do even with those tanks that have a twirler in the center spout.

3. If you're apt to forget what kind of film you loaded into the camera, and you have the type camera that has an accessory clip on top, fit a little card into this clip marked with the film you are using.

4. To clean stained trays pour in some acetic acid solution, add a little saturated potassium permanganate solution, empty and refill with old hypo solution, then wash thoroughly.

5. To keep an accurate check on the temperature of chemical solutions in your darkroom, keep the thermometer standing in a bottle of water near the other chemicals. A glance at the thermometer will tell you instantly the temperature of all solutions in the darkroom.

6. Film hung up to dry *horizontally* (instead of *vertically*) dries more evenly. Use wooden clips, which grip film by the edges and hang the clips on a horizontal rod or taut wire.

7. Developing solutions are likely to be mixed with air (and oxidized) when poured in the usual way. A better method is to use a stirring rod, touching the lip of the pouring vessel to the rod (which rests in the receiving vessel) and letting the solution run smoothly along the rod into the container below.

8. If you have trouble cleaning developer bottles, pour a nickel package of BB shot into the bottle, add some soapy water, shake well, and rinse. The shot can be reused.

9. Kodalk makes an excellent hand cleaner. Sprinkle a little on your wet hands, rub well, and rinse.

10. Don't leave film in your camera too long, especially in hot weather;

fog, grain, or streaks may develop. Plan your picture expedition so that you can use up full rolls; if there are a few blanks left over, use them for the experimental shots you have always been meaning to do.

11. To preserve developers in trays, cover with paraffin paper (the kind they sell for kitchen use, in rolls). Place the waxed tissue gently on top of the solution. If airbells form, move them to the edge and expel. The top of the tissue must be *dry* to make this trick effective. Preserved in this way, developers can be kept without harm for twenty-four hours or longer.

12. To cool chemical solutions quickly, pack a test tube with ice and salt and use it to stir the solution.

13. To preserve print developers that are kept in half-filled bottles, blow some carbon dioxide (from your lungs) into the bottle. The carbon dioxide will form a protective layer over the surface of the solution and seal out the air that oxidizes it. Chemists object to this crude method on the basis that carbon dioxide converts sodium carbonate to sodium bicarbonate, which is true. But experiments conducted by Eastman Kodak show that the bicarbonate acts as an antifogging agent, so decide for yourself. I've preserved my D-72 in this way—with the result that the stock solution has never discolored, and there's no perceptible difference between the action of a fresh solution one hour old, and a stored solution six months old. At any rate, I've made the necessary tests and have proved this to my own satisfaction.

14. To avoid fogged negatives with film-pack cameras: (1) don't tear off the tabs; just fold them out of the way until you get ready to develop them; (2) keep direct sunlight away from the tab end of the film pack; cover it with a hat or a newspaper or anything else that's handy.

15. Always dissolve acids *in* water, never the reverse, otherwise they may bubble over with explosive violence, throwing hot acid solution into your face.

16. Don't leave your enlarger uncovered. It will collect dust and grease, neither of which is good for it. Make a dust cover, or buy one of the ready-made kind.

17. Acquire the habit of washing up all darkroom equipment right after each developing session. *Leave nothing for tomorrow!* This may seem hard at first, but it's the only sensible way to work.

18. Too much washing of film is almost as bad as none at all. Five to ten minutes, with rapid flow of water, is usually sufficient.

19. *Desiccated, anhydrous* and *dry,* used interchangeably in chemical formulas, all mean exactly the same thing: *without water.* Chemicals in *crystal* form contain water in varying amounts and allowance must be made for this when substituting *dry* chemicals for the *crystal* form. Two

ounces of crystal sodium sulphite or 2¾ ounces of crystal sodium carbonate equals 1 ounce of the dry variety.

20. Always dissolve sodium hydroxide (caustic soda) in a little *cold* water. It creates intense heat when dissolving and the mixture may otherwise boil over. Add it last to the solution.

21. Keep such chemicals as potassium ferricyanide, potassium bromide, and sodium carbonate in 10 per cent solutions (1 gram in each 10 cc. of *distilled* water). Each cc. will then contain one tenth of a gram, and solutions can be made quickly by adding as many cc's. of stock solution as we need to make up gram volume. For example, if the formula calls for

| | | |
|---|---|---|
| Potassium ferricyanide | 6 | grams |
| Potassium bromide | 2.3 | grams |
| Water | 1000 | cc. |

measure out 60 cc. of the 10 per cent potassium ferricyanide stock solution, 23 cc. of the potassium bromide, and add water to make 1000 cc. Sodium sulphite can be kept in the same way, except that the concentration should be 20 per cent, using the *dry* form. Be sure to make these stock solutions with *distilled water* (which can be bought, delivered, in 5-gallon jugs from your corner druggist or the man who supplies him; the cost is about a dollar a jug, exclusive of the deposit).

22. Metol dissolves with difficulty in a strong sulphite solution. Dissolve about a tenth of the required sulphite in the water (to prevent oxidation), then the metol, then the balance of the sulphite.

23. Never pour water over chemicals such as sulphite, hypo, or carbonate; they will cake. Pour the salts into the water, a bit at a time, stirring vigorously as you do so.

24. Sodium sulphite is very soluble in cold water, still more in warm water, *not at all in very hot or boiling water.*

25. Two parts of Kodalk, weight for weight are equivalent to 1 part sodium carbonate in all formulas (except those containing Pyro) which do not contain bisulphite or other acids. Kodalk is borax which has a little caustic added to it, just enough to form sodium metaborate.

26. One part of citric acid by weight equals two parts of 28 per cent acetic acid by weight or one part of glacial acetic by weight.

27. For opening reluctant jar or bottle *screw caps,* get yourself a "Top-Off" opener. I bought mine in Woolworth's, but I think you can buy them at almost any hardware or house furnishings store.

28. Black spots on prints (due to pinholes in negatives) can be bleached out by touching them with iodine (the household tincture will do) applied with a brush or a toothpick. If the print is now placed in a

plain hypo bath, both iodine and spot will be removed. This will leave a white spot which can be retouched in the regular manner.

29. For the negative of *extreme contrast* that won't print on even the softest paper, try the following:

(*a*) Expose print as usual.

(*b*) Soak in plain water for 30 seconds.

(*c*) Soak in a solution of potassium bichromate, 2 grams in 1000 cc. of water for bromide; 5 grams in 1000 cc. for chlorides. Let it remain in the solution from 3 to 4 minutes; the longer the immersion, the softer the print.

(*d*) Wash this undeveloped print thoroughly (5 changes of water at least).

(*e*) Develop in usual way.

30. A quick and simple print reducer is made by adding some tincture of iodine to a tray of ordinary water. Place the dry print into this solution and remove it when the highlights take on a slightly blue tinge. A short soak in hypo will remove the blue tone. Wash and dry as usual.

31. Regardless of the percentage actually marked on the labels, the following chemicals are rated at 100 per cent when diluted, and are treated accordingly:

Ammonia 28 per cent
Nitric acid 45 per cent
Formalin 37 per cent

32. Except for such liquids as nitric and sulphuric acids, which attack both cork and rubber, use *rubber corks* in preference to regular cork or glass stoppers. They will not stick (as do these blasted glass stoppers), and they eliminate the hazard of explosions caused by expanding liquids or gasses.

33. To prevent them from getting stuck in the bottle, glass stoppers should be lightly smeared with vaseline. If you've got one that *is* stuck, tap it lightly with another glass stopper (or a glass rod) and it will come out easily. If that doesn't work, dip a strip of cloth or a wad of cotton in some very hot water and wrap around the neck of the bottle. This expands the bottle without affecting the stopper, which you can now remove.

34. The most stable form of sodium carbonate is the monohydrate. Use 15 per cent *more* of the monohydrate when the *dry* (anhydrous or desiccated) is specified in a formula; use 57 per cent less monohydrate when the *crystal* variety is specified. If you have the *dry* form, and the *monohydrate* is specified, use 15 per cent less of the dry.

35. Stock solutions of developers need *not* be kept in *brown* bottles. However, the brown bottles made for storing photographic chemicals are made of a glass that does not have an excess of alkali and are therefore preferred for storing *fine grain* developers.

36. Never fill bottles right up to the cork. Liquids expand and contract with temperature variations and may either blow caps off or suck corks in (especially if bottled when hot). Leave about one inch of air space between cap or cork and liquid.

37. There are three forms of tribasic sodium phosphate available:

(a) anhydrous (dry)
(b) monohydrate (1 molecule of water)
(c) crystalline (12 molecules of water)

Unless otherwise stated, the form generally supplied is the crystalline. Edwal's TSP is the monohydrate. If you are using TSP formulas which specify the crystalline (or fail to mention which form is to be used) use half as much as is specified. *Crystalline* is the same as *dodecahydrate*.

38. Films can be cleared of oil and finger marks with carbon tetra-chloride, Edwal Film Cleaner (which also neutralizes the static that at-tracts dust) and ammonia. *Caution:* Carbon tetrachloride is a deadly poison. Use it with care. Avoid its use entirely if ventilation is poor, or if you have cuts on your skin.

39. Manufacturers issue all sorts of free literature which is very help-ful. Make use of it. Most of them maintain service departments, to help amateurs with their problems. Write to them when you run into difficulty with any of their products.

40. To prevent air-bells, developer spots, and pinholes from ruining your negatives, and to be sure that your film subsequently dries evenly without watermarks and without curling, use a wetting agent. One of the best and least expensive is Aerosol OT Clear 25 per cent. You can buy this at Eimer and Amend in New York, or from any other reputable chemical supply house. Using the 25 per cent solution, dilute with 24 parts water to make a 1 per cent solution. *Be sure to filter the solution!* Add 1 ounce of the 1 per cent solution to each 32 ounces of developer but *not* if the developer is "maximum energy" or strongly alkaline. Aero-sol may be added, without danger, to *any* fine-grain developer. *Caution:* Diluted wetting agents decompose in a short time, especially in warm weather. You can prevent this by adding a small amount of formalin to the bath. The solution will then keep indefinitely. Formalin hardens film. If the amount of formalin is raised to 4%, and the film is left in the final rinse for 5 minutes, the gelatin will be protected against bacteria as well, according to *Leica Fotografie.*

41. Some chemical equivalents: (1) sodium sulphite, (2) sodium meta-bisulphite, (3) sodium bisulphite. You can substitute (2) and (3), one for the other and weight for weight. (2) is more expensive than (3). (2) and (3) are preferable in two-solution developers, since (1) is alkaline

while (2) and (3) are acid. (Oxidation proceeds more slowly in acid solutions.)

42. To photograph waterfalls, exposures should be fast enough to slow up action of the water without "freezing" it. Shutter speeds of 1/25 to 1/100 second are recommended. Faster than 1/100 second makes the water look glassy or icy; speeds slower than 1/25 second blur the water altogether. Diffused sunlight is best to avoid overexposure of the water and underexposure of the rocks and foliage.

43. The point to focus on, when trying to photograph a scene in which both foreground and background must be shown clearly, has always been a problem for the inexperienced amateur. Focussing on a point midway between the nearest and farthest object sounds reasonable, but doesn't work out in practice. The best way to find the correct distance requires a little bit of elementary mathematics. Multiply the far and near distance together, double that, then divide by the two distances added together. The result will be the distance to focus on. For instance: a man at 10 feet and a house at 22 feet. 10 x 22 = 220. Doubled, this gives us 440. Add the two distances and you get 32. 440 divided by 32 gives us 13¾ feet, the best focussing point. This does not mean that both points would be in focus at a large lens stop; merely that this way you will be able to use a larger stop than would otherwise be possible. This method is useful if you have no depth-of-field scale.

44. Against-the-light scenes are easy if you remember these three things: (1) Shade the lens with an adequate hood or by throwing a shadow across it with a hand, a hat, a tree, a sign, a flag. (2) Give ample exposure; two to four times normal is not too much. (3) Abbreviate developing time more than usual to avoid excessive contrast.

45. Reducing the aperture of a good enlarger lens will not sharpen your picture if the easel, lens board, and negative are all plane-parallel. Reduce the aperture only to increase exposure time and to allow for dodging and other manipulation. Depth of focus at the larger apertures is shallow enough to aid in avoiding scratches, hair, dust, etc. *Caution:* Sometimes the heat from your enlarger head will cause your negative to buckle. A small aperture may compensate for this to some degree.

46. Enlarger lens sharpness can be improved, generally, by printing through a blue filter such as the tricolor $C^5$. The printing time will be increased, but your pictures will be sharper. *Explanation:* Light from an incandescent lamp has radiations of all the visible wave lengths, as well as infrared and untraviolet. If all these rays are to be focussed sharply, the lens must be specially corrected. Few enlarger lenses are corrected that much.

# Supplemental Glossary[1]

ABRASION MARKS. Streaks and blotches occurring on bromide developing papers that appear much like pencil marks or scratches. They are probably due to the condition of the developer or the type of developer. They can be removed by rubbing them with a bit of cotton moistened in alcohol.

ACCELERATOR CONTROL. By varying the proportions of an accelerator in a developer, the time of development and the highlight details can be controlled. With overexposed highlights, much detail can be brought out by reducing the amount of accelerator and prolonging the time of development.

ACCENTUATION. An art term denoting special emphasis upon some particular part of a photograph. Accentuation may be secured by a strong highlight, a strong contrast of light and shade, or a dark mass in a relatively light area.

ACETONE SULFITE. $(CH_3)_2CO.Na$ $HSO_3$. A compound formed by mixing acetone and acid sodium sulfite. Used in some developer formulas as a substitute for sodium sulfite or potassium metabisulfite.

ACUTANCE. The measure of sharpness of a photographic image. It is not the same as "resolving power." The resolution of a photographic image depends as much on the resolving power of the lens as on the acutance of the emulsion. Both are necessary to produce a sharp image.

AERIAL IMAGE. An image existing in space which can be captured on a ground glass, film, or any other suitable surface. It can also be caught by another lens system.

AERIAL PERSPECTIVE. An impression of depth or distance in a photograph that depends upon the effect of the atmospheric haze in suppressing distant detail.

AGED DEVELOPERS. Certain classes of developers, employed for suppressing grain in miniature negatives, give much better grain suppression after they have been held or aged for several months after mixing.

ALUM, CHROME. $Cr_2(SO_4)_3.(NH_4)_2SO_4.$ $24H_2O$. A deep purple salt soluble in cold water and alcohol. It is used for hardening gelatin emulsions to prevent frilling in warm weather.

ALUM, COMMON WHITE. Same as potassium alum.

ALUM, POTASSIUM. $K_2SO_4.Al_2(SO_4)_3.$ $24H_2O$. Used for hardening and clearing stains from emulsion. Soluble in water but not in alcohol. Commonly used as the hardener in acid fixing baths.

ALUM, POTASSIUM CHROME. $KCr(SO_4)_2.12H_2O$. Plum-colored crystals used in the chrome-alum fixing bath to harden the gelatin of film.

AMIDOL. $C_6H_3(NH_2)_2OH.2HCl$. A developing agent (Diaminophenol hydrochloride) that will develop successfully without the addition of an alkaline accelerator. It does not keep well in solution and must be mixed when needed.

AMMONIUM BROMIDE. $NH_4Br$. Used in developer as a restrainer and also in preparation of gelatino-bromide emulsions.

AMMONIUM PERSULFATE. $(NH_4)_2$ $S_2O_8$. Used for reducing the density of negatives; a flattening reducer.

AMMONIUM SULFIDE. $(NH_4)_2S$. Used for intensification.

AMMONIUM SULFITE. $(NH_4)_2SO_3.H_2O$. Soluble, colorless crystals which may be substituted for sodium sulfite in pyro-ammonia developer, and to darken negatives in mercury intensification.

ANHYDROUS. Signifying "without water." Thus, anhydrous sodium carbonate is without water of crystallization.

ANNULAR. Ring form or ring-like.

APERTURE. The lens opening that is controlled by a diaphragm.

ASA. These letters, which stand for the American Standards Association, are now used (with a number) to indicate the emulsion speed of film. All American film and meter manufacturers, and most of the European ones, now use ASA figures. These film speeds have replaced the Weston, GE,

---

[1] Partially excerpted from *A Glossary for Photography* by Frank Fenner, Little Technical Library, copyright 1939 by Ziff-Davis Publishing Company.

Din, and BSI (British) film speed designations.

APOCHROMATIC LENS. Such a lens is corrected for chromatic aberration for three wave lengths of light (as compared with the two in the achromatic lens).

AUTOFOCAL. A term describing enlargers having a link mechanism which keeps the image in focus on the easel as the enlarger head is moved up or down to secure the necessary degree of enlargement.

AVAILABLE LIGHT. A system of photography which uses whatever light happens to be available, without resorting to additional artificial light. This requires fast films such as Tri-X and Royal X Pan, or medium speed films such as Plus X with speed-increase developers like Promicrol.

BACK CLOTH, BACK DROP. Any drapery used as a background in photographic work.

BACK COMBINATION. The half of a doublet lens nearest the film.

BACKLIGHTING. A style of photographic lighting which illuminates the side of a subject opposite the camera. Such lighting results in pictures with a "halo effect" around the edges of the subject.

BARE BULB FLASH. The use of flash without a reflector. The effect is a mixture of bounce and available light, less harsh and directional than reflected flash, not as soft as bounce light. *Caution:* Should not be used too close to the face of the photographer, to avoid injuring the eyes in case the bulb accidentally shatters.

BARREL MARKS. The lettering on a camera barrel that indicates the focal length, F-number, maker's name, and the serial number.

BARTOLOZZI RED. A red tone obtained by the use of a three-solution toning bath containing copper sulfate, ammonium carbonate, potassium ferricyanide and boric acid.

BAYONET MOUNT. A device used on some cameras to facilitate the exchange of lenses. Lens has prongs fitting into camera, and a lever locks them in place from within.

BED. The foundation structure of a bellows camera including bottom plate and the focusing slide rails.

BELITSKI REDUCER, MODIFIED. A single-solution reducer for dense, contrasty negatives; it keeps well.

BENZENE. $C_6H_6$. A light volatile aromatic and inflammable liquid distillate of coal tar, much used as a solvent and cleaning agent. It dissolves rubber, bitumen, matte varnishes, and many other gums or tars. It should be carefully distinguished from the "benzine" obtained from petroleum.

BENZINE. A light distillate of petroleum and consisting of a mixture of light hydrocarbons, frequently used as a solvent, but its use is more limited in photography than benzene. Benzine is now more properly known as naphtha.

BENZOL. Same as benzene.

BENZOLINE. Same as benzine; do not confuse with benzene or benzol.

BLISTERS. Small bubbles formed under the emulsion due to the detachment of the emulsion from the paper or film.

BLOCKING-OUT. Painting over portions of a negative with opaque paint (usually an uninteresting background) so that the portions so covered will not print. The backgrounds of machinery photographs are usually blocked out to eliminate uninteresting and distracting detail.

BLOCKED UP. Highlights in a photograph that are so over-exposed that no definition or detail is to be seen are said to be "blocked up."

BLURRED NEGATIVES. Any negative showing indistinct outlines of the image or double outlines is "blurred." This may be due to: (1) A poor lens, (2) Camera out of focus, (3) Holding the camera in the hands with a shutter speed of less than 1/25 second, (4) Object moving too rapidly for the shutter speed, and (5) Underexposure or underdevelopment.

BLURRED PRINTS. The loss of sharp detail and confused outlines on the print (when the negative is good) may be due to (1) Imperfect contact between the paper and negative, (2) The paper may be against the glass or celluloid back of the negative instead of against the emulsion, (3) Loose paper slipping over the negative, (4) The lamphouse or holder of the enlarger may vibrate during the exposure, and (5) The enlarger lens may be out of focus.

BORAX. $Na_2B_4O_7.10H_2O$. A white crystalline salt used in toners and as an important element in fine grain developers. It acts as a restrainer with pyro developers and as an accelerator with hydroquinone. Also known as sodium borate, biborate, tetraborate, pyroborate.

BORIC ACID. $H_3BO_3$. A slightly soluble, very weak acid used in the boric acid fixing bath. Boric acid in the fixing bath tends to prevent the formation of aluminum sulphite sludge and adds to the hardening properties of the potassium alum.

BOOM LIGHT. Light on a long arm or spar that is easily adjusted over model or set up at a height of several feet from floor.

BOUNCE LIGHT. A softer light than regular flash or flood, produced by reflecting the light from a ceiling, wall, or other surface. If color film is being used, make sure the reflecting surface is white or neutral, otherwise there will be an over-all tint to the light. The additional exposure required depends on the color and distance of the reflecting surface, usually from 3 to 5 times the regular exposure.

BRILLIANT. A term used to describe a print or negative with fairly strong contrast and sharp detail. In other words, a print with plenty of "snap."

BUFFERED. A developer so compounded as to retain its power and chemical balance while in use. Usually applied to a solution containing an acid and one of its salts. This increases the stability of the developer since the extra acid is brought into action only as it is needed.

BUILDS UP. A term applied to the gradual increase in density as metallic silver is set free in a print or negative during development.

BURNED UP. Badly overexposed.

BURNING-IN. A process used in enlarging. It means to give excessive exposure to certain portions of the print while other parts are held back by dodging. Used to darken light areas which detract, or to bring up detail in very dense portions of the negative without overexposing other portions.

CAMERA ANGLE. The point of view from which the subject is photographed.

CAMERA EXTENSION. Strictly, the distance between the exit node of the lens and the focal plane in which the film lies. When focused on infinity the camera extension equals the focal length of the lens.

CARBRO PROCESS. A method of making color prints in which the carbon and the bromide methods are combined.

CARTRIDGE FILM. A roll of sensitized film wound on a metal spool, the roll being encased in a metal casing (cassette) for protection against light and dampness. Film feeds out through slit in casing. Used mostly with 35 mm films.

CASSETTE. A container for roll film which may be loaded in the darkroom and used subsequently for daylight loading of the camera.

CATCH LIGHTS. Reflections, generally in the subject's eyes when portraits are being made, from the light sources used for illumination.

CENTILITER. A unit of capacity in the metric system; the hundredth part of a liter; 2.705 fluid drams.

CENTIMETER. cm. A unit of length in the metric system; the hundredth part of a meter; equal to 0.3937 inches.

CHALKY. Applied to negatives or prints which show excessive contrasts.

CHEMICAL DEVELOPMENT. Development by chemical action in a solution, in distinction to physical development.

CHEMICAL FOCUS. The point at which the actinic rays of light are brought together when focused by a lens that is not corrected.

CHEMICAL FOG. Fog produced on paper or films by chemical means, such as too energetic or contaminated developer.

CHIAROSCURO. The effect of the distribution of light and shadow in a picture.

CHROME ALUM. See alum, chrome.

CINCHING. Tightening loosely-wound film by pulling on the free end of it. Invariably causes scratches on the surface of the film which reproduce as black lines on the print or enlargement.

CIRCLE OF CONFUSION. The diameter of the circle created by a lens photographing a true point. The smaller the circle of confusion, the sharper the print will be when the negative is enlarged.

CIRCLE OF ILLUMINATION. The circular area on the focusing screen illuminated by light passing through the lens. There is no sharp boundary, as the amount of illumination decreases gradually at the edge of the circle.

CLOGGED. Term used in reference to shadow parts of a print or highlights (dense portions) of a negative when they are one heavy tone instead of showing differences in tone in the subject.

COLLAGE. A term used to designate a montage effect made by pasting up a composite photograph from portions cut from other photographs. The paste-up is usually copied on a new negative.

COMBINATION PRINTING. Combining parts of several negatives in one print; a method by which a sky can be printed into a landscape, etc.

COMBINED BATH. A mixture which both tones and fixes the prints.

CONCAVO-CONVEX LENS. A lens, one surface of which is a concave spherical surface and the other a convex spherical surface. Such a lens may be either convergent or divergent, depending on the radius of curvature of the surfaces. If the middle of the lens is thinner than the edges, it is divergent; if thicker, it is convergent.

CONTRAST FACTORS. The amount of contrast in a finished photograph may be attributed to several factors. These are: the exposure given the negative, the filter used, the kind of film, the duration of development, the duration of exposure and development in printing, the paper used in printing, and the developer used both for the negative and the print.

CONTRASTY. Applied to prints with very dark shadows and white highlights, due to underexposure or overdevelopment of the negative, or where the paper used is of the wrong contrast (too hard).

CONTROL PROCESSES. Photographic processes in which the operator exercises a considerable amount of control over the tone values. Not only can the tonal key be controlled, but the relative value of tones can be altered. Gum bichromate, oil, and bromoil processes are examples.

COVERING POWER. The capacity of a lens to give a sharply defined image to the edges of the plate it is designed to cover, when focused with the largest stop opening.

CROP. To trim or cut away a part of a print to eliminate some undesirable portion or to improve the composition.

CRYSTALLIZED. The form of a chemical produced either by deposit of crystals from solution or by solidification of a liquid into the crystalline solid form. Formation of ice is an example of the latter.

CUBIC CENTIMETER. cc. A unit of volume in the metric system equal to 1,000 millimeters ($mm^3$); 0.0610 cubic inches; approximately 17 drops. A cubic centimeter is almost exactly equal to a milliliter, or 1/1000 liter.

CUTTING REDUCER. See reducer, cutting.

DELAYED ACTION. An adjustment on a camera shutter by means of which the photographer may set the shutter and then take his place in a group or view so that he is included in the picture.

DESENSITIZER. An agent applied to films or plates in the dark after which development can be conducted in comparatively bright yellow light.

DENSITOMETER. An instrument (usually electrical, and with a comparison step-wedge) designed to measure the density of a negative.

DESICCATED. The dry or anhydrous form of chemicals as distinguished from the crystallized (cryst.) form.

DETAIL. In pictorial photography, detail includes everything which does not contribute to the motif of the photograph. In commercial photography, detail is desirable; in pictorial photography it detracts.

DEVELOPMENT. See chemical, finegrain, physical, and surface development.

DIAMINOPHENOL HYDROCHLORIDE. $C_6H_3(NH_2)_2OH.2HCl$. A substance commonly known as Amidol, the peculiar characteristic of which is that it will develop without the addition of an alkali.

DIAPOSITIVE. A positive image, as on a film; a transparency.

DICHROIC FOG. A condition in a negative where the film or plate looks red when seen by light coming through, and green by light reflected from it. Due to defects in the emulsion, hypo in the developer, etc.

DIFFUSION OF FOCUS. Also called "soft focus" or "soft definition." Lack of sharpness in the picture image due to a defective lens, imperfect focusing, or a special lens made to give soft effects.

DIN. A system of rating plate and film speeds generally accepted in Germany and other places on the Continent.

DIRECT POSITIVE. The positive image obtained by exposure in the camera with subsequent chemical treatment to develop and "reverse" the image.

DODGING. The process of shading a part of the negative while printing or enlarging.

DOPE. A varnish used on a negative to facilitate retouching, by giving a surface on which the pencil marks will "hold."

DOUBLE COATING. Many films, particularly those prepared for amateur use and X-ray photography, are coated with two emulsions, either one on top of the other, or one on each side of the base. One coating is a slow-speed and the other a high-speed emulsion. The slow emulsion provides correct exposure of the highlights and the fast emulsion provides detail in the shadows. The effect is to increase both the latitude and the tone scale of the film.

DOUBLE EXTENSION. A term applied to a camera or bellows which allows a distance between the lens and focusing screen about double the focal length of the lens.

DOUBLE FRAME. Some miniature cameras using standard motion-picture film make a negative of double-frame size— i.e., 8 pictures to each foot of film. In single-frame negatives the long dimension lies across the film; in double-frame negatives it lies along the film.

DOUBLE IMAGE. A duplication of the outlines of a photograph due to a movement of the camera or subject during exposure. Also used in reference to a print where the paper has been moved during printing.

DOUBLE PRINTING. See combination printing.

DRACHM, DRACHMA. Same as fluid dram.

DRAM. A unit of weight in the avoirdupois system, one sixteenth part of an ounce, or 27.34 grains. Also a unit in apothecaries weight, equal to $\frac{1}{8}$ ounce or 60 grains troy.

DRAW. The draw of a camera is the extent to which the bellows will permit the lens board to be racked forward.

DRYING NET. A sheet of thin, fluffless material such as mercerized lawn stretched out flat. Used for drying matte prints. The prints are laid on the net face down which prevents the formation of blobs of water as well as undue curling.

DYES, SENSITIZING. In 1873, H. W.

Vogel discovered that the sensitivity of the silver halides could be extended to include the longer wavelengths of light by treating them with certain dyes.

DYE TONING. The process of toning a photograph with a dye which will replace the silver image.

EBERHARD EFFECT. The name given to the phenomenon which darkens the edges of developed film, though the entire area has been uniformly exposed.

EAU DE JAVELLE. A reducer for negatives the active ingredient of which is sodium hypochlorite. It is also used to remove the last traces of hypo from film, and as a stain remover. Made by shaking together sodium carbonate and calcium hypochlorite then decanting the clear liquid.

EDGE FOG. The fog on film that is due to the leakage of light between the flanges of the spool on which the film is wound.

EDGE LIGHT. In portraiture, a light placed behind the subject to give a halo effect and illuminate the edges of the head and shoulders.

EFFECTIVE APERTURE. The diameter of the diaphragm of a lens measured through the front lens element. Sometimes this may be larger than the actual opening in the lens diaphragm because of the converging action of the front element of the lens.

EFFLORESCENCE. The process in which a salt gives up its water of crystallization to the air.

ELON. One of the many trade names for a developing agent the full name of which is para-methyl-amino-phenol sulphate. Elon is one of the constituents of MQ developers. See metol.

ELON-HYDROQUINONE DEVELOPER. Same as metol hydroquinone.

ELON-PYRO DEVELOPER. Any of several developing solutions compounded from pyro and Elon. To improve keeping qualities, this developer is generally prepared in three stock solutions which are mixed for use.

EMBOSSED MOUNT. A mount whose center portion is depressed with a die (plate-sunk) or an embossing tool (embossed), leaving a raised margin to frame the print.

EMPHASIS. Same as accentuation.

EMULSION. The sensitive coating on films, papers, and plates used in photography. It consists principally of a silver salt or salts suspended in gelatin.

EMULSION BATCH NUMBER. A number placed on the label of film and paper packages which identifies the batch from which that particular film or paper was made.

ENCAUSTIC PASTE. A wax paste used to impart a slight gloss to matte or semi-matte prints.

ETCHINGS, PHOTO. Photographic etchings differ from sketches in the subjugation of the photographic image, the main part of the picture being completely redrawn in pencil.

EVEREADY CASE. Camera case with drop front and openings to permit viewing film window and operating various parts, so that camera can be used without removal from case.

EVERSET SHUTTER. A shutter which does not require cocking or resetting between exposures.

EXPOSURE FACTORS. The difficulty encountered by beginners in photography may be attributed to the large number of factors which must be taken into consideration in arriving at correct exposure time. Following is a list of the more important factors: (1) relative aperture of lens; (2) kind of film used; (3) reflecting power of the subject; (4) season of the year; (5) time of day; (6) if artificial light is used, color of the light; (7) geographical location and altitude.

EXPOSURE INDICATOR. A device attached to plate-holders to show that the plate has been exposed.

EXPOSURE METER. An electrical or optical device that measures the amount of light reflected from or directed on a subject. This is done by converting or translating light energy to exposure units, thus indicating lens aperture and shutter speed.

EXTENSION. Extension of the camera is the distance to which the front of the camera (lens mount) can be drawn out from the back.

FEATHERING LIGHT. Letting only the soft, outside rim of light hit the object.

FERRIC SULPHATE REDUCER. A proportional reducer used in very dilute and slightly acid solution. It keeps well.

FERRICYANIDE REDUCER. Another name for Farmer's reducer; the active ingredient is potassium ferricyanide.

FERROUS SULFATE DEVELOPER. A physical developer using acetic acid as a restrainer.

FIELD. The space within which objects are seen on a viewfinder, lens, microscope, telescope, etc.

FILL-IN LIGHT. In portraiture or other photography by artificial light, fill-in lights are used (in addition to main lights) to fill in the dark shadow portions of the subject so that some detail will be recorded.

FILM CLEANER. (1) Any liquid which

may be used safely to remove dust and grease from film. One such is:

Ethyl alcohol ..................85%
Methyl alcohol ..................10%
Strong ammonium hydroxide ..... 5%

FILTER, CHEMICAL. A device used to remove suspended matter from a solution.

FILTER, NEUTRAL. A filter which has no color absorption or selectivity.

fl. dr. Abbreviation for fluid dram.

FINDER, ANGLE. A finder so arranged that the photographer may take a picture in a direction at right angles to the direction he is facing—used in candid camera work.

FIXING-HARDENING. A bath in which film, plates, or prints are freed from the unaltered silver bromide and at the same time the gelatin film is toughened.

FLARE SPOT. A fogged spot, generally near the center of the film or plate. It is usually circular or arc-shaped, and may be due either to reflection from the lens surfaces or from the interior of the lens mount.

FLASH EXPOSURE. A means of hypersensitizing film by exposing it very briefly, using an evenly illuminated subject such as open sky. This exposure overcomes the inertia of the film. An exposure of $1/300$ second at $f$ 16 is about right for most film.

FLATTENING REDUCER. See reducer, flattening.

FLATNESS. Lack of contrast in print or negative, generally due to flat, even lighting, overexposure, or incorrect concentration of developer.

FLUID DRAM. A unit of fluid measure in the apothecary's system; equal to 60 minims, .125 fluid ounce, or slightly less than 3.7 milliliters.

FOCUSING MOUNT. The lens mount which permits the lens to be moved toward or away from the film in order to focus it accurately on given distances. All fast lenses are in focusing mounts, and the slower ones may or may not be. Focusing is accomplished by moving a rotating collar which is calibrated in feet.

FOCUSING NEGATIVE or TARGET. A developed negative consisting of a geometrical design which may be placed in the negative holder of the enlarger for focusing. The extreme contrast and detail in the negative permit exact focusing, and the negative to be enlarged is substituted after the focusing is complete.

FOG FILTER. Actually not a filter, but a diffusion screen, used to give the effect of fog in a picture.

FORCING. Continuing development for a long time in order to get detail or density, or treating underexposed films or prints by adding alkali.

FORMIC ACID. $HCHO_2$. Sometimes used as a preservative for pyro.

FRILLING. A photographic defect in which the emulsion separates from the plate or film in folds and wrinkles. Frilling usually starts at the edges of the plate, during fixing, but may occur at other stages in the photographic process. It is caused by differences of temperature between solutions, etc. See reticulation.

g. (gm.) Abbreviation for gram.

GENRE. A type or style of photograph or other art which illustrates common life.

GLOSSY. The kind of photographic papers that can be ferrotyped to a high gloss.

GLYCIN. $CH_2(COOH) \cdot NH \cdot C_6H_4OH$. A slow, non-staining and particularly clean acting developing agent. Its chemical name is $p$-hydroxyphenlyglycin. It should be distinguished from glycine, an entirely different compound. Glycin may be used either as a one- or two-solution developer, and is often used for tank development. It is also used for producing various tones in chloride and bromochloride papers by direct development in dilute solution.

GLYCOLIC ACID. $HOCH_2CO_2H$. Added to amidol developers to improve the keeping property.

gm. (g.) Abbreviation for gram.

GRADATION. The tonal range in prints and negatives. If there are only a few tones between the deepest shadow and the brightest highlight, the gradation is "steep"; if there are many tones, the gradation is "long."

GRAIN. A unit of weight common to the avoirdupois, troy, and apothecaries' systems. It is equal to 0.064799 gram; there are 437.5 grains to an ounce avoirdupois; 480 grains to the ounce troy and the ounce apothecary.

GRAM (METRIC SYSTEM). The international unit of weight. It is almost exactly the weight of a cubic centimeter of pure water at its maximum density. It is equal to 15.432 grains avoirdupois.

GREASE PAINT. A flesh-toned cream used to provide a base for rouge, powder, and other make-up.

GREEN FILM. Newly developed film which, although apparently dry, still contains a considerable amount of moisture. Even in a warm room film does not become completely dry in less than six to twelve hours, and it is best not to attempt printing or enlargement of film sooner than this.

GREEN FOG. Same as dichroic fog.

HALFTONE. (1) In a photographic print, the darkest portions are called shadows, the lightest portions are called highlights, and all intermediate tones are known as halftones.

HALO EFFECT. A lighting effect secured by backlighting.

HARD-WORKING. Describes developing solutions which tend to produce contrasty negatives or prints.

HOGARTH'S LINE. A double curve in the form of a letter S, frequently employed in photographic composition; it is sometimes called the line of beauty or "S" curve.

HUE. That attribute of a color by virtue of which it differs from gray of the same brilliance, and which allows it to be classed as red, yellow, green, blue, or intermediate shades of these colors.

HYDROQUINONE. $C_6H_4(OH)_2$. A developing agent whose chemical name is para-dihydroxybenzene. It is commonly used in combination with metol, whose action it supplements. It is non-staining, produces high contrast, and keeps well in concentrated solution. It is also called hydrokinone, hydrochinon, and quinol.

HYPERFOCAL DISTANCE. The distance between a camera lens and the nearest object in focus when the lens is focused on infinity.

HYPERSENSITIZING. The process of increasing the sensitivity of a photographic emulsion by bathing it in distilled water or a dilute alcoholic solution of ammonia, exposing it to vapor (such as mercury), or exposing it to light *before* exposure. See *flash exposure,* above.

IMPRESSIONISM. That style of photography in which the essential features are brought out forcefully, while the rest of the picture appears indefinite, in a minor tonal key.

IRRADIATION. The spreading of light in an emulsion due to reflection from the surfaces of the silver halide crystals. The slight blurring due to irradiation should not be confused with the more noticeable and extensive blurring known as halation, which is due to reflection from the back surface of the plate or film on which the emulsion is supported.

ISOCHROMATIC. Synonymous with orthochromatic.

KEY. See tonal key.

kg. Standard abbreviation for kilogram.

KILOGRAM. kg. A metric unit of weight; equal to 1,000 grams, or 2.2046 pounds avoirdupois.

LATENSIFICATION. The process of increasing the sensitivity of a photographic emulsion *after* exposure. See *hypersensitizing,* above.

LATENT IMAGE. The invisible image, registered by light on a sensitive photographic emulsion, which does not appear until development.

LENS BARREL. The metal casing in which camera lenses are supported or mounted.

LENS CAP. A velvet lined covering for the protection of a camera lens. Also used for making exposures in the studio by momentarily removing the cap from the lens.

LENS FLARE. A light-flash on the film caused by using a very fast lens at a very small diaphragm stop. Usually happens only rarely with the better fast lenses.

l. Abbreviation for liter.

LIGHT TRAP. (1) An arrangement of doors or a curved passage by which one can enter a darkroom from a lighted room without permitting actinic light to shine into the darkroom. (2) Any arrangement for preventing light passage through an opening which must admit a moving part such as the felts on plate holders.

LINEAR ENLARGEMENT. When the degree of enlargement is figured on the basis of increase in one dimension, such as length, it is referred to as a linear enlargement of so many times. The alternate basis is the increase in total area. Enlarging a 4x5 in. negative to 8x10 in. is a two-time linear or a two-diameter enlargement, but a four-time area enlarging.

LITER. 0.908 quarts, dry measure; 1.0567 quarts, liquid measure.

LITMUS PAPER. A paper used for testing the acidity of solutions. It turns red in acid solutions, blue when they are alkaline. The paper is soaked in azolitmin, then dried and cut before use.

LOCAL CONTROL. Term which applies to dodging and burning in as practiced in enlarging.

LOCAL INTENSIFICATION AND REDUCTION. The application of an intensifier or reducer with a brush or swab to one portion of a negative or print.

LOW KEY. See tonal key.

m. Abbreviation for meter.

METER. m. 39.37 inches.

METOL. Trade name for the developing agent para-methylamino phenol sulfate. This compound is also available under such trade names as Elon, Pictol, Rhodal.

METOL-HYDROQUINONE DEVELOPER. Any developer compounded with metol and hydroquinone. These two developing agents have properties which supplement each other and consequently they are often used in combination.

METOL QUINOL DEVELOPER. Same as metol hydroquinone.

mg. Standard abbreviation for milligram.

MIDDLE DISTANCE. That portion of a scene, especially of a landscape, which lies between the foreground and the background.

MILK GLASS. Same as opal glass.

MILKY. A term used to describe the appearance of developed and unfixed film, or film which has been incorrectly or insufficiently fixed.

MILLIGRAM. mg. A unit of mass in the metric system; the thousandth part of a gram; equal to 0.01543 grains.

MILLILITER. ml. A unit of capacity in the metric system; the thousandth part of a liter; equal to 16.231 minims; almost exactly equal to 1 cubic centimeter.

MINIM. min. 1/480 fluid ounce, or just slightly more than 0.06 milliliter; roughly, one drop.

ml. Standard abbreviation for milliliter.

MONOHYDRATED. A term used to describe a substance from which most of the water of crystallization has been removed, leaving only one molecule of water combined with each molecule of the substance.

MONTAGE. See photomontage.

MOTIF. The theme or dominant feature of a photograph or other work of art.

MOTTLING. Marks which often appear on negatives when they are not sufficiently agitated to keep the developer in motion.

M. Q. TUBES. Containers of dry ingredients for making a given amount of metolhydroquinone developer. Generally used by amateurs.

NEAR POINT. The nearest object point lying between the camera and the object in critical focus which is reproduced without perceptible unsharpness.

NEWTON RINGS. These are the irregular colored rings that appear when two polished surfaces come into partial contact. The phenomenon is caused by the interference of light reflections from both surfaces.

OBJECTIVE. A term sometimes applied to the image-forming lens of an optical instrument; for example, the lens used on a camera or enlarging apparatus.

OIL TRANSFER PROCESS. A photographic process similar to the bromoil transfer or collotype processes, in which the pigmented image produced in the oil process is transferred to another support by means of pressure.

OPAL GLASS. A translucent milky glass used in enlargers to diffuse light before it reaches the negative.

OPTICAL AXIS. The imaginary line joining the centers of the two spherical surfaces of a lens; also called the principal axis. A ray of light entering the lens along this path will continue through the lens and emerge without being bent or refracted.

OXIDATION. The deterioration of a developer caused by its contact with air.

PAM (PAN) HEAD. The mechanism at the top of a tripod which permits the camera to be moved in horizontal or vertical planes. May be fixed to the tripod, or detachable.

PANCHROMATIC. Photographic emulsions that are sensitive to the entire visible spectrum, including red (as distinguished from orthochromatic, which is sensitive to blue and green, but not to red).

PAPER NEGATIVES. Negatives on a paper base rather than a film or glass base, generally used in enlarging. They can be made by two methods, one in which a small positive transparency on film is first made from the small negative. This is projected to the desired size just as a bromide enlargement is made, resulting in a negative on paper. Another method is to make a large positive (in reverse) on a smooth paper from which a paper negative is made by contact printing, the light passing through the paper base to the sensitized paper which has been placed in contact with it. The use of paper negatives permits a great deal of modification and retouching which is done with pencil. The mechanical grain due to printing through the paper base lends a pictorial quality to the finished contact print.

PARA-AMINOPHENOL. $C_6H_4NH_2OH$. A rapid soft-working developing agent of the Rodinal class which produces fine detail but yields contrast and density with prolonged development only. It is characterized by good keeping qualities in concentrated solution.

PARAMINOPHENOLATE. See sodium para-aminophenolate.

PARA-METHYLAMINO-PHENOL SULFATE. $CH_3NHC_6H_4OH.\frac{1}{2}H_2SO_4$. A developing agent with high reduction potential, generally used in combination with hydroquinone. It is marketed under a great variety of trade names, including Elon, Rhodol, Metol, Genol, Pictol, Photol.

PHOTOMONTAGE. A composite picture made by a number of exposures on the same film, by projecting a number of negatives to make a composite print, or by cutting and pasting-up a number of prints and subsequently copying to a new negative, or by any of a number of similar processes. See collage.

POLARIZED LIGHT. Light that is vibrating in only a single plane. Light can be polarized by a filter over the light source or, if that is impractical, by a filter over the lens.

PORTRAIT ATTACHMENT. A supplementary lens which shortens the focal length of the objective with which it is used so that near objects may be brought into sharp focus.

PORTRAIT PANCHROMATIC FILM. A high-speed panchromatic film whose color sensitiveness is approximately the same as that of the human eye. It is somewhat less sensitive to red than supersensitive panchromatic film.

POSITIVE FILM. (1) A non-color-sensitive film, much slower than negative film but faster than positive plates. It is used as an intermediate in making a copy negative.

POSITIVE IMAGE. An image that corresponds, in light and dark tones, to the original. (As distinguished from a negative, in which dark tones are light, and light tones dark).

POTASSIUM ALUM. See alum, potassium.

POTASSIUM CHROME ALUM. See alum, potassium chrome.

PRESERVATIVE. A chemical put into a developer to prevent oxidation, usually sodium sulphite.

PROCESS FILM. A slow film of steep gradation, useful in making photographs of line drawings, type matter, etc., in which there are no middle tones. It may also be used in copying monochrome originals when it is desirable to increase the contrast.

PRINTING-IN. Combination printing of two or more negatives on a single positive; especially the "printing-in" of some detail from one negative on the background from another negative.

PRISMATIC EYE. A device which may be attached to some view-finders permitting the scene to be viewed and filmed while the operator is facing 90° away from it.

PROPORTIONAL REDUCER. See reducer, proportional.

P. S. A. Abbreviation for Photographic Society of America.

RACK. (1) A metal strip with cogs on the upper surface. These cogs engage the cogs on a pinion, permitting the two to be moved relative to each other. Many camera and enlarger adjustments, such as focusing, are made by means of a rack and pinion. (2) Wood or metal frame upon which film is wound during processing. (3) Term applied to the movement of the camera lens toward or away from the film plane as the focusing ring is turned. The lens is said to be "racked" in or out.

RAID DEVELOPER. Any of several developing solutions which produce maximum density in minimum time. One such formula is:

| | | |
|---|---|---|
| Elon | 4 | grams |
| Sodium sulfite | 65 | grams |
| Hydroquinone | 2 | grams |
| Borax | 7.5 | grams |
| Water | 1,000 | cc. |

Time: Three minutes at 65°F.

RAPID FIXER. A fixing bath which dissolves the undeveloped silver halides in prints and films in minimum time. Such a fixer is useful in hot weather when the tendency of gelatin to soften is increased by long soaking.

RECIPROCITY FAILURE. At low levels of lighting, the reciprocity law (illumination decreases can be compensated for by proportionate increases in exposure time) fails to work. This failure has to be corrected by much greater increases of exposure at low light levels than would be expected on the basis of the reciprocity law.

RED FOG. Same as dichroic fog.

REDUCER CUTTING. An oxidizing agent which removes equal amounts of silver from all parts of the negative, therefore removing a larger proportion of the silver image from the shadows than from the highlights. Such a reducer will increase contrast, and is suitable for negatives which have been overexposed. Also called subtractive reducer.

REDUCER, FLATTENING. A reducer which reduces highlights without affecting the detail in the shadow; ammonium persulfate is most commonly used for this purpose. See also Belitski reducer; reducer, superproportional.

REDUCER, PROPORTIONAL. A reducer which acts on each portion of the negative in proportion to the amount of silver deposited. Since this is exactly the reverse of the developing process, a negative which is correctly exposed but overdeveloped should be treated with a proportional reducer. One may be made by mixing a cutting reducer, such as potassium permanganate, with a flattening reducer, such as ammonium persulfate. See ferric sulfate reducer.

REDUCER, SUPERPROPORTIONAL. A reducer which removes a greater amount of silver from the denser portions of a negative than from the lighter portions. Used to reduce contrast. See reducer, flattening.

RELATIVE APERTURE. The ratio between the effective aperture of a lens and its focal length. This ratio is usually given in numbers, not fractions. For example, a lens with a relative aperture of $\frac{1}{2}$ is known as an $f$ 2 lens.

REMBRANDT LIGHTING. Portrait lighting, three-quarter view, in which the shadow side faces the camera, named after the painter who used this kind of lighting for many of his portraits.

RETICULATION. A network of minute depressions or corrugations in a negative, produced—either accidentally or intentionally—by any treatment resulting in rapid expansion and shrinkage of the swollen gelatin. Reticulation may be produced by solutions which are too warm, or too alkaline, or by forced drying in an air current which is too hot. When a reticulated negative is printed, the corrugations show up as a network of fine lines due to the scattering of light by the uneven gelatin surface. See frilling.

RISING AND FALLING FRONT. An adjustment provided on some cameras which makes is possible to raise or lower the lens in relation to the film, in order to increase or decrease the amount of foreground included. This adjustment is very useful in photographing tall buildings. It is essential that the principal plane of the lens and the focal plane be kept strictly parallel in order to avoid distortion.

RODINAL. See *sodium para-aminophenolate*, below.

ROLL HOLDER, ROLL-FILM ADAPTER. An accessory permitting the use of roll film in cameras designed for plates or cut film.

R. P. S. Royal Photographic Society; founded in England in 1853, it was the first photographic society.

SAFELIGHT. A darkroom light that does not affect sensitive photographic materials.

SCALE. The full range of tones which a photographic paper is capable of reproducing.

SCREW MOUNT. Term applied to lenses or filters which screw into camera and lens, respectively.

SHORT-FACTOR DEVELOPER. A developer in which the image comes up slowly but builds up density rapidly when it does appear. Hydroquinone is an example.

SILK SURFACE. A term used to describe the texture of the surface of a photographic paper. This surface has a texture which simulates silk fabric.

SLUDGE. A muddy or slushy precipitate formed in a photographic solution, generally upon standing or when it has been used too long. The term is frequently used to describe the precipitate of aluminum sulfite which forms under certain conditions in potassium alum fixing baths.

"SNAP." See brilliant.

SNAP-ON-MOUNT. Method of mounting lens on camera by means of spring clips concealed within the camera housing.

SODIUM PARA-AMINOPHENOLATE. $C_6H_4ONaNH_2$. A developing agent; the substance formed when sodium hydroxide is added to a para-aminophenol developer. This derivative of para-aminophenol has been marketed under a variety of trade names: Rodinal, Citol, Azol, Activol, Certinal, Paranol, and Kalogen.

SOFT. Lacking contrast; having a short tone scale.

SOFT-WORKING. Developers or papers yielding a long tone scale from normal negatives or normal prints from contrasty negatives.

SOLARIZATION. A reversal of the image in a negative or print caused by great overexposure. Partial solarization is often intentionally obtained in a print for odd or pictorial effect.

SPILL. A colloquial term applied by photographers to the marginal rays from a photographic light. The concentrated light from a spotlight has no "spill"; a floodlight has a great deal of "spill."

STATIC MARKS. Dark streaks found on developed negatives, due to static discharge when the film was drawn too quickly from the pack, etc.

STREAMER MARKINGS. Dark strips in a negative in which the density of some long narrow object in the image is extended to adjacent parts; generally due to lack of agitation.

STRESS MARKS. Marks on prints due to mechanical contact or pressure. See also abrasion marks.

SUPERPROPORTIONAL REDUCER. See reducer, superproportional.

SURFACE DEVELOPMENT. Development in which only the superficial layers of silver in the emulsion are acted upon. Characteristic of fine-grain developers.

TONALITY. An art term, used to describe the effectiveness with which the photographer has reproduced the tonal gradations of his subject, or the effectiveness with which he has used tonal gradation to express an idea or feeling.

TONAL KEY. The balance of light or dark tones of a photograph. If light tones prevail with few or no dark tones, the photograph is said to be "high key"; if the opposite, "low key."

TRANSLUCENT. Permits the passage of light, but scatters it so that no image can be formed.

TROPICAL DEVELOPER. Any developer prepared especially for developing under tropical conditions. Such developers must yield satisfactory results when working at temperatures up to 90°F. or even higher.

VIGNETTE. The process of regulating the distribution of light in such a way that the image obtained fades out toward the edges, leaving no sharp boundaries.

# Index